# THE SAME BUT DIFFERENT

Frederick B. Taylor, *Hockey sur la rue Henri-Julien au coin de l'Avenue des Pins, Montréal*, 1948. Oil on canvas 24" x 30". © Estate of F.B. Taylor and Alan Klinkhoff Gallery

# THE SAME BUT DIFFERENT
## HOCKEY IN QUEBEC

Edited by
Jason Blake and Andrew C. Holman

McGill-Queen's University Press
Montreal & Kingston • London • Chicago

ISBN 978-0-7735-5054-4 (cloth)
ISBN 978-0-7735-5055-1 (paper)
ISBN 978-0-7735-5056-8 (ePDF)
ISBN 978-0-7735-5057-5 (ePUB)

Legal deposit second quarter 2017
Bibliothèque nationale du Québec

Printed in Canada on acid-free paper that is 100% ancient forest free (100% post-consumer recycled), processed chlorine free

This book has been published with the help of a grant from the Canadian Federation for the Humanities and Social Sciences, through the Awards to Scholarly Publications Program, using funds provided by the Social Sciences and Humanities Research Council of Canada. Funding has also been received from the Aide à la distribution d'un ouvrage à paraître en études québécoises program at the Association internationale des études québécoises (AIEQ).

McGill-Queen's University Press acknowledges the support of the Canada Council for the Arts for our publishing program. We also acknowledge the financial support of the Government of Canada through the Canada Book Fund for our publishing activities.

Library and Archives Canada Cataloguing in Publication

The same, but different : hockey in Quebec / edited by Jason Blake and Andrew C. Holman.

Includes bibliographical references and index.
Issued in print and electronic formats.
ISBN 978-0-7735-5054-4 (cloth).–ISBN 978-0-7735-5055-1 (paper).–
ISBN 978-0-7735-5056-8 (ePDF).–ISBN 978-0-7735-5057-5 (ePUB)

1. Hockey–Social aspects–Québec (Province)–History. I. Blake, Jason, 1972–, editor II. Holman, Andrew Carl, 1965–, editor

GV848.4.C3S22 2005 796.96209714 C2017-902066-8
C2017-902067-6

*For Nina*

*And with deepest thanks to Natalija Kranjc, Sabine Rona, Marcos Tatagiba, and the rest of that other kind of team*

# CONTENTS

# TABLES

# THE SAME BUT DIFFERENT

# INTRODUCTION

*Jason Blake and Andrew C. Holman*

A quarter-century ago, Michael Ignatieff wrote a curious vignette – little commented upon then and not much more ever since – that highlights concisely the problem of hockey and its relationship to national identity in modern Canada and Quebec. A decade before his return from American academia to Canadian public life to pursue the leadership of the Liberal Party of Canada, Ignatieff published his acclaimed book *Blood and Belonging: Journeys into the New Nationalism* (1993), a timely series of case studies from countries where ethnic nationalism had triggered contention, violence, civil war, and genocide. The book's real contribution lay not in any novel concepts in political economy, or new evidence, but in its popularization of the discourse on the "new" nationalism and in its juxtaposition of important hot spots.

Tucked away in his chapter on Quebec is a story about Dennis Rousseau, then an almost thirty-year-old paper-mill worker in Trois-Rivières, one of a great many everymen and everywomen whom Ignatieff used effectively to ground his discussion about ideas in real lives. Rousseau was a unilingual francophone nationalist who had embraced separatism not because of ideology but because of an economic downturn, American ownership of his plant, and what he saw as the unwillingness of the anglo-controlled Canadian government to act in Quebec's interest. "We need a jobs policy," Rousseau says, "but Quebec doesn't have the power … We need to get our hands on the levers."[1] Ignatieff interviewed Rousseau in his home, prodding the depths of his conviction about the separatist solution. Even more interestingly, the author then followed his Québécois slice-of-life tour to a local rink, where Rousseau's Wayagamack mill team was playing recreation-league hockey. There, sitting in the stands, surrounded by the familiar and the strange, the author ponders the essential Canadian conundrum: How it is possible that two peoples – sovereigntist Québécois and federalist anglophone Canadians – with such a long, shared, largely peaceful history and a similar outlook on what makes for a good life can feel so differently about the future of their political experiment?

Hockey is Ignatieff's metaphor. "I have hockey in common with Dennis, as any Canadian does. I grew up listening to NHL games on the radio … have all the same names in my head that he does – Geoffrion, Béliveau, Richard … I used to play in arenas like this." Ignatieff marvels at Dennis's play and longs for the emotional rush of being on the bench, and in the game. He feels a bond with someone who loves the game as he does, or used to, "wishing I still had my skating legs." But Ignatieff's initial rapture is suddenly checked. "We share all these things, and yet we don't. Language falls between us, even though I am bilingual … We play the same game, in the same arenas, and we cannot quite connect." Hockey, for Ignatieff, is too weak a vessel to resolve the differences in class and culture, "old resentments and a history of bitterness." As he closes his passage on hockey, Ignatieff laments that it is too much, perhaps, to suppose that individuals sharing the same rituals, the "same cold nights under the hockey rink," can feel a common belonging.[2]

Hockey (and all sport) has only ever offered a clumsy and awkward proxy for power politics, and Ignatieff's narrow use of the sport as evidence for his ideas about ethnic nationalism is a bit sloppy to scholarly eyes. Still, his final revelation states an important, elemental truth. The game of hockey in Quebec is the same as it is in the rest of Canada in a technical sense, and it has been since the game spread from its Montreal roots after it was founded there as a modern, rule-bound, indoor sport in 1875. But it is different, too. It conjures different meanings. This fact is one readily understood by players, coaches, students, and supporters of the game at all levels in francophone Quebec, though one understood hardly at all in English-speaking Canada. Hockey in our country inhabits a strange, bifurcated world. Though anglophones and francophones, Québécois and Rest-of-Canadians play and cherish the same game, we talk about it in different ways and in different contexts. We both speak of it as our national game, and yet our notions of nation contrast markedly – even if there is no strict binary involving a general francophone or anglophone attitude to the game. For years, there has been a popular myth in English Canada that the game is *really* played differently in Quebec, that it is less physical and more a game of finesse and puck skills. This hockey "truth" leads Marc Lavoie to ask: "Is it true that francophone players are too small, that they're not tough enough, that their defensive play is deficient, that they become invisible when the stakes rise?"[3]

The chapters in this book explore what hockey means in francophone Quebec, what it means, to paraphrase hockey historian and former prime minister Stephen Harper, to the *hockey nation within a hockey nation*. The book fills in some silent spaces in the growing scholarly literature on the game – "Hockey Studies." More than twenty years after Richard Gruneau and David Whitson's path-breaking *Hockey Night in Canada*[4] declared hockey fair game to serious scholars of Canadian society, there remains precious little published scholarship in English on the French Canadian context of the game, and only a few English Canadian scholars have cared to make it their study. *Coast to Coast* is the title of John Chi-Kit Wong's 2009 study of the game's various meanings, but, although the volume's chapters do cover Canada *a mari usque ad mare*, wide swaths of land are ignored. Wong acknowledges in his introduction, "Readers will find that certain regions of Canada and certain people's experiences are missing, most regrettably those of the French-speaking."[5] This is a curious lacuna, since Quebec hockey and French Canadian players feature prominently and regularly in the stories that English Canadian journalists, novelists, and filmmakers tell about Canadian society.

*The Same but Different: Hockey in Quebec* is, in another spirit, an antidote to the facile claim, which often passes uncritically in English Canada, that hockey among French Canadians is and always has been a fanatically followed social unifier – a vehicle onto which a society under siege has heaped its hopes and through which it has forged its collective sense of self. That is an old and infantilizing view, one that gives hockey in Quebec far too much credit (and Québécois too little). It holds that, for much of the twentieth century, hockey was a source of French Canadian salvation, a place where members of a francophone underclass could express their identity as a distinct society within a powerfully anglophone country. If they couldn't "win" in their daily material struggles in the English-speaking economic world, they could win (symbolically, at least) on the ice. French Canadian teams (and especially the Maurice Richard–led Montreal Canadiens of the 1940s and 1950s and Jean Béliveau's "firewagon" Canadiens teams of the 1960s) were the "porte-étendards" of the embattled Québécois nation and a lightning rod for national expression. This narrative has become orthodoxy. It received its most famous formulation in Roch Carrier's "Le chandail de hockey," an autobiographical short story about a ten-year-old boy's social disgrace when a mail-order error forces him to wear a Toronto Maple Leafs sweater amidst his cohort of small-town friends, all of them clad in the colours of the Montreal Canadiens. The story's message is that in Quebec hockey conveyed authority, and at the top of the hockey hierarchy were *Les Glorieux*. In this view, the Montreal Canadiens are central to an expression of Québécois culture, of vicarious social power; allegiance to them is a patriotic performance. The Canadiens are a talisman, more iconic in Québécois culture than paintings by Paul-Émile Borduas or Jean-Paul Riopelle, songs by Paul Piché, Laurence Jalbert, Georges Dor, or Robert Charlebois, poems by Félix Leclerc or Gilles Vigneault, or films by Claude Jutra or Denys Arcand. The claim continues to ring true to many today, albeit a little less loudly since the 1980s, as sport scholar Jean Harvey and others have argued correctly. Since then, globalization, a decline in francophone players and coaches, competition from a second National Hockey League (NHL) franchise in the province (the Quebec Nordiques), and, for a spell, an American owner conspired to make the Canadiens seem less symbolic of French Canada.[6]

Reality, of course, is more complex. Hockey has always been contested terrain *within* Quebec, among francophone Canadians for whom the sport meant different things. It was always politicized, divided, and troubled by religion, by class, by gender, and by language. Over time, hockey's multiple meanings were strung into a smooth and seamless narrative of identity, but, as the essays in this book seek to demonstrate, in fact hockey is a *problem* in Quebec.

Even during the hegemonic mid-century heyday of the Canadiens, the game's worth was pointedly challenged. In the 1950s and 1960s, popular reverence for the game disturbed an increasingly vocal middle-class francophone intelligentsia who saw the enthusiasm for hockey as an embarrassing parochialism, an impediment to modernization in a province seemingly slow to enter the twentieth century. In progressive journals such as *L'Action nationale* and *Cité Libre*, Quebec's intellectuals cast hockey as a reflection of the society's political infantilism and a faulty vessel for carrying a new, modern national spirit. The vaunted and revered Maurice Richard was as much a social problem to some as he was a cultural saviour to others, a barrier to social elevation. In a 1956 *L'Action nationale* article, Jean-Marc Léger writes of having to recognize "the ravages of a mentality of abdication" and the need to steer away from a national pride that depends on "the exploits of a hockey player."[7] Meanwhile, renowned essayist and novelist Jacques Godbout devoted a 1961 *Cité Libre* editorial to despairing of his countrymen, who prefer to "satisfy their pride ... with parish bingo [and] hockey heroes."[8] And just as troubling for these elites was the lexicon of hockey: an anything-goes repository where proper French terms were routinely anglicized and *joual* passed unchecked.[9] Too many pucks, too few *rondelles*. To some Quebec intellectuals before the Quiet Revolution, hockey embodied much of what was objectionable in their own national culture.

But even more hotly debated among Quebecers was the question of power, of who controlled the game of hockey. In much of Quebec until the 1940s, hockey was rejected by some francophone Catholic clergy, the powerful arbiters of traditional French Canadian culture. In their eyes, a sport created by anglo elite Protestant Montrealers and wildly embraced by English Canadians threatened to assimilate and contaminate francophone youth, as well as undermine Catholic morality and proper attitudes toward bodily modesty.[10] By the end of the Second World War, leading Quebec clergymen had begun to reverse their stance and to champion the playing of hockey (and other sports) by the French Canadian masses as an antidote to sloth and a way to develop useful skills and to honour God. Church-run *oeuvres des terrains de jeux* were places where generations of francophone children first learned sports such as hockey.[11] For mid-twentieth-century francophone youths, hockey, administered by parish priests, had become a performance of national culture. And yet that construction was short-lived. After 1960, when the election of Jean Lesage's Liberals ushered in new, modern values of statism and secularization, the organization of hockey in the province was affected, too. In time, youth sport became secularized. Recreational and minor hockey, first rejected, then embraced, by the church, was now co-opted by laymen who wrested control of it away from religious organizations and placed it instead in new civic ones, most notably the Association de Hockey Mineur du Québec (AHMQ). Founded in Trois-Rivières in 1968, the AHMQ used the collective power of its membership to relocate youth hockey organization from the church to town and neighbourhood communities.

By the late 1960s, identity politics in Quebec hockey had taken a new direction. No longer was it a question of whether or not the sport was a useful vessel for the expression of Québécois identity; that debate had been won. Now, the question was how to cement control of it for the benefit of the province's majority francophones. In the years immediately prior to the 1972 Summit Series (in French, La Série du Siècle),[12] that debate focused on the Quebec Amateur Hockey Association (QAHA), the governing body of the province's elite, adult amateur hockey organizations (senior, intermediate, and junior levels). Founded in 1919 by Westmount elites and McGill old boys at the Montreal Amateur Athletic Association, the QAHA suffered from the belief that it served first the interests of Quebec's anglophones. This was not mere administrative bickering; it was a matter of identity and there was much at stake beyond the rink. The QAHA was, after all, a regional branch of the Canadian Amateur Hockey Association, and though it had had several French Canadian presidents in its long history, the Montreal-heavy QAHA board and membership had always overrepresented the province's English-speaking community. "The QAHA," one document in the Royal Commission on Bilingualism and Biculturalism report noted bluntly (and probably overstating the case), "was an anglophone agency in which francophones had no power."[13] Relenting to popular pressure, it translated its name in 1969, becoming the Association de Hockey Amateur du Québec (AHAQ). Soon after the AHMQ began operations in 1968, it began to butt heads with the QAHA/AHAQ over jurisdiction and, especially, player transfers. Eventually, a mediator recommended the fusion of the organizations to create one governing council and dissolve constituent interests. Though the first attempt at fusion (1973–74) failed, a second one in 1976, encouraged by the Quebec state, succeeded. On 2 June 1976 representatives from the AHMQ, the old AHAQ, and the Quebec Ministry of Youth, Leisure and Sport brought into being the Fédération québécoise de Hockey sur Glace (FQHG).[14] Ultimately, one fact was plain: by the mid-1970s, French had become the language of hockey administration in the province and the FQHG (and its immediate antecedents) a symbol of Québécois control. Throughout this transition, hockey was a site for discussing national identity in Quebec and how to become *maîtres chez nous*.

For many, a logical next step in hockey's own Quiet Revolution in Quebec was (and is) the creation of a national team, to make hockey more than a metaphor for nation, to make it a sporting substitute. Since June 1976, there have been repeated attempts, led by Quebec City lawyer Guy Bertrand, to establish an Équipe Québec entry in men's ice hockey at the World Championships, Olympic Games, and other international tournaments. In the late 1970s, the Team Quebec project had no chance – stopped as it was by the intransigence of Hockey Canada (hockey's governing body in Canada), raw feelings in English Canada, and the daunting task of seeking International Ice Hockey Federation (IIHF) approval. Few outside Quebec could separate the hockey proposal at that time from the push for political independence in the province.[15] By 1981, Bertrand had recruited sports celebrities, including Guy Lafleur, to the cause, secured the support of the FQHG and the provincial government, and published a manifesto in *La Presse*.[16] This attempt also fizzled, but the idea has not died, and periodically since then new life has been breathed into it.[17] In 2006, prompted by Prime Minister Harper's statement in Parliament that Quebecers form "a nation within a united Canada," Bertrand revived the Équipe Québec campaign once more. He hired a Quebec polling firm – Léger Marketing – to survey Quebecers' views on the matter, and the results were revealing: 72 per cent of those polled supported the idea of a Team Quebec in the 2008 World Tournament.[18] But as with earlier attempts, the current notion of a Team Quebec separate from (and potentially competing against) Team Canada in IIHF competitions continues to rankle and confuse international hockey followers. Does Quebec, like every other entry in the IIHF tournament, have to work its way up the ranks into the elite division? Does it need the consent of Hockey Canada? Would elite Quebec hockey players choose to play for Quebec and not for Canada? In the end, there was no Team Quebec entered into the 2008 World Tournament in Quebec City, an outcome that did not sit well with many hockey-mad Quebecers. Today, the issue remains unresolved, though its prospects are positive. In August 2010 Hockey Canada authorized the creation of a Team Quebec to host and play in a tournament against national teams from France, Italy, and Switzerland in August 2011. In the end, the vaunted 2011 Coupe Québec hockey tournament never came to pass; plans foundered when the Swiss Confederation's national team declined the invitation.[19] But the idea won't die.[20]

Whatever its merits, the quest for a Quebec national hockey team formed to play in international tournaments is not a capricious endeavour. It is, rather, the product of a long train of events, driven and steered by many influences, among them the complex politics of Québécois national affirmation, the cult of personalities, and the desire to control the administration of hockey within the province of Quebec. "A Team Québec would ... create a sustainable and renewable sense of collective identity; it would contribute to a concrete and positive national affirmation," philosopher Tony Patoine wrote in 2009. "The 20 players on its roster would symbolize a Québécois *nous* ... which, one fine evening, could go head to head with the Canadian us, a duel that would arouse as least as much passion as that famous game against the USSR did in 1972."[21] And, as this book shows, the debate goes on.

*The Same but Different: Hockey in Quebec* contributes to the scholarly study of ice hockey in Canada and the world, a subject that has enjoyed a considerable growth in interest in the past two decades. Like much of this vibrant field, it is a multidisciplinary effort that engages the perspectives and methodologies of historians, literary scholars, sociologists, philosophers, and others – all those who have taken up the task of reading hockey seriously as a reflection of Canadian culture, behaviour, and identities. The book follows on the heels of John Wong's *Lords of the Rinks* (2005), Richard Harrison and Jamie Dopp's *Now Is the Winter* (2009), Whitson and Gruneau's *Artificial Ice* (2009), and Michael Buma's *Refereeing Identity* (2012), among other works, and aims to maintain the momentum that the field now enjoys. Building on these earlier studies, it adds hockey in Canada's francophone context to the meaningful discussions they have begun. Our analysis mixes perspectives – anglophone and francophone, Québécois and non-Québécois, male and female. It includes chapters that were originally composed in French and translated into English, as well as others composed as they appear here, in English. Throughout the book, the authors draw on the growing literature of sport studies published in both of Canada's official languages and treat the two bodies of literature as one. The chapters' notes demonstrate a comfortable literary juxtaposition: references to Benoît Melançon's masterful *Les Yeux de Maurice Richard* and the recent collection *Le Canadien*, for example, sit next to (and speak to) works more familiar to anglophone readers in the field.[22] In one respect, then, this book is a merging, or meeting place, of scholarly literatures on a subject that both binds and divides cultures in Canada.

Just as Melançon writes about events and occurrences that "go beyond Richard the person and can reveal something about Quebec society,"[23] the interconnected chapters in this volume go beyond Richard in considering hockey and hockey meanings in Quebec (no easy task given Richard's monumental status). Shifting the spotlight away from the Montreal Canadiens, Andrew C. Holman examines a less-celebrated and less-known form of hockey in Quebec: la Ligue de Hockey Dépression. A well-organized old-timers circuit dotted occasionally with ageing stars, the Depression Hockey League helped mould concepts of masculine identity in francophone Montreal in the years before the Quiet Revolution altered the definition of "manliness" in Quebec. Michel Vigneault's chapter returns to the roots of francophone hockey in Montreal, indeed the game's earliest days in all of francophone Quebec. As he shows, it took communal, though not always harmonious, effort and support from various groups in Montreal to make the "anglophone" game also one for the French Canadian people.

There are competing ideas of nationhood and identity involved in the symbolic role of hockey in Quebec, and many of the chapters in this work explore those ideas through new lenses. Emmanuel Lapierre's "La Soirée du Hockey in Montreal: National Stakes in a Cultural War" focuses on hockey as a cultural and constructed object and the way it is used to shape the contours of a Quebec nation, mostly through the Montreal Canadiens and the team's historiography. Fannie Valois-Nadeau's chapter examines the role of the Montreal Canadiens as a civic entity, in particular, as a contributor in the realm of social welfare through the Montreal Canadiens Children's Foundation. She uses the Foundation as a plumb-line to determine the meanings of sport spectacle and corporate citizenship, as well as the transformation of social-welfare activities beyond the state during an era of neo-liberal political ideology. Of course, younger generations of Quebec hockey fans have grown up without knowledge of another Quebec NHL team. As Terry Vaios Gitersos argues on the basis of newspaper reports in "Labour, *Francophonization*, and National Identity in Hockey's Battle of Quebec, 1980–1983," the fabled Habs, the familiar icons of a people, were challenged in social, linguistic, and political terms by the upstart fleur-de-lys-wearing Nordiques. After the demise of the Quebec Nordiques and the decline of the Montreal Canadiens as a "national" Quebec symbol, the highly politicized prospect of a Quebec national team has resurfaced. Such subnational teams already exist, placing a would-be Équipe Québec in the context of teams such as Wales and Scotland and England in international soccer.

The final chapters explore more traditional themes, looking at the sport's architectural shrine, the Montreal Forum (now the Bell Centre), popular culture, and artistic forms such as theatre and other literature. In Julie Perrone's "The 'House of Hockey': Spatialized Memories of the Montreal Forum," we are taken back to the Habs' former home as a *lieu de mémoire* replete with remembrances, language concerns, and, of course, hockey history, while considering how the "organized move" from the Forum to a newer venue attempted to transfer meaning and nostalgia. Especially in Quebec, gender politics have been understudied in hockey circles – even though, as Anouk Bélanger argues, hockey in the province "has undoubtedly acted as a place where males can receive gender training that supports the fragile process of masculinity."[24] Amy J. Ransom examines intertwined linguistic and gender concerns by directing our gaze to a popular television series. "'He Shoots! He Scores!': Language and Gender Politics in the Quebec Television Series *Lance et compte*" shows how roles are represented and staged in popular culture. Though hockey in fiction is no longer an area academics avoid, Frazer Andrews's chapter on Canadian historical theatre ventures onto entirely new terrain. Andrews points out how hockey has acted as a metaphor on the Canadian stage and – more importantly – how this common metaphor helps audiences access meanings about hockey as a cultural product, primarily regarding francophone struggle and *survivance* within Canada. Jason Blake's chapter reviews anglo-franco connections in hockey literature, highlighting recurrent themes (and absences) while pointing out both the advantages and disadvantages of using hockey as a literary pathfinder for Canada. The last chapter, by Paul Martin, examines the fascinating recent autobiographies of francophone Georges Laraque, one rendered in English, the other in French. Martin parses the meanings of the hockey lives of this quixotic enforcer and draws conclusions that shed light on the importance of language and race in the stories we tell about hockey in Canada and Quebec.

Together, these chapters reflect on the ways that Quebecers have projected competing identities into the playing and consumption of "notre sport national," while asking what "notre" refers to, and when. As is necessary for any study of hockey in Quebec, the book reinterprets the well-known narratives of the Montreal Canadiens, the Forum, and Maurice Richard. But it also skates beyond these subjects. It studies hockey's portrayal in popular media in Quebec, in television, in film and in theatre, and in both high and popular literature. And two chapters (Holman and Valois-Nadeau) study the relationships that hockey has with social welfare in the province, both before and after the critical changes made during the Quiet Revolution.

Two decades after hockey studies began in earnest, this book continues to invite scholars to take the sport seriously, and aims to expand interest in the subject. But it does not pretend to cover such a rich subject comprehensively. We need to know more, for example, about hockey's place in Québécois music and film, about the connections between the Quebec state and the governance of the sport, and about hockey culture outside Quebec's metropolitan centres, in rural areas and small towns. We also need to know more about the culture of hockey for women and girls – a subject that Lynda Baril has begun to analyze in detail in *Nos Glorieuses: Plus de cent ans de hockey féminin au Québec*, and that Élise Detellier touches on in her recent study of women's sports in Montreal[25] – at all levels from the semi-professional Canadiennes de Montréal to the province's university teams and throughout minor hockey. There is so much more to explore about this sport, which, in Quebec, is the same as but different from the hockey culture known in English Canada. This book puts us on that path, the same one that Michael Ignatieff experienced in a hockey arena in Trois-Rivières twenty years ago while watching a "Canadian scene" that was both *his* and not his at all.[26]

# 1

# THE DEPRESSION HOCKEY LEAGUE IN MONTREAL, 1932–1960: SPORT AND MASCULINE CIVIC PERFORMANCE BEFORE THE QUIET REVOLUTION

—

*Andrew C. Holman*

—

> A wag once said that there exist but two important companies in the world: the Canadian Pacific and the Catholic religion. He was mistaken because he failed to mention the Depression Hockey League.[1]
> *La Presse* journalist André Trudelle (1955)

> In this city hockey is the chief social cement.[2]
> Hugh Hood, "The Sportive Centre of Saint Vincent de Paul" (1965)

On 10 March 1947 an interesting event in the unwritten history of hockey took place at the Verdun Auditorium, in Montreal, Quebec. Five thousand people attended as the Ligue de Hockey Dépression (Depression Hockey League, DHL) celebrated its fourteenth annual festival of charity, an end-of-the-season extravaganza that featured novelty ice races, fancy skating, speeches and presentations from local dignitaries, and, most importantly, a championship hockey game for the league trophy, the Coupe Camirand. In 1947 the DHL's guest of honour was Canada's Sweetheart, Ottawa's Barbara Ann Scott – world figure-skating champion and, as Don Morrow and Kevin Wamsley have argued, one of the country's few true sport heroes.[3] Accompanied by her ever-present mother and later joined by Montreal's unsinkable mayor, Camillien Houde, Barbara Ann floated into the auditorium amid a press crush and, after receiving flower bouquets and addressing an admiring crowd, walked to ice level and dropped the puck. Her presence at this old-timers hockey game was telling: it granted authority to the doings of the DHL and helped its members raise $4,500 on the day, all of which was donated to the Société Saint-Vincent de Paul (SVP), Montreal's leading Catholic lay charity. That she accepted an invitation from a small francophone outfit unknown in English Canada was a significant social coup for the DHL. Just as interesting was the role that Scott played in the DHL ceremony. A world-class athlete herself, she was invited to Verdun not to perform but to observe. Her celebrity and feminine charm made an intriguing contrast to the relative anonymity and traditional masculine bearing of the DHL's players. She was resplendent in a "pale, blue dinner gown with sleeves," and her only regret, according to the *Montreal Gazette*, was that constant autograph-signing kept her from seeing much of the hockey game.[4]

There are many intriguing aspects to the history of the Depression Hockey League, perhaps Canada's oldest continually running old-timers "loop." Though serious and interdisciplinary academic study of hockey has grown remarkably in the past twenty years, almost all of its focus has been trained on elite athletes (in international competition and the professional ranks) and on children – especially the ways that hockey has mediated the experiences of childhood in Canada.[5] Scholars have examined much less what the experience of playing hockey has meant and means to Canadians who have passed their athletic prime but who routinely, religiously, perform their athletic identities, their sporting sense of self, weekly, in cold arenas and in front of desperately few interested spectators. While old-timers hockey (now often called "adult recreational hockey"[6]) in Canada is a perennial national phenomenon (and has been for a long time), it has evaded critical, scholarly study and we have allowed anecdote, nostalgia, memoir, and (sometimes patronizing) boilerplate journalism to take its place.[7]

This chapter examines the meaning of old-timers hockey in Canada, but it focuses only on one narrow slice: how hockey was used to reflect and construct a discourse about masculine identity in francophone Montreal in the 1930s, 1940s, and 1950s. Hockey masculinity is a subject that has been ably studied by a handful of Canadian scholars, most notably by Richard Gruneau and David Whitson, Stacy Lorenz and Geraint Osborne, Kristi Allain, and Matthew Barlow.[8] But this study revisits the subject in a different context: in French-speaking Quebec, among middle-class, over-the-hill hockey players in the decades before the Quiet Revolution. It contributes to the broader history of masculinity and male identity in Quebec, a subject complicated by language and ethnic difference and challenged, as recent scholars have noted, by a want of serious study. It tells some of the story of the DHL, a subject unknown in scholarly hockey literature and, more generally, outside Quebec. Between 1932 and the onset of the Quiet Revolution in the 1960s, the Depression Hockey League was a model of prescribed masculine behaviour for a generation of Québécois whose society was undergoing considerable change. Urban, middle-class, and francophone, the DHL conveyed a specific social and cultural message: that real manhood in the 1930s, 1940s, and 1950s could be located in gendered sportsmanship, the performance of fair play, and a commitment to marriage, procreation, and the welfare of one's own community.

The DHL was created in 1932, in the deepest trough of the Great Depression. On the surface, it was (and is) a modest enterprise.[9] The league has never had more than four teams in it at once: les Hobos and les Grads (both of which lasted throughout these years); le Wuk, which played for three years, before it was replaced by les Sages in 1936; and les Chromes – a team replaced in 1937 by Laval, which was itself succeeded in 1941 by the Junior Chambre de Commerce in 1941, the latter in turn being replaced in 1950 by le Totem.[10] League rules limited the number of players to eleven per team. Two games were played every Monday night at the new but modest cement-and-steel hangar-style arena located behind the Collège Saint-Laurent.[11] Between 1932 and 1960, the scope of the season expanded: from only nine games (plus playoffs) in 1932 to twelve in 1937, fifteen in 1948 (when artificial ice was installed in the arena), and eighteen in 1952.[12]

Despite its size, the DHL quickly developed into a prominent social institution. Several factors explain its rapid rise, not the least of which involved its chief avowed aim: the annual raising of charity funds, almost all of which were given to the SVP, an important symbol of Catholic community responsibility and lay leadership with a sterling reputation in the realm of poor relief. The league's motto made this plain: "We play for fun, while performing charity."[13] In these years, the DHL presented an unimpeachable public face, undertaking the basic spadework of community self-reliance in a province where redistributing wealth had important ethnic meaning. When coupled with another activity important to French Canadian identity – the playing of "notre sport national"[14] – the DHL developed into a potent local symbol. It is impossible to gauge what sort of real effect that DHL-raised dollars had for "les pauvres de la St-Vincent-de-Paul" in these years, but the league's annual subvention grew steadily from $300 in 1935 to $1,600 in 1949 and $2,500 in 1956. Yet it seems fair to say that the DHL's growing reputation in these years outpaced its real contributions to poor relief, especially after the Second World War, when Quebecers, as historian Dominique Marshall argues, began to look to the state as the legitimate provider of welfare.[15] Still, private, community efforts (like the DHL's) continued, buoyed by tradition and the strength of the narrative they told about community self-sufficiency and Catholic duty. Unlike bureaucratic operations, DHL efforts were local and newsworthy; hockey and charity had a complementarity that was irresistible both to prospective donors and to members of the press searching for a good story.

The DHL's climb to prominence was aided, too, by friends in high places. From its earliest days, the leaders of the DHL associated their league with the sport's institutional establishment. Throughout these decades, Montreal was the crown city of the hockey world: birthplace of the modern game, it remained home to the sport's most widely recognized organization – the Montreal Canadiens – and their home arena/cathedral, The Forum. The city was home, too, to the head office of the National Hockey League (NHL), which, by the end of the Depression, had become the most significant locus of power in the North American hockey world.[16] In the DHL's myriad associations with the Canadiens and the NHL, the social capital rubbed off. Canadiens and NHL brass were perennial honoured guests at the DHL's annual festival[17] and several members of the league held minor roles within the Canadiens' organization – two as goal judges for the NHL team's home games,[18] one as a penalty-box official,[19] and one who suited up as a practice goaltender when needed. Twice, the NHL head office was publicly consulted for advice when DHL league play produced situations that evaded the written rules.[20] But most conspicuous was the relationship that the DHL cultivated with current and former Canadiens players. One self-serving article in the 1954 DHL festival program, "En Causant de la LHD avec les Canadiens," reflected this impetus, soliciting compliments from current Canadiens (such as Doug Harvey and Jean Béliveau) and inquiring whether the DHL might be in their post-retirement futures. "In any event, the Depression League is proud to have among its admirers all the members of the Canadiens hockey club, the pride of sportsmen in the province of Quebec."[21] The overtures worked: in the years before 1960, seven former Canadiens suited up for teams in the Depression Hockey League after their pro careers had come to a close.[22]

The DHL owed its local prominence also to its ability to promote itself. Beginning in 1942, the league printed an annual start-of-the-season *bottin*, a brochure-sized booklet that ranged from twelve pages in the early years to twenty pages by 1960. Paid for by commercial advertising, it featured league statistics and trophy winners from previous seasons, a directory of names, occupations, addresses, and telephone numbers of all DHL members for the coming campaign, and a gossip column playfully called "Dépressionalités" written by notary and DHL player/publicist Pierre Bourgoin. The column sized up the league's teams and related anecdotes and apocryphal stories about the league's colourful characters. The *bottins* were meant for consumption beyond those who frequented the rink, to make the league and its aims known.[23] By the late 1940s, "Dépressionalités" was picked up as an occasional column by the francophone weekly *La Patrie*.

Recognizing the importance of media coverage to its mission, the league began to appoint its own official publicists after the Second World War. Among the first of them were Jean-Paul Hamelin, cartoonist Jacques Doyon, and Bourgoin himself, who spread the word about the DHL on the radio as well as in print. By 1951, the DHL had dispatched four publicists to do its PR work and added an official photographer to its staff in 1953.[24] These publicists prepared copy for journals willing to print it and courted favour with sportswriters by feeding them story ideas. Beginning in 1948, the DHL sponsored an annual lunch for Montreal hockey writers and honoured them, by name, in a special section of the annual festival program called "Bienvenue à Nos Journalistes."[25] Among the honoured was *Le Petit Journal* editor Charles Mayer, the doyen of mid-century Montreal sportswriters and one who wrote regularly about the DHL. As a result of all of this, DHL weekly game scores, annual festivals, and even biennial golf and tennis tournaments were widely covered in the francophone press – especially Montreal's *La Patrie*, *Le Canada*, and *Le Petit Journal*, and occasionally in the English-language *Gazette*. Held out by the press and the SVP as a model of charitable giving, the DHL formula spread beyond Montreal and was replicated in Quebec City, Verdun, Joliette, Sept-Îles, Sherbrooke, Cowansville, and Valleyfield.[26]

Montreal's Depression Hockey League, 1932–60, was much more than a peculiarly beneficent weekly "beer league." It reflected something bigger, beyond the field of play. As the Introduction to this collection argues, hockey was a site where ideas about national identity and aspiration, power and authority, and cultural affirmation intersected in twentieth-century Quebec. Until recently, there was precious little scholarly research on hockey and its importance in Quebec's history, though a great deal of popular discourse (in journalism, fiction, and film) maintains a common argument: hockey was one means by which members of a francophone underclass in pre-1960s Quebec expressed their identity. If they couldn't "win" in their daily material struggles in the anglo-dominated economic world, they could win – symbolically – on the ice. French Canadian teams (and especially the Maurice Richard–led Montreal Canadiens) became in the 1940s and 1950s an emblem of the embattled Québécois nation.[27] This narrative has become orthodoxy. It continues to ring true today though, as Jean Harvey has argued correctly, less so since the 1980s, when a variety of factors caused the Canadiens to lose their iconic aura.[28] But it is also important to note that the popular nationalist hockey story hides other, significant narratives about how hockey has shaped and reflected gender identities in Quebec. As Anouk Bélanger has argued in her essay "The Last Game?" Québécois hockey nationalism in the 1950s, 1960s, and 1970s may have compensated for the lack of real francophone power vis-à-vis anglophones, but that cultural construction had its own victims. Hockey nationalism in Quebec, she argues, has elevated (even celebrated) a hyperphysical, violent, and homophobic masculinity.[29] That form of nationalist expression marginalized many women and others who were given no role at the rink. And echoes of that social construction remain, as Amy Ransom shows in another chapter in this collection, in the depiction of Quebec hockey in the turn-of-the-twenty-first-century French-language television series *Lance et compte*.

Bélanger may be right about the influence of the Canadiens, the Rocket, and others on late-twentieth-century masculine nationalism in Quebec, but the Depression Hockey League shows us that there was more than one version of hockey masculinity in Quebec history. If hypermasculinity of the sort observed by Bélanger (and articulated by masculinity theorist R.W. Connell) prevailed in the late-twentieth-century hockey world in Quebec, a very different version, one more in line with Canadian sociologist Erving Goffman's idea of the "socially acceptable man," held sway among adult hockey players in the DHL from the 1930s to the 1960s.[30] In these years, DHL men were the proffered models of mid-century French Canadian manhood: on the ice, they performed manliness in a sport that was fast and physical; off the ice, they were family men who also raised money for their society's poor. Their model of masculinity was not the strident, martial, revolutionary strivings of an emasculated national underclass; theirs was the mature, solvent, respectable model of family and community provider: Ward Cleaver on skates. This mid-century "hockey man" was a version of the hegemonic masculinity that pervaded French Canadian culture more generally in the first half of the twentieth century, as Vincent Duhaime, Peter Gossage, Michael Gauvreau, and others have observed in their work on post-war change and the transformation of fatherhood in Quebec.[31] The DHL's traditional masculinity was crafted discursively in the accounts of its doings on and off the ice and had several important ingredients: ethnically Canadien and middle class, this fraternity was governed by a formal structure and exclusivity. But the DHL had cultural messages, too. Most conspicuously an *athletic* organization, it revered the male body and applauded physical performance. Equally a community association, the league's discourse honoured the institution of marriage and preached family responsibility and community fidelity.

## *ALL ARE "CITOYENS CANADIENS"*

Perhaps because its francophone nature was so conspicuous, this trait seldom entered into the public discourse about the league. There must have seemed very little need to extol it or declare it openly. The language of hockey in the DHL was French, and that mattered; it was a loaded cultural signal. In Montreal, a city whose neighbourhoods and socio-economic circles were divided by language, the DHL belonged to the city's respectable francophone population and was held out as a model of its characteristic values. Among those values in the years before 1960 was a commitment to the support of the Roman Catholic Church and its institutions. Though, as Harvey observed many years ago,[32] some Catholic clergymen continued to look dimly and with skepticism upon the value of organized sport among French Canadians until after mid-century, Montreal's DHL seems to have escaped that critique. It enjoyed a cordial (albeit arms-length) relationship with the church. Presumably, its annual contributions to the Société Saint-Vincent de Paul laid the groundwork for that relationship. And playing weekly in an arena that was owned and operated by the Congregation of the Holy Cross (Congrégation Saint-Croix, CSC), which ran the classical Collège Saint-Laurent, strengthened that bond. Priests from the CSC were always among the honoured invitees to DHL festivals and their names were listed among the politicians, judges, and other dignitaries in the front of the printed festival program.[33] That tacit approval of the DHL by local clergy helped congeal the ethnic imprimatur of the league and legitimize its operations.

The ethnicity of the DHL comes to light most recognizably, perhaps, in the way it identified and welcomed "others." Almost every year, the league included a small handful of anglophone players. Occasionally, their ethnic difference was noted, as it was in 1941, when the festival date fell on 17 March. "On the occasion of the festival of St. Patrick, the League offers its best wishes to its Irish friends."[34] It was important to recognize them as outliers, if only then to claim them as an honorary part of the group. Nowhere does this function surface more clearly than in a commentary included in the 1947 DHL festival program: "There are in the League 67 regular members, that is, 6 directors, 12 officials, 44 players and 6 coaches and managers, of this number, there are ten who have English-sounding names, namely: Russell Newell, J.P. McConvey, Bill O'Brien, Jerry Sullivan, Rod. Merrill, Earl Smith, Louis Ferguson, Paul Haynes, Jerry Heffernan and Henry Richardson; all are 'Canadian Citizens,' but five are French-Canadian, four Irish-Canadian and one English-Canadian."[35] The double-entendre of the term "Canadian Citizen" is important to emphasize. Canadian citizenship was a brand new status created with the Canadian Citizenship Act of 1946 and made effective on 1 January 1947. It reflected Canada's position, albeit belatedly, as a sovereign state (which it had become in 1931). But expressed in French, "citoyen canadien" conveyed another meaning: member of the French Canadian nation.[36] Unwittingly perhaps, the statement reveals an ambiguity among (and unease with) national identities within this decidedly Canadien sports institution.[37] Annual festival proceedings began (or sometimes concluded) with the singing of "O Canada," a tune that French Canadians shared with the rest of the country but whose words in French had special local resonance. Only once in almost thirty years did DHL festivities include "God Save the King!" – the anthemic homage to the country's British roots; that was in 1947, the year Barbara Ann Scott made her appearance and the year that Viscount Alexander of Tunis, the governor general and the king's representative in Canada, was among the festival's guests of honour.[38]

The organization was distinguished as much by social class as by ethnic identity. The DHL was a thoroughly middle-class construction. Virtually all of its players and organizers were businessmen and professionals – lawyers, doctors, merchants, bankers, insurance agents, and others. "This League … is entirely composed of young businessmen and professionals of Montreal," the 1935 *bottin* declared. By 1949, things had not changed: "The lawyers are the tops in the DHL, numbering twelve, while there are seven in insurance, five accountants, four engineers, two doctors, one notary, two dentists and one optometrist."[39] This class was a locus of French Canadian political and social leadership in the years before a new matrix of class power rose within the state and its institutions during the years of the Quiet Revolution.[40] Among this old elite were the DHL's first president, Dr Conrad Archambault, a Montreal dentist and one-time president of the Ordre des Dentistes du Québec. He was succeeded by Léopold Bernier, a commercial lawyer and erstwhile diplomat, who in turn was succeeded by optometrist Henry Richardson, a governor in the province's College of Optometrists. Among the league's leadership were some examples of impressive occupational achievement: Dr Guy Langelier, a long-serving DHL referee, elected president of Quebec's Société Dentaire; the Honourable André Montpetit, a Montreal lawyer while he served in the 1940s as a DHL referee and in 1951 a provincial Superior Court Judge appointee; and Maurice Rinfret, the president of the Montreal Junior Chamber of Commerce in 1945. Among DHL players was Léo Choquette, a widely known and successful movie-theatre entrepreneur in the province, who played DHL hockey into his forties and hobnobbed with Hollywood film stars of the era.[41] Below these examples were the dozens of other players and coaches who came from less decorated but still respectable white-collar occupations, from commercial travellers to insurance agents, all part of the urban middle class. "More than one important business was born" at the Saint-Laurent Arena, one 1946 memoir recounted. "What valuable contacts!"[42] As a class, DHLers were among, in Michael Behiels's words, Quebec's "traditional francophone professional petty bourgeoisie," respected but "virtually isolated" members of the local elite, whose entrepreneurial and social aims served "its own cultural community."[43]

League executives wished the organization to project a self-confident identity and prescribe a sense of social duty. "Parfaits gentilshommes,"[44] they aimed to create an incubator for the next generation of community leaders. Each year, the DHL *bottin*'s list of the players' and directors' addresses, occupations, and telephone numbers made it a networking "little black book" for budding members of the petite bourgeoisie. DHL directors believed the league to be a site for the reproduction of social class, both figuratively and literally. As the 1942–43 *bottin* proudly claimed: "In addition to being a sports and charitable organization, the Depression League has its place in the social scale … more than one marriage has been brought about."[45]

## A KU KLUX KLAN COMMITTED TO DOING GOOD

For an old-timers loop, the Depression Hockey League was remarkably formal and, ostensibly, exclusive. From its earliest days, its elected executive board governed the selection of players and disciplined misbehaving players and coaches.[46] Over time, the league added subcommittees that tended to a variety of functions, from festival organization to public relations. It held a general meeting each autumn at the Windsor Hotel in downtown Montreal, replete with a formal presidential address. The spine of the organization was a published constitution that contained a series of strictly enforced rules. Rarely amended, the constitution was nonetheless a subject of perennial discussion. The presidents' files are full of input from DHL coaches and players that took a variety of tones, from friendly suggestion to litigious demand. Moreover, league rules were communicated in formal contracts, signed annually by every DHL player and coach. Financially, the

DHL was a pillar of probity; its event summaries and annual reports detail revenue and expenditures to the last cent.

As mentioned, the DHL was, on the surface, exclusive – a closed shop. No player or coach could merely join up; one had both to apply formally and to have someone on the inside recommend his character and talent. One had to be at least twenty-five years old and an exemplar of masculine citizenship. One columnist endeavoured to capture the meaning of an invitation into this gentlemen's sports club in this way: "Being part of the Depression League is an honour, an award that even the most humble revere and with good reason. In being counted among its numbers, one gets the impression that he has joined quite a special group, nothing like the pride one feels in being a member of such and such club, social organization, Knights of this or that. It is a fraternity that resembles a sort of Klu Klux Klan [sic] committed to doing good."[47]

The writer's parallel was alarmingly clumsy (especially in light of the fact that the real Klan had targeted French Canadians and franco-Americans with their terror campaigns in the 1920s and 1930s), but the meaning of his comparison rings true. The league's exclusive admission policy and its narrow sport/charity purpose made it by nature a selective enterprise. Prospective players made formal applications, sometimes via well-worded missives on their companies' letterhead but more often via an application form that the league had printed for the purpose. Critically important to the process was the insistence that applicants be recommended by someone already in the league, or someone outside it well known in local hockey circles. At its own annual fall meeting, the executive committee reckoned the number of vacancies on each team for the coming season, weighed the talent balance in the league, and assigned roster spots to a lucky few successful applicants. By the 1950s, as competition grew and coaches insisted on having more say, decisions were negotiated and teams rebalanced by the coaches themselves at their own annual pre-season meetings. That said, outright rejection was rare; unsuccessful applicants were almost always assigned to a waiting list, to be called upon should resignation or injury create an unexpected opening. Moreover, if getting in was complicated and selective, getting out was marked by the same sort of officiousness. Players who no longer wished to play or whose jobs took them out of town were expected to submit formal resignations to the league.[48] Doubtless, many players must have departed unannounced, but it was clear that if one wished to re-enter the league at a later date, formal notice of departure was a must.

Among the DHL's more critical features was a thoroughgoing commitment to the amateur ideal. All league players were avowedly and strictly amateurs. Amateurism was a badge of respectability and an article of absolute certainty in a league whose earning power was steered solely toward charity. All players (regardless of their talent levels) paid to play: originally $5 each in 1932, the fee had risen to $40 apiece by 1955.[49] No director, referee, coach, or timekeeper was compensated. And all participants – players and non-players – paid for admission to the league's annual festival. The DHL constitution stipulated that no player could be currently "carded" by the Quebec Amateur Hockey Association (QAHA), the governing body of hockey in the province. The reason for this is never clarified in the DHL's documents, but it is implicit. Holding a QAHA card would have been doubly objectionable to francophone DHL governors. First, QAHA senior teams in the 1930s, 1940s and 1950s were anything but amateur and one running joke was that some of them (such as the Montreal Royals and Quebec Aces) paid better than NHL teams. Second, the QAHA, formed in 1919 at Montreal Amateur Athletic Association, was a creature of Westmount anglophones and McGill University old boys: the *other* solitude.[50] Still, the relationship between the QAHA and the DHL seems to have been respectful and cordial throughout this period. The QAHA occasionally informed the league when former DHLers went on to sign with QAHA teams, and when one of their own, former Sages player Wilfrid Duranceau, was elected QAHA president in the early 1950s, DHL solons made him an honorary member. "Although his organization is 'outlaw,' according to our constitution," the 1950–51 *bottin* noted, "Wilfrid will be welcome among us this winter."[51] Not an archaic trapping of days gone by, amateurism was a symbol of pride for DHLers. In 1942 NHL president (and Montrealer) Frank Calder called the DHL the "most amateur league in the world," a title that DHL officials interpreted as a glorious compliment (but may have been a clever double entendre). DHL executives were in earnest. They forbade their teams from having commercial advertising on their uniforms, as the Hobos found out when they were forced in 1947 to remove the Red Ball Brewery patches from their sweaters.[52] Finally, when the Canadian Amateur Hockey Association faced a conundrum about whom to send to the 1948 Olympic Games, the DHL, emboldened perhaps by Calder's declaration, made a serious application to supply the Canadian entry for the Olympic tournament in St Moritz. The application was politely rejected, but not dismissively, and nobody (in public anyway) ridiculed its bid.[53]

One might say that the DHL, whose aims after all were fun and charity, was *over*-governed and needlessly officious. But the formality of the league's structure reflected the seriousness of its mission as a middle-class community institution. When, in 1948, the league executive circulated among its members a proposition to transform the DHL into a full-blown, year-round service club (like Kiwanis or Rotary), the idea received a lukewarm reception. Those who objected feared it would spread the DHL's resources too thin and draw energy away from its original aim. "If you are looking to imitate organizations that already exist," lawyer Roger Lacoste wrote, "you will lose your prestige." The DHL's real social impact was rooted in its unique mission, as "a club … of a different sort."[54]

The formality of the league's structure and hierarchy was balanced by its lighthearted discourse and its commitment to fun. The annual festival demonstrated this best: the three periods of the championship game were interrupted by a variety of entertainments designed to keep league patrons amused: ice dancing performed by members of the Montreal Skating Club and the crowning of the festival queen were the highlights. Among the competitions staged were obstacle races for goaltenders, referees, and coaches (1936, 1937, 1940), barrel jumping (1936, 1937, 1947), ice acrobatics (1956), a "national" pie-eating contest (1938), a contest called "Fishing for Shoes" (1938), and a variety of gender-bending burlesques such as the "patinage de fantaisie par les 'BOYS'" – presumably DHL players – in 1936. In March 1941, in the heat of the Second World War, one festival act featured a "Coward Hunt" that had Winston Churchill and Ethiopian King Haile Selassie chasing Adolf Hitler and Benito Mussolini, with a public address announcer giving play-by-play description.[55]

## PLAYING THE BODY

The purpose that underlay all of this lighthearted play was openly expressed in the DHL discourse about the athletic male body. Individual hockey bodies were so many canvases on which community values and interests were projected and deliberated. For the sports-inclined among middle-class

Montreal francophones, the way DHL players looked and moved said a good deal about contemporary ideals of manliness. "Outward appearance and inward virtue," as George Mosse wrote in his classic work *The Image of Man* (1996), "were supposed to form one harmonious whole." Depression Hockey Leaguers became, in this way, cultural statements, or corporeal prescriptions writ small. Their bodies were a source of chatter about what real men should look like, and do, on the athletic proving ground.[56]

For example, one strain of homosocial banter in gossip columns such as "Dépressionalités" was ostensibly good-natured kidding about body size. Every year in the *bottin*, the DHL's collective physique was measured and named: heaviest and lightest players, tallest and shortest, oldest and youngest, along with averages for each category. There was no avowed purpose to this exercise beyond trivial amusement. Still, it had a cultural effect. The health of the DHL's collective body was open for public discussion. From their creation in 1942 until 1956, the DHL's annual *bottins* tracked the average heights and weights of its league members with statistics compiled from each season's player contracts. Over these years, DHL players did not grow much (they remained about 5' 7" on average), but they grew gradually heavier (from an average of 158 lbs 1942 to 173 lbs in 1956) as lean wartime diets were replaced by more prosperous ones of the 1950s.[57] The average size of these aging athletes was probably no taller and slightly lighter than the average thirty-year-old Montréalais. The resulting profile is less important, of course, than the fact that these numbers were gathered, published, and made to seem important.

Special comment was often reserved for two sorts: the stoutest players and the best dressed – those who adorned their bodies most stylishly. Stoutness was a gauge (then as now) of the inevitable male physical slide toward middle age, a process that sportsmen were ostensibly seeking to staunch or delay by playing old-timers hockey. Observations about the league's biggest players were meant as light-hearted, amusing labels of affection, but they were by no means empty or fatuous. *Bottin* authors identified, for example, "the mastodon Pitou St-Germain, who tilts the scales at 215 lbs"; "the 'Tub' of the League, Guy Lefaivre"; "the portliness of Bernard Couvrette"; and Jean "Hippo" Halde, "the fattest hockey player," who, according to the newspaper *La Patrie*, stood at 5'5" and weighed in at more than 265 pounds.[58] Veiled in jocularity, comments such as these targeted those whose appearance contested popular views about what an athletic body should be. They underlined the importance of body shape to middle-class ideas about the masculine self and served to gently police that norm. In addition to body size, the ways in which players clothed themselves off the ice also prompted occasional remarks. Proper middle-class attire was expected to be respectably cut and, of course, clean. In 1941 the league added to its annual individual player awards (most valuable player, top scorer, most improved, best goaltender) one for "Best Dressed Player."[59] Pete Daigle, of the 1946 *Commerce* hockey club, was one fine example. "Our 'Beau Brumel' [sic] is always the darling of the ladies."[60]

Regardless of how it was adorned, the body was seen as a key to athletic performance, a critical element to the social authority of the league. The calibre of athletic performance increased dramatically over the course of the DHL's first quarter-century, perhaps expectedly so. As the DHL's civic reputation grew, so too did its capacity to attract talented athletes. As it did, it became a tougher job to balance the league's stated aims and purpose with its increased ability to provide competitive spectacle.

In the league's first decade, the calibre of play in the DHL was good but not elite by any means. Almost all of its players had worn the sweaters of the province's classical colleges or local amateur teams; most were past their best days as players and most had not played for some time.[61] Before joining the DHL in 1946, insurance agent Raymond Caron skated for the Académie Saint-Léon in Westmount; the 1941 application of Jacques Thibault, agent for *La Patrie*, listed Collège Saint-François Xavier as one of his last teams. For players such as these, the goal was merely to relive college memories.[62] Post-war enthusiasm for the league and its growing reputation in the press, perhaps, changed the context and raised the stakes. Now, winning was an aim alongside having fun and raising money for the poor. It was at this time that the DHL began to permit ex-big leaguers to enter its ranks, and within a few years the league became known as a repository for a few well-known former NHLers, now reinstated as amateurs, including ex-Canadiens Hector "Toe" Blake, Buddy O'Connor, Paul Haynes, Gerry McNeil, Gerry Heffernan, and "Pit" Morin. Their prominence must have helped DHL fundraising; it certainly drew the attention of the local press. Their feats often headlined weekly DHL news stories.[63] Heffernan distinguished himself not only with his gentlemanly play (and lack of airs for an ex-pro) but also with his scoring touch. In 1948–49 he won all of the league's scoring trophies. Beyond the ex-NHLers, however, the talent level rose throughout the league. By the late 1940s, DHLers came to the league after having played for NHL-sponsored junior teams, such as the Oshawa Generals and the Montreal Junior Canadiens.[64] In 1957–58 Totem suited up Léon Bouchard, who was recruited by the Whitby Dunlops senior team to join them as Canada's representative at the World Ice Hockey Championship, and André Laperrière, a member of the Canadian National Hockey team of 1954.[65] As the league's reputation grew, there were consequences for weaker players. First-generation DHLers marvelled at (and lamented) the change in talent. The 1952–53 *bottin* quoted one amazed DHL graduate: "These are the passes professionals make … I wonder how I could play anymore."[66]

## "THE DEPRESSION LEAGUE SEEMS TO FAVOUR MARRIAGE"[67]

From its earliest days, the Depression Hockey League prided itself on the respectability of its members. A sturdy constitution and a raft of formal committees outlined the league's desire to be a model operation, but no less important was its ability to recruit men of character and moral compass. The DHL held itself out to be a community of mature, married (or, expectedly, soon-to-be married) family men. Reportage about the league expressed this ideal repeatedly in unsubtle ways.

An interest in measuring the maturity of DHL members may have been behind its fixation with age. Every year, the league compiled and published statistics on its players' ages, less as an index of their athletic abilities, perhaps, than as a gauge of their relative social standing. The league had a minimum age of twenty-five years, but the average age was always much older than that. In the war years, players' ages averaged twenty-eight to twenty-nine, but in the decade following 1945, the average age rose to between thirty and thirty-one.[68] The act of annually declaring the league's average age seems to suggest the type of representative men league directors were looking for: "jeunes gentilshommes." They sought men young enough to perform well on the ice, and express the league's vitality; but old enough to be employed and solvent, with a stake in the community – active but rooted men on their way to the respectability of middle age.[69]

DHL publicists were even more fixated upon players' marital status, and players and directors were expected to be family men.

"We will have the opportunity of experiencing the value of marriage this year," "Dépressionalités" mused in 1948; "the champion goalie Pierre Bourgoin, married last June, has become for the first time a member of the category of *serious people*."[70] To be married was to be serious and stable, a committed member of the community; conversely, bachelorhood connoted equivocation, hesitancy, even selfishness. Bachelors were often targets of the good-natured (but still pointed) jocularity in the DHL's regular newsletters, *bottins*, and carnival programs when they announced imminent nuptials.[71]

Like age, DHL players' marital status was tracked annually in the *bottins*. Married players always outnumbered bachelors and, as time progressed, increasingly so. Between 1942 and 1949, "les mariés" annually constituted on average almost 63 per cent of the league's players; between 1949 and 1955, they made up an average of 74 per cent.[72] Initially, in the 1930s, the Sages were the only team designated as one for married men, "much encouraged by their gentler halves," while the others contained a mixture of bachelors and "victims of Cupid."[73] By the 1950s, DHL commentators noted, bachelors were rare in the league: "the bachelors fall one after the other."[74] In all of this, the DHL was doing more than merely referencing an interesting bit of trivia about its ranks. League publicists were expressing their bias in favour of the married condition, the mark of full community membership and the incubator of family life. "More than one marriage was germinated" in the DHL, the 1956–57 *bottin* declared, and "business contacts established and friendships cemented."[75]

To be a family man in mid-century francophone Montreal (and in all of Quebec in these years, as historians Vincent Duhaime and Peter Gossage remind us) meant also to be a father.[76] Remarkable was the attention that the DHL's annual *bottins* paid to its players' abilities to procreate. Though the discourse was hardly poetic, one could not have missed the expectation or emphasis. Paternity was made to matter to these men. The statistics reveal an expected pattern (rise and fall) for an era than included the onset of the Baby Boom. Families grew in size during these years. DHL players were fathers to twenty-eight children in 1942; thirty-eight in 1944; forty in 1947; fifty-five in 1950; forty-seven in 1954.[77] The *bottins* even tracked the sex of DHL babies. Often singled out for special congratulations were the league's most productive procreators. "Bernard Couvrette et Eugene Brouillet," a 1942 edition of "Dépressionalités" noted, "are the champions with four babies each."[78] (Alas, there was no mention at all of the work of Mesdames Couvrette and Brouillet.) Even in such brief, obtuse, and lighthearted reports, important cultural prescriptions were being made. Part and parcel of being a model bourgeois masculine Montréalais was reproducing the DHL, the game, the class, and, perhaps, the race. In a column published in the 1950 carnival program, "Potins," an anonymous reporter, connected the Commerce team's dismal on-ice record the previous year to the fact that only two children had been born to its players: "Another proof that the birth rate affects a nation."[79]

In this discourse of social organization – an overtly male discourse – women were not entirely absent, but their presence and role in the making of middle-class hockey masculinity was assumed, limited, and marginal. They were recognized and valued, but mostly as witnesses and helpmeets to this project of masculine self-definition. Their presence at the games themselves was expected to help ensure that DHL hockey was trimmed of the sport's more brutish elements. Their work in and presence at the league's fundraising and social events assured DHL men of the respectability of their organization. But only rarely were women's voices recorded in this hockey talk.

Photographs from the DHL's annual dinner dances and fancy-dress trophy ceremonies at the swanky downtown Windsor Hotel in the 1930s, 1940s, and 1950s reveal the aura of these occasions. Women were there and the ceremonies were orderly. Not for DHLers the stereotypical homosocial beer-and-pepper-steak banquets in downtown taverns that characterized so many other old-timers' festivities. Women's presence, as dates and as co-organizers on fundraising committees, bestowed a bourgeois respectability upon the operation. During the Second World War, the DHL inaugurated a women's committee, which was lionized in annual programs for its moral support and for its sales of festival tickets. Reflecting the times, its married members were listed only by their husbands' names.[80] Where we do hear women's voices, they are filtered and appropriated. The presence of women and women's voices in this league served often as a foil, a gendered "other" (and an occasional voice of protest) to the exclusively masculine doings of Monday-night-hockey players. In 1954 the *bottin* claimed that President Richardson had received two pointed requests from the spouses of DHL members. First, they wished to have a room of their own at the rink on Monday nights in which to gather and socialize; second, they wished him to establish a midnight curfew for DHL players, when they must clear out of the dressing rooms and go home, "bière finie ou non."[81] Richardson granted both requests, as a family man would. This sort of gesture sought to reclaim hockey from popular constructions as overly violent, cultish, isolated, and lowbrow. In the DHL image, hockey was respectable and mainstream, its practitioners were married, solvent, employed (maybe even self-employed), and committed to bettering their community. Here was a variant of masculinity that flew in the face of the hockey warrior; here was the hockey player as masculine provider.

## LOSING ITS WAY

In October 1956, the Depression Hockey League opened its twenty-fifth season of play, with more than fifty of the league's alumni in attendance. The occasion gave league organizers a moment to consider how far the DHL had come, what it had accomplished and overcome. Pierre Bourgoin, long-time author of the league's gossip sheet, offered an historical look back, sparing no cliché: "Just like the story of a people, a nation, a country, the DHL has known beside its celebrated times less happy moments, such as the advent of the terrible world war of 1939 that decimated its ranks; it also knew intrigue and internal wars that even led to the expulsion of an entire team shortly after its foundation, and the worst unrest in several years last year; but as with an Olympic athlete, the last, most arduous mile ends with a resounding triumph; the DHL has survived the pitfalls that threatened its existence, to be used as a springboard to achieve, stronger than ever, its SILVER JUBILEE."[82]

From 1932 to 1957, more than 325 old-timer hockey players laced up the skates at one time or another at the Saint-Laurent Arena, six of whom, the program was careful to note, had gone on to their reward.[83] By the late 1950s, the record of the DHL was one of impressive growth in numbers, prestige, and finances. By 1959, the DHL had donated close to $40,000 to the SVP for the relief of the poor. It had become widely known in francophone communities as a cultural institution and a model for the expression of bourgeois masculinity in Canada's largest city.

Yet, even as the DHL rose to its highest point of strength and prominence, several sorts of change became manifest. By 1960, the meaning of the DHL's cultural work was challenged both functionally and symbolically, and it began to weaken. First, the organization aged. On one hand, age provided the DHL with the legitimacy that comes with continuous operation and, in its case, enduring both the Depression and the Second World War. Age gave the DHL a historical perspective, a long view, which by the 1950s it had begun to cultivate and celebrate in repeatedly retold lore in its own league publications and in the local press. The league created new social spaces for its own veterans, the 15-year Club in 1947 and in 1950 the Club Social des Anciens de la Ligue Dépression.[84] And with age, of course, came numerical expansion. By the early 1950s, with twenty years of operation under its belt, the DHL had had enough players, coaches, and executives pass through its ranks to cease being the personal, private, familiar community that marked the organization's early years. It had become large enough to become anonymous, and a sort of alienation crept in. By 1960, the Depression Hockey League boasted 108 active members (including players, coaches, on- and off-ice officials, and executive members) as well as 168 honorary members.[85] The arena was getting crowded. On its way out was the sense of immediacy, of personal knowledge, that cultivated male jocularity. Perhaps tellingly, the gossipy "Dépressionalités" disappeared from the league's *bottins* in 1957 and no more colourful caricatures – in print or graphics – adorned the league's literature any longer.

As it aged and expanded, the league moved away from its roots. New players began to resent the way the old guard ran things. In 1955 the DHL excised a long-standing constitutional rule that gave priority to former players who wished to return to the fold, thereby allowing the teams' coaches free rein to recruit only the best newcomers. The move trumped the feeling, spawned ten years earlier when veterans were returning from war, that *ancien joueurs* be given priority.[86] In 1958 a committee of players created an admissions committee, one now located in the hands of the players and coaches and outside the influence of the older executive. The festival program passed it off as a natural occurrence, a "child standing on its own feet," but the tension was hard to paper over.[87] Competition now trumped tradition. And the dream, oft-repeated in addresses by Léopold Bernier in the 1930s and 1940s, that the DHL's married players could assume that their sons would one day play in their fathers' league had become largely unfulfilled by 1960.[88] Among Bernier and his cohort, a feeling that their project was being high-jacked was hard to dispel.[89]

More than just growing pains, or the unavoidable lament that comes with passing the institutional torch, the DHL's culture of play was changing in ways that contradicted the league's original mission. First, even as on-ice competition increased, play among DHL teams was not enough for some. By the mid-1950s, a DHL all-star team was put together to challenge local college clubs and the all-star teams from other provincial cities, such as Quebec City, Granby, Sorel, and Hull.[90] The appetite for competition pushed the DHL several strides away from fun and charity.[91]

Even more concerning was a marked increase in rough play in the 1950s DHL. In the 1930s and 1940s, occasional rough play was tolerated and observed good-naturedly as an exceptional event but still within the margins of what was acceptable. A few characters were known for it, such as the Hobos' Gerry Desparois, who earned the nickname of "Bad-man" because of his "jeu robuste."[92] But rough play became alarmingly routine in the 1950s, and extreme violence escalated. Increasingly, league watchers did not like the way that things were going. In one 1953 match, DHL veteran (and former Quebec Senior League star) Maurice Bastien suffered a skull fracture, producing the sort of publicity that the DHL had never before experienced. In the *Petit Journal*, columnist Marc Thibault chastised DHL play: "The hockey is decidedly too rough."[93] Elevated from player to referee, Edmond Lareau declared in the 1954–55 *bottin* that neither he nor the league would tolerate "le jeu rude" in the coming season.[94] But the pattern continued. Writing in *Montréal-Matin* in January 1956, sportswriter Jacques Beauchamp made the point plainly: "We wonder if breaking apart your opponent, carrying sticks too high, starting fights on the ice fits well with the motto: 'WE PLAY FOR FUN.'"[95] Rough play symbolized, for many, the onset of anomie.

Beyond regular on-ice fracases, the tenor of relations among players and coaches started to sour by the late 1950s and the community of players had begun to disintegrate. Angered by poor officiating in a mid-season game against the Sages, Hobos coach Donatien "Jack" Laviolette pulled his team from the ice thirty-six seconds before the contest's final buzzer, a move that earned him both public reproach and a suspension from the league.[96] The DHL was losing its way. It was a sign of the times, perhaps, in 1956 when, for the first time in the twenty-four years of its existence, two players whose applications for admission to the DHL were accepted by league brass had the temerity to decline the offer.[97] All of this malaise informed the most regrettable event in the league's history. In April 1957, after a quarter-century of service to the DHL, Léopold Bernier resigned. In a private letter to his successor president, Henry Richardson, Bernier outlined his reasons: "Charity and sincerity, the two beautiful traditions that made the Depression Hockey League famous, have disappeared in a notorious and alarming fashion … The majority of new players in the DHL don't understand the purpose of the League, 'we play for fun and for charity.' Some coaches have not taken the trouble to explain to their players the duties of a member. With such a mentality, we have dangerously weakened the structure of our organization to the point of [doing] serious harm to its subsistence."[98] Bernier must have been convinced to remain connected to the league, his league, because he appears prominently in photographs of the DHL's twenty-fifth anniversary celebration in the fall 1957. Still, the letter shows that the meaning of the DHL had shifted, and the old middle-class culture of masculinity had begun to lose its purchase in amateur, old-timers hockey in Montreal.

It is hard not to see in all of this something bigger than just the routine activities of one small urban organization. The DHL experience 1932–60 seems likely to have been a microcosm of larger demographic and cultural changes that gripped all of Quebec society in the late 1950s and throughout the 1960s. The places and spaces where Québécois masculinity was made were being relocated, away from church affiliation, fatherhood and family, private enterprise, and maturity, and toward an active, open, and representative francophone statism, a stress on individual liberty, and a celebration of vibrant, restless youth. Hockey, of course, would still have a role in the making of Québécois manliness, but different men, younger men, were now to hold centre stage (and centre ice). One pseudonymous writer perhaps captured this best in a March 1959 letter to *La Presse*. Too much newspaper space was being given to "les ligues des 'has been' comme la Ligue Dépression," wrote "Rocket 500." His demand: more coverage of "les ligues junior (Metropolitain, Laurentian)."[99] Youth would be served, and hockey masculinity would come to mean something else.

2

# MONTREAL'S FRANCOPHONE HOCKEY BEGINNINGS, 1895–1910

*Michel Vigneault*

On 3 March 1875, at the Victoria Skating Rink in downtown Montreal, an event occurred that forever changed the Canadian sporting world. A group of young friends, most of them members of the Montreal Football Club (MFC), decided to rent the Victoria ice to play their winter game, "hockey." They had in fact already been meeting for some time before hockey caught the attention of local newspapers – with some support of MFC member J.G.A. Creighton, who provided the copy for stories in the *Star* and the *Gazette*.[1] And so, on that March day, the newspapers published a little article encouraging readers to come and enjoy this sporting novelty. The next day a brief description of the game appeared in Montreal's main English-language newspapers, the *Star* and the *Gazette*. Thus was modern hockey born. This chapter does not dwell on the origins of hockey – that subject on its own could fill a book yet still not provide a definite answer to the question of where Canada's national winter sport truly originated.[2] Instead, it limits itself to the beginnings of francophone hockey in Montreal, for which sparse literature exists in French and virtually none in English.[3] During the centenary of the Montreal Canadiens in 2009, there was much talk about the club's history and its beginnings, though hardly any about how this prestigious club came to blossom after ephemeral attempts by other francophone teams. Since all of the centenary celebrations focused solely on the Canadiens – ignoring even their 1980s rivalry with the Quebec Nordiques – it was as if the Canadiens were the only club in the history of francophone hockey, in spite of the rich francophone hockey history preceding the team's December 1909 birth. That said, not until twenty years after the famous 1875 game did the first francophone players begin playing together on wholly francophone teams. Though these players, like the majority of anglophone players, were middle-class students, they had the advantage of being mentored by the same players who came to dominate Canadian hockey a few years later.

The main hockey catalyst was the Stanley Cup, first donated in 1892 by then governor general Lord Stanley of Preston. The Stanley Cup became the symbol of the Canadian championship[4] and did much to spread Montreal-rules hockey across the whole country. This championship followed on the heels of the first competitions involving teams from Montreal, Quebec City, and Ottawa that took place at the Montreal Winter Carnival tournament between 1883 and 1886. Later, in 1886, there was a desire to extend these one-week competitions throughout the winter season – into what became the Dominion Championship. Competitive teams were organized into a league, the Amateur Hockey Association of Canada (AHAC, 1887–97). The anglophone Montreal Hockey Club, then affiliated with the Montreal Amateur Athletic Association (MAAA), was the 1893 champion of this league and the first to receive the Stanley Cup. In this unlikely context, the first francophone players and teams appeared in Montreal, supported unexpectedly by Irish Montrealers and the Catholic Church, an institution that did not generally welcome an anglophone sport as an avenue of cultural and moral growth for the French Canadian people.[5]

Beginning with an overview of the classical colleges' importance for early francophone hockey, and providing numerous empirical examples of rosters and "ethnic trading" within and between teams, this chapter traces the evolution of francophone hockey. It moves toward the culmination of that evolution – the creation of the Montreal Canadiens in December 1909 – while also highlighting the efforts of individuals and sports organizations in guiding a francophone team to the summit of Canadian hockey, the Stanley Cup. It argues that, though francophones were not generally welcomed into organized hockey, they entered it with the help of the Montreal Irish, an economically and socially marginal group that bore much in common with francophones in their respective relationships with anglo-elite society and sport. More importantly in terms of hockey, the Irish helped francophones find their balance in this new sport. It was a bumpy road on the way to the top league.[6] The importance of these ethnic origins is critical to explaining how hockey in Quebec became, as several chapters in this collection aver, "notre sport national."

## THE BEGINNINGS OF FRANCOPHONE HOCKEY AMONG STUDENTS

Before 1895, one could count the number of francophone hockey players on one hand, for there were almost none in anglophone sporting organizations.[7] The year 1895 saw the appearance of the first francophone club, but it also saw a large number of French-speaking players throughout the city, primarily in private educational institutions run by Catholic religious orders.

The vast majority of the first francophone players played the game at classical colleges, mainly at the collèges classique of Mont Saint-Louis, Sainte-Marie, and Saint-Laurent, institutions that have "over the centuries prepared Québec's social and intellectual elite for higher education."[8] These Catholic institutions were also open to Irish Catholics, who would receive their education in English (religion, more than language, being the dividing line between ethnicities back then). Though separated by language of instruction in the classroom, these young collegians shared recreational grounds and played in the same games. The francophones learned hockey from the Irish during free time on the college skating rink, since these Irish had their own team in the senior league, the Montreal Shamrocks. The Shamrocks, however, were best known for their prowess at lacrosse, and they repeatedly won Canadian championships between 1867 and 1910.[9] In 1892 Mont Saint-Louis and Sainte-Marie first squared off against each other in organized hockey games.[10] The college line-ups (available for Sainte-Marie from 1894 on and for Mont Saint-Louis and Saint-Laurent from 1895 and 1900 respectively) clearly indicate the mixing of Irish and French names on hockey teams. Though it must be admitted that presuming native tongue on the basis of names is speculative, a name such as William O'Brien hints strongly at an Irish background.[11]

TABLE 2.1. Numbers of Montreal francophone teams and players, 1885–1900

| Season | # fr. teams | # fr. players | # ang. players |
|---|---|---|---|
| 1885 | 0 | 2 | 69 |
| 1886 | 0 | 1 | 69 |
| 1887 | 0 | 1 | 55 |
| 1888 | 0 | 4 | 186 |
| 1889 | 0 | 4 | 168 |
| 1890 | 0 | 5 | 189 |
| 1891 | 0 | 5 | 190 |
| 1892 | 0 | 5 | 262 |
| 1893 | 0 | 6 | 240 |
| 1894 | 0 | 11 | 389 |
| 1895 | 2 | 37 | 562 |
| 1896 | 2 | 42 | 538 |
| 1897 | 0 | 30 | 533 |
| 1898 | 4 | 61 | 575 |
| 1899 | 8 | 72 | 874 |
| 1900 | 13 | 148 | 744 |

*Sources*: *La Presse* (1885–1900), *La Patrie* (1885–1900), *Montreal Daily Star* (1885–1900), *Montreal Gazette* (1885–1900).

Some Collège Sainte-Marie players on the 1894, 1895, and 1896 teams had previously played for other teams. In 1893 Hugh Semple and William O'Brien were with the Laurels, and in 1894 they played for the Orientals. Lorne Campbell played for Mowat's School in 1892 and for Crystal Jr in 1893, as did other top players, including Richard R. Boon, one of the founders of the Montreal Wanderers in 1904. Were these the players who introduced hockey to the Collège Sainte-Marie students? It is very probable. If not, the experienced trio undoubtedly helped to popularize the sport there. Collège Sainte-Marie's first francophone players appeared on the main team (not the intramural or occasional second teams) in 1896. In 1898 the creation of Loyola College signalled the removal of virtually all Irish Canadian students from French-language colleges in Montreal. However, the hockey links remained, along with those forged in other sports. An intramural league was organized in 1899 at Sainte-Marie, and Loyola's team participated in it. At Mont Saint-Louis after 1895, the franco-Irish team had as many French Canadian names on it as it did Irish. The same was true for Collège Saint-Laurent in 1900. In 1896 several French Canadian and Irish Canadian students from Mont Sainte-Marie and Saint-Louis colleges formed an independent team called the Orioles.[12] Five of its players later joined the senior Shamrocks.

These colleges hatched the future stars of senior hockey, among them Arthur Farrell, Harrey Trihey, and John "Jack" Brennan, who joined the Shamrocks in 1898 and who were themselves joined by Fred Scanlan and Ernest Pagnuelo of Sainte-Marie and Louis Belcourt of Mont Saint-Louis.[13] With another new recruit, Frank Tansey from Mont Saint-Louis, the Shamrocks won both the Canadian Amateur Hockey League (CAHL, [1899–1905], successor to the AHAC) and the Stanley Cup for two consecutive seasons in 1899 and 1900. After winning a third CAHL title, but losing the Stanley Cup against a team from Winnipeg, almost all of the Shamrocks players left, replaced in 1903 by other former Sainte-Marie students, most notably Louis Hurtubise and Théophile Viau. In short, the relationship between classical colleges and the Irish Shamrocks promoted the integration of francophones into elite, senior hockey, the most skilled level of the game before the creation of openly professional leagues. The Irish played a major role in disseminating hockey among francophones, both as instigators of collegiate hockey and as tutors to francophone players. However, it took ten years before the first fully francophone team became part of the "Old League."[14]

If the Shamrocks, an Irish-Catholic club, had Collège Sainte-Marie as a hockey nursery, the same held true for the Montreal branch of Université Laval.[15] The first francophone university team was formed in 1900. Its primary rival was the team from Université Laval's main campus in Quebec City, for whom another Sainte-Marie alumnus played.[16] Of the fifteen players wearing the Laval-Montreal uniform in 1900, seven were from Sainte-Marie, including Henri Ménard. Another player, J.R. Bélanger, was from McGill, not Laval.[17] Both players were invited to join because the Montreal team had lost the first match against the Quebec City-based team. Many of these players cracked CAHL line-ups a few years later, including the excellent Ménard, who, as goalkeeper, helped the Wanderers win their first Stanley Cup in 1906. In the meantime, nine players from Laval Montreal were training with the Montagnards hockey club in 1900. This club greatly helped the university over the next decade. Similarly, three of these players – Hector Dalbec, Louis Hurtubise, and Paul Laflamme – also played for the Shamrocks' team in the CAHL's intermediate league. The "feeder" classical colleges, especially Collège Sainte-Marie, played a major role in the beginnings of francophone hockey. It was thanks to their Irish fellow students that francophone students entered organized hockey, and the Shamrocks club was crucial in this development.

## THE NATIONAL, 1895–1900

The end of the nineteenth century saw the formation of the first francophone multi-sport club. Businessmen from Lachine and from Sainte-Cunégonde (in Montreal's Saint-Henri ward) created the Association Athlétique d'Amateurs Nationale de Montréal (the National) in May 1894 to promote gymnastics, athletics, and other sports for French Canadians.[18] This association was organized according to the model of the strictly amateur, anglophone MAAA.[19] In 1895 the National counted one lacrosse team, two baseball teams, one cycling team, and two hockey teams. In hockey, the National's senior team of twenty-one players included only eight francophones. Five of these players also played for another club, the Lilac, which claimed to be a club made up of students from Mont Saint-Louis.[20] Anglophones from the National had previously been members of a Scottish-sounding team called the Thistle that was folded into the new club. In 1895 the National's second, junior, team played against the Victorias' junior team, winning 4–2.[21] The seniors, meanwhile, tied Montreal-South, a south shore club, 1–1.[22] In short, the club's results in hockey and other sports were satisfactory enough for National president François-Xavier Dupuis to say at the club's first annual banquet: "Everything indicates that French Canadians are, in matters of sport, as in all other spheres of human activity, not inferior to other races."[23]

Though not inferior, they were definitely less experienced. Between 1895 and 1901, the National experienced several hockey failures. On 15 December 1896 the Ottawa Capitals approached the National and asked to create an independent league. The executive of the National refused the offer under the pretext of being suddenly disinclined to the sport of hockey.[24] The National did not make its hockey reappearance until 1901, despite a 1900 request that they join the CAHL intermediate league. As one spokesman for the club explained in 1898, lacrosse was the organization's sporting priority: "Forming lacrosse teams is the current preoccupation of the directors of the National."[25] This priority manifested itself when the National won the intermediate league championships in 1896 and 1897 as part of the National Amateur Lacrosse Association. In 1898 the National won the senior title, a feat it could not repeat until 1910.

The National tried to join the intermediate CAHL in 1900, propelled by the strength of its lacrosse success (indeed, many of the hockey players were also lacrosse players with an established culture of winning). Three Montreal clubs competed for the single available spot in this league. The procedure was rather simple: the delegates of the league examined each of the applications in turn. The league leaders rejected Club Pointe-Saint-Charles (PAAA), in which Irish Catholics formed the majority, by 12 votes to 4. Then, the National saw its application dismissed 9 to 7. Finally, Westmount was chosen, by a clear two-to-one majority.[26] The National recommenced the process the following year, and this time it was accepted, along with the PAAA and the Montagnards, another francophone club.[27] But this did not signal a grand entrance for francophones in organized hockey, nor did it herald a time of prosperity for French Canadian clubs.

## THE MONTAGNARDS, 1898–1900

The other francophone club accepted into the intermediate league in 1901 was no hockey newcomer. The Montagnards had more experience than the National in hockey, which accounted for their 1901 success in this league. Established in 1896, the Montagnards was initially a snowshoe club.[28] One year later, the Montagnards started in hockey, and did so in grand style. First, the club financed and built a skating rink at the corner of Saint-Hubert and Duluth.[29] Then, three Montagnards teams joined the hockey fray in three different leagues. The first team played in the Junior District Hockey League, the second in the City Hockey League (exclusively against railway company teams), and the third in the District Independent Juvenile Hockey League. Of the twenty-two players that the top two teams dressed in 1898,[30] only four had English names. In addition, many had played in previous years for Collège Sainte-Marie and, later, for Université Laval. On 30 January 1899, when the Shamrocks – future CAHL champions – visited the Montagnards at their home ice rink, there were two Irishmen in the Montagnards' line-up: Frank Stephen, a former Shamrock, and Eddy Cummings, a Loyola student. For the Irish, Hector Dalbec, a student at Collège Sainte-Marie, replaced Jack Brennan at forward. The referee of the match was C. James Hanratty, who had been a National in 1895.[31] The Irish-French Canadian linkage continued.

Before being accepted into the CAHL intermediate league in 1901, the Montagnards continued their apprenticeship during the 1900 season by playing challenge matches. The last meeting of the season was against the MAAA intermediate team, champions of its league. Even though the Montagnards lost the game 6–2, they put on a good show, especially when one considers that the MAAA had called upon two senior players just for this encounter. The strong performance helped the Montagnards reach the CAHL intermediate league because it was the first time that the directors of the MAAA saw this exclusively French Canadian club in action.[32] The Montagnards were able to limit themselves to francophone players more easily than the National, which often relied on Irish players.[33]

## IN THE INTERMEDIATE LEAGUE, 1901–02

In December 1899 the National tried unsuccessfully to gain entry into the antechamber of the Old League, now called the intermediate Canadian Amateur Hockey League. Though fruitless, this attempt did not go unnoticed. One reader, "an admirer of FAIR PLAY," wrote to the *Gazette*, supporting the bid vociferously:

> The coming season promises to be an interesting one in hockey circles. More especially in this city as our French-Canadian fellow citizens seem to be taking an interest in our country's greatest winter sport … I think Mr. Editor that the admission of the Nationals to the intermediate series would be a good thing for the other teams in the series, and help to create more interest in their matches … At present the teams playing in the intermediate and junior series of the Canadian Hockey Association in Montreal are all representatives of the west end of this city, and … it is about time that a team from the east end and Point St. Charles should have a place … The Nationals have won the championship of both the intermediate and senior lacrosse leagues, and now they are ambitious

> to make a name for themselves in Canada's national winter sport. The admission of the Nationals into the intermediate series, would not only add considerably to the gate receipts of other teams in the league, but would do away with the false impression existing among a great number of our French-Canadian citizens that the English athletic organisations in Montreal are prejudiced against anything French.[34]

Since one does not deny what does not require denying, the letter writer's vehement rebuffing of being "prejudiced against anything French" and his bold assertion of a "false impression" in fact confirms that anglophone clubs did not welcome francophone clubs. Indeed, many clubs saw no benefits for them, not even monetary ones. It took a 1900 game between the Montagnards and the MAAA, a team bolstered by two senior players, to convince anglophone clubs that francophone clubs' desire to be admitted into the intermediate league was genuine and that such skilled clubs' entrance was merited.[35]

At the December 1900 intermediate league meeting, the National and the Montagnards were finally accepted, along with the Pointe-Saint-Charles team (whose players were of Irish-Catholic origin). This is what the *Gazette* reader had desired the year before. Along with McGill, they formed the league's Centre-B section,[36] one of four sections: in the East, the Bulldogs II from Quebec, the Quebec Crescent, and Sherbrooke; in the West, two teams from Ottawa, the Senators II and the Aberdeens. The Centre-A section had the MAAA II, the Shamrocks II, the Victorias II, and Westmount.

The two francophone teams competed in the first game of the season, with the more experienced Montagnards winning 4–0. As *La Patrie* recounted, "the Montagnards team was superior to that of the National, as was somewhat to be expected … they [the National] have a certain degree of inferiority, though this inferiority, in reality, exists only in the lack of teamwork on the attack."[37] The National's lack of experience against more seasoned players was obvious. But the skill of the Montagnards is easy to explain: five players had already honed their skills at Université Laval, one at Collège de Saint-Laurent, and five at Collège Sainte-Marie. Only the goalkeeper Hurteau appears to have had no formal hockey experience. To be more precise, ten of the twelve Montagnards players came from Sainte-Marie. The National's inexperience proved disastrous – they lost not only to the Montagnards but also to McGill and the PAAA.

TABLE 2.2. Montagnards and National players' experience, 1901

| | 1900 | 1899 | 1898 |
|---|---|---|---|
| MONTAGNARDS | | | |
| [?] Hurteau | n/a | | |
| Théophile Viau | Sainte-Marie | Sainte-Marie | |
| Paul Laflamme | Shamrock+Montag. | Montagnards | Montagnards |
| Albert Prévost | Sainte-Marie | Sainte-Marie | Red Stars |
| Hector Dalbec | Shamrock+Montag. | Sainte-Marie | |
| Louis Hurtubise | Shamrock+Montag. | Sainte-Marie | |
| Rosaire Kent | Coll. Saint-Laurent | Sainte-Marie | |
| Émilien Brais | U. Laval+Montag. | Sainte-Marie | |
| Arthur Robillard | Sainte-Marie | Sainte-Marie | |
| Joseph Cousineau | Sainte-Marie | Sainte-Marie | |
| Chase Casgrain | U. Laval+Montag. | Sainte-Marie | |
| Paul Surveyer | Sainte-Marie | Sainte-Marie | |
| NATIONAL | | | |
| Paul Lavigne | International Business College | Columbians | |
| [?] Dupré | n/a | | |
| Alphonse Courville | Int. Bus. College | | |
| Albert Millaire | Int. Bus. College | | |
| [?] Lefebvre | n/a | | |
| Adolphe Roy | Int. Bus. College | | |
| [?] Jean | n/a | | |
| Pierre Champagne | Int. Bus. College | Columbians | |
| [?] Dupuis | n/a | | |
| [?] L'Heureux | n/a | | |

*Sources*: *La Presse* (1898–1901), *La Patrie* (1898–1901), *Montreal Daily Star* (1898–1901), *Montreal Gazette* (1899–1901).

The final standings for the Centre-B section stood: (1) Montagnards; (2) McGill; (3) PAAA; (4) National. The other section winners (teams played only within their section) were: in the East – Crescent; in the West – Aberdeens; and in Centre-A – MAAA. The East and West faced off in one semi-final, while two Montreal teams crossed sticks in the other semi-final. Although the teams won one game apiece, the MAAA prevailed on total goals scored. The MAAA won the first game 4–2, and the Montagnards won the second one 2–1; thus, the anglophone team won 5–4 on aggregate.[38] The results, however, were more encouraging in light of the first confrontation between these two clubs in 1900. The MAAA lost the final against the Quebec Crescents, who had eliminated the Ottawa Aberdeens in the other semi-final.

In the 1902 season important changes occurred in the intermediate league, foremost of which was the disappearance of the National. Because of the excessive competition from the Montagnards, some National players decided to join their francophone rivals. The National therefore found itself short of players. In addition, the team had no skating rink, since they were unable to rent the Ontario rink where they had played the previous season.[39] The Montagnards had its own rink but did not seem interested in renting it out to the National. The National was unable to survive these challenges.[40]

The Montagnards played against the PAAA and Trois-Rivières (McGill had also left the league). Two National players, Paul Lavigne and Lefebvre, joined the Montagnards team. Six players from the 1901 Montagnards team returned, while two new ones, Stephen Kent from Collège Saint-Laurent and Raoul Bonin, who had played for the MAAA seniors in 1900, rounded out the team. The PAAA won this section in 1902.[41]

The Montagnards decided to withdraw from the intermediate league in December 1902 in order to dispute a CAHL regulation about acceding to the senior league. According to CAHL regulations, no new team could join the senior league without having previously won the intermediate championship. The champion then had to defeat the last-place senior team for the right to play in the senior league the following season.[42] The CAHL had adopted this rule in 1899, at the time the league was created, and though the rule was amended for the 1902 season, it was never applied. The Ottawa Aberdeens, intermediate champions for the 1902 season, asked to be promoted to the senior league. The Aberdeens were denied this opportunity by the senior teams, including the Ottawa Senators, who were not keen on having another team in their region, presumably because they did not want to reduce gate revenues and – as shall be seen in the struggle for francophone players – talent pools.

For the French Canadian teams, this denial of the Aberdeens indicated that there was little hope of joining the senior ranks in the near future, since the senior-league teams did not want to add new members. After another victorious season, the Aberdeens withdrew for good from the intermediate league. Frustrated by the decision, the Montagnards also left before the start of the 1903 season, along with the PAAA and Sherbrooke. "It is absolutely useless to belong to a body where one cannot progress," the francophone team's manager explained. "So, what good is it to be part of a league that brings about nothing but costs? What's the good of developing players only to have them lifted from Old League clubs? … The Montagnards will nevertheless have a club this year, but it will be an independent club and it will arrange as many games as possible with clubs deemed suitable."[43] If the Montagnards complained about having had players poached, it was because two of its players benefited from another CAHL rule that allowed intermediate players to be called up for up to two games by a team in the senior league.

## FRANCOPHONES AMONG THE SHAMROCKS, 1902–03

The Montagnards began their second season in the intermediate league with much hope, since the regulations for gaining access to the senior league could allow the club to reach that league if it improved upon its performance from the 1901 season. To have any hope of winning regularly, the Montagnards would have to retain their two best players, Théophile Viau and Louis Hurtubise. In the meantime, the Shamrocks, who won the Stanley Cup in 1899 and 1900, had recently lost the cup to the Winnipeg Victorias in 1901. All of the Shamrocks players, except Jack Brennan, had left the club and retired; Fred Scanlan travelled to western Canada to continue his career. So, to form the team, Harry Trihey, now president of the Shamrocks hockey club, called upon intermediate players, including some from the Montagnards, to fill the vacancies. The Shamrocks invited Hurtubise and Viau to play a game, and with the help of these two stars the Irish club obtained its first victory, in January 1901. "Hurtubise and Viau, the two Montagnards players, worked wonders," *La Presse* reported: "The first made himself noticed as a forward with his brazen racing and his stunning dexterity … stealing the rubber from the opponent and launching himself with astonishing speed in the other direction … Viau on defence … excel[led] in clearing the territory, in … keep[ing] his opponents at bay … with a solid shoulder check."[44] The *Montreal Star* concurred: "The winning of Saturday's game by the Shamrocks, with two French-Canadians on the team ... was discussed all over town. Whether these two men, Hurtubise and Viau, will stick to the Shamrocks is a question, but it is hoped by the executive that they will ... Hurtubise and Viau can still play one more game with the Shamrocks ... Mr. Trihey had a talk with Hurtubise yesterday, and the latter stated that while he himself and Viau would like to continue playing senior, they did not like to throw their own club down. They would have a talk with the Montagnards, however, and see what could be done." The newspaper concluded: "Prominent French-Canadian gentlemen who take an interest in hockey "were pleased with the idea of having some of their own players in the senior ranks."[45] The argument, put forth in an anglophone forum, is that francophone players would be eager to join the English-speaking elite, even if there were doubts about whether the two francophones would "stick to the Shamrocks."

It would have been a difficult choice for these players. Apparently, helping the Montagnards win was more important to them than playing in the senior league, and, in keeping with league regulations, they played only one other game with the Shamrocks. However, when the Montagnards' 1903 season came to a close, both players now belonged to the Shamrocks, and Henri Ménard tended goal for the intermediate Shamrocks team. They were the only francophones to play top-level hockey in 1903.

In the 1890s, the Montagnards and the National were the two main predominantly francophone organizations to field competitive teams. However, given the limited number of experienced players, the two clubs waged war both for players and the support of the public; this battle raged from the time they entered the intermediate league in 1901. The rivalry ended with the disappearance of the two clubs and the creation of a new francophone club, the Canadiens, ten years later – a club that did not arise ex nihilo but from the early francophone hockey roots described here.

## THE RETURN OF THE NATIONAL, 1904–05

In December 1903 some players from the Victorias and MAAA decided to quit their respective teams to form both a new team, the Wanderers, and a new league, the Federal Amateur Hockey League (FAHL). They did this so they could be in control of their own aspirations, and make money under the table.[46] The new Wanderers, who declared themselves professionals after winning the Stanley Cup in 1906,[47] sought competition, and they thus turned to teams that had been rejected at various times by the Old League. They approached the National, the Cornwall "Seniors," and the Ottawa Capitals. In this new situation, an alliance was formed between the two main francophone clubs, the National and the Montagnards. The team wore the colours of the National, and the Montagnards provided the rink.[48] This agreement therefore allowed them to field the best francophone team possible. In addition, the Montagnards formed an independent team with players not retained by the National to play exhibition games against different intermediate teams; likewise, the National formed an intermediate team with players not selected for the Federal intermediate league. These two teams acted as "farm teams" of the National, providing players when it needed replacements during the season.

On the senior team were two future stars who had been playing together for some time – Jean-Baptiste "Jack" Laviolette and Didier Pitre. Only on rare occasions did they part company over the rest of their careers. The team also included the former Shamrock Viau, who was the only one with senior hockey experience. The other players were, for the most part, students from Université Laval. There were also four former Montagnards players. The National still managed to put together its best team yet to face this new challenge, finishing finished second in the FAHL, one spot behind the Wanderers.[49] The National intermediate team, which played in the FAHL, was composed of six former players from Sainte-Marie (five of whom were former Montagnards), who formed the group's core. Notably, only one player from the 1901 National, Albert Millaire, joined the 1904 intermediate team.[50]

After its first season in the senior FAHL, the National finally had a chance to enter the Old League, after the Ottawa Senators departed for the FAHL the following season.[51] Thumbing its nose at the Wanderers and the Senators, the Old League accepted the National and the Westmount teams in 1905.[52] To replace the National, the FAHL turned to the Montagnards. The two clubs once again raced to sign the best francophone players.[53] The 1904 agreement had been broken. And once again we can better understand what happened in 1905 by considering each team's roster.[54]

Jack Laviolette and J. Décary, two of the National's top players, left Quebec for the United States in 1904, joining the openly professional

International Hockey League. They were followed by Millette,[55] while Henri Ménard and Viau returned to the Montagnards. Eight Montagnards players were thus alumni of Sainte-Marie and all had studied or were studying at Université Laval. For the National, the situation was more complicated. Joseph Dostaler was a student at Université Laval and a former Collège Saint-Laurent student; Joseph Cattarinich was the goalie of the National's lacrosse team; Ernest Garon had previously played for anglophone teams.[56]

After playing two games with the National, Pitre accepted an offer to join Laviolette and make money playing on an International League team in Sault Ste Marie, Michigan.[57] The National had lost yet another talented player. After a third defeat in three games, the National decided to retire for the 1905 season, hoping to come back stronger in the Old League the following year. "Deprived of the services of the fine players on whom they had based their hopes, and abandoned by those who should have encouraged them for as long as they could have put together a team worthy of encouraging," *La Patrie* observed, "the directors of the National definitively resolved yesterday to withdraw from the league, from the CAHL, while reserving the right to belong to it again next year."[58]

The National, which had to cope with a shortage of talented players, rented the Victoria Skating Rink for its home games; the other local teams in the CAHL played at the Westmount Arena. Profits were higher at Westmount because it could accommodate five thousand spectators versus only two thousand in the dilapidated Victoria Skating Rink. The National's foray into senior hockey was over, though the club did try to return in 1906. At the dawn of the 1906 season, the CAHL reshuffled itself and changed its name to the Eastern Canada Amateur Hockey Association (ECAHA). The Old League repatriated the Wanderers and the Ottawa Senators. To make room for them, the Old League pushed out Westmount and the National, two latecomers to their ranks.[59] However, the National continued to play exhibition games for a few seasons.

## THE MONTAGNARDS IN THE FEDERAL LEAGUE, 1905–07

In 1905 the Federal League invited the Montagnards to replace the National, which had joined the Old League. They remained there for three seasons, but, as shall be seen, not without problems both for the other clubs in the league (all of which were outside Montreal) and for their former partner, the National.

Friction between the two francophone clubs resumed at the beginning of the 1906 season. Because the National was refused entry into the ECAHA (having dropped out the previous season), the club accused the Montagnards of not having supported their bid. A *La Presse* journalist defended the National's claim that it was strong enough to be accepted into the new league. The reporter reminded readers that four of its players were part of the American professional league,[60] which meant that they were banned from Canadian amateur hockey. According to the regulations of the Canadian Amateur Athletic Union that governed the Canadian amateur sport, including the ECAHA, it was impossible for professional players to play against or with amateurs, the punishment being that amateurs would then be deemed professionals.[61] They would be guilty by association, so to speak. In addition, the reporter advocated a union of French Canadian forces, a union that had not been possible until 1904, when the National joined the FAHL. Such a union would be feasible only if the National were to help out the Montagnards in the ECAHA.

But the Montagnards were not buying into prospects of union. As the club's chairmen, J. Firmin Bissonnette and H.J. Gagné, noted in *La Presse*: "What concern is that of ours, and how are we responsible for what has happened in the CAHL, to which we do not belong? … The National preaches harmony, union, by attacking us, booing us, attacking us personally, by proclaiming that the public are with them, though they do not even have [an] ice [rink] ... Mr. Mercier [president of the National] explains his club's defeat by the fact that there is a conflict of aims between certain English clubs and he takes out a [newspaper] column to explain it ... There only has to be one French-Canadian hockey club! Well, we are in the league, we have our players, we have our ice."[62]

As definitive as the reply was, it did not put an end to the conflict. On 29 January 1906 the National, which continued to play exhibition games, faced the Montagnards. The encounter should have, once and for all, determined who reigned supreme among the two francophone clubs. The newspapers highlighted the game's violence. The *Star* reported: "The Montagnard team fell before its bitter enemies, the National … Although an exhibition match, both teams were out for blood, and much rough play was the result."[63] The *Gazette*'s summary had it thus: "Players of both teams were being continually sent to the side [i.e., the penalty box] for rough play, and the referees, H.A. Watson and P. Foley of the Sterlings, had their hands full to hold the players in check and make them play the game according to the rules."[64] The result of the game explains the violence, as the National outclassed its rival 6–0. *La Patrie*, which seems to have favoured the National, wrote: "We have a French-Canadian club of the first order and measure to compete with … the current champions."[65] This challenge was not taken up by the holders of the Stanley Cup, the Ottawa Senators. However, the National team did play against the Quebec Bulldogs of the Old League, losing 7–4.[66] This loss to the National stung the Montagnards. The National, meanwhile, continued its momentum with wins against intermediate clubs and teams in the FAHL (though it did lose against Chicoutimi and its young goaltender, Georges Vézina).[67] The National played one final game against an ECAHA all-star team, the All-Point, comprised of Wanderers, Shamrocks, and MAAA players. These anglophone players hailed for the most part from the "Irish" Montreal neighbourhood of Pointe-Saint-Charles. Though the National lost this game, it was against a formidable opponent and it echoed a rivalry between French Canadians and Irish Canadians that stretched back to the creation of the two clubs and their affiliations with the colleges.[68]

A look at the composition of the teams that took part in the National-Montagnards game of 29 January 1906 reveals some surprises.[69] Former Montagnards players are found on the National, including Hector Dalbec and the Millaire brothers. Why? Perhaps better conditions were offered by the National? Joseph Dostaler, a National player, had played regularly for the Shamrocks in 1906, while the best francophone goalkeeper, Henri Ménard, played for the Wanderers, who were en route to their first Stanley Cup. Though several English names appear in these line-ups, some of them are potentially misleading. For example, Richard Duckett was a student at Université Laval in the Faculty of Law and was often to be found on francophone teams.[70] With the Kent brothers, things are more complicated and thus indicative of anglo-franco hockey connections. Rosaire was always associated with francophone teams, while his brother Stephen divided his career between anglophone and francophone teams. Wright, Doran, and Lunan are considered anglophones, the last two being Irish. These examples demonstrate the tenuousness of linking language to names. For their part, after another bitter defeat against Brockville (26–0), the Montagnards considered withdrawing from the FAHL for the rest of the season – owing to lack of support from francophone spectators, who preferred the National.[71]

Nevertheless, the Montagnards remained in the league and came back stronger in 1907, which proved to be its best season. What is more, it became the only francophone club to play. When the National was again refused entry to the ECAHA,[72] the club decided not to play in 1907. Because of this, the Montagnards' inherited all of the best available francophone players. Henri Ménard, Joseph Dostaler, and Édouard Millaire returned to the Montagnards. Six of the players were students at Université Laval, five studying medicine. Three anglophones were recruited to join the team, including Jack Marshall, who had played previously with Winnipeg, the MAAA, and the Wanderers. Having won the Stanley Cup with each of these teams, Marshall – who was born in Saint-Vallier on the south shore of the St Lawrence River and thus had a good knowledge of French – would win another cup in 1914, this time with the Toronto Blueshirts.[73] Joseph Leblanc also dressed for the Montagnards, but he had not travelled in the same hockey circles as the other francophone players. He always played for anglophone clubs: in 1898 and 1899 for Collège Sainte-Marie, between 1901 and 1903 for the Ontarios, in 1904 for the Garnets, and in 1905 for the intermediate Wanderers. He joined the Montagnards in 1906.[74] As these examples show, the anglo-franco delineations were by no means simple.

At the end of the 1907 season, the Montagnards won the FAHL championship, losing only one game along the way. However, three protests were filed against the Montagnards, one of them for dressing the ECAHA players Jack Marshall and Joseph Dostaler. Marshall had played only for the Montagnards in 1907, but he left after this complaint to join the Wanderers. Dostaler had played for the Shamrocks in an exhibition game before the start of the season. Though they had played in the Old League the previous season, they had not done so in the current season. The Cornwall team, meanwhile, had also used two former Shamrock players. What is more, several of the games themselves were rather bizarre affairs for the Montagnards. In Ottawa, against the Victorias, the two clubs were tied 6 apiece at the end of regulation time. Overtime, it was assumed, would determine the winner, but Théophile Viau, who had injured his foot in the first period, was unable to continue. Ottawa, contravening the rules, refused to remove a player to balance forces at the start of extra time. Not having a substitute player, the Montagnards left the ice, proposing to complete the game at another time. Ottawa would not hear of this and lined up alone for the face-off. When one of its men dumped the puck into the empty net, Ottawa declared itself the winner of the game.[75] The league officials confirmed the Victorias' victory a few days later at a meeting. On another occasion, in Cornwall, the Montagnards believed they had a won a game, but their victory was rescinded when the home team filed a protest over a goal and, unable to settle the dispute by committee, the league president ordered the game replayed.[76] *La Presse* described the club's ECAHA troubles in this strongly worded synopsis:

> After having been cruelly deceived many times by clubs of foreign nationalities, the Montagnards, in spite of the deficit its books show, was nevertheless determined to continue the fight because it anticipated the glorious title of Federal League champion, but in recent days its jealous opponents, who could not defeat our athletes on the ice, resolved to nullify their victories in league meetings. Nothing would be easier – and they understood this well – because the president of the league was simultaneously a representative of the Cornwall club ... Thus the Montagnards saw themselves robbed of three victories in a row by futile and ridiculous protests that nevertheless always found supporters. Recently, to cite but one example, the Montagnards beat Cornwall by a score of 7 to 3, and the latter protested in all seriousness that there was a Shamrocks player in the ranks of the Montagnards, while they themselves had two throughout the entire season and while the Victorias [Ottawa] want now to have the entire Ottawa [Senators of the ECAHA] instead of them ... In these circumstances it was useless for the Montagnards to continue to defeat [opponents] on the ice only to be later defeated by the league magnates, but it will always be a glory for them to be able to proclaim loudly that they suffered only a single defeat this year, as well to add that this was inflicted upon them by a partisan referee and not by a team of players.[77]

This decision meant that the Montagnards had lost the chance to face the Wanderers for the Stanley Cup.[78] Cornwall, whose team director, George A. Stiles, was also league president, became champion of the FAHL. The team's challenge for the Stanley Cup, however, was not accepted by the

Wanderers and the cup trustees. The Montagnards again challenged for the league title at the beginning of the 1908 season, knowing in advance that their challenge would be for nought. In any case, the francophone club had already given up on senior hockey in order to embark on a new adventure in university hockey.

Uniting francophone forces proved challenging, while also demonstrating that ethnic solidarity is not a given. This union between francophone teams had been made possible in 1904 when the National, bringing together players from the National and Montagnards, finished second behind the Wanderers in the Federal League. However, it crumbled in 1906 when the two clubs clashed and the National, a club that played only exhibition games, defeated the league-based club. Meanwhile, the Montagnards were not able to succeed until 1907, as their opponents made risible and litigious off-ice challenges to the Montagnards' league championship victory – and the league backed up the dubious contentions. Was a definitive union of francophone hockey players indeed in the works?

## THE NEW RETURN OF THE NATIONAL, 1909: TOWARD PROFESSIONAL HOCKEY

In 1909 the successful anglophone senior team, the Wanderers, agreed to meet a selection of the best francophone players at the Jubilee Rink, at the corner of Moreau and Sainte-Catherine in Montreal's east end. The rink was the property of Patrick J. Doran, one of the shareholders of the Wanderers. Since the Wanderers had just lost the Stanley Cup to the Senators, the trophy was not at stake; and yet the challenge remained an important one. Within a few days, a team of francophone players, almost all of whom were known to the public, was established.[79]

The purpose of this encounter was to show it was possible to form a francophone professional team of a calibre that could compete against the best in the next Eastern Canada Hockey Association (ECHA; by now the league had dropped the "Amateur" tag) season. Though openly professional hockey existed in Montreal as early as the 1906–07 season, no professional francophone team had ever been formed; players had to head to anglophone squads to make money. In the event, the game offered some surprises for spectators. One concerned the uniform worn by the French

Canadian players. How would they be dressed? Another concerned their coherence as a team, since none of the players had played together during the season. Despite bad weather enveloping Montreal, there were about one thousand spectators in the stands. There were three amateur players on this francophone team.[80] In the words of *La Presse*'s editor:

> Last night about a thousand people saw the French-Canadian team playing in the colours of the National put up a valiant fight against the Wanderers at the Jubilee Rink. The former champions emerged victorious from the encounter by a score of 10 to 9, but the Canadien [i.e., French Canadian] players showed they were up to battling the most powerful clubs in the professional league. As can be imagined, our team's game was slightly lacking in teamwork, because its members were recruited rather haphazardly. There is no doubt that if the same players were to practice together for any amount of time they would form a formidable group. [Alphonse] Jetté was a surprise. This was his first senior game and he worked wonders. He's a future star … Last night's game showed that the Professional League [sic] would be making a good acquisition next year by accepting the National into its ranks.[81]

The *Gazette*, meanwhile, declared: "The principal object of the match was to demonstrate that National could place in the ECHA a team of their own nationality which would be able to hold its own with the best sevens in the game."[82] Anglophone spectators were very impressed by the francophone players, some of whom were not known to them – notably Alphonse Jetté and Robitaille. The *Gazette* continued: "The ECHA would make a popular and profitable move by taking in [the] National next season. The team would have a backing that would benefit the other clubs and at the same time they could place an all-French team on the ice that would be fighting it out near the top all season."[83] The National supported this last-minute team in the aim of returning to high-level hockey, but it had to amend its constitution because only amateurs could be members of the Association Athlétique d'Amateurs Nationale.[84] Everything was sorted out by December 1909, when the Old League readmitted the National to its ranks.

But the National was not the only club desirous of a professional team. The newly created Canadian Athletic Club,[85] whose purpose was to promote professional sports such as wrestling and boxing, wanted to buy the Wanderers and transform it into a francophone team – that is, to make money from francophone spectators who would pay to watch their fellow francophones.[86] However, the approach of its president, Dr J.P. Gadbois, and its secretary-treasurer, George Kendall (better known by his wrestling name, Kennedy), was not initially successful. Still, by 1909 there was a clear demand for a francophone professional hockey team in Montreal.

## TWO FRANCOPHONE PROFESSIONAL CLUBS

The 1910 season saw a highlight: the existence of two francophone clubs. The Canadiens and the National had many run-ins in their struggles to attract the best players. The March 1909 game between the Wanderers and the National announced new beginnings, but nobody would have thought there would have been changes as important as those of November 1909. At the beginning-of-the-season meeting of the Old League (now the ECHA), Patrick Doran, owner of the Jubilee Rink and Wanderers shareholder, expressed his intention that the Wanderers play on his ice. The other teams in the league refused to play in east Montreal, for both economic and cultural reasons. The Jubilee Rink accommodated fewer spectators than the Westmount Arena, and it was too far east in the city to attract regulars from Hochelaga ward. Citing these reasons, the league leaders expelled the Wanderers, and the ECHA changed its name, becoming the Canadian Hockey Association (CHA).[87] By the beginning of the 1910 season, five teams made up the league: the three teams from the Old League – the Montreal Shamrocks, Ottawa, and Quebec – as well as the All-Montreal and the National. The All-Montreal was a team formed around Art Ross, a player who had left the Wanderers. It filled the vacancy created by the retreating Wanderers. After its March 1909 game against the Wanderers, the National was invited to join this league.[88]

On 26 November 1909, at the same meeting where it was decided that the Wanderers would be expelled, another team submitted its application to join the Old League – the Renfrew (Ontario) Creamery Kings, owned by J. Ambrose O'Brien of the Ottawa Valley Hockey League (OVHL; previously the FAHL). This application was rejected by the directors of the Old League. The bosses of the Wanderers and the Renfrew team then decided to convene in a neighbouring room in the Windsor Hotel, the very hotel that was hosting the CHA meeting. They came to an agreement to form a new league, the National Hockey Association – with the other teams being Cobalt and Haileybury, both from the OVHL and both situated in northeastern Ontario. James Gardner, who represented the Wanderers, proposed the formation of a francophone team to attract audiences from this community to the Jubilee Rink.[89] This new team was to be called Les Canadiens. Since the withdrawal of the Montagnards, francophones had not had a team in the senior ranks. And yet, for the 1909–10 season, francophones had two skilled teams, professional ones at that.

A struggle to hire the best players commenced among the five Montreal professional teams. The problem was most acute among francophones. Jack Laviolette was offered $5,000 by the Canadiens' first owner, J. Ambrose O'Brien, to run the Canadiens as a player-manager-instructor. Of course, this amount had to suffice to pay salaries, buy equipment, and cover other operating expenses.[90] He had to find top players interested in joining this new team. In order to accept professionals in its ranks, the National had to amend its constitution, which had in place strict regulations regarding amateurism.[91] The new situation motivated a change. "Nevertheless, and notwithstanding the above," the amendment reads, "the Association may employ one or more professional players who must not be members of the Association, and they may play for the Association or against clubs and associations which may be opponents of the association, and this without prejudice to the amateur status of members of the Association."[92] A professional player could not become a member of the National, but he could represent the club at sporting events, especially hockey and lacrosse. Thus began the National's rather unusual search for the best players. Both the National and the Canadiens publicly claimed to have signed contracts with the same players. One Montreal *Star* piece comparing the two francophone teams on the basis of information provided by their managers showed that each seven-man roster claimed three players in common.[93] As dubious as the source may be, it points to how bitter the struggle to sign top francophone players was.

Of those on this list, only Didier Pitre had actually signed with both teams. The National intended to sue Pitre to prevent him from playing with the Canadiens, summoning former Shamrocks player Harry Trihey to represent the National. The Pitre "saga" began on 12 December 1909 while Pitre was heading to Montreal from Sault Ste Marie, Ontario. Laviolette and Cattarinich waited for Pitre in Ottawa to get him to sign a contract. In the meantime, Alphonse Lecours, president of the National, headed to North Bay to put Pitre under contract after having caught wind of the player's imminent arrival in Montreal.[94] Lecours thus cut off the Canadiens in the attempt to hire Pitre. Pitre, on arriving in Ottawa, informed Laviolette that he had signed for the National. Laviolette was ready to go to court, and offered him $1,700 to sign with the Canadiens. The National had offered him $1,100.[95]

On the eve of the Canadiens' first match, Pitre lost a round in court against the National. The club obtained an injunction against Pitre. If he played, he risked a fine of $2,000 and six months in prison. Pitre appealed the decision. Trihey advised him not to play.[96] On the evening of 5 January 1910, Pitre lined up for the Canadiens on the Jubilee ice against Cobalt; he remained in the Canadiens' blue uniform for the rest of the season. Finally, in February 1910, Pitre won his appeal against the National, putting an end to this affair.[97] In the meantime, the National had withdrawn from professional hockey. The National suffered $293 in costs in this case.[98] After the retreat of the National, the Canadiens remained the only francophone team playing at the professional level.

## THE 1910 CHA-NHA MERGER

The battle for professional hockey supremacy concluded in just a few days, with the newcomer Canadiens emerging victorious. And so the 1910 season was mired in controversy from the outset. There were two professional leagues – the Canadian Hockey Association and the National Hockey Association – each composed of five teams.[99] Five of the ten teams were in Montreal. The three Montreal clubs in the CHA played in the Westmount Arena, on Sainte-Catherine Street West, and those of the NHA played in the Jubilee, on Sainte-Catherine Street East. But the public was not able to buy tickets for so many games. After just two weeks of activity, the two leagues decided to merge. Ottawa and the Shamrocks left the CHA ranks to join the NHA on 14 January 1910. That marked was the end of the Old League. Three teams ceased operations: Quebec, the All-Montreal, and the National. Quebec returned to the NHA the following year. The All-Montreal club proved ephemeral. The Canadiens franchise was offered to the National, but under four conditions, as *La Patrie* detailed: "1) that the association make itself responsible for all debts incurred to date by the Canadiens; 2) that the association play all its games at the Jubilee for 3 years; 3) that the association pay the sum of $1400 or thereabouts, the debt incurred to date by the Canadiens; 4) that the association pay the Canadiens players the sum of $6200, which is the salary of the Canadiens players for the season."[100] From the creation of the Canadiens, O'Brien had wanted to rid himself of the team as quickly as possible, aiming to sell it to francophone buyers. The National, however, found the conditions too difficult to meet, seeing that they were already in a precarious financial situation. Thus, O'Brien kept the Canadiens for the time being.

O'Brien retained the team but "lost" his best Canadiens player, Edouard "Newsy" Lalonde, by enticing him to join Renfrew – another team O'Brien owned. Despite having Lalonde, Renfrew did not become champions. Lalonde returned to the Canadiens the following season, when the club passed into the hands of the Club Athlétique Canadien (CAC) in the fall of 1910 following an agreement between O'Brien and Kendall, as the CAC had filed a lawsuit against the hockey team for the exclusive use of the Canadiens name. On 10 March 1916 the team took the name of the Canadian Hockey Club Incorporated,[101] just a few weeks before winning its first Stanley Cup at the Westmount Arena against the champions of the Pacific Coast Hockey Association, the Portland Rosebuds.

## CONCLUSION

Modern hockey was invented in the late nineteenth century by a group of Montreal anglophone friends. Within a few short decades, the sport's pinnacle was the Dominion Hockey Challenge Cup, a competition proposed by Governor General Lord Stanley in 1892 but known since 1894 as the Stanley Cup. So it is that this sport, which had been played only in a triangle of cities with vertices at Ottawa, Montreal, and Quebec City, began to spread across Canada. But the sport remained the preserve of an anglophone elite until francophones decided to join their ranks. The journey was long and arduous.

Thanks to their Irish classmates at Montreal's classical colleges, francophones began to play inter-college matches. When other francophone sports clubs embraced hockey, they had no choice but to ask these students to join their ranks. And, again, thanks to the Irish, the francophones were able to gain admission into the senior league by joining the Shamrocks teams. With this experience, they were able to help francophone clubs join the ranks of organized leagues, in the hope of one day joining the league that awarded the Stanley Cup. But once that goal was attained, everything collapsed, be it through the loss of key players or because of other teams' jealous ways. The professionalization of francophone hockey and the creation of a francophone team integrated into the anglo commercial-sport structure culminated in the Montreal Canadiens' victory in the 1916 Stanley Cup championship. In time, this is the club that would become the standard bearer of a Quebec nation. But it is not true that the Canadiens alone embody the history of francophone hockey. And we must not leave to oblivion clubs like the Montagnards and the National, and colleges such as Mont Saint-Louis, Sainte-Marie, or Saint-Laurent, in the history of hockey.

# 3

# LA SOIRÉE DU HOCKEY IN MONTREAL: NATIONAL STAKES IN A CULTURAL WAR

*Emmanuel Lapierre*

"What does it mean to be Canadian?" asked hockey scholar Andrew Holman in 2009.[1] The same question could be asked within Quebec. What does it mean to be Québécois? If Canadians find hockey along the path guiding them to an elusive collective identity, Québécois travel the same path and discover the same treasure. Or is it, in fact, a different path? In any case, hockey is a useful and important element in contributing to the construction of national identity in Quebec and in Canada. But has it been put to use in the same manner? This chapter aims to demonstrate that, in Quebec, Montreal Canadiens hockey has been the focus of a cultural war between the English Canadian and French Canadian (later Québécois) nations. Reflected in the history of the Montreal Canadiens, two very distinct nationalisms prescribe opposing views of what the prevailing cultural identity in Quebec should be.[2]

Starting with a definition of the concept of cultural nationalism, this chapter demonstrates that francophones have used sport, and especially the Montreal Canadiens, as a symbol to assert their cultural identity and their national aspirations as Québécois. It is here that one can find the reason for the team's popularity and success. On the other hand, much of the anglophone media and the Montreal Canadiens organization have actively denied the existence of this link in their communications regarding the team. By doing this, they implicitly suggest that the Montreal Canadiens should reflect a *Canadian* cultural and national identity.

## CULTURAL NATIONALISM

A great deal of academic effort has been expended recently on defining nation and nationalism, with perhaps the best of it being articulated by Anthony Smith and Umut Özkirimli.[3] Since the 1990s, a growing number of researchers have suggested that classical nationalisms (that is, civic and ethnic) are insufficient for defining the phenomenon of nationalism. The post-classical movement includes such diverse proposed concepts as cultural nationalism, communicative nationalism, socio-political nationalism, and banal nationalism.[4] These ideas have in common the notion that collective identity is fundamentally built on the sharing of a language community and a culture within a given area, rather than solely on citizenship or a biological relationship.[5] The post-classical movement, which is encompassed here under the umbrella term "cultural nationalism," is defined in the context of this research as the will to match national identity to a given cultural identity.

Cultural nationalism has been manifested in all nations since the creation of modern states in the late eighteenth century and into the mid-nineteenth century. Among researchers, there is a consensus that states are built on the basis of diffusion by a group that is in a position of power and/or in possession of the majority language, collective memory, customs, values, and ways of living in society in a common territory.[6] At the same time, cultural nationalism entails eradicating the culture of peoples or nations that are under the state's control or that are in the minority. In France, for example, at the time of the Revolution of 1789, 50 per cent of the population expressed themselves not in French but in another language, notably Occitan, Provençal, Picard, and Breton. Through various measures, primarily the mandatory use of French in the school system, these languages gradually waned.[7] Today, they have all but disappeared, and French is the dominant language of the land. Since the nineteenth century, a similar phenomenon of cultural nationalization has been reproduced in nations the world over. In Great Britain, Scots, Gaelic, Welsh, and Cornish ceded national use, to the benefit of English.[8] In the United States, dozens of Amerindian languages and the French language have disappeared from or been pushed out of the public arena,[9] and a similar sort of linguistic atrophy has occurred in other American countries, such as Peru, Mexico, and Brazil. For all practical purposes, this is a worldwide phenomenon. As Ernest Gellner underlines while considering countries of the East,[10] this process is what makes linguistic blocks relatively homogenous, or puts them on the path to becoming so.

As elsewhere, cultural nationalism has been a powerful force in the territory that is now Canada. After 1760, the proportion of the population whose mother tongue was French fell by about 70 per cent over the course of a century,[11] as a result of various measures. For example, the Act of Union brought together Upper and Lower Canada in 1840, and English was declared the sole official language of a united Canada. As well, in several parts of Britain's Canadian possessions (New Brunswick, Manitoba, and Ontario), 1848–1927, francophones' rights to be educated in French were systematically curtailed.[12] Though rarely addressed by Canadian historians, nineteenth-century efforts of the Orange Order in Canada to intimidate and terrorize francophones in several provinces certainly contributed significantly to their assimilation.[13] In spite of the popularity of French immersion in schools, and in spite of bilingual New Brunswick, in most Canadian public spaces outside Quebec one cannot see any French-language presence. In Quebec, meanwhile, French Canadians have succeeded in resisting English Canadian cultural nationalism and preserving their language, culture, and customs.

Moreover, cultural nationalism in Canada has had a special characteristic in that it has been particularly polarized around language. In Marcel Martel and Martin Pâquet's view, language was a political issue after the Conquest of 1760, and this set in motion a long train of linguistic conflicts throughout Canada. The assimilation project in the 1840 Act of Union, school crises resulting from provincial legislation that significantly reduced or abolished instruction in French, the conscription crises in the two world wars, the demands among immigrants to be educated in English in Quebec, and the wave of lawsuits to reduce the scope of Law 101 in that province have historically polarized the population into two linguistic camps. Claiming one's language in Canada also means claiming solidarity.[14]

Put simply, then, Canadian cultural nationalism since the eighteenth century has sought to equate the identity of the Canadian nation with English speakers (the dominant identity within a professedly "multicultural" nation) and the French Canadian nation with the French language; since the 1940s, Québécois cultural nationalism has also strived to associate national Québécois identity with French. In Quebec itself, this battle between English Canadian cultural nationalism and French Canadian – later Québécois – cultural nationalism has been fought in many arenas, including the sports arena.

## SPORTS AND CULTURAL NATIONALISM IN QUEBEC

Scholars in both sport history and post-colonial studies have shown how sport has been used to impose or claim a cultural and national identity, particularly in countries whose history has been marked by colonization. Whether used to discipline or to assimilate populations culturally, or, conversely, to disseminate a threatened national identity in a spirit of protest, resistance, and emancipation, the meaning of sports has gone beyond the boundary of the game – for example, in French and British Africa, the Basque country, Catalonia, India, Australia, Scotland, Ireland, New Zealand, or the former dependencies of the Soviet Union.[15] Though national contexts should not be automatically conflated (there is a difference between an Indian playing cricket against England or the Irish playing Gaelic games in Ireland), the phenomenon of sport as a site of identity and surrogate resistance is also true for Quebec. French Canadian cultural nationalism has stridently expressed itself through sport from the start.

Several authors have effectively shown that, since the beginning of modern sport in the nineteenth century, French Canadians have used their bodies as a means of resistance, recovery, and affirmation of their national identity. Jean Harvey[16] quotes, for example, an 1848 speech by Sir Étienne-Paschal Taché addressed to the French Canadian elite, urging them to establish physical education in the classical colleges: "Through lack of exercise, and consequently of strength and toughness, our youth becomes timid, irresolute, sheepish; and how could it be otherwise? Are not courage and daring born of confidence which, in the individual, is nothing but the deep conviction that he is able to overcome all obstacles, to triumph over all dangers? Thus, without exercise, no strength; without strength, no self-confidence; without self-confidence, no valiant men, but feeble, cowardly and pusillanimous beings."[17] According to Gilles Janson, repeated crises such as the 1871 abolition of funding to Acadian Catholic schools in New Brunswick, the Riel affair in 1885, the 1890 prohibition of the use of French in Manitoba schools, and the restrictions on teaching French in Ontario between 1890 and 1912 stimulated French Canadian nationalism in Quebec, particularly in sport.[18] As Michel Vigneault has shown in detail in another chapter of this book, the year 1894 saw the foundation of l'Association Athlétique d'Amateurs de Montréal (the National). Made up of French Canadians, the National was created to compete with anglophone teams in sports as varied as baseball, hockey, cycling, soccer, running, and lacrosse.[19] Janson points out that the main motivation of the club was to counteract the dogged prejudices regarding the superiority of anglophones and lack of initiative among francophones. In 1914 the secretary of the National wrote: "We who love sports, healthy and honest pastimes, reasoned physical exercise that creates muscles of steel, want strong athletes, *Canadiens,* who through doing sports acquire the spirit of discipline, daring and the tenacity indispensable for triumphing over life's obstacles. Our football, hockey and lacrosse champions will rout the adversaries of the French language."[20] The aim was thus to form sports organizations that would be the pride of the French-Canadian "race." In seminaries and colleges after 1870, efforts to develop sports received the support of clerical administrations, which provided the resources and equipment necessary to carry out hockey, baseball, or basketball projects.[21] This initiative is inscribed in the logic of education but also in the logic of adherence to French Canadian nationalism in the face of the risk of assimilation. In the framework of such activity, the clergy were defending French.[22] Élise Detellier shows that, in addition to the Catholic Church, the medical corps joined those voices calling for the use of sports to produce "golden souls in bodies of iron" and "strengthen national power."[23] Raoul Masson, a professor of pediatrics at the University of Montreal, explained at an academic conference in 1927[24] that "the struggle for life is becoming increasingly bitter and difficult, and the hesitant, the weak, the timid, are very soon relegated to inferior posts, while the bold, the brave, the hardy, assert themselves and ensure themselves good positions where they persist through their energy, their tenacity at their fighting spirit … On the one hand, the Anglo-Saxon is positive, hardy, tenacious, cold, authoritarian, wilful … but grasping; on the other hand, the Latin is polished, more flexible, somewhat dreamy, reserved, idealistic, passionate."[25]

### *From Joliat to Desharnais*

As elsewhere, in the nineteenth and twentieth centuries, sport was used in Quebec as a means of resistance and national affirmation, of waging a cultural war between a dominant group and a dependent group. In this context, why do the Montreal Canadiens make for such an interesting object of study? Nationalism is an abstract concept that is embodied in reality by means of concrete symbols such as national borders, passports, currency, national anthems, and, often, a national sports team. In the absence of a sovereign state, foreign relations, or the prospect of a national hockey team, Québécois nationalism necessarily has had to seek an embodiment elsewhere. It found that embodiment in the Montreal Canadiens. Many francophone supporters use it to dramatize a liberation fantasy, and to affirm their Québécois identity.

In the early twentieth century, "Canadiens" meant something different than what it means today. To call oneself "canadien" was to designate oneself as non-English, or even anti-English.[26] Moreover, the Canadiens team colours were chosen to refer to the motherland, France. All of the players from the first (1909–10) edition of the team were francophones, at least by heritage – among them, Newsy Lalonde, Didier Pitre, Georges Vézina, and Eugène Payan. This idea of boosting national spirit was a great success, and the francophone population of Montreal quickly identified with the Canadiens players. Supporters did not want anglophones on the team, as was evident in the scandal that erupted when the Canadiens attempted to sign defenceman James "Rocket" Power.[27] A *Le Devoir* article from 13 February 1911 reads: "Several newspapers and, above all, a considerable number of sportsmen protested against the hiring of Rocket Power as a 'Canadien player.' It's not that Rocket is not a good hockey player. On the contrary, he is a professional who has his value and if the public finds his hiring strange, it's because the 'Canadien' is felt to represent on the ice solely the French-Canadian colours. What is more, that's what gives [the team] its character and what *keeps it in our interest*."[28] In the view of *Le Devoir*, the Power affair was a "serious insult," "a blunder," "a dishonour" to the French Canadian nation. For this people struggling for over a century and a half against Anglo-Saxon assimilation, this event raised passions.[29]

If it is true that many intellectuals do not wish for their compatriots to attach themselves to such a sport, as Jason Blake and Andrew Holman remind us in the Introduction to this book, from the 1920s on the Canadiens nevertheless became a national symbol for the majority of French Canadians.[30] The Maroons (1924–38), a National Hockey League (NHL) team symbolizing English-speaking Montreal, stoked the rivalry between English and French, as outlined by Allan Turowetz and Chrystian Goyens: "How bitter was the Canadiens-Maroons rivalry? The answer best comes from Maroons defenceman Red Dutton, a western cowboy … Getting antsy before a game while the referee hunted for three ounces of black, vulcanized rubber, Dutton offered the famous line: 'Never mind the goddamned puck, let's start the game!'"[31]

Starting in the 1940s and 1950s, respectively, radio and television broadcasts in Quebec and the rest of Canada made it possible for French Canadians to follow live the exploits of Canadiens players. Fans travelled to the Montreal Forum "as if the nation's future were at stake" and, starting in the 1955–56 season, *La Soirée du hockey* held first place among the twenty top television shows in the Montreal region.[32] Stan Fischler and Maurice Richard summarized the popularity of the team – "Thanks to Vézina, Lalonde, Laviolette and Pitre, Les Canadiens rapidly obtained a distinctive image, which they have retained to the present day" – and Fischler quotes journalist Peter Gzowski to back up his point: "And the headlong, passionate way they have always played hockey has helped to make them *the* national team of French Canada in a way no team representing *all* of Canada, with its diverse, unmelted ethnic strains, could hope to parallel."[33] French Canadians identified with francophone players because these players were emblematic of their cultural identity, as a great many researchers and historians have argued.[34] The Canadiens embodied a form of political expression that the populace lacked. Christian Poirier, for example, underlines the exploits of francophones Bernard Geoffrion, Jean Béliveau, and Maurice Richard, who contributed so much to Stanley Cup victories in the 1950s and 1960s. In the 1970s, it was the Larocques, the Lafleurs, the Lemaires and others who collected an exceptional six Stanley

Cups within a decade. As Poirier argues, hockey in Quebec facilitated differentiation from Canada. French Canadians appropriated hockey *in their own manner* and used it to tell a story about themselves.[35]

That said, one must emphasize that this imagined liberation found much of its significance in identifying with the French language. As Lisa Anne Gunderson points out, hockey nationalism allowed French Canadians to affirm the importance of their language in the pitched battle they were fighting for survival.[36] The intimate link between national identity, the French language, and francophone Canadiens players is most evident in the marked popularity of francophone players among supporters, but it can also be seen in Quebec's many hockey-themed cultural products. Whether at the movies, on television, literature, or in songs, the tight link that has always united Québécois to francophone players is more than obvious. For example, Charles Binamé's film *Maurice Richard* is something of an allegory for the arduous rise of French Canadians at the dawn of the Quiet Revolution through the gains and setbacks of their idol. In another vein, Daniel Boucher fantasizes in the song "Boules à mites" that he has replaced Guy Lafleur as a hockey hero. In a key scene from Louis Saia's *Les Boys*, the figure of Ti-Guy, played by Patrick Huard, magically transforms himself into the *Démon blond* (i.e., Guy Lafleur). Galvanized in his mind by a Canadiens sweater bearing the number 10, he imagines himself racing up the ice, swiftly sweeping in a dramatic crescendo toward the opponents' goal. In another chapter in this book, Amy Ransom describes, in the same spirit, the series *Lance et compte*, in which French dominates the dressing room of the National, a professional hockey team. The most striking cinematic example of this link is undoubtedly the animated National Film Board of Canada film based on Roch Carrier's "Le chandail de hockey," in which each of the young boys emulates Maurice Richard.

Finally, is it possible that this close and special relationship between francophone players and the Québécois nation has had an effect on the Montreal Canadiens' on-ice performance? Between 1926 and 2012, when the team was at least 50 per cent francophone, it won the Stanley Cup every two or three years on average – an almost unimaginable achievement. In contrast, when less than half of the Canadiens players were francophone, the team's success rate proved to be average, that is, on a level comparable to that of the other five "Original Six" NHL teams.[37] The strength of this positive relationship between the proportion of francophone players and the incredible frequency with which the Canadiens won the Stanley Cup suggests that the team's winning ways and the international reputation that followed is very much due to the expression of French Canadian, and then Québécois, cultural nationalism. At the very least, such success is of great symbolic import for a team so closely allied to its home province.

The worth of the Quebec nation was, it seemed, sublimated into the courage and the athletic prowess of francophone Canadiens hockey players precisely because they were francophones. If their victories and their Stanley Cups acquired such significance, and if francophone players were so popular, it is because these achievements were superimposed onto the fantasy of liberation from anglophone domination and because the team and its players were living proof of the French Canadian nation's capacity to escape demise, misery, and mediocrity, to achieve the greatest success by being true to itself, its language and its culture. The example par excellence of this resilience is undoubtedly Maurice Richard. No other Canadiens player better symbolized the strength and courage of the entire French Canadian nation. Nonetheless, in this context it should be underlined that cultural nationalism is not about political independence (though it may lead to it), but about independence in terms of collective identity and of a cultural specificity of the French Canadian, then Québécois, nation.

In Quebec, the symbolic significance of francophone players' past exploits is taken for granted (and has been a common touchstone throughout this volume). And yet divergent interpretations from anglophone Canadian culture attest to a cultural war that exists precisely when imbuing Montreal Canadiens' players with meaning. Even in the case of the Rocket, there is much to say, or, in the competing narrative, to pass over in silence.

## MAURICE

The funeral of Maurice Richard was held on 31 May 2000. More than a mere legend, from the Quiet Revolution to today, the *myth* of Maurice Richard has supported Québécois aspirations for national affirmation. In Quebec, it is self-evident to say that Maurice Richard is culturally unique because he was *l'idole d'un peuple*. Many have situated his 1955 suspension as the starting point of the Quiet Revolution,[38] and he received a tremendous, sixteen-minute standing ovation at the closing of the Montreal Forum in 1996, just a few years before his death. One can read the following tribute in the website archives of French television network Radio-Canada: "His achievements, his spectacular goals and his desire to win have raised him to the rank of hero of the French-Canadian nation."[39] This is undoubtedly in recognition of the status that the government of Quebec offered to the family of Richard, since it underlined Richard's exceptional contribution to the construction to the *nation québécoise* by providing him with a state funeral. It was the first time in the history of Quebec that the government had decided to deviate from protocol in providing a ceremony usually reserved for premiers – complete with flying at half-staff "all flags subject to the Regulation Respecting the Flag of Québec" and the Quebec flag draped over the coffin.[40] To mark the occasion of his funeral, Radio-Canada broadcast the funeral live from Notre Dame Cathedral in Montreal, with Bernard Derome, the broadcaster's most seasoned news anchor, handling the reins for the French-language commentary.

The Canadian Broadcasting Corporation (CBC) – the anglophone side – also covered the funeral of "Rocket Richard." The now-defunct *National Magazine* presented excerpts from the ceremony in a short report: "Paul Arcand, one of the Rocket's closest friends, was determined that all Canadians, not just Québécois, could share in this moment of history." An extract from Arcand's account was then broadcast: "I also know that Maurice had many good English friends all around Canada … In your name, I will send a message to Maurice. In your name, I will say: Rocket, enjoy. Enjoy as much as you can. Et je dirais, en français, Maurice, jouis de cette paix, de ce repos éternel. Nous te le souhaitons tous de tout notre cœur. Merci."[41] The report concluded with a series of anecdotes told by Richard's former teammates, including Jean Béliveau: "There was so much pressure on him. By nature he was an introverted guy … We understood how Rocket was. Like we always said, he was leading us on the ice and that was the most important part of the group [sic] … He was a fine example, if you wanna succeed in any career … put a little passion in, work at it, I think he was a great example."[42]

Placing emphasis entirely on his sporting achievements, the CBC report made *no* mention of the myth of Maurice Richard as a source of inspiration for French Canadians during their quest for emancipation.

On the contrary, the emphasis fell heavily on the pan-Canadian aspect of the sport, brushing over the specifically Quebec nationalist aspects of Richard.[43] Was this tendency not to want to recognize the real reason for his popularity, namely his strength as a national symbol in Quebec, an isolated one? Given the importance that hockey assumes in Canada – it has the reputation of being more than a sport, of being, in Doug Beardsley's formulation, "an allegory of our life in Canada"[44] – this made for a rather surprising reading of the reality transmitted by myth.

According to Howard Ramos and Kevin Gosine, profound differences in fact marked the media coverage of Richard's death in anglophone Canadian newspapers compared to French-language Quebec ones. In their analysis of the main Canadian print media, for example, 97.4 per cent of articles in *La Presse* recounting the death of Richard and 88.5 per cent of those published in *Le Devoir* appeared in the first section. Only 47.9 per cent of articles in the *Montreal Gazette* and 34.4 per cent of those published in the *Winnipeg Free Press*, the *Calgary Herald*, and the *Vancouver Sun* appeared in the first section,[45] indicating that English-language newspapers clearly gave much less importance to the event (which is not to say that Richard's death went unnoticed in the Canadian press). Ramos and Gosine also note that the country's English-language media tended to rely on pre-written articles from news agencies such as Associated Press, Southam, and Canadian NewsWire instead of assigning their own journalists to the story. Moreover, the *Gazette* and the *Globe and Mail* were slower than others to publish articles on Richard's death simply because they had not entirely recognized the importance of the event at the time it was announced.[46] In terms of content, the authors also point out that the English-language newspapers mainly presented Richard's statistics, avoiding his personal life and his political resonance in Quebec. Quebec francophone media tended to do exactly the opposite.[47]

For Ramos and Gosine, the death of Maurice Richard provided proof that hockey, though a "supposedly unifying symbol," does not bridge the "enduring cultural gap between Canada's two solitudes" since coverage of this important event was characterized by profound linguistic differences.[48] Their article underlines particularly well the existence of a cultural war between two cultural nations, one denying the emancipatory project of the Québécois (even the cultural one), the other producing the identity of the Quebec nation. But is this propensity of Canadian and

Quebec communities to seize upon the symbol of Maurice Richard and assign it certain meanings over others a recent phenomenon? No. In fact, the first notable polemics stretch back to the "l'affaire Richard" – that is, to the Richard Riot of 17 March 1955.

At the time of the riot, various observers arrived at diametrically opposed conclusions about its causes and consequences. Four days afterwards, the journalist André Laurendeau wrote a famous article in *Le Devoir*. Entitled "On a tué mon frère Richard," the article alluded to nineteenth-century politician Honoré Mercier's reaction to the death of Louis Riel:[49]

> French-Canadian nationalism seems to have taken refuge in hockey. The crowd that roared its anger on Thursday night was not driven only by sporting rivalry or by a sense of the injustice committed against its idol. It was a people frustrated, protesting against its fate … But here is Mr. [Clarence] Campbell to arise to stop the momentum. One deprives French-Canadians of Maurice Richard. One breaks the momentum of Maurice Richard, which was going to clearly establish his superiority. And this "one" speaks English, this "one" decides in haste against the hero, provokes, incites. Well, he will see. One is suddenly tired of having always had masters, of having been bent double for so long. Mr. Campbell will see. One cannot be in the hands of bad luck every day; one cannot wring one's neck for misfortune every day.[50]

But others did not necessarily see things the same way. For example, Montreal journalist Nick Auf der Maur, who himself witnessed the riot, drew very different conclusions from those of Laurendeau, expressing them in a 1985 article published in the *Gazette*:

> One of the kids on the street phoned me and suggested we checked what was happening. My mother wouldn't let me go. I begged and pleaded. Finally, I snuck out of the house just as the game was starting. We went over to the old Atwater baseball park, where Alexis Nihon plaza stands today … People started throwing things. Rocks shattered the windows in the Forum. We saw a streetcar surrounded by the mob. Its windows were broken, and people were trying unsuccessfully to tip it over. They had better luck with a police car. Then we saw one of

those old wooden newspaper kiosks on Cabot Square go up in flames. At first, we kids on the sidelines felt a sense of excitement. Then fear. We went home … Some pundits claim the Rocket Riot was the start of the Quiet Revolution – the first howl of rage by oppressed French Canadians. But I don't at all remember it having an English-French connotation.[51]

A few months after the riot, Sidney Katz voiced substantially the same opinion as Auf der Maur in the Canadian weekly *Maclean's*. Conceding that "some germ of truth" could be behind the argument that it was the French Canadian nationalism that was the engine of revolt, Katz nevertheless concluded that none of the observations was sufficient to "explain satisfactorily what happened in Montreal on St. Patrick's Night."[52]

Suzanne Laberge and Alexandre Dumas examine in detail the wide gap between anglo-Canadian and French Canadian communities' antipodal responses to "l'affaire Richard."[53] *The Globe and Mail*, the *Montreal Gazette*, and the *Toronto Star* applauded the firmness of NHL President Campbell while unanimously condemning Maurice Richard, whereas francophone newspapers such as *Le Devoir*, *Montréal-Matin*, and *La Patrie* denounced the injustice committed against Richard. The stakes were clearly political, as was shown by the antagonism between the anglophone and francophone communities.

Laberge and Dumas's view is shared by David Di Felice, who has also researched the symbolic construction of collective identities in Quebec after the Richard Riot.[54] He claims that the controversy only channelled French Canadians' growing national sentiment in the face of the injustices to which they were subjected. Several clues can be found in the demography of the 1940–60 era. The subordination of French Canadians is evident if one compares their socio-economic position to that of the anglophone community. In 1961 francophones' annual salary was still on average 33 per cent lower than anglophones'. What is more, 69 per cent of anglophone non-agricultural workers had no high school or university education, whereas 54.2 per cent of their francophone counterparts did not go beyond the elementary level of education. Few French Canadians owned property.[55]

The sharp ethnic divisions and social injustices were also reproduced in professional hockey. Indeed, the image of the Canadiens had been formed on an ethnic basis by its first owner, Ambrose O'Brien.[56] Moreover, in professional hockey's first generation, few French Canadians reached the pro level, whether as players, referees, members of the NHL Board of Governors, or as league president.[57] According to Di Felice, injustice on the rinks, as in the NHL's offices, coupled with the league's resolutely Anglo-Saxon character, reflected, in hockey, the larger ethnic tensions and the nationalist claims of French Canadians.[58]

As well, Montreal and Toronto were the only two Canadian cities in the NHL at the time Maurice Richard was playing. If the Canadiens were the team that had the most francophone players and administrators, the Toronto Maple Leafs, English Canada's team, was the one with the fewest throughout the Richard era (1942–60). Beyond ethnic composition, even the personality of the two teams reflected the two nations. The Leafs were known for playing in a conservative Anglo-Saxon style based on strength and defence, whereas the Canadiens aimed for finesse and speed, "the flying Frenchmen," as the anglophone press were wont to describe them.[59] It was in the 1940s that the symbolic identities of these two teams become politically coloured. Significantly, given their great rivalry, they faced off in seven separate Stanley Cup finals. While conscription during the Second World War was dividing the country, the Maple Leafs organization took the political position of publicly supporting the policy, which was in keeping with Canadian support outside Quebec for the war effort. Owner and war veteran Conn Smythe pressured his players to act out their patriotism by enlisting in the Canadian armed forces.[60] The Canadiens team, meanwhile, was the least affected by the war and subsequently faced criticism about this from Toronto and, more stridently, from Boston.[61] Thus, if the Richard Riot initially resembled a trivial case of hooliganism, more in-depth analysis reveals that it had more to do with an already existing tension between the two nations.[62]

In Canada outside Quebec, there is relatively little ambiguity in the symbolism of hockey as a playing-out of a simplistic national identity. The robust process of naturalization surrounding the sport has been a powerful and effective way to promote the political and cultural unity of the country.[63] Today, the simple act of playing hockey constitutes a patriotic gesture – since hockey is the national winter sport of Canada. In Quebec, however, the symbolism of hockey is more problematic. As the various examples of the Maurice Richard myth show, and as the *specific* popularity of other francophone Montreal Canadiens shows, hockey has been transformed into a theatre where the cultural war between two competing national identities – English Canadian and Québécois – play themselves out. The successive language crises the team has had from the 1980s until very recently, as well as the severe critiques francophone fans and journalists alike have levied at the Canadiens management, make it clear that the war is still ongoing in Quebec.[64] This invites the question: What role has the Montreal Canadiens organization, a business corporation, played in the cultural war?

### *The Montreal Canadiens and the Manufactured Forgetting of Québécois Nationalism*

Ever since the first intellectual forays into play and sport by Johan Huizinga, Pierre Bourdieu, and others, most of the research on sport and society has tended to emphasize the intimate relation between sport, identity, and politics. Similarly, labour history and the histories of women, African Americans, and nationalism are replete with examples taken from the sporting realm. For example, in Canada, research into sports, especially hockey and the construction of Canadian nationalism, by a number of scholars – Jean Harvey and Hart Cantelon; Don Morrow; Alan Metcalfe, Donald Macintosh, Tom Bedecki, and C.E.S Franks; and Bruce Kidd and John Macfarlane – has proved authoritative on the topic.

And yet even today there are "naturalists"[65] who propose that sport is apolitical and serves only to mark social consensus. For Allen Guttmann, this stream of thought has been fed particularly by the various presidents of the International Olympic Committee,[66] who, since Pierre de Coubertin, have unceasingly repeated that politics has no place in sports, that the two do not mix (or at least should not mix), as well as by sports journalists who nevertheless thrive on political controversies.[67] In *Sport, Culture and the Modern State*, Hart Cantelon and Richard Gruneau explain the place that sport occupies in this apolitical perspective: "Sport is, in short, assumed to belong to an ideal realm of unrestrained voluntary action, expressive meaning and cultural creation, and state intervention is seen to be an unjustified intrusion into this realm. According to this view, sport should be an area of life that is somehow set-off from the realities of politics and government."[68] It is understandable why a sports organization such as the Canadiens, being concerned about managing its anglophone and francophone ticket buyers, might claim that its activities have nothing to do with nationalism. In response to yet another language-based criticism in 2010 – namely, that the Canadiens cared little about French or francophone players – owner Geoff Molson explained: "We don't do politics, we play hockey."[69] Officially, the Canadiens organization has always claimed not to meddle in politics, instead focusing just on hockey and the community. But from the point of view of cultural nationalism, this position is untenable.

Since their last Stanley Cup victory in 1993, the declining popularity of the Canadiens has led to poorer financial results and to public criticism. Because the new economic context of the NHL meant it was now extremely rare for players to spend their entire careers with the same organization, the Montreal Canadiens made a significant marketing turn. It had to convince the Québécois that it was no longer the players that made up the Canadiens but that the organization was *in and of itself* a Quebec institution. The Canadiens was to be not only part of Quebec culture; it was now to *be* Quebec culture. It was not necessary for the Québécois to be able to imagine the existence of Quebec without the Canadiens, despite the fact that its players are increasingly interchangeable and, as a group, less and less able to speak French. The organization has tried to achieve this result by organizing a broad marketing and communication campaign over several years of which the profits have been harvested in the long term.

For this, the team has been associated with community projects such as the construction of hockey rinks in disadvantaged neighbourhoods of Montreal, hockey programs for youth, and fundraisers to raise money in support of healthy lifestyles. The organization has also linked its players to charities such as the Montreal Canadiens Children's Foundation and organized well-publicized visits to sick children at, for example, the Sainte-Justine hospital centre.[70] As Fannie Valois-Nadeau argues convincingly in her chapter in this book, this vast operation has been very successful. Today, who in Quebec could seriously dispute the fact that the Canadiens organization is not only part of Quebec culture but one of its key institutions? Since 2010 the team has even had a street named after it: l'avenue des Canadiens de Montréal. However, these activities make the Montreal Canadiens' official position of cultural neutrality indefensible. It is indeed difficult not to meddle in politics while trying to become a pillar of a nation's culture. In fact, the Montreal Canadiens organization has wanted to do much more than this. It has tried – and continues to try – to reorganize the collective memory of the Québécois to *change* their national identity.

In spite of the recent intensification of such efforts, the first attempts to modify fans' memory took place in the 1930s. Julie Perrone hypothesizes that the legend of the anglo-Ontarian Howie Morenz was manufactured entirely by the Canadiens organization and the NHL in order to create an artificial popularity. Although he was a great offensive player for the club, and was the Canadiens' leading scorer for seven consecutive seasons, Howie Morenz was not particularly popular in the media. Perrone says there was little talk of him in the newspapers between 30 January 1937, the day after he suffered a serious leg injury in a game against the Chicago Black Hawks, and 8 March, the day of his death.[71] On 10 March, the Forum was transformed into a funeral venue and the general population was invited to come and gather in front of Morenz's coffin. The funeral was nationally broadcast on radio, and, since radio was then paid for by commercial sponsors, the fact that the Canadiens were footing the bill for the funeral broadcast would have been widely perceived as an altruistic gesture.[72] As Perrone writes, "the NHL and the Canadiens covered the full costs of this ceremony, a surprisingly altruistic move for a corporation," especially given that it occurred during the Depression.[73] The Canadiens also organized, with the Maroons, a benefit game in honour of Morenz a few months later, though this was not a great success. There is much evidence to suggest that Morenz did not necessarily have the status of a star player and that the idealized and artificially produced image of the player did not resonate among the public. There were thus two images of Morenz existing beside each other in 1937 – the one presented to the public and the one that was publicly perceived.[74] As Morenz is now accepted as an important figure in the pantheon of hockey, the Canadiens organization was clearly successful in shaping collective identity by creating an artificial popularity.[75]

The idea that the Canadiens organization would have a lasting influence on collective memory has also been explored by Anouk Bélanger. Her PhD thesis "Where Have the Ghosts Gone? Sport Venues and the Political Economy of Memory in Montreal" explores the Canadiens' 1996 move from the Forum to the Molson (now Bell) Centre. At the heart of Bélanger's thesis is a reflection on memory. The "historical process" and the production of identities are largely determined by the way in which social groups remember history. In this sense, the ability to control the memory of a society determines the hierarchy of power when members of a given social order all share a certain memory. Privileged groups are in a better position than others to make valid their representations of time and space, to disseminate and popularize particular ways of understanding the past and the present. The holders of political and economic power create, according to Bélanger, a hegemonic interest bloc capable of exercising cultural "leadership" in the state. In Quebec, the past was thus rearticulated by Molson at the ceremony marking the move from the Forum in order to recreate some traditions and to forget others.[76] The old Forum was an important place for counter-culture in Montreal, where particular ideas associated with Quebec nationalism could circulate.[77] But the ceremonies surrounding the closing of the Forum and the move to the Molson Centre rearticulated memory in a manner that voided it of controversial ideas associated with the emancipation of Quebec and, more specifically, with Quebec nationalism. The marketing campaign's ultimate aim was to orchestrate forgetting in a manner that would recreate continuity of memory from which any form of potential opposition or resistance to the new social order resulting from global capitalism would be absent, even memories of the past.[78] Several marketing operations were organized in this pageantry of homogenization that manifested the colonization of memory by means of ceremonies, parades, and festivals, presenting the inevitability of companies such as Molson in the cultural and civic life of Montreal.[79] Enjoying a great success, they had the effect of organizing the forgetting of various memories, including that of the francophone nationalist project.[80]

This omission also marked the activities surrounding the team's 100th anniversary in 2008–09. Alongside a host of other activities, the organization produced for this occasion a box of four special edition DVDs entitled "100 ans des Canadiens de Montréal / Hundred Years of the Montreal Canadians," revisiting important moments in the team's history. It is interesting to note that there are several direct and indirect references to the French Canadian and Québécois nations in the film. Interestingly, the national aspect is emphasized more in the French version: "La mort de Vézina et d'autres événements subséquents au Québec ont prouvé sans l'ombre d'un doute qu'à la fin des années 20, les Canadiens étaient devenus plus qu'une équipe de hockey, *ils faisaient partie de la culture d'un people.*"

In the English version the reference to becoming "part of the culture of an [unidentified] 'people'" disappears; it is replaced by the catch-all term "culture": "Vézina's death and the subsequent events in Quebec made it clear that by the late '20s the Canadiens were more than a hockey team. They were part of the culture." And the relation between Maurice Richard and the fans is described thus: "L'humanité de Maurice Richard l'a rendu plus qu'un joueur de hockey pour les partisans des Canadiens. Les événements l'ont fait passer de joueur étoile à celui *d'idole pour tout un peuple*." In the English version, one learns that "perhaps most of all his humanity made him more than a hockey player to the fans of les Canadiens," but there is nothing about Richard being an "idol of an entire people." That phrase is rendered as "[events] moved him from hockey star to near deity." Again, the reference to a people disappears, to be replaced by "near deity." A third, veiled, reference to the "province" and thus the people of Quebec, meanwhile, remains the same. However, it is mitigated or perhaps diluted by the addition of "the city": "l'équipe, les partisans, la province, sont interreliés. Cette relation est aussi profonde que complexe"; "the team, the fans, *the city* and the province are interwoven. This relationship is as deep as it is complex."[81]

Province? People? But which people are being spoken of? Nowhere is that stated. Everything transpires as if there were an effort to forget that, through its supporters' exceptional fervour and the prodigious exploits of its players, the history of the Canadiens has long been intimately linked to the project of cultural and political empowerment of francophone Québécois. Even today, the Canadiens organization is attempting to modify the collective memory of the Quebec nation by concealing or neglecting to name its symbolic raison d'être – a raison d'être that exists alongside and in the service of the purpose of selling hockey – for a vast majority of fans throughout history. This is a dynamic process: even as the organization taps into collective popular memories, it modifies those memories to serve its needs. The identity of the Canadiens was abandoned when the Maroons disappeared, in order to respond to a business imperative: to conquer the anglophone market.

Finally, it is worth highlighting the evolution of the Canadiens' language policy since 1938, because it is closely linked to the strategy of forgetting that the organization has orchestrated. It is known that, as a means of conquering the anglophone market in Montreal, the specifically French Canadian identity of the Canadiens was jettisoned when the Maroons folded. As has been discussed, until then the Canadiens was a team of French Canadians. However, just as in the case of Howie Morenz, there was an attempt to manufacture and make popular a new cultural identity for the Canadiens – that of a bilingual team. In the 1940s, 1950s, 1960s, and 1970s, the Canadiens teams were made up of approximately equal numbers of francophone and anglophone players, albeit always with a slight francophone majority. Yet the environment of the team was essentially anglophone, from the dressing room to the coaches and the corporate offices. By changing things, the organization was moving against the trend to make the public space in Quebec French.[82] Francophone fans, however, continued to read a proud symbol of the Québécois nation into the team. English supporters, meanwhile, tended to associate the team primarily with the city of Montreal and its bilingual character. And so two images of the Montreal Canadiens have come to exist side by side – the one that had been manufactured by the Canadiens organization, and the one that has been held by francophones.

It took competition from the Quebec Nordiques in the 1980s, which was threatening the market share of Molson's (the Canadiens owners') brewery, to force the organization into changing its corporate practices in matters of linguistic policy by making it correspond to the image of the Canadiens held by the vast majority of its fans. After they entered the NHL in 1979, the Nordiques foil spurred the Canadiens to francophonize its front office and pay particular attention to recruiting francophone players – even more than they had had to do since the introduction of a universal draft in 1963.[83] After Serge Savard had replaced Irving Grundman as general manager in 1983, and after Jacques Lemaire succeeded Bob Berry as coach in 1984, there was no longer a question about the general manager or the coach being anglophone. But the Canadiens organization's language policy changed once again after the Nordiques left Quebec for Colorado in 1995. The economic threat having disappeared, the requirements to speak French within the organization were soon relaxed. Since that time, games have always taken place in a bilingual environment and the announcer can never address the crowd in French only. Since the 2000s it has no longer been a requirement that the team captain be able to speak to the media in the language of Molière – something that would have been unthinkable just ten years earlier. Many supporters and journalists have also noted that the environment in the Centre Bell is becoming increasingly English. The organization has, for example, been criticized because the songs played there are increasingly English-language (up to 95 per cent by some estimates)[84] and because it has not drafted enough francophones. In 2010 management appointed an anglophone coach who could not speak French. This decision was frowned upon by several influential players in the public square, including the former general manager Serge Savard, as well as by Minister of Education, Recreation, and Sports Line Beauchamp and Minister of Culture Christine Saint-Pierre.[85] In 2012 the team owner publicly stated that bilingualism was a feature of Quebec culture.[86] This confirms that the strategy of forgetting orchestrated by the Canadiens corporation since the mid-1990s is being deployed in a cultural context. The organization has attempted to show not only that the Canadiens are bilingual but that Québécois *should* be.

## A DOUBLE TRUTH

Two main conclusions can be drawn from this study. First, it seems clear that this hockey team has been employed to nourish the cultural war between Quebec and Canadian nationalisms. Unquestionably, francophone fans have historically made a direct and powerful link between francophone players and their collective identity as Québécois. The on-ice successes of Maurice Richard, Jean-Claude Tremblay, Guy Lafleur, Patrick Roy, et al. were closely related to the expansion of cultural nationalism in Quebec. This link has been transferred to the Canadiens themselves and continues into the twentieth-first century – despite the fact that the team has almost no Québécois players or others who are capable of speaking French in interviews with the media. Ironically, many Canadian and Quebec anglophone media outlets have actively ignored the existence of a national French/Québécois identity that is specifically francophone and nationalist and that is symbolized by the Canadiens; indeed, a person studying the activities and communications of the team popularly known as the "Flying Frenchmen" could arrive at the conclusion that Quebec nationalism simply does not exist and that there is no grand "Flying Frenchmen" tradition.

The Montreal Canadiens are a canvas upon which contradictory cultural meanings have long been projected. In this context, it is possible for outside observers to perceive the organization as sending contradictory and ambiguous signals. While it has historically incorporated more francophones – both on the ice and in the front office – than any other team in the NHL, it has never recognized the link between its historic popularity and the project of cultural emancipation of the francophone majority, much less defended a national Québécois project. If scholarly work focusing on the Montreal Canadiens and its players speaks inevitably and abundantly about the tie that links them to Quebec cultural nationalism, it is revealing that, like many in the English media, the Canadiens organization itself has avoided the subject – for example, in the several important ceremonies that accompanied the 1996 move from the Forum to the Molson Centre, or the video commemorating the club's 2009 centennial. The activities of the Canadiens corporation are, of course, not coercive and do not have a direct effect on politics. But they do exert an influence on reality and identity. In Quebec society, the Canadiens are a figure of authority. Though this corporation does not foment any conspiracy to oppress or to assimilate Québécois, it does radiate the desire of powerful economic interests that express themselves in cultural and political terms. By silencing the cultural-nationalist discourse in Quebec memory, the Canadiens corporation wants to establish the values, tastes, and imaginings of French Canadians and Québécois differently. In doing so, it has also revealed a profound duplicity.

The Canadiens organization is disseminating a discourse that is based on a double truth. On the one hand, the team presents itself as a Quebec institution. The Molson Centre was a Québécois masterpiece, that of a people, said former Canadiens executive Ronald Corey.[87] On the other hand, the organization seems to avoid any staging of the Quebec national narrative and bans the unilingual use of French – that hallmark of Quebec francophone culture and society – while presenting bilingualism as a natural trait of Quebec society. These actions betray the desire of the Canadiens corporation to change the very meaning of what it means to be Québécois. It takes part in the cultural war in Canada by actively participating in the cultural assimilation of the Québécois people, by doing everything in its power to make Quebec identity and Canadian identity synonymous.[88]

The success of Quebec as a nation has in fact nothing to do with hockey or the discourse of the Canadiens corporation on the Québécois. It has everything to do with national affirmation in French.[89] But the fact that the Montreal Canadiens organization took an active part in the cultural war in Quebec is obviously not without consequence for the fans or for the collective identity of all Québécois. As Bélanger writes, a close connection binds the Montreal Canadiens to the process of identity construction.[90] We have also seen how fans have historically identified with francophone players and have played out and staged their performances in order to keep alive the project of broadly illuminating, of blossoming, the success and the independence of a French-speaking Quebec.

In another chapter in this book, Jason Blake, following Benoît Melançon, stresses that the Maurice Richard myth is not stable and can be imbued with many different meanings and senses. Significantly, this malleability of myth shows that the discourse depicting two cultural identities in Canada is by no means outdated. If we are actively changing the myth of Maurice Richard, it is precisely to give it more of a pan-Canadian dimension. There is no longer a core of francophones on the Canadiens, "sensationalism" is rampant, and Canadiens hockey is becoming a point of convergence between identities. All this is true. But that does not mean that these changes are any less charged with meaning in terms of national identity. The Canadiens organization is not yet ready, it seems, to drop its label of national symbol or to be relieved of its iconic standing.

The ceremonies and communication campaigns of the Canadiens dismiss Quebec cultural nationalism, thus making it a marginalized, inferior, exotic, *other* counter-culture, a form of subnationalism. Fundamentally excluded, the francophone fan then faces the challenge of reconciling two incompatible collective identities – that of his or her own community, the francophone culture of the Quebec nation, and that which the Canadiens organization wants to impose, the anglophone culture of the Canadian nation, in which his or her national identity is impoverished. This cultural colonization in which the "Habs" actively participate reshapes the identity sphere of the Québécois people and has important cultural consequences for the relationship between commerce, the state, and sport. These issues remain to be fully explored.

4

# HOCKEY AND PHILANTHROPY: THE LEGACY OF THE MONTREAL CANADIENS CHILDREN'S FOUNDATION

—

*Fannie Valois-Nadeau*

—

Thinking of hockey in Quebec usually leads one to the Montreal Canadiens. And for good reason, since the team occupies a hegemonic position in popular representations of Quebec hockey. For fifty years or more, movies, paintings, and popular songs about hockey have underscored an attachment to this team and its history. The ubiquity of the Canadiens in Quebec's public life, particularly in Montreal, reinforces this link. Besides Quebec-wide radio and television game broadcasts and the advertising visible in the mediated landscape, this public presence has taken new forms. This chapter proposes that the social importance and significance of the Montreal Canadiens hockey club has become more than that of a symbolic attachment linked to the political history of the French Quebecers, as Suzanne Laberge,[1] Tony Patoine,[2] and Emmanuel Lapierre (in this volume) argue. Rather, through the development of its philanthropic actions, principally through the work of the Montreal Canadiens Children's Foundation, this hockey team has transformed its concrete and effective presence in the public life of Quebec and in the ways by which the fans, the team, and the city/province are connected.

In addition to the traditional visit to a children's hospital during Christmas time, well established since the days of Jean Béliveau and Maurice Richard, Canadiens players also participate in the Annual Blood Donor Clinic to benefit Héma-Québec, a program that pre-dates the Children's Foundation by decades. As stated in the Foundation's report, "from the very beginning, each player who has worn the Montreal Canadiens uniform has lent support to sick children and their families. Moved by the youngsters' ordeals, the players have brought comfort and times of joy through their visits at the hospitals."[3] Each year, well-known players distribute T-shirts and autographed hockey cards, and add their signatures to various objects meant to help people get through their difficulties.

In recent years, especially since the advent of the Children's Foundation, the Canadiens have extended their areas of intervention beyond health care, thereby making the hockey club's name and logo widely visible. For example, in 2011 some players, with the collaboration of their spouses and the popular television chef Ricardo, launched a recipe book. Coordinated by Amy Moen, the wife of then-Canadiens player Travis Moen, this project aims to raise funds for the Children's Foundation; moreover, as she said, "it's the occasion to learn how to cook new dishes."[4] The book represents an opportunity to find out the preferred dish of one's favourite player, but it is also an aid in developing new eating habits. Another example of the diversification of the Canadiens' interventions is the creation of the program Bleu Blanc Bouge ("Blue Red Move"). With this program, the Montreal Canadiens hockey club has begun collaborating with other civic organizations in several venues and has built six community outdoor rinks in what it calls "disadvantaged neighbourhoods." The main goal of this philanthropic intervention is to help children fight obesity by engaging in sport. For the past several years, the Canadiens have thus become a progressive and forward-looking actor in health promotion in Quebec and not merely one providing remediation, moral support, and compassion for disadvantaged people. Through the support of its Foundation, the hockey club is becoming in its own way a leader in the community and, consequently, more than just an abstract national symbol or popular spectacle.

This chapter examines the links between professional hockey and the culture of philanthropy, and explores how, in the Canadiens' case, they have brought about and entrenched a sense of community belonging," especially since the team's centennial anniversary in 2009. Today, "Corporate Social Responsibility" (CSR) discourse is widespread among teams throughout the National Hockey League (NHL), and many of the league's professional franchises have sought to make and cement community roots through charitable enterprise. This chapter recognizes that hockey philanthropy is not unique to the Quebec context[5] and neither, as Andrew Holman notes in his chapter, is the connection between hockey and philanthropy wholly new. Still, its presence has been accentuated in the province in recent decades,[6] which have been characterized by the rise of a neo-liberal context in which citizens' responsibilities are increased and the presence of the welfare state is declining.[7] And the particular success of the Canadiens' community-through-charity initiatives makes them especially worthy of study.

Although the Montreal Canadiens Children's Foundation was officially created in 2000, the team's centennial celebrations in 2009 were the trigger for increasing its presence in the community. Presented notably as a legacy offered to a community that has loyally supported the team throughout the years, the Canadiens have implemented multiple philanthropic practices in the Quebec social landscape. From this perspective, the Canadiens are necessarily more than just a professional hockey club; the team is already a national symbol and in addition, through the social implications of the Foundation, the Canadiens have become a politically effective social actor.

This chapter investigates more specifically how these philanthropic initiatives have made the Montreal Canadiens a social leader in Quebec, while exploring the effects of this new role on fans and on the way that belonging is constructed through a conception of community – one that is quite new in the history of this team, even though it is the oldest in the NHL. Therefore, the Montreal hockey club contributes to the definition of the idea of a community in which youth and health issues occupy a prominent place, and makes concrete connections between various actors who would probably otherwise not meet.

Because many scholars (notably Terry Gitersos in this volume) have dealt with the Canadiens in terms of national belonging, my angle of analysis is a significantly new way of comprehending the bonds to the current, widely beloved team.[8] This chapter broadens the aperture by examining the production of a sense of popular belonging, both to hockey and to the Montreal Canadiens. Recognizing that philanthropy is an important tool of community outreach for many franchises across the NHL, and more generally across professional sports, it argues that the Canadiens are a special case. This is because their legacy as a *national* team provides them with a unique position from which to use their philanthropic activities to encourage others to give and participate – to build a robust sense of "we." Based on a media review and a contextual analysis, I investigate how, through the actions of the Montreal Canadiens Children's Foundation, hockey in Quebec is considered a vector for social change inscribed by a particular economic and political context and moulded by the will of the famous hockey organization.

## HOCKEY AND PHILANTHROPY: A FERTILE MIX FOR BECOMING A SOCIAL LEADER

> The Montreal Canadiens Hockey Club is more than an accomplished and legendary sports organization. (Montreal Canadiens Children's Foundation, *Report*, 2011–12)

It is through the Montreal Canadiens Children's Foundation that the hockey club shines in public activities in Quebec, with an annual operating budget of more than $1 million. In reaching more and more donors, the Foundation has given $16 million to charitable organizations since its creation.[9] The creation of the Foundation is part of a changing context in Quebec in which citizens and governments have begun to consider creative ways to increase the commitment of private enterprise in social life.

The Canadiens' community involvement reflects the phenomenon, including the discourse, of Corporate Social Responsibility, a term that describes the multiple ways in which private corporations have entered into public life. Such corporations have particularly shaped the discourse through philanthropic projects. In the domains of business ethics and community enterprise, and more recently in sport business, CSR is becoming a major keyword and receiving a great deal of attention.[10] Indeed, as one sports-focused administrative newsletter cited by Hela Sheth and Kathy Babiak has claimed: "There is no doubt that there is an increase in emphasis on CSR and philanthropy in professional sport.

Sport philanthropy is an emerging sector within corporate philanthropy through which professional sport organizations forge partnerships and strategically invest in the health and well-being of their communities by dedicating and leveraging both financial and in-kind resources to address local issues."[11] The goal here is not to outline the genealogy of this concept, and neither is it to find better strategies for improving community involvement by sport enterprises. Rather, it is to trace the contours of this new tendency and assess its implications for professional sports teams such as the Montreal Canadiens.

Community involvement is widespread among the teams in the National Hockey League. Certain recurrences in the types of fundraising events can be found among them (such as lotteries, golf tournaments, and silent auctions). Furthermore, some of the philanthropic activities of other teams are similar to those of the Montreal Canadiens Children's Foundation. For example, like the Canadiens, the Ottawa Senators have created a kind of refrigerated outdoor rink, called "Rink of Dreams," and the educational program Canadiens@School has been mirrored in projects run by the Ottawa Senators and Toronto Maple Leafs. The NHL thus seems to offer a specific framework for stimulating local commitment, one within which teams can decide where and to whom to donate. Since 1986, when the first foundation was established in the NHL (by the Vancouver Canucks),[12] involvement in the community has become a common endeavour all around the league. As a member of the NHL, the Canadiens have followed this parade while maintaining their own specific agenda.

In this context, the centennial commemoration activities, which extended over almost five years, were the perfect occasion to honour the longevity and rich history of the hockey club but also to give back to the community. Philanthropy found a central place among these celebrations and greatly contributed to the reputation and the visibility of the team. Spread over a range of activities and articulated through several spectacle forms, the practices of philanthropy initiated during this time reached different actors in Quebec society. For instance, some star players were honoured for their accomplishments by having their jersey numbers retired. To mark this special event, the Montreal Canadiens Children's Foundation gave $25,000 to each player to donate to the cause of his choice. Eight formers players were selected to make donations and some of them, including Bob Gainey, decided to give this money to their own charitable foundations.[13] These donations demonstrated that philanthropy frequently overlaps with the performance of celebrity, or, to quote Margrit Talparu's statement in a 28 May 2012 *National Post* article, "it's no longer good enough that you're good at something, you've won something, you have to give at least part of it to charity."[14] The circularity of these sorts of donation practices serves to reinforce the greatness of the players.

In Montreal, however, the centennial was also the trigger for initiating and increasing new partnerships, reinforcing the Canadiens' physical presence in the community, and spreading the name and the logo of the team across the Montreal region and the province of Quebec. For Sheth and Babiak, the purpose of CSR is not only to donate funds and in-kind items, but also to partner with other organizations and build strong networks for the betterment of the entire community. In this way, being a "partner" allows teams to address social issues faced by communities where they operate – needs that would not be addressed otherwise.[15] Becoming a philanthropic social leader entails, first and foremost, weaving links with leading social actors, which essentially means powerful corporations, governmental institutions, and other organisms already involved in community. To achieve their philanthropic goals, sports teams must find new partners and collaborators who will take them beyond the entertainment and hockey universes.

The case of the Montreal Canadiens Children's Foundation follows this logic; indeed, the Foundation is very active in the creation of all sorts of partnerships, with both international companies and local administrations. As evinced by the report on the outdoor-rink project launched during the centennial, this initiative has been the perfect pretext for new collaborations:

> The initiative is part of BLEU BLANC BOUGE, the Foundation's flagship project with the objective of building five refrigerated outdoor multipurpose community rinks that can accommodate various sports activities in less privileged neighbourhoods in the greater Montreal area. Eager to provide high quality infrastructure, the Foundation works closely with Roustan United, a leader in the area of arena products and services, in the implementation of this type of playing surface. With this aim in view, the Foundation agreed to

> a five-year partnership with the FTQ (Fédération des travailleurs du Québec), the Fonds de solidarité FTQ, City of Montreal blue collars, FTQ construction workers and local entrepreneurs which contribute to the project by providing material and manpower ... Over and above the infrastructure, the borough benefited from the generosity of Bauer Nike which donated 100 pairs of skates, helmets and sticks to create a bank of supplies to be able to fill the needs of various local organizations that work with children.[16]

Over the past decade, the Canadiens hockey club has created notable partnerships with FTQ-Construction, City of Montreal blue-collar workers, the hockey equipment manufacturer Bauer, and the chef Ricardo. We can also add to this list the grocery-store chain Metro, Rio Tinto Alcan, and Desjardins (the largest financial cooperative in Canada). While their philanthropic activities focus primarily on children's health, these partners (except for the organization Québec en Forme) are neither directly involved with children nor experts in the improvement of social conditions. However, partnering with influential actors in Quebec society who possess considerable financial means seems to have brought about win-win situations. These new forms of visibility benefit each partner involved, who become more powerful through their collaboration, regardless of their original areas of expertise. The benefit of social acknowledgment redounds to all those organizations that work alongside the Canadiens on charity projects. As the mayor of the LaSalle district, Manon Barbe, said at the inauguration of the outdoor rink funded by the Canadiens Foundation: "I am very happy to see this incredible project come to fruition. It's a legacy for our youth that could not come at a better time as we are about to celebrate our centennial. It truly reflects the will of the elected members to establish meaningful partnerships in order to provide our citizens with a state-of-the-art and accessible facility that makes us all proud."[17]

According to Sheth and Babiak, sport philanthropic organizations tend to look for long-term partners, including, and perhaps foremost among them, those in government. This kind of long-term partnership was manifest in the creation of *Canadiens@School* in 2007, an educational program aimed at elementary students. Allowing a private intervention into what had been a public domain, the Quebec government funded *Canadiens@School* for more than two years. However, because some considered the collaboration to be both a form of privatizing welfare-state functions and, especially, a form of disguised advertising, this particular partnership and specifically its public funding sparked controversy during the centennial year. As Pierre Saint-Germain, president of the trade union Fédération Autonome de l'Enseignement, claimed, any form of interference in public schools is inadmissible.[18] In response, Jean-Pascal Bernier, the press secretary for the education minister, justified the initiatives of the hockey club by claiming that "the Canadiens are not a private enterprise like the others. They are a part of history. They are an institution rather than an enterprise."[19] For Bernier, the fact that the Canadiens had been part of Quebec's mediated landscape for a century was enough to trump the team's essentially commercial orientation and its use of public education to market the team.

In the year after the controversy erupted, government funding to the program was rescinded. Nevertheless, the program still exists and has been adopted by teachers from every one of the province's school boards.[20] This example therefore shows how the powerful aura of the team (based particularly on its longevity) remained unscathed and its privileged position in Quebec society unshaken. The historical character of the Montreal Canadiens was evoked as an argument legitimizing its penetration into a "sacred domain" (such as the public education system), while its multiple and widespread partnerships further established the hockey team as an important actor within Quebec society. However, to some, the Montreal Canadiens crossed a line with *Canadiens@School*, perhaps because of the overtly national character of the educational system, which arises out of a different form of belonging in this province. Here, where the modern education state apparatus is comparatively new and the product of Quiet-Revolutionary ideals, and where schools are an essential locus for constructing national identity, citizens are especially wary of mixing private interest with public prerogative. This case highlights the limits in the Quebec context to the amalgamation of private and public endeavours, especially ones that might be interpreted as a business's co-option of an important public function.

The general discourse of CSR and the philanthropic initiatives undertaken by NHL teams, then, are not always successful. That said, when NHL teams' CSR initiatives are connected in a more direct way to their sport, the initiatives have had a greater measure of success.

The same pattern is evident in the case of outdoor rinks and other venues in Quebec's public space.

## A LEGACY OF VALUES

> With over 100 years of history, the franchise taps into its resources to spark interest among Quebec's youth in school. Discipline, dedication and determination are all values embraced by professional hockey players, and they are also values that the Montreal Canadiens want to pass on to young people so that they may grow in their educational and personal journeys.[21]
> (Montreal Canadiens Children's Foundation, *Report,* 2008–09)

In presenting its message on the importance of education, and in promoting behaviour such as discipline, dedication, and determination, this quotation puts forward an image of a team that values moral virtue. As the Foundation's reports show, being a philanthropist is not only a matter of giving money or reaching partners; it is also a way of educating, changing children's habits, and inculcating a way of life. The Canadiens' legacy is consequential, and not only in terms of materials and funds. It is also a matter of passing down certain values, which might in turn affect the image of the donor and the behaviour of the receiver. Adding a signature to a cheque or organizing a charity event is no longer a surrogate for heroism; in promoting CSR values, the Montreal Canadiens Children's Foundation aims to bring about permanent social transformations in its followers' ways of life. But it seeks to embody them too. In pursuing the promotion of moral virtue, the Canadiens' legacy plays on other dimensions of CSR discourse.

As might be obvious, becoming a role model through CSR can ameliorate the public image of the players, to remove them from the images of luxury, scandal, and performance-enhancing drug use that have generally coloured modern professional sports and that, as Amy Ransom shows in another of this book's chapters, have entered into the depictions of hockey heroes in popular culture. Over the last two decades or so, major sports teams have sensed a social responsibility for its players to behave better, and to be seen to be behaving better – to cultivate an image of morality to whitewash some of the more sordid aspects of life in the entertainment industry. By placing the team at the heart of the community, philanthropy lends a ubiquitous "positive" visibility. Through direct and indirect marketing of the franchise, philanthropic work helps create, to quote scholar Rebecca Robinson, "an image of a team as a solid corporate citizen worthy of support."[22]

In Montreal, this positive visibility is generated by more than the Foundation and the team's players themselves.[23] Image-making is also performed, as Canadiens' CEO and co-owner Geoff Molson has said, by the wives of the players who participate in the Santa's Christmas Basket program and the alumni who attend their Radio-Telethon and Golf Tournament. "The role our company plays outside the arena is one we take seriously," Molson stated in 2010. "It is a role that fits with our objective of actively participating in the development of healthy lifestyles."[24]

In this singular manner, one big, legendary Canadiens family is thus mobilized to perpetuate a will to act for social change. The weight of tradition is frequently reiterated by the team and gives the impression that the Canadiens (all of its members, near or far) have always been a social leader, concerned with their role in the community and with modelling what it means to be a good citizen. In creating a direct connection with the fans through donations and the promotion of specific behaviours and values, the hockey club now does more than merely give money to worthy causes; it provides direction for Quebec society, especially for youth, and has become, intentionally or not, a powerful actor in Quebec society.

## FANS AS VOLUNTEERS

As we have seen thus far, the Montreal Canadiens Children's Foundation has carved out a peculiar CSR strategy. Premised on the hockey team's unique inscription in the history of the province and its avowed commitment toward Quebec's future, philanthropy for the Canadiens constitutes more than a strategy to earn a profit; it also shapes *how* one might become attached to the team. Because their revenue depends on popularity, all sports teams develop an affective relation to their audience and supporters through their performances on the field, court, or rink. Via philanthropy, sports teams' reach extends beyond the stadiums in which they play and into the broader community. Philanthropy constitutes, in this sense, a profitable way to reach fans and to develop a wider series of connections within their milieux. Besides helping offset negative popular concerns about astronomical player salaries and high player turnover that sometimes undermine fans' connection to the team (as Robinson notes, "athletes rarely stay in one city, they have to build new support every time they move, essentially starting over each time"[25]), philanthropy is part of the mediated landscape and assists in strengthening the links of attachment between professional sports teams, places, and fans. As Sheth and Babiak observe, "reaching out to a community through philanthropic efforts generates interest in a team and builds a fan base. These fans, in turn, may be more likely to follow the team and become life-long fans, which may affect purchasing decisions."[26] Recruiting new fans has been a notable part of recent philanthropic activities undertaken by the Canadiens.

Being a fan is not just a matter of taste, preference, or knowledge about the statistics and the history of a team. In playing upon loyalty and mobilizing intimate citizenship, philanthropic actions transform one's status as a fan and the general framework through which the team is seen. One of the effects of integrating moral virtues into the marketing plans and the philanthropic goals of sports teams is, to quote from Lauren Berlant's analysis of mediated compassion, a "claim on the spectator to become an ameliorative actor."[27] As we can see with the case of the Foundation, the call to participate in philanthropic activities has been accentuated in recent years; fans are now also a part of the process of fundraising and they have simultaneously become a way to render it more visible. The shift to conspicuous giving affects everybody: even non-heroes are invited to do more than just sign a cheque. Because it evokes moral duty and entails close engagement, the new philanthropy establishes proximate links between corporate organizations and the community.

The charitable event "Street Hockey de Rue" provides a good example of this new philanthropy. In May 2012 the Montreal Canadiens Children's Foundation, with the collaboration of YM-YWHA (the Montreal Jewish Community Centre), launched a massive street-hockey tournament to raise funds in a playful manner. The participation fee was fixed at $200 for adults (with a team commitment to raise $2,000) and $100 for youth (with a team commitment to raise $1,000). In this context, being a great hockey fan means being implicated in, involved with, concerned about, and dedicated to finding money for the Foundation. In the process, fans are gradually transformed into volunteers and fundraisers, and fandom into a space of activism for the team. Articulated through a discourse promoting physical activity and nostalgic feelings associated with "playing outside like in the old days," this fundraising event aimed, moreover, to encourage the practice of hockey. Here, the financial legacy of the Montreal Canadiens is thus connected to both the history and the playing of the game of hockey.

Giving tips for increasing fans' ability to reach their fundraising goals, the "Street Hockey de Rue" website calls personally on young fans to improve their fundraising abilities:

> Be passionate about your mission to play hockey, help kids and have fun! Friends and family are happy to support someone who believes in their cause.
> Reach your email contacts with a personal message. Use powerful words to emphasize your belief in the cause.
> Write a strong statement on your player page! Include a picture.
> Get organized! Make a list of those you would like to approach and keep track of your follow-up list.
> Be specific! Know what you are asking for and don't be shy to mention a dollar amount.
> Learn about the cause. An informed fundraiser is a successful fundraiser!
> Make a personal donation! It is easier to ask if you have contributed yourself.
> Challenge other teams, or your teammates, to raise as much as you!
> Invite your friends to our Facebook Fan Page.
> Spread the word and link to our Twitter![28]

This example demonstrates how philanthropy mobilizes belonging to the team and the community on a small scale, in an intimate manner, while cultivating fan dedication. It also highlights how this relation becomes not a passive or abstract feeling but rather an active practice in which, as Samantha King says, "subjects are addressed and understood as individuals who are responsible for themselves and for others in their 'community.'"[29] Through the promotion of the practice of an "old" or "traditional" sport, in *playing* hockey (or a version of it), this philanthropic strategy shows a new way to be a fan. In playing street hockey for a good cause, fans themselves participate in a redefined citizenship, a sort of belonging formed around individual responsibilities in fans' hearts and consciousness.[30] However, these charitable events develop belonging not just between the fans and the team, but also among the fans themselves who participate in the fundraising and consequently propose a different kind of collectivization than the one usually theorized through national lenses.

Through this call for involvement in community, the practice of philanthropy is materialized through the promotion of a corporate and intimate citizenship, in which fans themselves are responsible for its maintenance. Maintaining that sense of citizenship means passing on its meaning and mentality to the next generations of fans. One way of doing that, as Sheth and Babiak suggest, is through collective projects, such as the construction of outdoor rinks in 2009.

And it is the continued *collective* aspect of philanthropic citizenship that, in the end, matters most and ensures legacy. The legacy of and responsibility for this kind of community belongs not only to the Montreal Canadiens organization. In the case of the outdoor rinks, it also belongs to the blue-collar volunteers who build them, the partners who finance them, and the people who live in the "disadvantaged" neighborhoods who must ensure the rinks' maintenance. This form of legacy demands their "accountability" and implies a responsibility for the perpetuation of hockey playing in the community. In transforming public spaces, affecting public budgets, and developing personal involvement, the Montreal Canadiens cannot be seen merely as empty entertainment that moves citizens away from political life. On the contrary, through its Foundation, the Canadiens (and other sports organizations like them) keep citizens close to social issues in an everyday and intimate manner, albeit on a different scale than through traditional political involvement.

## FROM NATIONAL TO COMMUNITY BELONGING

As stated at the opening of this chapter, the attachment expressed to the Canadiens through philanthropic activities constitutes a significant shift in the way fans belong to hockey in Quebec, which has usually been understood in a national (and identity-based) framework.[31] While co-existing with this form of belonging, these practices challenge the common way of examining belonging and hockey in Quebec because, as we have seen, philanthropy gives rise to an abstract concept of community in which members are seen to be relationally involved, regardless of their language or political affiliation.

The dominant conception of hockey as a symbol of the nation is not exclusive to Quebec's academics and fans; it is also meaningful in Canada as a whole. Paradoxically, the relation between hockey and nation underwent a good deal of examination in the academy at the very moment when its existence seemed challenged by the growing "spectacularization" and commodification of hockey in the 1990s.[32] Inspired by a political-economy approach, Richard Gruneau and David Whitson developed a critique of this new tendency among NHL hockey teams. At the beginning of the 1990s, the emergence of new hockey markets was seen to be a threat to belonging and to already existing hockey teams, especially Canadian ones. As Gruneau and Whitson wrote: "The agenda of 'global culture' has nothing to do with cross-cultural understanding and everything to do with the larger profits to be gained by expansion into new and affluent markets. Indeed, as cultural products become directed at international markets rather than at national or regional markets, many traditional connections between cultural practices and national identities threaten to be lost in the process – with the connection between hockey and Canadian 'national' identity as a prime example."[33]

From this perspective, the cultural (and climatic) specificities that once linked hockey and Canada might be broken, with the link being adversely affected by the delocalization of the sport. The attachment to hockey can also be seen as being interchangeable with other sports (already widely broadcast on cable channels), which renders it susceptible to losing its historical place. Even if Gruneau and Whitson do not consider hockey to be a natural practice in Canada, they definitely conceptualize hockey as a cultural practice which conjures up and evokes the nation, while reinforcing the obviousness of this association. In Quebec social discourse, the decrease in the number of francophone players playing for the Canadiens and the purchase of the team by the American George Gillett at the beginning of the 2000s produced the same feelings of loss and dispossession and consequently triggered a similar discourse.[34]

However, as the multiple examples depicted above have shown, sports teams' philanthropic interventions do not directly challenge the idea of declining senses of belonging. Rather, they serve to unify fans and help to concretize a collectivity, and even push fans to imagine themselves "one of the team," or, in this case, the Canadiens' community. In linking fans to another form of collectivity, and as a significant and shared cultural practice, philanthropy gives birth to another way of being together – that is, other than one based on national terms or intrinsic identity. Even as the Canadiens organization's discourse refers often to a "common past" and asserts its place in Quebec's historical landscape – highly politicized terrain indeed – its philanthropic activities put forward the idea of a community outside of or above politics. Through the practices of giving and receiving, the Montreal Canadiens claim to pursue moral and collective goals. This is in line with Raymond Williams's 1976 claim that, even if its signification is never consensual and never stopped, the term "community" designates direct relations organized around actions performed to benefit others: "In some uses this has been given a polemical edge, as in community politics, which is distinct not only from *national politics* but from formal *local politics* and normally involves various kinds of direct action and direct local organization, 'working directly with people,' as which it is distinct from 'service to the community,' which has an older sense of voluntary work supplementary to official provision or paid service."[35] In showing solidarity with their fans (while giving specific directions and establishing a kind of leadership), the Montreal Canadiens perform this concept of community, one that offers us another reading of belonging and hockey markedly different from the one oriented by nation.

There is no denying completely the spectacularization of sports and the ways this affects attachments – national allegiances – to hockey teams, in particular. But the sort of attachment that this chapter identifies – in the sense of belonging to a hockey community – appears to be a consequence of these processes, one that displaces the national framework. This displacement can be interpreted as a decline of the hegemony of the national framework, but it does not mean that all forms of belonging are completely disappearing.

This transition away from national considerations is not without consequence for the Montreal Canadiens hockey club's image and its presence in public life. For example, the emphasis the team puts on the notion of community building through philanthropic events evades the singular linguistic (and therefore national) debates around the low proportion of French speakers on the team and francophones' feeling of dispossession mentioned above. Through the Montreal Canadiens Children's Foundation, the hockey club professes to take care of all children – regardless of whether they are francophone, anglophone, or allophone. Following Benedict Anderson, the concept of community is generally less polemical than the one of nation, because community puts the emphasis more on the relations of the everyday and asserts a "status quo." And, as Raymond Williams has stated, "what is most important, perhaps, is that unlike all other terms of social organization (*state, nation, society,* etc.), it seems never to be used unfavourably, and never to be given any positive opposition or distinguishing term."[36] The Montreal Canadiens' community presents itself as careful and inclusive – that is, at least for those who practice sport and integrate its values into their lives. In the community for which the Montreal Canadiens are working, everybody speaks the language of hockey. This is the language of a social guide that circumvents existing debates by proposing other issues or factors – childhood, for instance. To be sure, the remediation of belonging and displacement of critical debates should not be interpreted as signs of the waning importance of the team's political dimensions.

In fact, the philanthropic actions of the Montreal Canadiens are a kind of *re-politicization* of the team, notably because the hockey club is becoming a social leader in Quebec by giving direction to society and creating other political spaces (such as the bodies of children) and other political actors (such as powerful partnerships and fan activism). As the political and cultural riot triggered by the 1955 Maurice Richard suspension showed,[37] hockey in Quebec has for a long time been considered more than mere leisure and entertainment; it has been attached to the project of emancipation. Hockey in Quebec has been seen as a national and a cultural symbol, and for many years now, because of the emergence of foundations and structured philanthropy among professional sports teams, it continues to be political. Through the "community of the Canadiens," projects continue to move, funds circulate, and behaviours and the cultural landscape are transformed. Finally, even if national belonging undergoes transformation, it does not mean that it disappears totally. Both ways of being attached to the hockey club (as nation and as community) can co-exist, and, as Lauren Berlant states, "the remediation of national life away from the federal state does not blank out the nation but sees patriotism as a feeling of abstract intimacy practiced from the ground up."[38]

## CONCLUSION

Examining the Montreal Canadiens Children's Foundation brings to light the implications in public life of professional sports teams' philanthropic activities. As the examples presented above show, the practice of philanthropy by professional sport organizations is now common and has become more structured and well organized. Although the Montreal Canadiens organization shares with other professional sport teams similar principles and ways of being involved in their communities, philanthropy does not necessarily affect or mobilize fans in the same way. Since the centennial anniversary, many philanthropic practices have been woven into a discourse on legacy, because, as is noted in the Foundation *Report* of 2008–09, "the Montreal Canadiens are part of Quebec's rich heritage." These activities have thus reinforced the promotion of hockey and legitimized the accentuated presence of the team in the public space, on behalf of its specific traditional dimension. During the centennial and ever since, the organization has referred to its own unique past, a past integral to the history of the province, to explain its community involvement.

The aim here has been to identify some of the main issues involved with the Canadiens' particular kind of philanthropic legacy, notably the (not always successful) pursuit of partnerships, the team's promotion of moral virtue and new ways to express fandom, and the shift in the collective framework of belonging. The representations of "goodness" that the team promotes are intertwined with its marketing strategy, and this examination has therefore explored the transformations that have occurred in public life (in promoting certain kinds of behaviours and commitments to special causes) and the way these transformations make use of and rely on intimate support. These shifts are significant to the specific linkages among hockey, belonging, and Québécois identity, if only because they open and multiply the forms by which these concepts are now expressed. Nevertheless, many issues remain shadowy after this exploration, appearing more as questions than conclusions. For example, why have the Montreal Canadiens decided to make such a significant commitment to children? Is there something about the status and place accorded to childhood in Quebec society that has led it to attract so much attention?

The increased presence of philanthropic activity also has consequences for Quebec's public life. The Montreal Canadiens Children's Foundation, through its extensive resources, is giving visibility to some selected causes and participating in the social discourse on childhood, and thereby establishing a moral model. Through its Foundation's activities, the Montreal Canadiens hockey club is clearly becoming a social leader with considerable impact. The embodiment of this new role invites another set of questions that need to be clarified – notably what it means for a sports organization to be a social leader in the style of a political leader, and whether that role is relevant for other NHL hockey franchises. Political and social leaders alike distribute resources for disadvantaged people, coordinate projects and partnerships, and promote good values. There does not seem to be a great difference in the way each proceeds. But the major point that distinguishes them is this: even if they each endeavour to transform public space and initiate programs for helping people, they do not have the same accountability among the community. As Paul Tracey, Nelson Phillips, and Helen Haugh have noted, dialoguing with the members of the community is not necessarily at the core of philanthropic organizational procedure.[39] Many projects financed by the Foundation are coordinated by NGOs which have their own aims and relevance in their communities. What happens with the kinds of projects specially conceived and promoted by the Foundation, such as the outdoor skating rinks and Canadiens@School? Have "disadvantaged" neighbourhoods that received outdoors skating rinks been consulted about this investment in their community and asked whether it meets a real need? Who is really convinced, beyond the Montreal Canadiens, that children want hockey – want to play it, and to pursue this tradition? All of these questions suggests that, in the ways that corporations (and especially sports teams) declare themselves responsible, societal stakeholders, a new form of governance is emerging. And this emergence can be seen as the intersection of the sports-spectacle system, the neo-liberal transformations of citizenship, and (in the specific case of the Canadiens) the discourse of legacy.

5

# LABOUR, *FRANCOPHONIZATION*, AND NATIONAL IDENTITY IN HOCKEY'S BATTLE OF QUEBEC, 1980–1983

—

*Terry Vaios Gitersos*

—

In April 1982 Quebec's two National Hockey League (NHL) franchises, the historically dominant and culturally iconic Montreal Canadiens and the upstart Quebec City–based Nordiques, faced off for the first time in the Stanley Cup playoffs. Across the wall-to-wall media coverage of this inaugural "Battle of Quebec," one newspaper column stood out. In the weekend tabloid *Dimanche-Matin*, sportswriter Jerry Trudel cast the Nordiques and Canadiens as characters in the historical second Battle of Quebec, fought by British and French forces on the Plains of Abraham in Quebec City in 1759:

> September 13, 1759, second siege of Quebec where Wolfe and Montcalm perish. And the day arrives when the English become masters at home and found *The Gazette* and later the Maroons. The Maroons die an honourable death before the Canadiens and flee up the 401. But the phantoms of the Plains of Abraham prowl again. The Fleurdelysés seize Quebec and insidiously the Maroons are reborn in the guise of the Canadiens. Cunning, guile and gumdrop! And here we are at the siege of Quebec III. But Bergeron's troops were decimated on the

> eve of the great battle. A week earlier, General Berry had ordered his redcoats to demoralize the enemy with sneaky incursions … Still, the thunder rolls and the natives are restless. Intendant Filion in Quebec [City] tries to fortify his forces with battle-hardened soldiers such as Wilfrid Paiement, Marc Tardif, Michel Goulet, Réal Cloutier, Alain Côté, Daniel Bouchard, a phalanx of descendants of the settlers of New France, to whom, for good measure, three mercenaries from the old country were added. Meanwhile, back on St. Catherine St. West, the Maroons inspect their troops for the Battle of Quebec and for the repatriation of the Constitution. It is with pride that the gauntlet goose steps before Governor Grundman, the Robinsons, Shutts, Napiers, Wamsleys, Actons, Wickenheisers, Langways, Engbloms, Brubakers, Nilans, Risebroughs to whom are added a Lafleur, a Tremblay, an Houle, to comply with the section of the law that says that Frenchmen are acceptable "where the number warrants."[1]

Militaristic representations are not unprecedented in Quebec's hockey culture: the first act of Rick Salutin's celebrated play *Les Canadiens* (1977) also used war as a metaphor for hockey, but it placed the Canadiens in the role of the French forces on the Plains of Abraham, in line with their historical role in the province as representatives and standard bearers of the French Canadian nation.[2] While hockey's first Battle of Quebec occurred only five years after the publication of Salutin's play, it is clear from Trudel's column that Quebec's pro-hockey landscape had changed dramatically in that time. In 1982 it was the Nordiques and their "phalange de descendants des colons de la Nouvelle France" who symbolically defended the nation. The Canadiens, sporting British military red coats, represented a colonial force.

Through a detailed analysis of the hockey content in Montreal's and Quebec City's French-language newspapers in the early 1980s, this chapter argues that the issues then debated through the medium of professional hockey were linked to broader discourses of labour, language, and identity. With a stated policy that favoured, assuming equal talent, francophone players, the Nordiques were positively represented as having gone beyond neo-nationalist legislation by conducting *francophonization* – preferential hiring to ensure the dominance of francophones (and consequently, the French language) in the workplace – of their hockey club.[3] The Canadiens, meanwhile, were severely criticized for failing to follow the Nordiques' lead. It was only after the purge of the Canadiens' front office and the appointment of a francophone brain trust that this criticism ceased. The nature of the French media's coverage provides valuable insight into the nature of Québécois identity: it implies that neo-nationalism, despite its stated emphasis on language and territory as the touchstones of Québécois identity, continued to be permeated by notions of identity rooted in ethnic particularism.

## THE QUEBEC LABOUR MOVEMENT AND THE POLITICS OF *FRANCOPHONIZATION*

This examination must necessarily start with a consideration of the relationship between the Quebec labour movement and neo-nationalist language legislation in the 1960s and 1970s.[4] The Canadiens' and Nordiques' players and managers were, after all, employees of Quebec-based enterprises, and media coverage of the demographic composition of the Canadiens and Nordiques was clearly linked to the discourse of linguistic and economic colonialism promulgated by the Québécois labour movement in the push to establish French as the primary language of the workplace. This discourse postulated that the use of language in the workplace could not be separated from structures of social, cultural, and economic power. And, indeed, this argument was backed by facts. Various reports, most notably the Canadian government's 1969 Royal Commission on Bilingualism and Biculturalism (RCBB), starkly described a cultural division of labour in the Quebec workplace, where material wealth and upward mobility were tied to knowledge of the English language. The RCBB's report provided statistics showing that those who knew the most English were usually much better compensated than those who knew the least (unilingual French speakers). Unilingual anglophones were found to have the highest average salary of any socio-linguistic group in the province, suggestive of a virtual monopoly over white-collar managerial positions; in contrast, unilingual francophones were nearly at the bottom of this salary hierarchy.[5] These conditions persisted throughout the 1960s, despite the decline of Montreal's anglophone business elite and the creation of state enterprises such as Hydro-Québec that provided managerial jobs for a growing francophone white-collar middle class.[6]

In the early 1960s, Quebec's three largest unions – the Confédération des syndicats nationaux (CSN), the Fédération des travailleurs du Québec (FTQ), and the Centrale de l'enseignement du Québec (CEQ) – were part of the broad social consensus that characterized the inaugural years of the period of rapid social change known as the Quiet Revolution (1960–66).[7] Yet, by 1972, all three major unions had declared their uncompromising support for French unilingualism and Quebec independence. A series of bitter strikes – the foremost among which involved francophone journalists at *La Presse*, *Le Soleil*, and *Le Devoir* – hardened union attitudes against the political and economic status quo. Just as importantly, the leadership and rank-and-file membership of the three big unions began to understand Quebec through the lens of empire. Like many journalists and radical nationalists, they came to perceive Quebec as a colony: both an internal colony of anglophone Canada but also, drawing on the economic theory of scholars such as Andre Gunder Frank and Kari Levitt (both of whom worked in Montreal in the early 1960s and 1970s), an economic colony of the United States.[8] Levitt, for instance, argued that capitalism in Quebec was inextricably linked with structures of colonialism, that Québécois workers were linguistically and economically dominated by English speakers (especially those from Montreal's historically ascendant anglophone community), and that national domination was rooted in capitalist exploitation.[9] These views are also clearly identifiable in the works of the era's leading radical nationalists. To give one example, the journalist and writer Pierre Vallières contended that "the nationalism of a dominated people is the expression of antagonistic relations of exploitation which can only be resolved through political and economic independence."[10]

According to Vallières and many other radicals, national liberation was the sine qua non for any meaningful social or structural economic change in Quebec: only national liberation could overthrow the cultural division of labour that privileged anglophones and oppressed francophones. This was the perspective adopted by the Quebec labour movement in the 1970s. All three major unions endorsed Quebec independence as part of their official platforms by 1972, and were actively involved in nationalist struggles such as the battle for French unilingualism. Other than Quebec independence, unilingualism was the most significant political change sought by Quebec labour. The three big unions understood language as a labour issue because the dominance of English affected the ability of francophone workers to find jobs, keep them, and be adequately compensated for them: French unilingualism was, according to a CSN communiqué, "a lever in the fight against capitalist domination."[11] It was with this in mind that the CSN officially gave its support to French unilingualism in 1969, urging the provincial government to make French the sole language of work in the province; the FTQ and the CEQ soon followed.[12] Labour was also intimately involved in the bitter struggle against the province's first attempt at language legislation, Bill 63 (1969), which stopped well short of instituting French unilingualism.[13]

In effect, the first official state acknowledgment of the gravity of Quebec's cultural division of labour came from the province's Gendron Commission (inquiring into the situation of French in the Quebec workplace) in its 1973 report. Reiterating and confirming the stark findings of the RCBC, the Gendron Commission argued that French probably would not be spoken in the workplace unless there was an influx of francophones into those workplaces: "The use of French as the language of work and the bilingualization of English-speaking senior personnel will become truly possible only when there are larger numbers of French-speaking individuals working at all administrative levels (francophonization). The overrepresentation of the English-speaking element and the segregation of the two groups on the basis of language constitute obstacles which, if not removed, will prevent any change in language usage within enterprises."[14] To stimulate the use of French in the workplace, the Gendron Commission urged the institution of a policy of affirmative action that would favour francophones over non-francophones (francophonization). The commission's report argued that only this kind of coercive legislated action, similar to race-based programs already adopted in the United States and elsewhere in the world, would begin to undo English-language dominance in the Quebec economy, unravel the linguistic division of labour that had become entrenched, affirm the French-speaking majority, and guarantee that French became the lingua franca of the Quebec workplace.[15] Although Bill 22 (1974), the province's second attempt at language legislation, implemented some of the suggestions of the Gendron Commission, it was, like Bill 63 before it, vague about the prospect of a francophonization of the workplace, and as a result was rejected by most nationalists as well as by the three largest Quebec unions.[16]

Workplace language redress had to wait until the 1976 election of the Parti Québécois (PQ), a bourgeois neo-nationalist party whose interests converged with radical labour on the issue of French in the workplace. The PQ selectively utilized radical labour's rhetoric of linguistic oppression and social justice in order to frame and justify the language legislation it would adopt: Bill 1 (1977), based largely on a policy "White Paper"; and Bill 101 (1977), a revamped version of Bill 1 that was eventually signed into law and is now called the Charter of the French Language (La charte de la langue française). The White Paper – officially, *Québec's Policy on the French Language* – was the theoretical underpinning of the PQ's subsequent language legislation. Like Quebec's labour unions, the White Paper identified the long dominance of English in the halls of corporate Quebec as one of the foremost factors that structured the subordination of Quebec francophones. It therefore presented language legislation as a remedial measure concerned as much with the liberation of French Canadian wage earners as it was with the language they spoke: the White Paper announced that PQ language initiatives were not just limited, like Bill 22, to strengthening the French language, but would be structured to secure social justice for the people who spoke it and worked with it.[17] Central to these plans were statutes designed to make French the language of commerce in Quebec. And, while the White Paper offered few hints about the practical implementation of the language legislation to come, it did make clear that a francophonization program would be part of it: "Business firms could set themselves the following definite objective: to reflect, at every level and in every function of their personnel, the ethnic make-up of the population of Québec. There is nothing revolutionary about this; it is such an elementary principle of social justice that the United States, that paradise of private enterprise, had adopted it as the basis of its social hiring policy. Common sense must prevail here, in particular over manoeuvres that tend to mask it or water it down."[18] Contrary to its contentions, the White Paper did indeed propose a revolutionary understanding of Québécois identity in the form of the reference to "the ethnic make-up of the population of Québec." This was the first time that an official government document had applied a specific and restrictive definition to the term "Québécois." Rather than denoting a citizen of the province who could speak French well enough to use it at work, a Québécois was identified as a French speaker of French Canadian descent, making a distinction between the intended beneficiaries of the ensuing language legislation and other citizens.

Bill 1 provided clarification and concrete legislation where the White Paper provided relatively vague ideas. Bill 1 became notorious primarily for an unabashed support for francophonization that was rooted in the definition of "Québécois" elucidated in the White Paper. Like the White Paper, Bill 1 identified francophonization as the most efficient means of ensuring the presence of French in Quebec workplaces. In calling for increased numbers of Québécois at every position, Bill 1 also made it clear that, for its purposes, "Québécois" was equivalent to "ethnic French Canadian," excluding anglophones and allophones (those whose first language was neither English nor French) who had been born and raised in Quebec, no matter their proficiency in French.[19] Not surprisingly, Bill 1 was forcefully attacked by those who rejected the notion that Québécois identity should be built upon an ethnic base.[20] On the other hand, scores of Quebecers, especially neo-nationalists and trade unionists, heartily supported Bill 1. For these groups, Bill 1 signified the most logical and concrete step in the cultural, economic, and linguistic emancipation of the province. The CSN, for example, congratulated the government for putting "a brake to the specific subordination of francophone workers as francophone workers."[21] In this same vein was the reaction of Les Fils du Québec, a nationalist organization: it understood Bill 1 as "the supreme affirmation of the French fact in America, the victory of the Quebec nation over the anglophone occupiers, the wiping clean of the defeat of the Plains of Abraham, and the cultural Magna Carta of the Québécois."[22]

Despite a solid base of support from the above-mentioned groups, francophonization was abandoned in Bill 101, Bill 1's watered-down successor, signalling the beginning of Quebec's statutory commitment to an identity rooted in citizenship and language usage rather than ethnicity.[23] Bill 101 defined a "Québécois" essentially as a resident of Quebec who could speak French, a much broader and less restrictive definition than that outlined in Bill 1. But, while official government discourse has consistently emphasized this vision, it would be naive to conclude that Bill 101 produced a consensus regarding francophonization, the nature of Québécois identity, or the Quebec social project.[24] Instead of consensus, there has been an almost uninterrupted debate on the nature of Québécois identity as well as the desired shape of Quebec society, a debate in which artists, writers, academics, politicians, and journalists have served as major actors. Quebec's activist francophone sport journalists, heavily influenced by trade-unionist labour discourses, took an active part in these deliberations.

## THE NORDIQUES: QUEBEC INC.?

By 1980, the French media had constructed the Nordiques as an important institution in the struggle for the affirmation of the French language by virtue of the team's French-only arena communication policy.[25] But the Nordiques' language initiatives did not stop with a rejection of bilingualism: the club, by its own admission, also claimed to strive to secure as much French-speaking talent as possible, both on the ice and in management positions. The club was eager to trumpet that its player recruitment policy favoured, to a certain extent, Quebec-born francophones. "Given equal talents, we will choose a francophone," repeated Nordiques officials on many occasions.[26] And, indeed, the team's nucleus, at least for the first few years of its National Hockey League tenure (1979–95), was composed mostly of francophones. Early Nordiques triumphs were interpreted by the francophone press as vehicles for Québécois affirmation and as proof that enterprises with francophone workforces could indeed flourish. The outpouring of support for the Nordiques during the 1982 playoffs as the team advanced to the NHL semi-finals is a case in point. A *Le Soleil* editorial lauded the team for proving that an enterprise controlled by and composed of francophones could be successful.[27] Figures associated with Quebec hockey openly thanked the Nordiques for placing their confidence in Quebec players;[28] by the same token, an anticipated increase in the number of Quebec teenagers selected in the 1982 draft was chalked up to the Nordiques' success with Québécois players.[29] Parallels between the success of the Nordiques and the ongoing neo-nationalist project did not go unnoticed by politicians: one Parti Québécois legislator compared the Nordiques' entry into and rise up the NHL ranks to the inevitable accession of Quebec to political independence,[30] while Premier René Lévesque publicly announced his allegiance to the Nordiques on account of their "Québécois" image.[31]

The Nordiques' reputation for nurturing francophones applied equally to managerial positions. Team President Marcel Aubut and General Manager Maurice Filion were the only francophones serving in their respective positions in the entire league during the first years of the 1980s; head coach Michel Bergeron was the first alumnus of Quebec's foremost junior hockey league to graduate to the NHL when he was hired in 1980;[32] assistant coach Simon Nolet, upon joining the organization in 1982, publicly thanked the Nordiques for being the only organization in the NHL that provided job opportunities to francophone coaches.[33]

The Nordiques' perceived preference for francophone personnel was constructed by the French media as a vindication of the neo-nationalist project, and the Nordiques themselves as a model neo-nationalist enterprise that had enacted francophonization (as stipulated in the aborted Bill 1). The best example of this is the media coverage of the allegations made against the team by three anglophone ex-players. The first episode occurred at the end of the 1979–80 season when veteran defenceman Gerry Hart warned, in the words of a *La Presse* headline: "Anglophones don't feel at home in Quebec."[34] His argument revolved around two central premises: first, that in order to buttress their francophone image, the Nordiques did not always ice the team's best players and that deserving anglophone players were held back in favour of undeserving francophones; second, that anglophone players felt uncomfortable with the club's adoption of unilingual public-address announcements.[35]

In response to Hart's concerns, journalists conceded that the Nordiques very likely had a serious integration problem. Yet this "problem," rather than being depicted as unacceptable or undesirable, was presented as a function of Quebec City's unilingual French character and, as *Le Soleil*'s Claude Larochelle put it, "the *naturally* francophone dimension of the team."[36] Larochelle put this into context by contrasting the Nordiques' situation with the Canadiens': "The integration [of anglophones] takes on a particular character with the Nordiques, a dimension which up to now the Montreal Canadiens have managed to avoid. In Montreal, the English-speaking players have the West Island to share, and if there are star francophone players like Guy Lafleur raiding all the trophies, there are also athletes from Quebec to do much of the dirty work ... In Quebec, the humble and backbreaking labour is the lot of a few anglophones who are uncomfortable in their skin in light of the stars' lavish income."[37] The last sentence contends that the Nordiques had inverted Quebec's long-standing cultural division of labour; instead of unilingual anglophones monopolizing the best positions and the most material rewards, Larochelle agreed with Hart that the top positions in Quebec City were reserved for francophones. Larochelle and other commentators disagreed with Hart on one crucial point, however: what for Hart was a worrying and unacceptable situation was depicted in Quebec's French newspapers as a desirable, normal, and unavoidable state of affairs for a professional hockey club operating under Quebec's language laws.

Claude Bédard of *Le Journal de Québec* reinforced this discourse by unfavourably comparing Hart's plight to the legions of francophone players who had migrated to play hockey in other parts of Canada and the United States.[38] Larochelle, in a second column, repeated this comparison: "Many athletes from Quebec and their families have had to live through this rough transition. Many of them were plunged into a different cultural environment across North America. They finally got out while the going was good, a fate that nobody could change. As I have reported to Gerry Hart recently, the Québécois athlete who sets out for Winnipeg or Vancouver would never expect to have many francophones around him and to ask for announcements in French at the rink!"[39] In evoking the plight of others, Larochelle posited that anglophone players such as Hart should accept the prevailing situation as a matter of social justice. Francophones, confronted with the socio-linguistic realities in English-speaking cities, never asked for concessions or for special accommodation in French; instead, they remained silent, accepted the prevailing linguistic arrangements, and did their jobs. Hart and others like him, Larochelle argued, in effect, would be better served by accepting the dominance of the French language in Quebec City. So, while Larochelle on one hand acknowledged that Hart's concerns were legitimate and should be considered seriously, he simultaneously positioned dissident anglophone players as troublemakers seeking to subvert Quebec's legislated linguistic order.

This analysis was vigorously reiterated the next time an ex-Nordique questioned the team's orientation. During the team's 1980 training camp, anglophone player Reggie Thomas strongly criticized the team for its personnel policy immediately after losing his roster spot in Quebec City.

"I wouldn't be surprised if before the end of the year they trade three or four English players for two or three French players," Thomas said. "Honestly, I don't think there's an English player that's happy." Thomas also claimed that the Nordiques had broken up a successful unit because it was comprised entirely of anglophones: "It's still in the back of my mind that they did that because we were an all English line and we were going well. We've never been back together."[40] Finally, Thomas blasted the Nordiques for overt prejudice and insinuated that his release was the beginning of a purge of the team's anglophones: the organization, according to him, was sabotaging its anglophone players purposely. Soon thereafter, Dave Farrish, another ex-Nordique who ironically had been traded away from the club in the transaction that brought Thomas to Quebec City, chimed in. According to Farrish, there was a virtual conspiracy afoot in Quebec City to drive anglophones from the team. He himself claimed mistreatment at the hands of both the front office and prominent francophone players. Poignantly, Farrish pinpointed the Nordiques' language policy as the thing that left anglophone players most bemused: "How are Anglophone players supposed to feel at ease? We felt like strangers."[41]

The line parroted by the French-language hockey press was in agreement with the Nordiques' interpretation of the accusations as "a real farce."[42] Bédard, writing in *Le Journal de Montréal*, argued that Thomas simply was not good enough to make the grade with a much improved team, and reminded his readers that "Quebec is a city different from all the others in America," chastising Thomas and those who agreed with him for not considering the plight of francophones plying their trade outside Quebec.[43] The article's central thesis was summed up in its headline: "If Francophones Had Been So Fortunate." Through this headline and the ensuing article, *Le Journal de Montréal* identified Quebec's anglophone minority as having enjoyed a charmed existence, in contrast to francophones, who elsewhere on the continent were subordinate in the workplace and subjected to assimilationist pressures. The Nordiques, in this line of reasoning, were simply providing opportunities for francophones to work in their native tongue, thereby helping them avoid the pitfalls of assimilation and linguistic domination. Rather than the club, it was up to Thomas, Farrish, and like-minded people to acclimatize to this new reality, argued an editorial in *Le Soleil*.[44]

The press reactions to Hart's, Thomas's, and Farrish's allegations reproduced many of the assumptions of the neo-nationalist discourse that emerged from social and legislative debates about the use of French in the workplace. First, reporters reinforced the normality of the Nordiques' presumed francophonization program; it was depicted as largely uncontroversial that a Québécois enterprise should strive to reflect the province's demographic realities. Next, such a policy was identified as being critically important in order to reverse the subordination that francophones had suffered in the North American labour market. And, finally, the ideal role for anglophone workers was elucidated somewhat as well: while anglophones should be accommodated, there were limits to this accommodation, and anglophones themselves (as represented by Hart, Thomas, and Farrish) were warned to keep in mind that they enjoyed privileges in Quebec that francophones had long been denied elsewhere in North America, and urged to accept silently the linguistic status quo.

## THE BALLAD OF "LES MAROONS": MEDIA REQUIEMS FOR A FRANCOPHONE INSTITUTION

Despite these controversies in Quebec City, the main battleground for francophonization in hockey was Montreal, where the Canadiens, particularly when juxtaposed with the Nordiques, were accused of purging their long-established francophone players in favour of anglophone replacements in the early 1980s. Inspired both by Thomas's rant and by the Canadiens' release of two francophone players, Gilles Lupien and Normand Dupont, *La Presse*'s chief sports columnist, Réjean Tremblay, insisted that the Canadiens, like the Nordiques, had a "moral obligation" to field the best francophone players because of the linguistic domination suffered by francophone players in the hockey workplace.[45] While agreeing that accusations of racism were ridiculous, Tremblay argued that one could certainly criticize the Canadiens for "imprudence," and concluded with a call for the Canadiens to adopt the Nordiques' recruitment policy, which favoured francophone players over anglophones of equal talent.

While Tremblay hesitated to accuse the Canadiens of prejudice, his colleague at *La Presse*, Canadiens beat writer Bernard Brisset, penned a blistering report arguing that the team's "French fact" was quickly disappearing, and accused club management of causing this predicament in part through institutional anti-francophone prejudice.[46] Employing logic that recalled the forecasts of demographic and cultural Armageddon underpinning so much of neo-nationalist discourse, Brisset argued that anglophones would very soon form a majority in the Canadiens' line-up if the Canadiens' drafting and recruitment policies continued to favour them: the "frogs," said Brisset, using an anglophone slur of French Canadians, were in danger. Brisset went on to ponder a question that would preoccupy francophone sports journalists for the next few years. One-half of the Canadiens' roster, he noted, was composed of francophones, while the other half was comprised of anglophones: Was this an acceptable proportion? Brisset began to answer this question by citing the Canadiens' historical importance in the province: "Evidently, the Expos and the Alouettes are not preoccupied with a language division in their ranks. But fans identify with their hockey team in a way that is not the case with the two others, which are made up largely of American players."[47] Brisset, echoing political reports, submitted an argument based on imperatives and "moral obligations," concluding that the Canadiens had a responsibility to match the Nordiques' commitment to Québécois players. A half-anglophone, half-francophone roster fell short of the proportional representation urged in documents such as *Québec's Policy on the French Language*, and Brisset and Tremblay both argued that anything less constituted a breach of the Canadiens' "moral obligation" to work toward the emancipation and affirmation of Quebec francophones.

Despite public assurances that they, like the Nordiques, would choose a francophone over an anglophone if the players' talents were equal, the Canadiens were continually depicted as failing to work for the affirmation of Quebec francophones in the workplace.[48] Francophone players' departures were met with requiems for the Canadiens' status as a pre-eminent Québécois institution. The retirement of Serge Savard in December 1981 prompted Tremblay to lament that "in two or three years, the Canadiens will be just a team like the others," and warn that the club risked losing its popularity if it continued to jettison francophones.[49] Similar protestations followed the trade of Pierre Larouche to Hartford a few weeks later.[50] Standout defenceman Guy Lapointe's trade to St Louis in 1982 prompted *La Presse*'s Brisset to lament that "clearing out the frogs continues with the Canadiens," the use of the epithet "frog" driving home the Canadiens' perceived hostility toward Québécois players.[51] Meanwhile, *Le Journal de Montréal* reminded its readers matter-of-factly that "it must be recognized that les Glorieux are less and less francophone" and that, after Lapointe's exit, "the list grows longer."[52] Likewise, the appointment of Bob Gainey, an Ontarian who had learned French during his tenure in Montreal, as team captain in 1982 was presented as evidence of the erosion of francophone players' influence in the club.[53]

The French-language media most graphically drove home the team's failure to establish an appropriately francophone workplace by comparing it to the Montreal Maroons, the Canadiens' erstwhile anglophone NHL rivals from 1924 to 1938. Francophone journalists began calling the Canadiens "Les Maroons" beginning in December 1981, and did so consistently for the better part of the next year.[54] The use of this epithet was intended to underscore forcefully that the Canadiens were now representative of Montreal's anglophone minority; similarly sarcastic references to the Canadiens as the "Glorious," an English rendering of the team's traditional nickname *Les Glorieux*, had the same effect.[55]

In this atmosphere, the Canadiens' ethnic composition became a press obsession. Journalists monitored the number of francophones featured in the Canadiens' line-up, and routinely published head counts in their newspapers. For instance, the arrival of US-born player Jeff Brubaker was commemorated in *La Presse* as the moment when francophone players became a minority in Montreal.[56] Canadiens' games versus the Nordiques tended to prompt a count, which usually proved uncomplimentary for the Canadiens.[57] Comparisons with other francophone-staffed teams further underlined the Canadiens' failure to fulfill their "moral obligation" to work toward francophonization. A Canadian Press report from January 1982, written after a game that pitted the Canadiens against the Buffalo Sabres, demonstrated this. The Canadiens iced five francophones in that game, while the Sabres, coached by ex-Canadiens coach and alleged francophobe Scotty Bowman,[58] iced six; this fact was taken as evidence that the Canadiens needed to remake their image.[59] Letters to the editor in French-language newspapers also engaged in these head counts, while linking events in the hockey sphere even more explicitly to wider socio-political contexts than the stories that prompted them. One case in point was a letter that was published in all three of Montreal's daily French-language newspapers, *La Presse*, *Le Devoir*, and *Le Journal de Montréal*.

It began by explicitly linking the Canadiens' demographic composition to the neo-nationalist language project: "At this moment, in the era of francophonization, the team that represents the second-biggest French-speaking city in the world comprises 12 francophone players and 14 anglophones."[60] After criticizing the Canadiens for not hiring enough francophone players, the reader proposed a solution: "It's not a matter of eliminating the English from Montreal … but simply of respecting the demographic proportions of the Metropolis … for example, we should have within the Tricolore at least 14 francophone players out of a total of 21, since Montreal is 70% majority French-speaking."[61] The solution proposed was a strict program of francophonization, complete with affirmative-action quotas, as suggested in Bill 1 and its associated White Paper. According to this view, the Canadiens' demography should correspond *exactly* to the related percentages in Montreal.

## IRVING GRUNDMAN: THE "USURPER FROM HIGH FINANCE"

In essence, the French press criticized the Canadiens for failing to adhere to the spirit, if not the letter, of neo-nationalist language legislation. The blame for this failure often fell on Irving Grundman, the team's general manager in the early 1980s. Interestingly, Grundman's identity was presented as an explanation, possibly *the* explanation, for why the Canadiens had failed to restock the team with Québécois players – a line of argument that took for granted that Grundman, born and raised in Montreal to Jewish-immigrant parents and fluent in French, was *not* Québécois. Instead, the media consistently depicted Grundman as linguistically, ethnically, and culturally foreign. This usually entailed portraying him as an anglophone, but Grundman's Jewishness was also flagged. For example, a profile in the prominent news magazine *L'actualité* constructed Grundman as neither francophone nor anglophone while quoting a Canadiens employee who referred to the team's home area, the Montreal Forum, as "la Synagogue";[62] another report described how some team observers had taken to describing the Forum as the "Closse Street Synagogue."[63] This referential strategy, employing religious metaphors, is illustrative. The Forum was, because of the Canadiens' historical association with the traditional, catholicized version of French Canadian nationalism, considered a "temple" of hockey, and attending a hockey game a religious experience.[64] By contrast, by describing the Forum as a synagogue under Grundman's leadership, journalists constructed it as a place for others to worship, not Quebec francophones; it became a Québécois sanctuary that had been hijacked by Jews.

Similarly, another profile in *La Presse*, pondering why Irving Grundman was so unpopular in comparison to other prominent Montreal sports figures, concluded that, in part, it was because Grundman was Jewish. While one local sports impresario was depicted as warm, enthusiastic, and passionate – qualities deemed typical of "Latin" cultures – the article, drawing on centuries-old anti-Semitic stereotypes, speculated that Grundman's unpopularity was due to the perception that he was "a usurper of high finance."[65] Nor was this an isolated depiction: an earlier column in *La Presse* argued that the Canadiens comprised a microcosm of society, with "francophones, anglophones, Jews who control the licence."[66] Grundman himself evidently believed that his image problems were due in some part to anti-Semitism.[67] Indeed, on at least one occasion, during a 1982 game in Quebec City, Grundman and his family were subjected to anti-Semitic abuse.[68]

Whether or not Québécois nationalism was expressly anti-Semitic is beyond the scope of this chapter (though other commentators have made precisely that claim).[69] However, the above examples illustrate that francophone sports journalists often wrote about Québécois identity in a way that limited it to ethnic French Canadians. It is therefore unsurprising that these journalists frequently represented Grundman as an impediment to francophone affirmation and francophonization. In this vein, the language Grundman used on the job was heavily scrutinized. Grundman was fluent enough in French to conduct interviews with francophone reporters entirely in their language; yet instances where he was reported to have used English were interpreted as evidence that the team's general manager was an obstacle to a French workplace. A good example came at the end of an hour-long interview between a *La Presse* scribe and Grundman, which had been conducted entirely in French (the English translation follows in the endnotes):

> Avant de quitter le Forum, je suis allée saluer le nouveau patron d'Irving, M. Corey en personne.
> On jasait depuis peu, debout au centre de son bureau, quand

M. Grundman a fait son entrée.
On venait tout juste de terminer une long conversation d'une heure.
En français.
"Excuse me, Ron, the lawer [sic] is waiting for us. We should go."
– I'll be there in a few minutes.
Compris?[70]

This passage, through the parting, sarcastic "compris?" clearly represented the use of French as a smokescreen, something utilized for journalists and public relations only, while English dominated in office communication. Most significant is that Grundman *forced* Ronald Corey, the Canadiens' new francophone president, to use English as his workplace language: Corey only switched to English because of Grundman's presence in the room. So Grundman's presence was understood not only as an example of the continuation of anglophone dominance in the Quebec workplace, but also as a factor that prevented the Canadiens' francophone front-office employees from using their own language.

## PLEASE CALL ME ROBERT: UN GARS DE CHEZ NOUS?

Grundman's most contentious action was the hiring of Bob Berry as head coach of the Canadiens in 1981. Berry was a Montreal native who had been reared as a player in the Canadiens' organization before beginning a coaching career with the NHL's Los Angeles Kings. He did not speak much French upon his hiring; he did, however, promise to commence French lessons immediately.[71] Despite this, his hiring was universally panned by francophone journalists who had been vocal in their desire for a francophone head coach.[72] Berry's Montreal roots were deemed to be largely insufficient, or even irrelevant. A column written by ex-Canadiens player and Québécois cultural icon Maurice "Rocket" Richard in *Dimanche-Matin* provides a good example of this thinking: while accepting that Berry was indeed "un gars de chez nous," a term frequently used to denote someone who is Québécois, Richard still declared himself disappointed that a francophone had not been hired and argued that Berry *must* now ensure that he hired francophone assistants.[73] Similarly, in *Le Soleil*, Claude Larochelle noted that while Berry could utter a few words in French thanks to "ses origines québécoises," the Canadiens had still conformed to their tradition of hiring "citizens of the Anglo-Saxon tradition, pervasive in this environment where the English language is the instrument of work."[74] Berry's identity, while on one hand rooted firmly in the territorial Quebec nation, was simultaneously reduced to the language of work utilized by his cultural group; Larochelle reinforced this discourse with a comparison to the Nordiques, who relied on "gens du pays," a reference to Gilles Vigneault's iconic nationalist folk song.[75] Even ostensibly positive portrayals of Berry branded him as irredeemably English. When seeking to underscore that loyalty was one of Berry's positive personality traits, *La Presse* called him a "loyaliste," a reference to the English-speaking settlers loyal to the British crown who migrated en masse to Quebec following the American Revolution, linking Berry to the long history of British imperialism in Quebec.[76]

In the end, Berry's candidacy and hiring were opposed not on hockey grounds but because his presence ultimately would continue the subordination of the French language at the Forum. "More than ever," wrote Larochelle about Berry's hiring, "the working language of Montreal's hockey team will be English."[77] Citing the debates about the Nordiques' language policy, *La Presse*'s François Béliveau explained Berry's hiring as an unwelcome result of the Canadiens' bilingualism, which secured the team's Englishness: "The Canadiens, who are of many traditions, chose to remain in line with the Pollocks, Toe Blakes and Bowmans in hiring Bob Berry as head coach and continue, in line with the Trudeau Government, the dream of a happy marriage between francophones and anglophones. A dream, because in fact, in the small memos, the paperwork among employees, discussion between players and coach, English will predominate. The exterior image, however, the one that the public affairs department conveys, will be a stamp of bilingualism."[78] Béliveau placed Berry in the tradition of other anglophone managers (Pollock, Blake, Bowman) and described his hiring as consistent with the federal government's official bilingualism scheme, which was largely rejected by neo-nationalists as detrimental to the French language. Béliveau dismissed bilingualism as an institution that would prevent the affirmation both of the French language and of francophones: as with Grundman's presence as general manager, Berry's hiring as coach was submitted as evidence that bilingualism was merely a smokescreen behind which the day-to-day operations of the Canadiens would continue in English. In this frame, Béliveau unequivocally portrayed Berry's hiring as a step back from francophonization and deepened the team's image as an essentially anglophone institution. As Béliveau later wrote, the Canadiens had abandoned their francophone fan base to the Nordiques by having failed to "respond to the aspirations of the people."[79]

## "UNE PURGE JOYEUSE": THE FRANCOPHONIZATION OF THE CANADIENS

The unenthusiastic reaction to Berry's hiring as coach stands in sharp contrast to the unrestrained glee that characterized media reactions to the Canadiens' hiring of Ronald Corey, who, despite his English-sounding name, was accepted unreservedly as a francophone by both the French- and English-language media, as club president in 1982. Corey, a former sports journalist, had previously been an executive at Carling O'Keefe, the brewery that owned the Nordiques; his hiring was so unexpected that *La Presse* described it "as if the Ayatollah Khomeini converted to Buddhism."[80] Not surprisingly, given the discourses generated around the personae of Grundman and Berry, the most important factor for the Quebec media was that Corey was, according to Claude Larochelle, "the francophone that the Canadiens had to get."[81] Report after report implied that, or perhaps hoped that, Corey's hiring was the beginning of the much longed for francophonization of the Canadiens. *Le Soleil*, for example, reported that Corey's hiring was evidence that the Canadiens planned to build a "more representative" hockey team.[82]

Thus, Corey's appointment was heralded as the coup that returned the Canadiens to their fans and to their Québécois roots. Claims that he had "saved" the team were commonplace in French-language newspapers. For example, *Dimanche-Matin* described fans accosting Corey on the street "as if he was to save an historical monument from demolition."[83] *La Presse*'s Réjean Tremblay described a similar phenomenon: "Corey's image, that of a go-ahead and modern Québécois, contrasts sharply with that of [his predecessor as team president, anglophone lawyer] Mr. Morgan McCammon ... Ronald Corey allows a sort of identification between the fan and his team. In the popular imagination, it is possible to make believe that the Canadiens belong to the citizens."[84]

These examples made clear exactly for whom the club was "saved." Tremblay wrote approvingly of Corey quickly organizing team excursions into Montreal's francophone east end for public appearances at stores that typically catered to a French-Canadian clientele. Here, Montreal's geography was crucial. Tremblay clearly implied that the Canadiens previously did not venture into the overwhelmingly francophone east end, instead staying close by the Forum in the English-speaking west end.[85] By stressing that the Canadiens had returned to the east end, Tremblay constructed the Canadiens as agents in the francophonization of the city's urban life: the club itself was participating in the migration of socio-economic power from the west end of the city to the east end.[86]

As enthusiastically as Corey's hiring was heralded by the French-language media, those reactions paled in comparison to the euphoria that greeted Corey's first major act: the dismissal of Grundman and scouting director Ronald Caron, the main architect along with Grundman of the Canadiens' player-recruitment policy. They were soon replaced by the team's former star Serge Savard as general manager and former Canadiens' coach and scout Claude Ruel as director of scouting. Though Berry was ultimately reappointed as coach, he was stripped of his ability to assemble his own staff. Former Canadiens player Jacques Lemaire was imposed as assistant coach and, essentially, head-coach-in-waiting.[87] Significantly, all three new appointees were Quebec francophones. Savard's hiring was especially praised: French-language newspapers depicted him as a model Québécois and emphasized his nationalist credentials. A highly favourable *La Presse* profile of Savard emphasized his nationalism and his business credentials.[88] Another profile in the same newspaper depicted Savard (and Corey) as emblematic of the post-Quiet Revolution francophone managerial class.[89]

This "joyous purge," as *Le Soleil* called it, was presented as irrefutable evidence of the triumph of the neo-nationalist project at the Forum. *Le Soleil* exulted that after "an interminable eclipse … French will be the language of work at the Forum."[90] Corey, who had instigated these changes, was portrayed as an agent of francophonization, as the catalyst in the decolonization of the Canadiens. *Le Soleil* depicted him as a courageous figure who "shook the pillars of the temple, the long tradition of the Gormans, Selkes, Pollocks, Bowmans, Grundmans."[91] Tremblay described the purge as a complete reversal of the Canadiens' direction under Grundman's leadership: the liberation of an oppressed population's cultural institution. "For decades, the people had the unpleasant impression that the Canadiens belonged to 'others,' that it was directed by 'others,' and that he, the ordinary sort, was not tolerated in the Sanctuary."[92] Corey's intervention in effect became an allegory for the neo-nationalist project itself: long dominated by "les autres," its institutions co-opted, the nation had taken strong remedial action to end francophone subordination.

*Dimanche-Matin*'s Jerry Trudel may have depicted the Canadiens as British colonizers in 1982, but by 1983 a different kind of military metaphor was *de rigueur*: the Canadiens, led by "General Corey," had commenced the "reconquest" of Quebec.[93] If not quite a return to their historical status as undisputed champions of French Canada, the Savard- and Corey-led Canadiens were no longer deemed an impediment to the use of French at the Forum. This was the end result of three years (1980–83) of intense media scrutiny of the Canadiens' and Nordiques' ethno-linguistic compositions. The Nordiques, with their francophone management, francophone coaches, and stated policy of favouring (assuming equal talents) francophone players, were lauded as a model neo-nationalist enterprise that adhered to both the letter and the spirit of neo-nationalist language legislation: they had in fact gone *beyond* the legislation by conducting a francophonization of their club, a policy of preferential hiring ensuring the dominance of French (and francophones) in the workplace. Accusations levelled by former Nordiques, alleging systematic anti-anglophone discrimination, only confirmed this image. In contrast, the Canadiens, who, after the hiring of Bob Berry in 1981, had anglophones as owner, general manager, and head coach, and, in the estimation of some journalists, an increasingly anglophone player roster, were lampooned as representative of anglophone hegemony, and constructed as an institution that worked against the establishment of French as the lingua franca of the workplace. Only after the remaking of the Canadiens' front office and the appointment of Corey and Savard did this criticism end.

The discourse produced by French-language media coverage of the Nordiques' and Canadiens' personnel decisions also provides valuable insight into the never-ending debate about the nature of Québécois identity. Canadiens General Manager Irving Grundman, identified as the main culprit in the Canadiens' *anglophonization*, spoke fluent French, having been born and raised in Montreal. Yet he and fellow Montrealer Bob Berry were denied Québécois identities and were portrayed instead, in various ways, as the ethnic, cultural, and linguistic *other*: as English-speakers, Jews, Anglo-Saxons, even British redcoats. This suggests the continued salience, through the early 1980s, of a Québécois identity rooted in ethnic particularism. Despite a firm statutory emphasis on a national identity rooted in common citizenship and use of the French language, Québécois identity was constructed through NHL hockey coverage in such a way that excluded, in some form or another, some of the province's citizens.

6

# THE "HOUSE OF HOCKEY": SPATIALIZED MEMORIES OF THE MONTREAL FORUM

—

*Julie Perrone*

—

Home of a legendary team whose record for Stanley Cup wins has yet to be broken, the Forum, built in 1924, grew with and within the city of Montreal, becoming an integral part of its landscape and culture. But in 1989 Ronald Corey, president of the Montreal Canadiens hockey team, made a sad but expected announcement: the "Habs" needed a new home because the Forum had become seriously outdated. The "house of hockey"[1] was undoubtedly a source of pride for Montrealers, but they seemed to understand the need for a new and improved facility, at least right after the announcement. Between 1989 and 1996, this attitude of "acceptance, observation and/or a growing excitement"[2] slowly evolved into an increasingly emotional and nostalgic attachment to place. What makes the story of the Forum different from other organized moves from old arenas to state-of-the-art facilities is the complex and intertwined nature of the memories it brought back in Montreal. Class struggle, language issues, and, as Emmanuel Lapierre notes in his chapter, the central place of the Canadiens in hockey history all contribute to explain the deep attachment to the Forum. Each of these factors was also embedded in the discussions about the closing of the building and the construction of a new arena.

According to Montreal sports journalist Red Fisher, hockey represented "our hopes, our dreams, our culture, our national identity. And nowhere else has it been played with more success and more passion than in this building."[3] The Forum in Montreal was perceived as representing not only hockey in general but also the city, the province, and even the country. Hockey was, Fisher added, an intricate part of the lives of Montrealers: "It has provided Montrealers with direction and purpose. When the Canadiens won, the people … also have won. When they lost, the people lost – at least for a little while."[4] Given this intimate relationship between the team and the people in the city, the deep attachment expressed about the home of the Habs cannot be that surprising, and neither can the wave of memories that were brought back when it closed.

As a reflection on hockey in the Quebec context, this chapter focuses mostly on what two leading Montreal newspapers, the *Gazette* and *La Presse*, had to say about the closing of the Forum. Of course, these were only two of the many information sources that participated in and shaped the public conversation, and they conveyed a mediated version of the past that should be read with caution. However, to be fair, the public's nostalgia for the building was real, as the crowds drawn by the closing events demonstrate. I have elected to train my attention on these two newspapers simply because they were the ones spilling the most ink on the topic: both closely followed the negotiations surrounding the choice of the new location, the design of new building itself, and the fate of the old building. What is argued here is that the memories expressed in the context of its closing conceptualized the Forum as a space in which physical attributes of the building were imbued with significance as well as a representation of lived experience. Beginning with a short history of the Forum, the chapter then looks at the 1989 announcement and the events of 1996, before diving into these spatialized Forum memories. This is, in some ways, a "sportscape," a study of "human geographical configurations that provide the context and possibilities of sports experiences."[5] The texture of these "configurations" is what makes Quebec hockey the same ... but different. It is indeed not immensely surprising that Montrealers expressed such a deep attachment to a not-so-great-looking building: no other city has played such a critical role in the development of the sport, and no other city has seen the Stanley Cup hoisted in its streets as often as Montreal has. The Forum was indeed the "house of hockey."

## THE MECCA OF HOCKEY: A SHORT HISTORY

The construction of the Montreal Forum began in 1924, paid for by the Canadian Arena Company (CAC). The project was the result of intense lobbying by CAC founders William Northey and Senator Donat Raymond, who managed to convince Edward Beatty, then chairman of the Canadian Pacific Railway (CPR), to support the construction of a new arena.[6] Montreal hosted two professional hockey teams between 1909 and 1918: the Montreal Canadiens, a primarily French Canadian team, and the Wanderers, its anglophone counterpart. Both teams played in the Montreal Arena in Westmount, but they played against each other only a few times overall, and never during playoffs.[7] Built in 1898, the Montreal Arena featured artificial ice for the first time in 1914 and seemed to be the up-and-coming place for an up-and-coming sport. Unfortunately, the building burned down in 1918, forcing Sam Lichtenhein, owner of the Montreal Wanderers, to fold the team because of significant losses.[8] The Montreal Canadiens, now the only hockey team in town, played for a while in the very small Jubilee Arena, which burned down as well. The team eventually took on a lease at the new Mount Royal Arena and thus went back to playing on natural ice.

The city desperately needed a new arena, given the propensity of these buildings to "go up in smoke."[9] The necessity for an arena was, of course, a product of its time. Indeed, the 1920s mark a period in Canada (as well as in the United States) where there was "an increase in the free time and disposable incomes that could be devoted to consumption, including the consumption of commercial sporting entertainment."[10] The development of the National Hockey League (NHL) into a "continental business"[11] certainly illustrated the growing appetite for entertainment and the increased capacity, at least for some, to spend money on such leisure activities. In Montreal's case, it appeared that this appetite could not be satiated with only one team. Indeed, one of the arguments for building a new arena was the "need" for an anglophone team to compete against the French-speaking Canadiens. Montrealers were quite interested in watching these epic battles between the French and the English. As Michel Vigneault tells us in his chapter, a game between the Wanderers and a team made up of the best francophone players in 1909 was able to attract some one thousand people despite bad weather, a telling sign that such polarizing events had great commercial potential. Hence the CAC executives argued that, since the Wanderers had folded, a new anglophone team needed to be created. They argued successfully it seems, because the building of the Forum coincided with the creation of the Montreal Maroons.[12] The 10,000-person-capacity arena project raised such enthusiasm that everything – foundation, structure, and interior design – was completed in 159 days and ready for a puck drop between the Montreal Canadiens' Howie Morenz and the Toronto St Patricks' Jack Adams in 1924.

The CAC renovated the Forum twice, both times to add more seats, in a sense "shoehorning" them into the existing building, as a *Gazette* journalist explained.[13] In this way, the nostalgia expressed by Montrealers was for a building that somewhat resembled the original one and had kept many of its original components, such as the bright red seats, the standing-room area, and the hallowed ice rink. In 1949 a second storey was installed on top of the existing building to add about 3,000 seats. In 1968, too late for Expo '67, the CAC added another 3,000 seats, but this time the primary objective of the makeover was to remove the immense pillars supporting the structure, thus clearing the previously obstructed view for 6,000 seats.[14] The addition of ten VIP boxes, quickly snagged by the CAC, Molson Brewery (future owner of the team), and Ford Canada among others,[15] may have been a testimony to the gradual gentrification of hockey, but it also demonstrated that the Forum was developing with the city and with the sport, thanks to a growing population and the gradual rise of hockey as a national pastime.[16]

Although used primarily by the Montreal Canadiens, who became the arena's only tenant after the Maroons folded in 1938, the facility also served as concert hall, theatre, exhibition hall, trade-show venue, funeral home, and even church. Indeed, annually between 1950 and 1953, the midnight mass on Christmas Eve was celebrated at centre ice by Cardinal Paul-Émile Léger. This particular use explains perhaps in part the religious connotations one can find in later comments and editorials about the Forum.[17] The funeral of Howie Morenz, a hockey great who died from complications stemming from a hockey injury,[18] also added to the mystique of the Forum, which became, on one special day, a space of quiet devotion.[19] The Forum was an important space in Montreal, not only because it was the home of a legendary hockey team, but also because it was the location of many significant events in the lives of Montrealers and Quebecers: "We can say, unmistakably, that a majority of Quebecers have set foot in the Forum at least once in their lives."[20] The decision to close the Forum brought about both lament and a collective need to remember the place publicly.

## TOO OLD AND TOO SMALL

The 1989 announcement by Ronald Corey was fraught with justifications, perhaps because he and the organization he represented expected the worst. The Canadiens administration had asked Lavalin, a well-known engineering firm in Quebec, to perform a feasibility study for the complete renovation of the Forum. The conclusion of that study was gloomy, to say the least: only 2,300 seats could be added to the structure, at a staggering cost of $30,000 each. This would have brought the number of seats to a respectable 17,000, but Corey wanted at least 20,000 to cater to the ever-increasing demand.[21] In addition, the Canadiens would have had to be relocated during the hockey season, which simply did not make sense to Corey: "We can't have the Montreal Canadiens play in Hamilton or Ottawa."[22] Concerns over the memory issue were readily addressed, as Corey felt the need to underline that "the next building will have to pursue the Canadiens' tradition of excellence."[23]

There were no significant arguments against this decision in the following days, weeks, or years. Indeed, the newspaper comments and editorials focused instead on the location of the new venue. While the English-speaking side of the hockey community reflected on the sadness of it all (progress versus tradition), the French-language newspaper *La Presse* prepared its readers for what it thought would be a "East-West, Francophone-Anglophone rivalry,"[24] at least in terms of the choice of location. A few weeks after the announcement, much noise was made about moving the Forum close to the Olympic facilities, and a group was formed to campaign aggressively for this to happen.[25] There was enough noise for journalist Jack Todd to address the issue, in the form of a message to Réjean Tremblay (who was later appointed as director/producer of the closing ceremony): "And please, please, Réjean, don't make this a French-English thing. I'd hate to see the Forum in the wilds of Pointe-Claire as much as I'd hate to see it parked out by the Big O [Olympic Stadium] or near Blue Bonnets [Raceway]."[26] Despite this expected conflict (which never materialized), the promise of a state-of-the-art facility, built as much for hockey games as for rock shows, was enticing: "It's like changing an old '57 Chevy for a brand new 1995 Oldsmobile."[27] The team's coach, Pat Burns, was definitely on board, commenting a few months after the announcement that the Forum ice was in such poor condition that cracks in it were "so big, and his players so small, [that he was] afraid of losing" someone.[28]

In the end, Molson, the Canadiens owner, decided to build the new Forum in the square formed by Peel, de la Gauchetière, de la Montagne, and Saint-Antoine streets. This meant that the construction project had to take the surrounding buildings into account: "The challenge was to create a coherent and urban whole from the site's components, which include the new Forum (the generating element), Windsor Station, the train stations, the Terminus tower building and the public plaza called Cours Windsor."[29] The project entailed the restoration of Windsor Station, a train station turned historical site.[30] More than three hundred workers helped build the arena and journalist Yvon Laberge suggested that these men would probably never be able to afford to pass through its doors: "Wearing helmets and warm clothes, they don't drag their feet. In fact, they are at the other end of the spectrum from those young millionaires, wearing helmets too and flannel – holy or not – that will be living there in March 1996."[31] The new Forum project was to cost between $160 and $180 million, fit close to 21,500 fans, and include 125 luxury boxes. It also included the construction of two office towers, the Windsor Tower (forty-eight floors) and the Canadiens Tower (forty floors) a few years later.[32]

As the new Forum neared completion, concerns began to arise. Molson found itself in dire financial straits owing to restructuring in the beer industry and lower earnings from its chemical division. The credit rating of the company was lowered by Dominion Bond Rating Service, and the Canadian Press reported (wrongly, as it would turn out) that Molson would consider any "serious" offer for the legendary Montreal Canadiens.[33] Lengthy evaluations and redrafting requests from the City of Montreal, along with public criticism from Phyllis Lambert, head of the Montreal-based Canadian Centre for Architecture, and many others, all threatened to slow down dramatically the construction of the new Forum. Concerns also began to grow over what would become of the area surrounding the former building: "What will happen to the old Forum at the corner of Ste. Catherine St. and Atwater Ave., the western edge of a part of town that is looking more and more like a war zone?"[34] One could read such discourse in the *Gazette* throughout the Forum saga, while *La Presse* started asking these questions only once the location of the new arena was announced. This discourse is not unknown to labour and oral historian Steven High, who studies the perceived consequences of deindustrialization in Canadian and American cities. In a dramatic way, the closing of an industry in a small town displaces the people and the place connected to what he and David Lewis call "the cultural periphery."[35] To a certain extent, there was a similar concern among merchants situated in the vicinity of the Forum. The traffic created by the hockey crowds was a vital source of revenues for them[36] and the move of the Forum to a new area meant that hockey fans would no longer be their clientele. But, despite all these concerns and the heated debates they produced, the construction of the new Forum continued as planned.

In short, the general attitude prior to the Forum's closing was one of surprising complacency, as the expected public outcry never came: "Not one letter … maybe Ronald [Corey] got one, but I [François Seigneur, marketing consultant for the Canadiens] don't think so."[37] Mostly, this move was examined through an economic lens: it would undoubtedly hurt the old area, but it made sense because it was fiscally inevitable.[38] Not to provide a new arena to the Montreal Canadiens was like being "ostriches with their heads in the sands … wanting to keep the status quo."[39]

As the new Forum neared completion, the sentimental value of the Forum began to rise dramatically. With the closing ceremony fast approaching, people slowly realized that the space in which the powerful hockey dynasty had evolved for some seventy years was on the verge of becoming history. Particularly at this moment in time, in late 1995 and early 1996, there appeared in the pages of the *Montreal Gazette* and *La Presse* a collective sharing of memories about the Forum.[40] The events held in the week before the new building's opening, planned to illustrate the move both tangibly and symbolically, served as a catalyst of sorts for Forum nostalgia. It became more than a "place" just about the time it closed down: the process that occurred was the gradual sanctification of a building described otherwise "as distinguished architecturally as an M[etro] [grocery] store."[41]

## THE END IS NEAR: MARCH 1996

March 1996 was a sad month for many hockey fans in Montreal. The countdown to the last game played at the Forum was almost over and it was finally hitting home: the Forum was gone. To be sure, the attractiveness of a brand new arena, with perfect ice for the players and comfortable seats for the fans, was undeniable. Nevertheless, in Montreal newspapers the days before and after the closing ceremony, one could sense heightened nostalgia, and perhaps a bit of dampened anger toward the inevitability of progress. Molson knew there was a deep attachment to the Forum and, for this reason, organized a week-long celebration to mark the opening of the new place instead of mourning the closing of the old one. The company was also conscious that the decision made about the name of the building was sure to annoy many Montrealers. Indeed, the Forum was to become the Molson Centre, following a new trend in the NHL to give corporate names to arenas. Needless to say, when the news became public around the time the new Forum was almost completed, many wondered about the name change. The *Gazette*'s Pat Hickey was one of them: "As for the new Forum being a shrine, can you imagine some marketing type trying to sell the Air France Shrine at Lourdes or going to midnight mass at Mary, Queen of Trans World Airlines?"[42]

The last game played at the Forum (on 11 March 1996) pitted the Canadiens against the Minnesota North Stars, a one-time expansion team with a bland record and a short history, albeit one that did employ Guy Carbonneau and Bob Gainey, two former Habs players. A ceremony took place after the game to make official the closing of the Forum. A torch was carried on the ice by legendary figures, including Maurice Richard, Jean Béliveau, and Guy Lafleur, among others. It offered a reminder of the slogan featured in the players' dressing room, an excerpt from the First World War poem "In Flanders Fields," by the Canadian John McCrae: "To you from failing hands we throw the torch; be yours to hold it high." When Maurice Richard appeared on the ice to receive the torch, fans went wild. The entire ceremony was in effect subsumed by the public reaction to the presence of Rocket Richard, as demonstrated by a long ovation and several pleas from the teary-eyed Richard for people to stop clapping.[43] The ceremony clearly aimed at underlining the long-standing hockey tradition in Montreal, a visible reminder to fans of the Canadiens' former glory and also a clear message that what was important was the team, not the place. The event indeed focused on the players and not on the building itself.

The Canadiens administration organized an auction the day after the game, ripping apart whatever was inside the building and offering the pieces to those who were willing to pay. This created a public uproar: somehow people expected the building to stay the way it was, a dust-collecting house of sports memorabilia. Fans could bid on prized items such as the shiny red seats, original Stanley Cup banners, practice hockey nets – even a hot-dog stand. Of course, for the ones who were lucky enough to leave with a piece of hockey history, the auction represented a chance to own a piece of the Canadiens' past. For most, however, this was sacrilege: the sharing with a few of what seemed to belong to a much larger group. Many denounced the auction as the ultimate encroachment of commercialism: "Money has spoken and the ghosts have stopped talking."[44]

After the auction, Molson prepared the team's move to the new premises by organizing a parade to bring the "ghosts" from the old place to the new. Who were these ghosts? For most, they were the Canadiens' players who had passed away: Howie Morenz, Aurèle Joliat, and so many others. "It's tough to get a good look because they're moving fast and they fade in and out. But there can be no mistake. These are the ghosts," said Jack Todd, imagining what a conversation among all the past Canadiens stars might sound like: "Morenz: Ah, since Blake got here he's gotta run everything. Blake: That's cuz you need somebody to stay on ya, Morenz. Harvey: At least Toe, he's always polite, he never shows you up in front of the crowd. He looks up at the clock and he's talking, people think he's just mad because we're running out of time."[45] Players who were alive and well were likewise considered ghosts, and Maurice Richard, who was asked to take part in the parade, hated this: "I don't like being taken for a ghost."[46] For others, the ghosts were memories not of people but of specific events such as memorable on-ice fights or legendary Stanley Cup wins. Michael Mayerfeld Bell argues that ghosts are what give meaning to a place. "The ghosts of place are fabrications, products of our imagination, social constructions ... Although we generally experience ghosts as given to us, it is we that give ghosts to places."[47] The legendary players and the memorable moments were indeed the ghosts that Montrealers fabricated to populate a space about to be destroyed.

## THE FORUM AS A MEMORY "SPACE"

The many articles, letters to the editor, and editorials published between 1989 and 1996 speak of very different Forum memories, but it was the very fact of remembering, the nostalgic reminiscence prompted by the Forum's closing, that transformed the building into a lived and experienced space. According to Kathleen Stewart, nostalgia is a relational discourse: people narrate themselves into a story and through this they create an "interpretive space."[48] The Forum, in this way, is a place fabricated by nostalgia and shaped by the consumers of that nostalgia. As Anouk Bélanger demonstrated so well in her 1999 PhD thesis "Where Have the Ghosts Gone? Sports Venues and the Political Economy of Memory in Montreal," there were considerable efforts made by the Canadiens administration, and by the media as well, to construct a hegemonic version of the Forum's history.[49] But there also remained discursive space for Montrealers to tell their own stories. That space deserves examination.

The concept of "place" is more intricate than it might at first appear. A sense of place – *genius loci* in Latin – originally referred to a place with an aura of divinity, one that "derived much of its unique quality from the presence or guardianship of a supernatural spirit."[50] To make the case for the Forum as a place in that original sense, let us point out that the Montreal (but also broader Canadian) media, between 1989 and 1996, kept hammering on this idea of the Forum as an "inviolable shrine,"[51] a "sanctuary,"[52] a "spiritual centre,"[53] a "high altar,"[54] or a "mecca,"[55] notwithstanding the significant presence of ghosts in the building's story. The Forum's identity was being formulated during the process in which the sacred place was changed for a new (and presumably profane) one, confirming Steven High's argument that "when the places that define us change we ourselves change."[56] In other words, fans of the Forum changed the way they perceived the venue, or at the very least started expressing these perceptions about the venue, only because of a stimulus, that of the impending closing. Not until the sanctified arena started to shift away from the present "reality" and toward memory and "the past" did awareness of the Forum as a site of sentimental importance really take hold.

The sense of place of the Forum is embodied in the remnants of its past. In this context, the Forum is a *lieu de mémoire*, of the sort French historian Pierre Nora has so brilliantly identified. According to Nora, there exists a liminal space between the past and the present, where memory is still alive, an "ultimate embodiment of a memorial consciousness that has barely survived in a historical age that calls out for memory because it has abandoned it."[57] A *lieu* is a space where memories are still vivid and shifting but on the verge of becoming part of a more static historical narrative. However, while some *lieux*, like those mentioned by Nora, seem to emerge naturally, the Forum as a *lieu de mémoire* was wholly constructed by fans and the media for a specific reason (its closing) and for a certain time (until the Molson Centre opened and became accepted). Before this process of construction, the Forum was simply an existing space. It was its loss that breathed life into the ghosts and gave a voice to memories inhabiting the building. Memories of the Forum may have existed before, but its closing served as a catalyst to express them.

Steven High and David Lewis argue in *Corporate Wasteland* that a mill becomes an "actor" in a worker's life: in their study, "several narrators spoke of the time when 'the mill' called to offer them a job."[58] Because of the close relationship between the worker and the building he worked in, the mill became a living thing: it was the embodiment of years of hard work, of course, but it could also become the repository of memories about a worker's life outside the mill. Similarly, some saw the Forum as a living organism, a "beautiful lady"[59] who was going to be "dismembered"[60] unabashedly, one who had been issued a death sentence.[61] For more optimistic fans, it was possible for the Forum to experience a "rebirth" in its new location.[62] Despite Molson's insistence that the Canadiens were more important than the arena they played in, Montrealers were expressing the idea that, for them, the Forum was a living thing: it was breathing in memories and exhaling ghosts. Jack Todd wrote that "you could feel it – last night the old Forum coming undone from the rafters where the ghosts live down to ice level,"[63] as if the Forum "knew" it was "dying." Ian Borer explains that a place can become alive in people's memories because "places are not only the settings for a culture's myths, narratives, rituals, and ceremonies. Sometimes, they become their main characters."[64] Hence the Forum *was* as important as the hockey rituals taking place inside. This can explain the harsh criticisms voiced by some about the destruction of the Forum, such as this one: "It would be tragic if we destroy the things that have given us our identity and our history. Rome never made such a mistake."[65] Comparing the Forum to a Roman structure, Michael Fish argued that buildings should not be destroyed but instead protected for their historical value.

Several key elements of space emerged in the different pieces published about the closing of the Forum. Among the most prominent were comments about the space's organization, or its seating arrangements. One of the noticeable changes in the new facility was the removal of the standing-room area, which Gare Joyce of the *Globe and Mail* called "one of the time-honoured traditions of the Montreal Forum."[66] This section of the Forum was where tickets were the cheapest: there were no reserved spots and one claimed whatever he or she could after running through the gates. In this competition for prime space, trips to the washrooms were to be avoided at all costs. While the removal of the standing-room area was required by law because of the fire hazard it represented, many linked this to the addition of sixty-one luxury boxes, rented annually for anywhere between $50,000 and $125,000.[67] Walter Buchignani of the *Gazette* decried the change, because he "always had the feeling at the Forum that it was peopled by fans."[68] No more standing room meant no more cheap tickets, and its replacement with private boxes illustrated all too well the gentrification of a sport that had been, for a time, a poor Frenchman's job.[69] As Michael Farber summarized, there were additional seats for "the 'ordinary Joe,' assuming the 'ordinary Joe' is friends with a corporate vice-president or is willing to pay triple the face value to somebody in a corduroy jacket who barks, 'Tickets, billets.'"[70]

Besides the end of the standing-room area, fans also criticized the colour choices for the seats: the traditional red seats became burgundy. They reminded journalist Francine Grimaldi of the logo of the Société des alcools du Québec (SAQ), a somewhat fitting reference.[71] In a sense, the colours had structured people's memories: red, white, and blue seats each had a different price tag, status, and surrounding crowd attached to it. Class boundaries were deeply imbedded in the seating arrangement and colours came to have a specific meaning over the years. In fact, the seats were one of the most popular items at the auction that took place after the Forum closed. People willing to spend between $300 and $600 could bring home an authentic seat, a true piece of history reminiscent of the tens of thousands of "hockey bums" who spent a few hours living and breathing hockey. Todd reported that, a few games before the end, fans actually started pulling seats out and bringing them home. And, while he did not want “to encourage this sort of thing,” he wrote that “better the seat goes to a real fan with a pair of bolt-cutters and some moxie than some Molson lick-spittle with a BMW, a gold card and the right connections.”[72] Underlying these comments about the seats, and those about the standing-room area as well, was the issue of the increasing gentrification of the venue, and of the entire sport. “Real” fans apparently could not own BMWs and certainly could not afford to watch their team sitting on a red/burgundy seat.

The Forum seats were bright red, one of the colours on the team's jersey and perhaps the same shade as the fire in Rocket Richard's eyes. But they were also “shiny,”[73] with the kind of patina enhanced only by memory. The distant past makes our memories more vivid and the “glow” of the seats is one such example. David Johnston remembered that “shinyness,” but it related to the ice rather than the seats: “the way the ice glistened just so under the television lights.”[74] Lysiane Gagnon recalled the inside of the Forum as “too cavernous, too noisy, too shiny and too metallic.”[75] Even though the lighting at the Molson Centre undoubtedly enhanced the shiny finish on the brand new seats, it could not rival the glow of the original ones. The relation between the well-maintained seats and pride is interesting; after all, what was so special about the seats? But, as scholar Kathleen Stewart points out, nostalgia creates these multiple relations as many social referents:[76] the seats, as only one among many other physical elements of the Forum, came to be imbued with and related to pride and historical meaning.

Another material aspect of the Forum became drenched in immaterial nostalgia: the Stanley Cup banners, which were also sold at the auction. For many, Molson was going too far by selling these timepieces: “Those banners are really the property of all those ‘true fans.’ They're among the first things a parent points out to a son or daughter on their first visit together to the Forum.”[77] It seemed that whoever could afford to bid on these banners was by this very fact not a “true” fan at all. The banners were being purchased by people who could afford it (“to hang in my bar,” as one purchaser quipped[78]), thus making this story even more about the gentrification of the Forum. Two *Gazette* readers made this very argument in letters to the editor, with one wondering if “the owners worried that the banners may obstruct the view of occupants in the expensive box seats?”[79] The banners, just like the seats, were imbued with nostalgic power; they were “historical symbols of Les Canadiens,”[80] “family treasures.”[81] In the end, they were only pieces of fabric, and very old and dusty ones. There is something to be said about the power of an "original," an object or an event whose importance and significance is solely related to it being the first of many. Historian Paul Zumthor calls this the "fetishization of origins,"[82] whereby greater importance is attached to an object or an event because it represents or symbolizes the first sign of greatness. The banners were not only the material sign of the Canadiens' greatness; they also represented past victories in a time of Stanley Cup drought.[83] They were the tangible testimony of a triumphal era in the history of the Canadiens, and illustrated in quite a vivid manner the fascinating evolution of a legendary team.

### *When I Was a Kid, the Forum Was ...*

While some people's memories focused on specific physical aspects of the Forum, others used the space as a repository for their own memories. In this case, the Forum served as background for personal stories. In articles and letters to the editor, many shared family memories of experiences in the building. As Derek Drummond mused in 1992, the Forum was part of many childhoods: "The children of Montreal dream of going to the Forum to see Les Canadiens play."[84] Many people (men and women) who attended the closing ceremony went with their fathers. *La Presse* and the *Gazette* were saturated with these stories, such as that of Pierre Sauvé, who stated that "for me, the Forum is my dad and me as a kid"; of Sylvie Marchand identifying the Forum with the stories of Maurice, not Maurice Richard but Maurice Marchand, her father; of Serge Gariépy telling readers that the building reminded him of his parents, who had both passed away.[85] For fans who had lost their fathers, like Serge Gariépy, the Forum was frozen in time and transformed into a personal *lieu de mémoire*. The discontent felt about the Forum's closing was compounded by the sadness over the loss a loved one. The association between the closing of the Forum and childhood memories explains some of the nostalgia, but it also points to the construction of the Forum as a liminal space.

We could surmise that the overwhelming number of father-and-son commentaries is an expression of nostalgia about the Forum as a (perceived) masculine enclave. As Andrew Holman and Amy Ransom each observe in this volume, hockey was for many the epitome of what it was to be a man: a violent and intense sport in which valour, courage, and team spirit were the expected norm. In an interview with the *Gazette*, anthropologist David Howes had this to say about hockey: "We're in a male domain that valorizes male aggressivity ... That sense of a male identity comes out of a male context, a male space."[86] While this longing for a male-only environment may have featured in some comments about the closing of the Forum, *La Presse*'s Nathalie Petrowsky proposed a different, but still gendered, memory of the building, because the Forum, as a public space, "also belongs to us girls." She recalled going to a concert at the Forum as a form of rebellion and concluded, against the perception of the Forum as a masculine space, that the arena was also significant for Montreal women. It was in the Forum that many had witnessed the emancipation of women, one rock show or feminist rally at a time.[87]

### *When I Was a Teenager, the Forum Was ...*

While a good many people talked about father-and-son memories, an almost equal number spoke of "shenanigans" they committed at the Forum or of having attended some event as teenagers. Yves Létourneau of *La Presse* wrote: "As young fanatics, when we had a chance to approach the Forum doors and to purchase a ticket, even if it was standing room, we had only one thing in mind: go through the door as quickly as possible and go watch what was happening on the ice."[88] One woman remembers getting into the Forum with cheap tickets and finding her way to the red seats, until a "smart usher" found her and her friends and asked them to leave the premises.[89] She was there to meet boys, just like another reader who stated that "what we were looking for were the looks, the whistling and other appreciative behaviours from the finest specimens of the all-male classical colleges."[90] A former telegram boy remembers lying to a Forum doorman by telling him the telegram he had was for Dick Duff, a Canadiens player, and needed to be delivered "by hand."[91] Thanks to this fabricated story, the fifteen-year-old was able to watch Jean Béliveau hoist the Stanley Cup. Hockey analyst François Gagnon tells the tale of a group of young men combining their allowances to buy one standing-room ticket and the rest of them waiting at an entrance to be let in illegally.[92] Another *La Presse* reader recalled that he and his friend were able to strike a deal with a Forum employee, putting a few bucks together as a bribe to let them in at an Elton John concert: "The environs of the Forum are deserted. We ask an employee at the turnstiles. 'No problem,' he says."[93] As a place, the Forum reminded people of the freedom they felt at an age when they had no responsibilities ... and no money. The closing of the Forum threatened their memories about these days, when, not yet weighed down by the responsibilities of adulthood, they were more carefree. With the building gone, it meant that their children would never be able to experience the Forum in the same way. The Forum reminded people of specific times in their lives, times that "smelled like beer and patchouli"[94] for some, and became the repository of meaningful personal memories. These memories existed on their own, but they were brought back to life by the closing of the Forum.

### *When the Canadiens Were Good, the Forum Was ...*

Another memory permeating the walls of the Forum was that of the Canadiens' winning tradition. This one drew on the team's dynastic performances of the distant past. The Forum was thus not only about personal memories of past ages or shiny seats, but also embodied a collective memory of what the Canadiens meant and how important their performance was for Montrealers.

Was it the same story for the Maple Leafs in Toronto and their arena, Maple Leaf Gardens, which was replaced by the Air Canada Centre in 1999? Of course, place attachment is not a phenomenon unique to Montreal. And yet the reaction to the closing ceremonies in the two cities differed greatly. In Lisa Anne Gunderson's analysis, "the underwhelming reaction given by many columnists to the ceremonies held in Toronto" is explained by "the predominant refusal to fall under the sway of the nostalgic promises that the ceremonies seemed to offer."[95] What makes this hockey story different in Quebec than elsewhere is that the Forum was the place where fans enjoyed the most Stanley Cup victories. Conversely, the tepid reactions to the closing ceremonies for Maple Leaf Gardens, according to Gunderson, were prompted by the public perception that "the night's festivities just served to shine a spotlight on the unavoidable evidence of so many years of failure."[96]

Despite the team's varying degrees of success over the course of its history, it remains true that Montreal is a significant place for hockey in general. The first-ever documented hockey game was played in that city in 1875, the National Hockey League was founded there in 1917, and the team that won the most Stanley Cups in history has been there for over a century, making it the oldest and most successful team of the NHL. For any avid hockey fan, Montreal represents the origins of organized hockey, the beginning of it all. Hockey in Quebec is the same as everywhere else in many respects, except for this key point: an attachment to a team that reflects so closely the history of a province and the history of a sport. And this attachment percolates in anything related to the team, remotely or not, including the place in which they play. Indeed, as Emmanuel Lapierre explains in his chapter, the Canadiens are not just a hockey team in Montreal, they are a cultural symbol. Whatever happens to them is newsworthy, and not always buried in the sports pages of newspapers.[97]

## A NEW BEGINNING?

The Forum as a *lieu de mémoire* is now very much split in two. There is the Molson Centre (now the Bell Centre),[98] which is in a way the New Forum. It is sold out every game and it is the prime location for any large-scale event in the city. It is now the new home of the Montreal Canadiens and, as such, a new space for fans to create new memories. For Sophie Gironnay, the new arena is "not pretty, not ugly, not amazing, not catastrophic … kind of nice, a little potbellied but welcoming. A real good average Quebecer!"[99]

The other "half" of the Forum is, well, the old Forum, which is now an entertainment centre with a movie theatre, stores, arcades, and restaurants. The builders have recreated centre ice, albeit not in the original location, and have left a section of the seats in the middle of the building. People can sit there and reminisce, although the sound of videogames is a tad overbearing for some. For Canadiens fans, there is a faint feeling of unease when looking at the seats, lone vestiges of a glorious past, plunked in the middle of a shopping area and decorated with faux spectators made of paper mâché. A reader of the *Gazette* described the new centre as a "whiz-bang mini-Sodom and Gomorrah,"[100] a statement that is testimony to the strident reactions to the Forum being gutted and now serving a purpose so far from hockey. For the merchants in the area, the AMC Pepsi Forum, as it is called, is a good thing because it helped them survive the closing of the sports facility. For many others, however, it would have been better simply to let it go.

There is an interesting difference between this sports nostalgia and the nostalgia that workers feel for a destroyed or decayed mill. In the latter case, the building is either gone or beyond recognition; memory is thus free to roam and recreate the images of the past. In the case of the Forum, there are two buildings, one that does not look like the Forum anymore, and another one that is supposed to replace it. Long-gone childhood and teenage years cannot be recaptured, but the long-gone glory of the Canadiens might (someday). Indeed, it is up to the Montreal Canadiens to usher in a new glorious era which would then allow the Bell Centre to become itself a repository of new memories. After all, it is the players who have won Stanley Cups, not the building: "The soul is not in the bricks but in the team's spirit."[101]

7

# "HE SHOOTS! HE SCORES!": LANGUAGE AND GENDER POLITICS IN THE QUEBEC TELEVISION SERIES *LANCE ET COMPTE*

—

*Amy J. Ransom*

—

C'est drôle les joueurs de hockey sans leurs costumes. On dirait des hommes ordinaires. (It's strange to see hockey players without their uniforms on. You'd think they were ordinary men.)
Marilou, *Lance et compte*, season 1, episode 4

When producer Claude Héroux pitched a television series to Radio-Canada in the 1980s, his translation of Foster Hewitt's well-known exclamation "He shoots! He scores!" as *Lance et compte* (1986–91; 2002–09) was not considered proper French by the French-language branch of Canada's state-owned broadcasting corporation, Radio-Canada.[1] The phrase did not apparently bother francophone viewers since the show became one of Quebec's most popular and long-lasting dramatic series. While the French title lacks the sexual double entendre of the original English, the inextricably linked themes of sex/gender and hockey dominate its narrative trajectories. Set in Quebec City and based on a fictionalized

National Hockey League (NHL) franchise (le National, possibly named after the first francophone multi-sporting club in Canada, as described by Michel Vigneault in chapter 2, and purposefully modelled on the Nordiques, the *real*, neo-nationalist-cum-separatist organization that Terry Vaios Gitersos examines in chapter 5), the series revolves around the lives of hockey players, coaches, agents, and sport journalists. A female cast of mothers, sisters, wives, lovers, and daughters supports (and often antagonizes) this largely male cast. As Élise Detellier demonstrates, sport in Quebec has traditionally been a male domain, and this is particularly true of hockey, as its relative absence in her path-breaking study, *Mise au jeu: Les sports féminins à Montréal* (2015), reveals.[2] Although it most often reinscribes the compulsory heterosexuality and male-dominant gender roles of patriarchal bourgeois capitalist society, *Lance et compte* occasionally grapples with the conflict caused by challenges to that order represented by women entering into the androcentric world of hockey.

French feminist theory has long stressed the essential relationship between language and gender,[3] and more recently scholars have linked gender to nationalist politics in the Quebec context.[4] This chapter examines the connected issues of language and gender politics in *Lance et compte*, focusing on the series' dialogue choices (between French and English, as well as between standard international and vernacular Quebec French) and its representation of gender roles for contemporary franco-Québécois through depictions of, and relationships between, its various male and female characters. Drawing on the gender theory of Jeffery Vacante, R.W. Connell, Diane Lamoureux, and Denyse Baillargeon, the chapter addresses the series' construction of specifically Québécois forms of masculinity and femininity, as well as how those roles and relations have changed (or not) from the original series and telefilms of the mid-1980s through 1991 and to the series' reprise in the first decade of the new millennium.

## *LANCE ET COMPTE*: WINNERS NOT LOSERS

Independent producer Claude Héroux conceived the idea of a hockey-themed prime-time drama in hopes of good ratings.[5] Given hockey's popularity and its meaning for Québécois national identity,[6] he expected positive responses to "this dyed-in-the wool Quebec story,"[7] a cultural product that played on the concept of recognition[8] while at the same time taking advantage of new developments in Canadian broadcasting regulations.[9] In addition to being able to fulfill the Canadian-content specifications of state-sponsored television, Héroux was also energized by the incentives for private-sector media productions,[10] a corollary to the privatization of crown corporations occurring during the free-trade Mulroney regime,[11] an ideology largely mirrored by Quebec's Liberal Party provincial premier, Robert Bourassa.[12] Used to working in film, Héroux also wished to offer viewers higher production values than were typical of made-in-Quebec television in order to compete with the highly popular American exports *Dallas* (1978–91) and *Dynasty* (1981–91).[13] His engagement of film director Jean-Claude Lord was instrumental in ensuring the necessary levels of both narrative and visual quality.[14]

Héroux's memoir, *Lance et compte: Les Dessous d'une grande réussite* (2006; He Shoots! He Scores!: The Underside of a Great Success), reflects the series' central discourse of winners and losers, an increasingly meaningful discourse against the backdrop of flagging nationalism, the Montreal Canadiens' Stanley Cup drought (which began almost as soon as the series aired), and Quebec City's eventual loss of its NHL franchise. "The National" offered post-referendum Quebecers a compensatory fantasy of success in a period of tense constitutional negotiations with federal Canada and a dearth of victories by their real teams on the ice, particularly in the series revival.[15] It also perhaps fulfilled the repeatedly expressed desire for a Quebec national hockey team as described in the Introduction to this volume. With plots and dialogue co-written by hockey journalist Réjean Tremblay, in consultation with a hockey expert, and incorporating stock footage of NHL games, *Lance et compte* apparently got the hockey right, at least right enough to satisfy prime-time viewers. Its ratings[16] and the show's longevity demonstrate that *Lance et compte* and its fictional hockey heroes are definitely winners. As seen in the table below, three consecutive seasons of the original series (1986, 1987, and 1988) were followed by six telefilms (1990–91). Then a revival series began with *Lance et compte: La Nouvelle Génération* (LCNG; 2002), which has survived four more seasons to date (2004, 2006, 2008, 2012); a final series that aired in 2015 (but not yet available on DVD at the time of writing); and a big-screen feature film (2010).

TABLE 7.1. The Various avatars of the *Lance et compte* phenomenon

| Aired | Title | Abbreviation |
|---|---|---|
| 1986 | *Lance et compte*: original tv series, episodes 1–13 | LCI |
| 1988 | *Lance et compte II*: episodes 14–26 | LCII |
| 1989 | *Lance et compte III*: episodes 27–39 | LCIII |
| 1990 | *Lance et compte: Tous pour un* | *Tous* |
| 1990 | *Lance et compte: Le Crime de Lulu* | *Crime* |
| 1990 | *Lance et compte: Envers et contre tous* | *Envers* |
| 1991 | *Lance et compte: Le Moment de vérité* | *Moment* |
| 1991 | *Lance et compte: Le Choix* | *Choix* |
| 1991 | *Lance et compte: Le Retour du Chat* | *Retour* |
| 2002 | *Lance et compte: La Nouvelle Génération* | LCNG |
| 2004 | *Lance et compte: La Reconquête* | LCRec |
| 2006 | *Lance et compte: La Revanche* | LCRev |
| 2009 | *Lance et compte: Le Grand Duel* | LCGD |
| 2010 | *Lance et compte: Le Film* | LC*Film* |
| 2012 | *Lance et compte: La Déchirure* | LCDec |
| 2015 | *Lance et compte: La Finale* | LCF |

Each season offers a complete story arc with several dramatic threads, following key characters. The first season traces the rise of rookie Pierre Lambert (Carl Marotte) from the minor leagues to the NHL, along with the National's battle to reach the Stanley Cup finals. It introduces a cast of characters and actors, many of whom reassume their roles nearly two decades later in *La Nouvelle Génération* and its sequels: the Lambert family, including the widowed franco-Russian matriarch Maroussia (French actress Macha Méril) and girl-next-door-pretty, intelligent Suzie (Marina Orsini), Pierre's mother and sister respectively; and aging star and then coach Marc Gagnon (Marc Messier) and his family (and many girlfriends). In particular, his son, Francis Gagnon (Michel Goyette/Louis-Philippe Dandenault), works so hard at the game that the seemingly talentless child (*LCI:* 9) grows up to become a star himself with the National (*LCNG*), then the Montreal Canadiens (*LCGD*). A number of additional characters remain for the entirety of the series, including: the team's relentless coach, then media commentator, Jacques Mercier (Yvan Ponton); its general manager,

Gilles Guilbeault (Michel Forget); key players, most notably Bob Martin (Robert Merrien) and Mac Templeton (Éric Hoziel); and sport journalist Lucien Boivin, known affectionately as Lulu (Denis Bouchard). Part of the franchise's success lies in building fan loyalty with these compelling and engaging characters cast with familiar local actors and actresses.

## LANGUAGE CHOICE IN *LANCE ET COMPTE*'S DIALOGUE[17]

In order to reach as many markets as possible, Héroux initially filmed *Lance et compte* in both French and English and sought co-production status with France and later Switzerland.[18] This complicated the issue of language during all phases of the production process. Héroux planned to film, simultaneously, French- and English-language versions of the series, confident that hockey's popularity in the rest of Canada would ensure a sale to Canadian Broadcasting Corporation (CBC), the English-language branch of Canada's state-sponsored broadcasting network. He thus cast Quebec actors whose English was relatively unaccented.[19] Unsatisfied with the results, however, the CBC required the series to be redubbed by anglophones.[20] Perhaps indicative of the phenomenon pointed to in the title of this volume, that the same game of hockey holds different meanings in Quebec and the rest of Canada, *He Shoots! He Scores!* survived only two seasons in English Canada in spite of its meaning-laden title, and Héroux never realized his goal of selling the series in the United States.[21] The producer expresses disappointment with a system that claims to desire bilingual/bicultural products but then fails to support them: "We're doing what the CRTC [Canadian Radio-television and Telecommunications Commission] says it wants: broadcasting a pan-Canadian production adopted by television watchers from one ocean to the other."[22]

Other issues arose regarding the European French version of the series, including its unhappy title *Cogne et gagne*,[23] roughly translatable as "hit and win," which invokes the sport's violence. For co-production with France's state-sponsored TF1, Héroux had to cast three roles with French citizens;[24] since few French hockey players could be found, women's roles would have to suffice. These included Maroussia Lambert, Marilou (Sophie Renoir), and Lucie Baptiste (although the character is of Haitian origin, she is played by Martinican actress France Zobda). The (eventually futile) intention to film an undubbed English version added further difficulties in finding French actresses competent in English.[25] Furthermore, it was felt that the European audience would not be able to understand colloquial Québécois, Vernacular Quebec French (VQF), so a Parisian version was dubbed in Standard International French (SIF). In a bizarre twist due to Canadian language law and trade-union politics, the producers could not dub directly from French into French; happily, the English-filmed version existed, and it was this version that was dubbed into metropolitan French.[26] In addition, German, Portuguese, Italian, Russian, and Spanish versions were made.[27]

Apart from the obvious choice of casting local actors, one of the main strategies to infuse the series with the *pure-laine* Québécois character that Héroux sought was the use of dialogue in VQF.[28] Language debates in Quebec went beyond the issue of French-English conflicts addressed with the 1977 Charter of the French Language, also known as Bill 101.[29] Controversy during the 1960s revolved around the use of French itself. Known as *La Querelle du joual*, the joual debate – referring to working-class Montreal French in which "horse," *cheval*, was pronounced *joual* – revolved around whether or not the province should adopt SIF, or whether it should express itself in its own vernacular.[30] In the context of the visual media, writing in 1984 just before the release of *Lance et compte*, Denyse Therrien traces the growing acceptance of VQF in the province's cinema, linking it to the rise of cultural and political nationalism since the 1960s.[31] While television journalists today generally employ SIF or its closer relative, Standard Quebec French (SQF),[32] Quebec film and fiction television reflect a range of linguistic expression, adopting a register appropriate to a character's education, social class, age group, subregional origins, and, of course, gender. Such is the case with *Lance et compte*.

## *Do Men and Women Speak a Different Language?*

John Christian Sanaker argues that, in post-colonial contexts, including those in Quebec, such language choices are not innocent and arbitrary but rather bear cultural and political significance.[33] Sanaker analyzes big-screen films with artistic aspirations and limited releases even in Quebec, both of which lend themselves to political readings. In contrast, the publicly broadcast television show *Lance et compte*, also aspiring to Héroux's profit-based goal of appealing to the largest audience possible (including anglophone Canada), largely eschews overtly franco-nationalist discourses. Indeed, during season two's depiction of the World Cup of Hockey, team members acknowledge, "We play for our country and that country's called Canada!"[34] Nonetheless, it marks its lead characters as very specifically franco-Québécois through its use of language, particularly as this relates to gender. The following analysis of language choices made by the show's writers reveals the gendered nature of language in Quebec, the reality (and acceptance) of the incorporation of English into VQF, and the continued aspiration of franco-Quebecers for their language to be dominant in a territory perceived as their own. In addition, it uses language to establish difference between North American French-speakers and metropolitan French people, reinforcing to a certain extent the *américanité* (Americanicity)[35] of a franco-Québécois identity.

Apart from the distinct pronunciation of certain vowels and a lexicon reflective of the New World environment, including terms from Aboriginal languages and French archaisms maintained from the pre-Conquest era, one of the key characteristics of VQF is its idiosyncratic cannibalization of English terms.[36] We see this at work throughout the original series with the fans' motivating slogan for the team: "Go! Go! Go!" In particular, the winner-loser dialogue occurs largely in English. Mercier variously encourages his team with phrases like "Let's go!" (*LCI:* 2) and disparages them as a "Buncha losers" (*LCGD:* 6). While it naturalizes the presence of English, the series at times underscores linguistic tensions between North American and metropolitan French. In its very first episode, Suzie's Tunisian-French roommate, Marilou, challenges Pierre to a contest of "pompes," and the illustrative exchange merits repeating:

PIERRE: Des quoi? (What?)
MARILOU: Des pompes. (Push-ups. [continental French])
PIERRE: C'est quoi, des pompes? (What's that, "pumps"?)
MARILOU: Eh, ben, c'est ça. (Well, it's this. [she performs a push-up])
PIERRE: C'est pas des pompes, c'est des push-up. On appelle ça des push-up. (Those aren't "pumps," it's push-ups.

You call that push-ups.)

MARILOU: Ah, non, on dit des pompes. (No, you say "pompes.")

PIERRE: On dit des push-up. (You say "push-up.")

MARILOU: Des pompes, des pompes.

PIERRE: [interrupting] Push-up*s*. [The last time he explicitly pronounces the plural "s"]

The presence of such anglicisms has traditionally been a bone of contention for purists who, as Jason Blake and Andrew C. Holman show in this book's Introduction, have wished to purge them from Quebec French,[37] and in the 1980s the series was critiqued for co-opting the American-style soap-opera television genre.[38] At the same time, as distinct markers of *québécitude*, an open acknowledgment of the daily reality of North American French-speakers' contact with the continent's dominant language, *Lance et compte*'s insertion of such incidences of linguistic and cultural confusion underscores the difference between, for example, two French speakers – the metropolitan French Marilou and the Québécois Pierre. Rather than marking Pierre as an uneducated, even "colonized" individual, his unapologetic insistence on the appropriated English term signifies pride in his presence in North America, suggesting that here in Quebec the metropolitan French visitor Marilou must adapt to his ways rather than correct his French, thus reversing the usual colonial power dynamic. In addition to these nationalist stakes, the linguistic exchange also reflects the gendered rivalry that infuses this couple's relationship, through which they seem incessantly to be competing for dominance over the other. The series appears to code Pierre's (albeit anglicized) Quebec French with an aura of masculinity absent from Marilou's French "from France." The incorporation of anglicisms into VQF, and their increasingly shameless presence in Québécois popular culture texts, seems so extensive, and unique, that they should be read as appropriations, and thus markers of a Quebec-specific form of French rather than erroneous borrowings from English.

Of course, the vocabulary of hockey itself is largely bilingual thanks to English being the official language of the NHL, the migration of Quebec players into English markets, and the presence of English-speaking fans in Montreal, Quebec's only remaining NHL market. In the early days, well-meaning clerics – who, after initial opposition to the sport, played a role in its development in Quebec, as we see both in Roch Carrier's popular story "The Hockey Sweater" and in Sheldon Cohen's film adaptation of it – attempted to gallicize the vocabulary of hockey. The term "gouret" offered a non-English derived alternative name for the sport until the 1940s;[39] French names for equipment also exist: la rondelle (*puck*), le palet (*stick*), le filet (*net*), and so on. However, over the years, hockey has become the one area in which perhaps all franco-Québécois are bilingual, as the nouns *puck*, *goal* (most often as an exclamation after one is scored), and the verbs *scorer, coacher,* and *skate* have entered VQF, offering a more varied lexicon for a topic frequently discussed by both fans and broadcasters.

Thus, characters in coaching and managing positions are clearly portrayed in the series as bilingual, or at least as functional speakers of English. For example, the general manager of the National in the original series, Gilles Guilbeault, speaks a very regional form of Québécois French that is marked particularly by his rolled Rs. As a member of the business class, his French is generally grammatically correct, but because of his position in the NHL, he must also be bilingual; frequently, he speaks Quebec-accented English in the owners' box with Allan Goldman or on the phone when discussing a trade. However, coach Jacques Mercier even more frequently switches codes from VQF to colloquial, but accented, English. These particular language choices for Mercier's characterization reflect both his domestic situation – he is married to an anglo-Canadian – and the reality for francophones working in the NHL.

However, Mercier – who is described as "the National's coach with the colorful language"[40] – also swears more often than Guilbeault. Not only does this add to his characterization as the stereotype of the ill-tempered coach who often resorts to abuse to motivate his team, it also enhances his construction as a figure of hegemonic masculine leadership. Sociolinguist Jennifer Coates confirms the common-sense notion that "swearing and taboo language have historically been used by men in the company of other men as a sign of their toughness and of their manhood."[41] *Lance et compte* provides the perfect context for this intersection, staging a vision both of the "macho" sport of hockey *and* of Quebec, a province noted for its distinctive form of swearing derived from terms for the instruments and sacraments of the Catholic Church. Indeed, *calvaire, ostie, sacrament, sacrifice*, and *tabarnak* occur repeatedly in male cast members' dialogue; whereas series' producers justified the language as adding to the realism of the narrative,[42] this was another source of criticism from Quebec's *bien pensants* or cultural elitists, according to René Payant.[43] Pierre Lambert, like other young players, speaks in typical VQF, something that also reinforces his characterization as a provincial innocent abroad (he comes from the smaller city of Trois-Rivières). For example, on discovering that the sleeves of his undershirt and the legs of his long-johns have been truncated prior to his rookie initiation ritual in the National's locker room, he exclaims: "Voyons, sacrifice! Quel sacrifice de cave a fait ça, alors?" ("What the hell?! Which bloody idiot did this, then?")[44] Marc Gagnon, however, swears even more frequently than others in a manner clearly coded as Québécois. When the phone rings during an argument with his first wife, Nicole, a rare incidence of both sexes swearing occurs as Marc commands her to answer – "Réponds, calvaire!" – and she replies in frustration, "Shit!" (*LCI:* 4). Although Maroussia also swears in a fashion that signals her continental origins ("Les salauds!" [Those bastards]; *LCI:* 1), Nicole Gagnon offers an exception that proves the rule – she appears to be the only woman in the series' eight seasons who swears *and* uses an anglicism. Across the board, male characters in *Lance et compte* speak a form of French marked as specifically Québécois through an increased frequency of both VQF terms appropriated from English and swear words unique to VQF. When female characters swear in exceptional situations like these, their linguistic practice is estranged; expressed in English and metropolitan French respectively, Nicole's and Maroussia's expletives distance them from the masculine, Québécois norm.

While the series thus enhances, on the one hand, the authenticity of its franco-Québécois characters through their populist use of VQF, language choices made for English-speaking characters, on the other, involve a certain element of a reverse assimilationist fantasy attributing to the hockey world a French-language presence that is simply not plausible. Certainly, a number of anglophone characters appear in the series and they, as one would expect, often speak English. For continuity's sake, however, nearly all of these anglo-Canadians are depicted as fully bilingual, fluently following the rapid-fire VQF dialogue of others and, before or after the sentence or two uttered in English (subtitled for unilingual francophones), participating in the remainder of the conversation in French. Thus, the ongoing presence of unilingual English-speaking hockey players in Quebec is almost completely elided; indeed, the series' foregrounding of the French language resists the clearing of French from the national space that, according to Emmanuel Lapierre in this volume, has occurred across the history of Quebec's real NHL franchise, the Montreal Canadiens.

Furthermore, unlike Martin Ward (Colm Feore), the cultivated Toronto officer who speaks Parisian French in the hockey-themed film *Bon Cop, Bad Cop* (2005),[45] these anglophone characters in *Lance et compte* speak French with a distinctive provincial accent and vocabulary. They include owner Allan Goldman (August Schellenberg), season-one goalie Gary Bennett (Timothy Webber), a racist player named Steve Bradshaw (David Nerman), the beloved team goon, American Mac Templeton (played by Éric Hoziel, whose accent sometimes betrays the actor's franco-Québécois origins), and, in the revival series, team captain Mike Ludano (acted by Peter Miller, who, in spite of his name, clearly coded as non-francophone, was born in Chibougamau). Of course, the quantity and quality of French used by these anglophone characters must to a certain extent simply represent a convenient device in a program developed first and foremost with francophone viewers in mind. In fact, the international context of season two's World Cup of Hockey story arc requires that Russians and Americans speak French in private conversations with each other. Nonetheless, the predominance of the French language in an NHL locker room also suggests a level of assimilation to franco-Québécois culture that reflects a wish-fulfillment fantasy about the dominance of French in the territory of Quebec, an issue that still concerns franco-nationalists today.[46]

To cite a few examples, the first series realistically portrays the situation of Jacques Mercier's son Jimmy (Andrew Bednarski). Attending French schools, he is fluently bilingual, although his mother is English-speaking; the couple uses both languages alternately in their home. For children growing up in post-Bill 101 Quebec, this seems natural, but for adult anglo-Canadians in the 1980s, like an unnamed scout (Harry Hill) who tries to sell members of Prince Albert's junior league team to the National's management (*LCI:* 1), it is less realistic. In the later series in the first decade of the new millennium, the children of the first series are now young players, so it also seems logical that Ludano would speak French fluently in spite of his English-language heritage. It is less reasonable to expect, though, that all of the players on an NHL team, albeit a fictional one, could follow the coach's speeches and instructions in French. Although for the past forty years the Montreal Canadiens have with few exceptions hired head coaches who speak French, the fact remains that Montreal is a largely bilingual market with many avid anglophone Habs fans and a history of star anglophone players, such as Ken Dryden and Steve Shutt. To be sure, the 2011 appointment of unilingual anglophone Randy Cunneyworth led to a media blizzard, and he was replaced by francophone Michel Therrien after less than one season at the helm. Yet the team's composition, even in its earliest, explicitly francophone iterations, has always reflected a range of ethnic diversity.[47] Even with the highest figures for drafting French Canadian players, the Canadiens and Nordiques never surpassed an average of 2.63 and 2.38 francophone draftees per season.[48] Viewed in light of those numbers, the high proportion of National players whose jerseys sport ethnically French Canadian names surely reflects a fantasy team, parlaying the Canadian dream of playing in the NHL into the Québécois dream of playing for the National, a discourse explicitly recognized by Pierre Lambert and Denis Mercure (Jean Harvey), both drafted from the Trois-Rivières Dragons (*LCI:* 1). Imbedded in the linguistic performance of this series, then, is an imagining of a fictive Quebec secure in its francophone North American identity, yet often by eliding the *fait anglais*, an imagining that is reiterated in the social construction of the (real) Montreal Canadiens as marketed to francophones, as we have seen in Emmanuel Lapierre's and Julie Perrone's respective chapters.

## GENDER POLITICS IN *LANCE ET COMPTE*

Language choice in *Lance et compte*'s dialogue, then, goes beyond producers' desire to reach a broad market or writers' depictions of its characters' cultural or national identities; it is also integral to the construction of those characters' fictional gendered identities. Obviously, many other aspects of plot and characterization also feed into their construction as "masculine" and "feminine" in relation to evolving social norms in Quebec and across Western society. As I discuss at greater length elsewhere,[49] with its two iterations, the original series and its more recent revival, *Lance et compte* offers a unique window onto Quebec in the 1980s and the first decade of the new millennium in its efforts to present a highly contemporary, "realistic" drama to its viewers.[50] As such, it engages many of those two periods' compelling questions, including what Diane Lamoureux terms "an unexpected reconfiguring of social sex roles" in Québécois society.[51] Because the series features many of the same characters, but at two different points in time, its comparative potential is rare in the history of Quebec television. Before we turn to an analysis of *Lance et compte*'s representation of gender roles for franco-Québécois in the 1980s and the twenty-first century, a brief overview of these changing gender roles and relations, as well as the relationship between gender and nationalism in the province, would be useful.

As is widely understood, across the 1970s, feminist movements developed in France, the United States, and Quebec itself, where they worked in tandem with the growing nationalist movement, achieving additional specific gains for *les Québécoises*.[52] Women thus participated in the rise of the Parti Québécois and René Lévesque's victory in the 1976 provincial elections; however, as Jeffery Vacante explains, a number of factors led various intellectual and political figures to blame women and/or feminism for the failure of the 1980 referendum on sovereignty-association. Harking back to an old tradition of patriarchal authority inherent in the Catholic Church's past role as the guardian of French-language culture in North America, including "a long history of blaming women for the challenges arising from economic dislocation and political failures,"[53] the 1980s and 1990s represented a paradoxical time in terms of gender roles and relations. On the one hand, not only had the liberal social values associated with the neo-nationalist movement in Quebec freed women from the anti-divorce, anti-contraception, pro-natality ideology of the earlier clerico-nationalism, but increasing numbers of women entered the workforce, a trend embraced on the surface through, for example, the adoption of feminine forms of professional titles absent from the French language and not yet in use in France.[54] On the other hand, after the failed referendum of 1980, an increasing sense that "the result somehow reflected the state of Quebec manhood" fuelled a perceived crisis in masculinity,[55] which in turn fed a latent misogyny.

Mirroring the "backlash" and actual rollbacks in women's and family legislation since the Reagan-Bush era in the United States, therefore, media representations of men's and women's roles, along with normative images of masculinity and femininity, appear to have changed very little in Quebec between the 1980s and the first decade of the new millennium, at least as they are depicted in *Lance et compte*. The original series and telefilms both consistently engage the hot topics of their day, often lending a veneer of progressiveness. Various episodes engage such issues as the first female sport journalists in men's locker rooms; women's roles in the masculine domain of ice hockey; two-career families and their challenges; non-traditional families; sexual relationships between men and women, including increased sexual freedom and even promiscuity, as well as a lower age at which Western young people are having sex, resulting in questions over abortion and birth control; and, finally, the demands of homosexuals to live their lives without stigma. Even the question of AIDS appeared briefly in *Lance et compte I*, as Lucie Baptiste lists the negative stereotypes of Haitians.

In spite of this apparent progressiveness, both series (1986–91 and 2002–12) project ambivalent attitudes toward the breakdown of the bourgeois, patriarchal norms that have been in place for centuries in Western societies, toward the continued impact of the so-called sexual revolution, and toward the evolution of the contemporary family. The series offers images of men as whole individuals capable of being loving, equal partners and fathers for the women and children in their lives, like those promulgated by early proponents of masculinity studies, such as R.W. Connell.[56] And yet, in its male leads, the series continues to reward strength and aggressiveness, traits traditionally considered proper only to the masculine, even implying that these traits are necessary for their true success as men. In terms of the feminine, I find a similar ambivalence in the portrayal both of domestic women and of professional women. A few well-rounded characters stand out as balanced female role models, eschewing at times "the established sex/gender order" of female domesticity and taking on the part of "transitional feminine cultural figure[s]," as Bill Marshall reads Emilie (not coincidentally played by "Suzie Lambert," actress Marina Orsini) in *Les Filles de Caleb* (1990–91), a contemporary television success.[57] Nonetheless, *Lance et compte*'s various iterations clearly objectify the female body, implicitly disparage the housewife's contribution to the family economy, and portray certain secondary female characters in the tradition of the vamp, "the exotic and wicked seductress who cast irresistible spells over men with her sexually aggressive behaviour and intriguing, relatively unclothed body."[58]

## THE PARADOXES OF QUÉBÉCOIS MANHOOD: HEGEMONIC MASCULINITY AND THE NEW MAN

In *Lance et compte*, prowess on the ice becomes intricately connected to prowess in the bedroom, but it cuts both ways. While the hockey player's attractiveness to women represents one of the fringe benefits of the profession – a notion explicitly stated by the National's young, Black star goalie, Alex Beauchesne[59] (*LCRec:* 4) – sexual activity and relationships with women often undermine his game performance. Mercier harangues his young recruits, "Those make-out sessions with your girlfriends are over, so forget about it,"[60] and after practice Pierre Lambert admits to his amorous girlfriend that "I don't think I even can."[61] The most famous and skilled players get more – and more beautiful – women, as well. The womanizing of the National's senior star, Marc Gagnon, appears legendary; although he is married, a beautiful woman awaits him in every away city, including Winnipeg (*LCI:* 2) and Toronto (*LCI:* 5). Even the biggest stars, however, eventually suffer the consequences of placing their sexual attraction to women over the sport. When Marc falls in love with eighteen-year-old Suzie Lambert and contemplates divorce, the shambles of his personal life leaves him distracted on the ice and the team's general manager livid: "Leave the little girls alone! You don't have the legs for it anymore ... Marc, hockey's a beautiful game; stop mucking it up!"[62] The series thus values a highly active heterosexuality as enhancing players' masculinity, while at the same time positing women as a distraction from the ostensibly more important homosocial realm of the game.

In spite of this blatant exploitation of time-worn clichés about sexual activity undermining athletes' performance and athletes' use of their position to obtain sexual attention from women, *Lance et compte* nonetheless offers viewers a glimpse of the new Québécois man. Diane Lamoureux argues that the modern nationalist-sovereigntist movement in Quebec may be seen as "a movement of men's virilization,"[63] through which pre-Quiet Revolution, subaltern French Canadians became the Québécois "Maîtres chez soi" (Masters in their own house) by the turn of the twenty-first century. Having shrugged off the role of the typical Québécois loser, by the time of even the first iteration of *Lance et compte*, new images of a confident Québécois manhood can be seen in popular culture. With this confidence also comes a new sensitivity. Thus, while they may be tigers on the ice, in the locker room, or at the negotiating table, Pierre Lambert, Jacques Mercier, and eventually even Marc Gagnon offer models of loving sons, brothers, and husbands, an echo of the sort of traditional masculinity that, as described by Holman in chapter 1, players in the pre-Quiet Revolution Depression Hockey League exhibited. Additionally, team captain Bob Martin offers an alternative leadership style to the negative motivation largely seen in the series' portrayal of the professional hockey world. Yet these same kinder, gentler hockey heroes at home perpetrate clear-cut acts of "hegemonic masculinity" – a concept to which we will return shortly – in order to further their careers in the sport, to establish dominance over each other, and to objectify women in a manner that reinscribes traditional images of female passivity. Such images of masculine strength work, then, to combat the perceived crisis in masculinity that Vacante describes in 1980s Quebec and to reconstruct a "link between national affirmation and manhood" that appeared to have been broken.[64] In the new millennium, a so-called "post-national" era, such images of vigorous masculinity suggest that although sovereignty per se has not been realized, the men of Quebec have nonetheless achieved "the full political, economic, and social power that is usually associated with that manhood."[65]

With a now idealized dead father, raised by his widowed mother, and deeply attached to a sister only two years younger than him, Pierre Lambert offers the most well-rounded image of a young man who eventually learns to negotiate contemporary society's expectations of masculine aggressiveness in the workplace while also showing an ability to express emotion and caring at home. At first, Pierre appears to be the stereotypical product of the society described just a few years after the series' debut by Guy Corneau in *Absent Fathers, Missing Sons* (1989). Headed by a matriarch, the Lambert family embodies Corneau's popular theory, which concluded that Quebec was populated with incomplete men struggling to come to terms with their masculine identity because the father figure had been literally or metaphorically absent. Corneau proposed that, for many Quebec men, hockey fills a role for the development of male role models and inter-male bonding.[66] In the first series, still very much a boy, Pierre finds comfort in his mother's reassurances, but he also offers in turn comfort to his sister when she suffers the emotional pain of a break-up (*LCI:* 8). While he works to distance himself from his mother, cutting the proverbial apron strings, he remains attracted to women who mother him, although sometimes this mothering appears in unconventional ways – for example, when Marilou, the free-spirited French girl, takes him on a New Age journey to restore his positive wave-lengths (*LCI*: 2, 4, 5). Lucie, an aspiring physician in her residency, helps him mature by offering Pierre a more sophisticated, intellectual vision of the world. As Pierre – ever so slowly to keep the drama alive – matures, however, he breaks this mould and offers viewers an image of the new, complete Québécois man. Growing comfortable in his masculinity, he eventually settles down and marries a franco-Québécoise career woman. The central plotline of the telefilm *Le Retour du chat* (The Cat's Comeback, referring to Lambert's nickname) involves Pierre's successful struggle to accept his wife's public activities while he has been sidelined by an injury and early retirement. Much later, in the series revival, Pierre, now widowed, has successfully raised three children on his own – thus reversing the absent father trope – and starts a second family with a new wife, embracing the lifestyle of an equal-partnership couple. His second wife, Michelle Béliveau (Maxim Roy, *LCNG*; Julie McClemens, *LCRec-LCDec*), is also a career woman, working in the hockey world as the first woman to serve as assistant coach on an NHL team. Yet, in order to achieve stardom, Pierre Lambert also must wield the tools of what R.W. Connell terms "hegemonic masculinity."[67]

Defined as "the culturally idealized form of masculine character" which links masculinity with "the subordination of women, the marginalization of gay men, and … toughness and competitiveness,"[68] the term vividly suggests a sense of encroaching aggression that seeks power and control over others, a gender model in keeping with critical assessments of the sport of hockey. In spite of – or perhaps to compensate for? – all of his "positive" qualities described above, Pierre is an imperfect (that is, human) being who is nonetheless capable of expressing the full range of emotion and empathy. He thus resorts to the strategies of hegemonic masculinity to succeed in the hockey world; paradoxically, self-assertion through violence is both punished and rewarded, and in this respect the series reflects the reality of the hockey world itself. At times, the storylines suggest that the system causes such behaviour; for example, the immense pressure upon the young rookie, including repeated browbeatings by Mercier and demands for attention from his girlfriend, coupled with his fear of being cut at the National's training camp, lead Pierre to apply an excessively forceful body check to the already injured Denis Mercure during a practice session. While his cut-throat actions appear rewarded, since he stays in Quebec with the majors, for his best friend they result in two months' recovery time and, instead of a slot with the National, a berth with the Chicoutimi Saints (*LCI:* 1). Grappling with the moral ambiguities of his actions, Pierre seeks out the team captain, Bob Martin. The latter offers a management style that includes first listening to the problem, then attempting to console, and, finally, after communication has occurred, offering sound advice (*LCI:* 3). Although he is not openly misogynistic like Marc, Pierre's heterosexual desire, including the objectification of the female body, appears clearly through his sexual affairs and his enjoyment in watching a stripper sent by teammates to his hospital room (*LCI:* 7). Most of all, his need to demonstrate not only the skills of a skater and scorer but also an ability to fight (he refuses the aid of team enforcer Mac Templeton, insisting on taking down the Bruins' fictional "goon" himself; *LCI:* 3) constructs Lambert's hegemonic masculinity.

The most obvious example of the seemingly contradictory roles that contemporary society expects men to take on in the public versus the domestic realms appears in the case of Jacques Mercier. Referred to as "the castrating NHL coach,"[69] Mercier at least remains consistent in his motivational techniques for the National, nearly each episode involving a harangue inevitably peppered with such "Franglais" expressions as "gang de losers" and "sans *guts*" (*LCI:* 6). Even his catchphrase, an instance of positive motivation, "Let's go, les boys!" infantilizes his players, establishing his own superiority. The players describe him as being on a "power trip," using the English expression (*LCI:* 2). Camera work and editing play up his characterization as a sadistic coach who revels in the punishment of his players, with close-ups, for example, as he leers while Pierre performs a set of push-ups allotted because he arrived a few minutes late to practice (*LCI:* 2). On the ice and in the locker room, Mercier's behaviour bears all the hallmarks of hegemonic masculinity gone awry, and yet privately he is portrayed as a loving husband and caring father, preparing breakfast for his career-oriented wife and patiently nurturing his paralyzed son during painful physical therapy (*LCI:* 2). Mercier faces the greatest challenge to his love for his son when Jimmy (Robert Brouillette) comes out as gay in the telefilm *Le Moment de vérité* and he rises to the occasion, reflecting the province's developing ideology of inclusivity.

In contrast with Pierre Lambert and Jacques Mercier, male characters who do not conform to the dominant image of hegemonic masculinity in the public realm, such as reporter Lucien Bouchard (Denis Bouchard) and Pierre's nerdy younger brother Hugo Lambert (Jean-Sébastien Lord), frequently appear as comic foils. For example, within the first fifteen minutes of the series, Hugo cooks for the family, a device that becomes a running gag in subsequent episodes. The series thus reinforces a heteronormative ideology that identifies masculinity with both physical and social power through the depiction of its heroes as successful hockey stars who command others' respect, relegating those who fail to meet that standard to the margins of both the series and the society it proposes to reflect. Significantly, in a recent commentary on the omnipresence of hockey-themed programming on Québécois television screens, Pierre Barrette observes an overall trend toward eliding the sport's violence and commercialism, portraying both real-life and fictional hockey players as family men and benevolent volunteers (an aspect of professional hockey life addressed by Fannie Valois-Nadeau in this volume) and so contributing to "the great family portrait constructed around the national sport."[70]

### *Embracing Changing Roles for Women?*

Similarly, just as the series serves as a vehicle for conflicting images of masculinity, it also reveals an ambivalence toward changing roles for women in Quebec society – not least because the central role of the vamp figure in *La Reconquête*, Valérie Nantel, suggests perhaps an even more negative attitude toward feminine power after the new millennium than in the 1980s series. In her *Brève Histoire des femmes au Québec*, Denyse Baillargeon titles the chapter on the period leading up to and including the production of *Lance et compte*'s debut as "La Révolution féministe (1966–89)." As Baillargeon recounts,[71] for the most part, Quebec's second-wave feminists saw sovereigntist nationalism as a force for the province's modernization, including updating the role of women. Changing roles in the real world also meant creating a sort of feedback loop in which women needed to see themselves assuming roles other than those of daughter, wife, mother, or nun in Québécois cultural production. The visual media played an active role in this process of offering "a vision of women that shatters traditional cinematic stereotypes,"[72] including the documentary series *En tant que femmes* produced by the National Film Board and fiction films by women directors such as Léa Pool.[73] Also, Bill Marshall asserts that "it is a commonplace to ascribe to television a crucial role in the creation of a 'modern' *Québécois* national identity,"[74] and the creators of *Lance et compte* consciously participated in that project in terms of their depictions of Québécois women, while at the same time often failing to escape the traps of the television genres from which they borrowed.

Prior to season one, director Jean-Claude Lord asserted that, whereas the original script depicted Pierre Lambert's mother as yet another "maman Plouffe" (after a well-known pre-Quiet Revolution French Canadian fictional family), he lobbied for "the role of a forty-year-old woman, much more dynamic."[75] That trend continued for season two (premiered 7 January 1988 to 2,621,000 viewers),[76] as the series' new director, Richard Martin, requested more strong women characters, "strong-minded, intelligent women, independent professionals."[77] The Lambert women lead the vanguard in this area across both iterations of the show. The matriarch Maroussia's French-Russian heritage allows producers to celebrate Canada's official multiculturalism (adopted back in 1971), invoking the Canada-is-a-land-of-immigrants image. While the daughter of the family, Suzie, lacks any real domestic skill – she, too, will prove to be a businesswoman later in life – she nonetheless offers the perfect image of wholesome femininity for the 1980s. Her beauty, however, often appears objectified for a male gaze, occasionally even as a *mise en abyme* of sorts, for example, when Marc Gagnon gazes directly upon her lingerie-clad body. Editing and framing techniques further reify and fragment her body, as when first we see Suzie's naked legs, then her torso in a high-cut leotard, her breasts, and only then her face, effectively delaying any sense of her as an individual subject rather than an object of sexualized beauty, as the camera reveals her posed in a headstand (*LCI:* 3).

As a mature, forty-year-old woman in the series revival, Suzie comes into her own, forced to untangle her late mother's disorderly estate (it should be noted that Maroussia's business failures undermine the viewers' perception of her status as a *femme de tête*). The series stresses the adult Suzie's equality and independence, as when, for example, she confronts a patronizing "businessman" (he belongs to the Russian mafia), insisting that he call her Mme Lambert – note also the province's legal and social convention that married women retain their maiden names – and not "ma petite Suzie" (*LCRec:* 2). In addition to her intelligence, Suzie is a model of inner strength, since the next season's title, *Le Grand Duel*, refers not only to the rivalry between the National and the Montreal Canadiens in the race for the Stanley Cup but also to her personal battle with breast cancer. The largely naturalistic portrayal of Suzie's reaction to the bodily changes forced on her by chemotherapy (loss of hair and weight) and a partial mastectomy reveals the ambivalence faced by women of her generation who have internalized feminist discourses about independence and strength but who also carry the burden of traditional discourses about feminine beauty. The latter appears mitigated in Suzie's insistence that she wants to be beautiful not only for Marc but also for herself; the series thus sidesteps her appearance only as an object of desire for the male gaze, treating her as a self-respecting subject in her own right.[78]

One of the most apparently progressive moves made in the post-millennium series revival, *Lance et compte: La Nouvelle Génération*, was the casting of Maxim Roy – well known for her role in Quebec's other hockey-themed media franchise, *Les Boys*[79] – as a female assistant coach hired by the National. In her master's thesis, "La Représentation du genre masculin et du genre féminin dans le téléroman québécois: Le Cas de *Lance et compte*," Sophie Émond analyzes the series' portrayal of Coach Jacques Mercier in season one and Michelle Béliveau's characterization in *La Nouvelle Génération*. Not surprisingly, Émond's results reveal that, even when portrayed in very similar professional positions, the female character is clearly presented in personal and relational situations to a much higher degree than the male character.[80] The same can be said about Maroussia and Suzie Lambert, whose professional lives remain in the background of the series' various narrative arcs. Indeed, after a heart-break in season one, Maroussia consoles her daughter by explaining that they share the gift (and curse) of feeling things more deeply than average people, thus implying that, while male heroes excel in the public arena of the ice, exceptional females are defined by the private emotion of love. In the end, then, the series' so-called *femmes de tête* are after all governed by their hearts.

Perhaps because of the series' intent for viewers to identify with and emulate modern, independent career women like Maroussia and

Suzie, the series offers up – both during the 1980s and the 2000s – a sequence of problematic images of housewives, beginning with Pierre Lambert's high-school sweetheart, Ginette Létourneau (Marie-Chantal Labelle). Audiences first meet Ginette merely as an appendage to Pierre; accompanying him to Quebec City for the National's training camp, she not only is humiliatingly denied entrance to the masculine realm of the Colisée but then stays in their hotel room and waits for him all day. When he returns "home," her demands for attention do not correspond with his needs for relief from the professional pressures he feels as a young player struggling to make the team (*LCI:* 1). Like a traditional housewife, she at first keeps the tiny room neat and tidy, even mentioning that she has "fait du ménage" ("cleaned up"; *LCI:* 1), but, as she grows increasingly bored and lonely, Pierre returns to find the bed strewn with magazines and food wrappers. Only later do we see that Ginette is gainfully employed in Shawinigan, but even there her boss's patronizing reminder that "work comes before affairs of the heart, Ginette"[81] subverts our sense of her work ethic. The series ambivalently undermines the social and economic gains accomplished by Quebec's women across the 1970s by calling into question its female characters' suitability for the economic sphere. At the same time, it devalues the contribution of the stay-at-home wife and mother, revealing her to be an unproductive lay-about. Similarly, another hanger-on, weight-around-the-neck hockey wife, Nicole Gagnon (Lise Thouin), is portrayed as shrew-like and increasingly an alcoholic, a characterization that seems to justify her husband's infidelities.

Of perhaps greater concern is the persistence of the negative stereotype of the housewife in the early twenty-first century. In *La Reconquête*, Annie (Véronique Bannon) becomes increasingly worried about the frequent absences of her fiancé, Danny Bouchard (Patrick Hivon), the National's new rising star. (Annie's last name, "Girard," is barely mentioned and this denies us a sense of her full identity.) Again, rather than sympathetically presenting what turn out to be well-justified concerns about his neglect of financial responsibilities, the stories' writers stereotypically characterize the pregnant woman as clingy and overly emotional. Other instances of hockey wives' pathological behaviour include a shopping addiction and a case of kleptomania. Futhermore, in this post-millennium, supposedly post-feminist era, the series invokes a female antagonist that was already a stock character a century ago: the vamp, Valérie Nantel (Julie Du Page), into whose clutches Bouchard falls.

Valérie appears in *La Reconquête*'s first episode exchanging lustful eye contact with Danny, accompanied by his very pregnant fiancée. While her luxurious ash-blonde hair, striking blue eyes, and glaringly white teeth suggest ideals of feminine beauty, her extremely sculpted body suggests an excess of fitness that verges on the masculine, as does her aggressiveness on the volleyball court (*LCRec:* 1). Valérie is a math professor who plays high-stakes poker for fun, and her professional and leisure activities further place her in male domains, as does her active, sexualized gaze. She not only openly initiates affairs with Danny but also toys with his teammate Mathias Ladouceur (Karim Toupin-Chaieb). She revels in defeating and humiliating her wealthy male opponents at the poker table in the VIP room of the Montreal Casino and cites Nietzsche, professing to live above the normal standards of morality. That philosophy spurs her to challenge Danny to a fatal game of Russian roulette (*LCRec:* 7), proving that she is literally a *femme fatale.* Furthermore, she is explicitly linked with demonic forces – harking back to traditional French Canadian tales – by the series' male protagonists. Indeed, when Danny describes having sex with Valérie to Mathieu, he says it's like descending into hell and going up to heaven all at once; to seal the vamp's damnation by an audience that still maintains some aspects of its Catholic tradition, a team trainer refers to her as "un vrai démon" (*LCRec:* 6). Bouchard's failure to man up and his obsession with this predatory woman who usurps agency and other prerogatives associated with the masculine reflects the visual media's tradition of the vamp, one often present in sport films.[82]

Thus, the popular television series reproduces a political discourse endemic to the province which links men's failures to women's self-advocacy. Furthermore, although most overtly misogynist in the wake of the 1980 referendum's failure, this discourse continues into the new millennium under the guise of masculinity studies, according to Vacante. As recently as 2005, Mathieu-Robert Sauvé's *Échecs et mâles* rehashes the thesis of a crisis in Québécois masculinity linked to a lack of strong male role models.[83] Vacante concludes that "the Quebec literature on masculinity, then, links the supposed crisis of masculinity to the political failures of certain nationalists and to the perceived gains women have made over the last three decades."[84] Whereas *Lance et compte* does offer many strong, even hegemonic masculine role models for two generations of Québécois men, it, too, blames its male characters' failures – as seen most clearly in the case of Danny Bouchard – on women who have gained access to spheres formerly the privileged domain of men, such as the casino table and the cerebral discipline of theoretical mathematics.[85]

In contrast with the semi-angelic Suzie Lambert and the demonic Valérie Nantel, *Lance et compte* does depict an array of women caught in the middle, struggling to remain feminine while their careers force them into spheres formerly reserved for men. Journalist Linda Hébert (Sylvie Bourque) most clearly represents social ambivalence about the career woman in the 1980s, an ambivalence that seems hardly to have disappeared in the 2000s with her carbon copy, Nathalie Renault (Catherine Florent). Proudly introducing herself as Canada's only female hockey reporter, Linda faces the challenges of women breaking into the particularly male-dominated profession of sports journalism. Only in 1978 did a federal judge grant *Sports Illustrated* reporter Melissa Ludtke equal access to Major League Baseball locker rooms, a decision that affected all of professional sports.[86] The Lisa Olson affair, in which a female reporter was sexually harassed in the New England Patriots locker room,[87] occurred in 1990 at about the same time that the *Lance et compte* telefilms aired.

As a woman who has trespassed in the male domain of the locker room, Linda's femininity is called into question; for example, in season two, media playboy Erick Murdock (Bob Harding) – apparently a fictional avatar of Rupert Murdoch – insinuates, "If you were a real woman …"[88] Earlier, Pierre Lambert confessed that some players think her "cold" (*LCI:* 4), implying frigidity, and a spiteful Marc Gagnon called her a "lesbienne" both behind her back (*LCI:* 4) and to her face (*LCI:* 5). After three seasons of the show, in direct response to actress Sylvie Bourque's insistence that her character be more complex or she would not accept the role, Héroux, writer Réjean Tremblay, and his new co-writer, Jean Jacob, sought to offer a more nuanced portrait of Linda in the telefilm *Envers et contre tous*.[89] Once again, however, her sexuality is portrayed as non-normative, as she falls in love with Steve Richard (Pierre Gendron), a player fifteen years her junior, making herself and her lover objects of ridicule. The film's conclusion, in which a blissful, post-coital Linda drives off to meet her lover rather than leave him for a business trip, exorcizes the image of a strong but castrating woman it has created for her precisely by restoring her to a state of "true" submission to a dominant male and placing domestic happiness over a career in the public sphere. The telefilm's treatment of this reverse May-September romance provides insight into the relatively unchanging attitudes toward women's desire and agency as Linda's character appears in an increasingly positive, though also more traditionally feminine, light.

## CONCLUSION

Such constructions of gender in popular culture feed into constructions of national identity, particularly in Quebec, where, as Vacante's account reveals, arguments about masculinity have long been linked to nationalist discourses.[90] Tim Edensor makes that very point, claiming that, not only is "the national … constituted and reproduced, contested and reaffirmed in everyday life," but today more than ever, national identity is "shaped through shared points of commonality in popular culture."[91] Like the sport of ice hockey itself, the hockey-themed television series *Lance et compte* incontestably represents a shared cultural icon, offering franco-Quebecers a reflection – albeit one distorted by the conventions of the dramatic television serial – of everyday life in the imagined community of Quebec. In this chapter, I have specifically considered how that series reflects two interrelated and core aspects of a national society: language politics and gender roles.

In terms of its linguistic choices, including its comfortable relationship with English and its more distanced relationship to metropolitan French, *Lance et compte* reflects the reality of French speakers on the North American continent, offering an image of Québécois national identity that embraces a certain *américanité*. The image of *québécité* that it projects speaks the language of Molière proudly, but on its own terms, not those of the Académie française. Furthermore, the series' characters have no reservations about taking their rightful place alongside and in communion with English speakers. Indeed, rather than an exclusionary separatist nationalism, the series espouses an inclusionary view of Quebec as part of Canada, not only in extraordinary events like the World Cup of Hockey but also in everyday life as players and their families – from both solitudes – work and socialize together. Above all, its discourse of winners seeks to counter a certain received image of the "French Canadian loser."

With respect to the show's depiction of gender roles, not only do men and women sometimes appear to "speak different languages," as revealed by dialogue choices, but, as in anglophone North America, Quebec – in spite of real gains by women's movements – continues to grapple with a heritage of patriarchal images of male supremacy, the over-valuation of hegemonic masculinity, and the continued objectification of women's bodies and the demonization of women who claim the status of full subjectivity. *Lance et compte*'s chosen décor is the hypermasculine domain of an NHL franchise. While it offers viewers in the province a fantasy of dominance, it does so, unfortunately, at the expense of a more harmonious and progressive image of gender roles and relationships.

8

# TWO HUNDRED YEARS FOR FIGHTING: "A HISTORY OF RESISTANCE" IN TWO BILINGUAL HOCKEY PLAYS

*Frazer Andrews*

Love it or hate it, hockey is woven into the fabric of Canadian society. It is one of Canada's strongest national emblems – transcending language and occurring in every part of the country. The game captures the hearts and minds of many Canadians and is, in turn, reflected in many forms of Canadian art. In 2008 the Art Gallery of Nova Scotia commissioned *Arena: The Art of Hockey*, an exhibition showcasing a plethora of visual artistic representations of hockey that toured other Canadian galleries as well.[1] Alison Pryer posits hockey as "a form of dance that embodies the spirit and passions of Canadians."[2] Music is brought to mind by author and anthologist David Gowdey when he views the game. "Hockey," he muses, "is as intricate as jazz or a classical fugue,"[3] and the game has often been the subject of Canadian popular music.[4] Roch Carrier credits an unnamed friend with the notion that the best of Canadian literature "was written on the ice, by the hockey players, in the sophisticated calligraphy of their skates."[5] There have been volumes of academic and popular books published on the subject of hockey, including countless examples of non-fiction chronicling and celebrating the rich history of the sport as well as many works of hockey fiction by authors among the first rank of Canadian literature, from Mordecai Richler's hockey-infused *Barney's Version* to

Wayne Johnston's *The Divine Ryans*, from Paul Quarrington's *King Leary* and *Logan in Overtime* and Diane Schoemperlen's "Hockey Night in Canada" to Mark Anthony Jarman's *Salvage King, Ya!* and Cara Hedley's *Twenty Miles*.[6]

In keeping with the manner in which these other art forms comment on, critique, and celebrate hockey as a Canadian cultural phenomenon, there have also been important plays in Canadian theatre devoted to the subject of the sport. The bilingual hockey plays discussed in this chapter[7] – Françoise Loranger and Claude Levac's *Le Chemin du Roy* and Rick Salutin's *Les Canadiens* (the latter with an assist from hockey legend Ken Dryden) – are among the oldest examples of hockey used in performance as cultural representation. *Le Chemin du Roy* was produced in 1968 by la Compagnie de L'Égrégore, and the most recognizable title, *Les Canadiens*, which premiered at Centaur Theatre in 1977, has been produced nationally and has been available in print since that same year. These dramatic works are two seminal examples of a unique, largely unresearched, subgenre that has developed in lockstep within Canadian theatre.[8]

In *The Death of Hockey*, Bruce Kidd and John Macfarlane extoll hockey as the "Canadian metaphor, the rink a symbol of this country's vast stretches of water and wilderness, its extremes of climate, the player a symbol of our struggle to civilize such a land."[9] According to Ken Dryden, "hockey helps us express what we feel about Canada, and ourselves. It is a giant point of contact in a place, in a time, where we need every one we have – East and West, French and English."[10] Conversely, Mary Louise Adams rejects this common use of hockey as a representative and laudable national symbol: "If hockey is life in Canada, then life in Canada remains decidedly masculine and white."[11] Michael Robidoux, meanwhile, incorporates these negative elements of hockey into his understanding of what the game represents: "Hockey does speak to issues of gender, race, ethnicity, and region in this nation, albeit not in an entirely positive manner. For this reason, hockey moves beyond symbol and becomes more of a metaphoric representation of Canadian identity."[12] The dramatic works discussed in this chapter perpetuate Robidoux's thesis, using hockey as a symbol of socio-political struggle among Canadians. At its essence, hockey is a struggle between two sides, the game itself carrying significant cultural weight in the province of Quebec. *Le Chemin du Roy* and *Les Canadiens* are hockey-based theatrical representations of cultural conflict, struggle, and war in *la belle province*, evidenced in both stagecraft elements and text. The two works have the same goal, explaining Quebec nationalism within Canada as a whole. Further, through the incorporation of hockey into the *mise en scène* and references in the script as dramaturgical elements, these plays collectively relate two hundred years of French struggle within Canada: starting on the Plains of Abraham, shifting to the Riel Rebellion, moving on to the conscription crises of the First and Second World Wars, then proceeding to the 1955 Richard Riot, Charles de Gaulle's 1967 visit, and, finally, the election of the Parti Québécois (PQ) in November 1976. By "captur[ing] the tradition, skill, and ambiance" of hockey, Salutin, Loranger, and Levac effectively attracted an unconventional theatre audience,[13] the relative universality of hockey being pivotal in accessing the potentially difficult topic of Quebec sovereignty. Decades after *Chemin du Roy* and *Les Canadiens* premiered, it is this accessibility or this "giant point of contact," to use Dryden and MacGregor's words[14] – which stems from the game's widespread appeal – that has given these pieces enduring historical and educational relevance.

## LANGUAGE AND AUDIENCE

As is evident from their respective dominant language, these bilingual plays use hockey to relate Quebec politics to ideologically opposed audiences. *Le Chemin du Roy* is a predominantly French-language, pro-separatist work and *Les Canadiens* is a largely English-language play concerned with explaining the prevailing sentiment in Quebec surrounding the election of the PQ in November 1976 to the rest of Canada.[15] Although both bilingual, these plays are near-perfect foils of each other in that they have opposite dominant languages and intended audiences: *Les Canadiens* is an English-language play that contains some characters who speak French, while *Le Chemin Du Roy* is a French-language play with some English-speaking characters. As Elaine F. Nardocchio pointed out in *Theatre and Politics in Modern Quebec*: "[Setting *Le Chemin du Roy*] in a hockey rink, a place that is so closely linked to Quebec culture, was not only a clever device (actually suggested by Montreal's Paul Buissonneau), but also an effective way of bringing home to the Québécois audience the concrete, cultural dimensions of the federalist-separatist political "game" that was taking place between

Ottawa and Quebec."[16] The play was written in Quebec, for a francophone Québécois audience. *Les Canadiens* was also written in Quebec but was commissioned by Montreal's English-language Centaur Theatre Company. According to Salutin, it "found its audience" in English Canada when remounted at Toronto Workshop Productions.[17] Francophone Montrealers did "appreciate the sympathy of the play toward Quebec nationalism, particularly since it was coming from an anglophone source ... [however, the play's point of view was] nothing new to them."[18] *Les Canadiens* then played to the rest of English Canada – with productions at Neptune Theatre in Halifax and the Arts Club in Vancouver, and a tour mounted by Theatre Passe Muraille of Toronto.[19] As Mary Jane Miller states in the conclusion to her *Canadian Drama* article "They Shoot! They Score?": "The play is not about or for separatists – or even for Quebec Anglophones."[20] For English Canadian audiences, Salutin's use of the Montreal Canadiens, on stage, was a clear and accessible metaphorical representation of Quebec.

## STAGING THE HOCKEY METAPHOR(S)

Though these works share the hockey metaphor, they utilize it in different ways. *Le Chemin du Roy* satirizes the political "game" at play between Ottawa and Quebec, while in *Les Canadiens* Salutin presents the team as a symbol of a conquered Québécois people. Both plays stage historical events through the use of historical and (mostly) political figures involved in a symbolic hockey game. Loranger and Levac feature a game "to play out the aftermath of ... General de Gaulle's memorable visit to Quebec in 1967,"[21] and in Salutin the Canadiens take on "all comers"[22] from the Plains of Abraham to the election of the PQ – that is, from the so-called Conquest to the political victory of the *indépendantiste* cause. In *Le Chemin du Roy*, the people of Quebec, led by the PQ, achieve a decisive 4–2 victory over Ottawa. With the prevailing metaphor in the play relating politics to a hockey game, "[PQ leader] René Lévesque's 'goal' is independence. His team successfully makes a mockery of Ottawa's policy and the blundering plays for unity by politicians such as John Diefenbaker, Lester Pearson, and [long-time Liberal MP] Jean Marchand."[23] Although Loranger and Levac use the hockey metaphor in a broad sense, applying it to a "political game," their work is much more historically specific than *Les Canadiens*, focusing on the entirety of de Gaulle's 1967 visit, including the events leading up to his reception in Quebec City and the reception itself; his visits to towns along le Chemin du Roy (the highway between Quebec and Montreal, from which the play's title is derived); his speeches in Montreal; and his departure and the political aftermath.

According to Ken Dryden, the Montreal Canadiens are "perhaps the most visible and accessible symbol of Quebec." He goes on to explain in the preface to *Les Canadiens* that "they are more than just a hockey team" and that "the team has an impact and imparts a depth of feeling to their public that extends well beyond the result of the last game or the last season."[24] This is the essence of the central metaphor of Act 1 in Salutin's play, which establishes "the myth of Les Canadiens [as] standard bearers of the Quebec spirit."[25] The origins of this metaphor were related to Salutin by former *Montreal Star* sports editor Red Fisher, who explained that "ever since the Plains of Abraham, the French people have been number two, but on the ice, they're number one."[26] According to Salutin, the Québécois see themselves as living under occupation: "Since Wolfe's victory [a] sense of being a conquered people, ruled by a foreign power, has remained in Quebec."[27] He considers the history of Quebec to be a continued "history of resistance," where French-speaking people have fought but never won.[28] Salutin then refers back to Fisher, who surmises: "If you fight but don't win – the battle against the real rulers – then you may try to win elsewhere, in a form where you are successful."[29] This is how the Montreal Canadiens (the most successful franchise in National Hockey League history) have become a symbol of pride in Quebec, "*porte-étendards* of the French presence in North America," which in turn explains why "it was so important that the Canadiens were a winning club, a club that could beat the Anglos, and especially the Toronto Maple Leafs."[30] In Salutin's play, once the Canadiens as symbol of the Quebec metaphor has been established, Act 2 serves to show how it has been overcome by the political rise of Quebec nationalism. As Miller explains, "the play ends with the implication that the 'torch' of Canadien nationalism ... has passed into the hands of the Parti Québécois."[31]

The torch Miller refers to is the supporting symbol of *Les Canadiens*, a hockey stick that is first used as a rifle passed on through the generations after the Plains of Abraham, and eventually to the Canadiens. Before passing the rifle to his son on the Plains of Abraham, the father character in Salutin's play quotes John McCrae's First World War poem, "In Flanders Fields": "To you from failing hands we throw the torch, be yours to hold it high." These words appear in English and French in the Montreal Canadiens' dressing room – formerly in the Montreal Forum and now in the Bell Centre. The use of McCrae's words ties the Canadiens legacy to the rifle/torch/hockey stick symbol of the script. This symbol implies that the "weapon" of Quebec nationalism and resistance has been passed between generations and has changed from rifle to hockey stick, eventually landing, symbolically, in the hands of the Parti Québécois. After the PQ was elected in 1976, Bills 63, 22, and 101 were enacted to "reinforce the status of the French language in Quebec."[32]

## HOCKEY IN THE *MISE EN SCÈNE*

Just as the iconic tricolour uniform of the Montreal Canadiens is easily recognizable to hockey fans, putting hockey sticks and pucks onstage is an immediate and unmistakable identifier to a Canadian theatre audience. The fourteen roles of *Le Chemin du Roy* are divided into three categories: seven players, four majorettes, and three referees. All of the players wear numbers on their backs (from 1 to 14) and these numbers are often used in lieu of character names in the script.[33] The players all wear basic white body suits under hockey equipment that consists of shin pads, pants, hockey gloves, elbow pads, shoulder pads, and helmets.[34] There are chest plates worn by players and referees showing either a maple leaf or a fleur-de-lys; this interchangeable bit of costume conveys whether the actor is portraying an anglophone Canadian or Québécois character. The referees, who at times wear either the maple leaf or fleur-de-lys, are costumed as a common hockey referee with a black-and-white vertical-striped shirt and black trousers.[35]

In contrast to *Le Chemin du Roy*, there is little or no costume description provided in *Les Canadiens*; the characters are described simply as "players."[36] In sartorial harmony with the name of the piece and the setting in the Montreal Forum, players are dressed in the red, blue, and white Montreal Canadiens uniform. This is confirmed as the play progresses and we are introduced to famous Canadiens players such as Georges Vézina, Howie Morenz, and Rocket Richard. There is no mention of skates or roller-skates being worn by the actors in Salutin's script; a

*Toronto Star* review mentions "actor-players on roller-skates miming shots" as the audience enters,[37] while the *Vancouver Sun* explains that the actors are "skating on rollers, rather than blades."[38] Miller verifies this feature of the Toronto production, noting that director "[George] Luscombe coaxed his actors onto skateboards and roller skates for much of the action, giving the performance the speed, grace, skill and hazards of the game."[39]

Both plays are set in imaginatively reconfigured Montreal Forums. The Forum of *Le Chemin* boasts some notable additions: between the stylized bleachers stages right and left is an enormous iron frame representing the feet and legs of General Charles de Gaulle, with the rest of his body extending up, unseen, into the flies of the theatre. The fact that de Gaulle is literally too big to be put on stage suggests mythologization of the general, a mythologization that runs counter to the trends in Québécois drama of the time.[40] Supported on the stage-right bleachers is a giant Stanley Cup. To create an authentic environment, a soundscape was recorded from the Forum, with organ, crowd noise, and echo. Vendors selling popcorn and soft drinks shout their wares, as the stage directions explain; the intention is that, before the show begins, the audience should forget they are in a theatre and be immersed in the well-known atmosphere of a hockey game.[41] Max Wyman similarly described the pre-show scene of the 1978 production of *Les Canadiens* at Vancouver's Arts Club: "It's ten minutes or so to faceoff. Kids in striped jackets are selling peanuts and popcorn. A gum-chewing cop is nonchalantly eyeing the crowd. Cheerful tunes are pouring nonstop from the organ."[42] In the text, Salutin simply describes the setting: "The theatre is the Montreal Forum. The stage is the ice. There are stands, a time-clock, a broadcast booth and an electronic message board."[43] Salutin cleverly uses the time-clock to denote the year in which the current scene is taking place. During the Plains of Abraham scene, for example, the time-clock reads 17:59, matching the year of that famous battle.

## A CHRONOLOGY OF RESISTANCE IN *LES CANADIENS*, ACT 2

At the beginning of *Les Canadiens*, the time-clock starts at 20:00 and counts down, stopping on the historic date. The stage directions read: "A fight breaks out. Suddenly, the situation is transformed."[44] Despite the realism of the pre-show setting, within minutes, the ice surface has become the Plains of Abraham, site of the battle between the English soldiers of General James Wolfe and the French of Montcalm. Among French Canadian nationalists, this battle is seen as "the root of over two centuries of national oppression," even if Montreal wouldn't surrender until 1760.[45] The scene sets up the French as a "conquered people, ruled by a foreign power,"[46] and puts the previously mentioned rifle/torch/stick symbol of resistance in motion. The stage directions read: "With his last breath, [the Father] throws the rifle to his Son. As his Son catches it, it turns into a hockey stick."[47] From there, the time-clock jumps over one hundred years to the time of Canadian Confederation. Here, we see John A. Macdonald discussing the construction of the transcontinental railway and expressing his reluctance to include Quebec in the Dominion of Canada even though, according to John Dickinson and Brian Young, "Quebec was [already] an integral part of [the] larger Canadian state" in 1867.[48] In this way, Salutin presents the high politics of the Victorian era through Macdonald and other historical figures "in a parallel structure which symbolizes the shaping of Quebecois consciousness … [in this same historical context], the game of hockey also develops."[49] For example, in the same scene that features Macdonald, the Farmer's Son takes a ball to play hockey and slices off two ends, effectively inventing the hockey puck[50] and alluding to the first documented use of the puck (during the first documented indoor game) at the Victoria Rink in Montreal in 1875.[51]

The scene then shifts to the North-West Rebellion of 1885, just before Louis Riel is set to go to trial for treason, having led Métis and First Nations peoples in open revolt against the government of Canada. Riel was a polarizing figure among English and French Canadians: to the English he was simply a "dangerous traitor" while the French felt he was expressing "the just grievances of the francophone Catholic Métis [although he was thought to be a] deranged person."[52] The Farmer's Son has improved his hockey skills considerably since inheriting his hockey stick in 1759; he "unleashes a vicious slapshot" at Prime Minister Macdonald.[53] This improvement in offensive skill represents the rebellion itself; as the English regiment chases the Farmer's Son offstage, they yell at him as though he were Louis Riel: "Murderer! Degenerate! Halfbreed! Avenge the Death of Thomas Scott! Fire and Bloodshed! And Canada First!"[54] Salutin portrays the North-West Rebellion as a hard slapshot aimed at the head of Sir John A. Macdonald, one that he was, however, able to avoid.

The plot of *Les Canadiens* then shifts to focus on the Canadiens hockey club, and Salutin dramatizes the formation and naming of the club in 1909:

O'BRIEN: I want a team here. A French team.

RINK OWNER: A French team? You don't know what you're letting the lid off. The French hate the English. They'd go wild ... It might work.

*O'BRIEN starts to exit.*

Hey, where you going?

O'BRIEN: Buy some Frenchmen for the Montreal ... Frenchmen?

RINK OWNER: Sounds English.

O'BRIEN: Trappers? Peasants? Missionaries? The Montreal Missionaries?

RINK OWNERS: Canadiens.

O'BRIEN: Canadians?

RINK OWNER: Like they say it. Ca-na-dyens.

O'BRIEN: The Ca-na-dyens.

RINK OWNER: *Les* Canadiens.[55]

The team's first owner, J. Ambrose O'Brien, was an anglophone whose family had struck it rich mining in Ontario. He already owned or partly owned teams in Renfrew, Cobalt, and Haileybury when he was approached by Jimmy Gardner, owner of the Montreal Wanderers, a rival anglophone team. Gardner saw the potential in starting an all-French team in Montreal and "thus were the Canadiens formed not by French-Canadians but by a sharp English speaking cookie who was looking to exploit the burgeoning francophone community of Montreal – then 54 per cent of the residents of the city."[56]

The Canadiens are then seen in a match against their cross-town rivals, the Wanderers, representing the "fissure"[57] between English and French Montreal. By 1910, the Canadiens have their first star player, goaltender Georges Vézina (portrayed by the same actor who plays the Farmer's Son, perhaps indicating a continuation of the francophone tradition), who carries the hockey stick/torch.[58] The time-clock then moves to 19:16, indicating the year when nearly one-sixth of professional hockey players enlisted in the First World War.[59] The attitudes of English

Canada are represented in this scene by an English fan who suggests that the Canadiens' Stanley Cup win was "'cause all the English boys went off to fight the war!"[60] Late in the war, riots erupted between the RCMP and anti-conscription protesters in Quebec City, and, to avoid conscription, hundreds of Québécois men went into hiding. In the course of the war, the Montreal Wanderers folded and some of their players were absorbed by the Canadiens.[61] This gave English Montrealers little choice but to take an interest in the Canadiens. The play then leads into the Second World War, where Salutin introduces Rocket Richard, who receives the stick-torch. With the time-clock reading 19:43, an English fan remarks, "I think of them as the Montreal Canadians,"[62] showing that support for "les Habitants" was no longer only francophone. Although Quebec society was now united in support of its hockey team, it was starkly divided once again by the prospect of conscription. In this wartime scene, the Mother at first does not rise for the playing of "God Save the King" at a hockey game; she then reluctantly does so but sings different lyrics: "À bas la conscription."[63] Again, conscription was not taken lightly; people within the province of Quebec "reacted with anger and riots to Bill 80, which empowered the government to introduce conscription."[64] In these scenes, Salutin has twice used crowds at hockey games in Montreal as a showplace for the sharp contrast in attitudes toward fighting for England and the slogans of resistance used by the Québécois.

As the time-clock ticks to 19:55, a scene involving Maurice Richard, a Toronto Maple Leafs player, and a referee attempts to exhibit linguistic and racial issues. The two English-speaking men try to explain to Richard when it is acceptable to fight during a hockey game, and when it is not. Richard draws the line at racial slurs, specifically "frog,"[65] while the anglophones try to convince him otherwise. With great irony, the supreme hockey player of the time is disciplined and educated in the ways of the game. Next, we are introduced to Clarence Campbell – the score board reads: "Soldier, Scholar, Businessman, President of the NHL."[66] Campbell and Richard discuss the Rocket's assault of a referee, dramatizing the real meeting between the two men that was held before Richard was suspended in 1955. The two struggle to find common ground and have difficulty communicating. Campbell says at one point, "Two different languages," to which Richard retorts, "Like a war."[67] Campbell sees their differences as linguistic, and Richard sees them as fundamentally racial. In 1955

Richard was suspended for the rest of the regular season and the playoffs for his on-ice actions against a referee. When Campbell attended the next Montreal Canadiens home game, he was pelted with vegetables, eggs, and a pickled pig's foot. He was verbally assaulted; the crowd in the Forum began to chant, "Shoo Campbell, Shoo Campbell, Va-t'en, Va-t'en."[68] In *Les Canadiens*, the bilingual Forum crowd similarly insults Campbell before a tear-gas bomb is thrown onto the ice:

CROWD: À bas, Campbell!
Vive Richard!
Did you sleep well last night, Campbell?
Cochon anglais!
*A tear gas canister explodes in the Forum.*
Lacrymogenes!
Tear gas![69]

The resulting incident, known in English Canada as the "Richard Riot," left Montreal in an uproar. In Salutin's play, as we hear the riot continue, the time-clock and scoreboard spell out the remainder of the decade, and "dates rush by at a dizzying pace"[70] leading up to the October Crisis of 1970:

19:62: Thousands Protest in Front of CNR Headquarters.
19:64: Bombs in the Streets of Westmount.
19:65: Protest Against the Queen Crushed by Police.
19:67: Huge Crowd Cheers "Vive Le Quebec Libre."
19:68: Beatings, Arrests in Anti-Trudeau Riot.
1969: Riot Act Read in St. Leonard.
1970: War Measures Act Proclaimed.[71]

Salutin's stage directions read: "It is as though the Richard-Campbell riot was only the opening shot of the Quiet Revolution."[72] The riot concludes Salutin's Act 1 and, when Act 2 begins, twenty years have passed. The major events leading up to the election of the Parti Québécois are not staged but merely highlighted on the scoreboard. As Benoît Melançon points out, the concluding act "would deal not with the violence of Nationalism, as one would have expected [given some of the lines in the play], but with its peaceful triumph."[73] The tear gas that explodes on stage, in the Forum of the play, builds and swirls between 1962 and 1970, and when this literal and figurative smoke of nationalist violence clears, after the intermission, it is 1976 and Act 2, the act in which the fateful election victory will occur.

## THE POLITICAL GAME OF *LE CHEMIN DU ROY*

Among the escalating events flashed on the scoreboard in *Les Canadiens* is "19:67: Huge Crowd Cheers 'Vive Le Quebec Libre.'"[74] This is the basis of *Le Chemin du Roy*, described as "a rollicking political satire that recreates the climate of excitement and collective euphoria inspired by General de Gaulle."[75] The piece "transposed the political events of the time and reset an emotional reality,"[76] as Jean Royer wrote in *L'Action*. This deep-rooted sentiment associated with the de Gaulle visit seemed lost on Montreal's English media, which was more focused on the form of *Le Chemin* than on its content. Zelda Heller of the *Gazette* wrote: "It's even harder to describe what went on. A political satire. Somewhat like a revue. A kind of historical document."[77] Joan Irwin of the *Montreal Star* described *Le Chemin du Roy* as "an entertainment rather than a play in any formal sense."[78] In other words, she found it more of a "show" than theatre and apparently did not know just what to call this non-traditional theatrical production.

In *Le Chemin du Roy*, there is significantly less focus on specific dates and times compared to *Les Canadiens*, but there are notable events that are presented within the drama. There is no time-clock in *Le Chemin du Roy*; instead, the game (or play) is divided by goals scored by each side. The first goal is scored after Prime Minister Lester Pearson places a French-speaking soldier in command of the English-speaking regiment that is to receive the French president (as per his insistence) at Quebec City in 1967[79] – as opposed to his being received in Ottawa as is customary for visiting foreign heads of state. Placing a francophone in command was an attempt to "do something nice" for de Gaulle since he had consented to be greeted by the governor general in Quebec. The politics are complicated. This first goal of the game is seen as a concession by Ottawa to appease Quebec and de Gaulle – that is, since Ottawa had agreed to receive the visitor in Quebec rather than in Canada's capital.[80] Yet, at the same time, as the character of Liberal MP Judy LaMarsh says in the play, "even if it [the reception] takes place in Quebec, Canada would be first to receive him."[81]

A moral victory, the second goal, is scored after some English tourists are insulted with a lusty rendition of *Alouette* and a fight breaks out.[82] The voice of the general stops the fight from on high, as he says, "Je vous vois, je vous entends, je vous aime" [I see you, I hear you, I love you]."[83] These words are derived from de Gaulle's speech at Quebec City on 23 July 1967, when he said, "Elle [France] vous voit. Elle vous entend. Elle vous aime,"[84] signifying France's sympathy for the cause of Quebec sovereignty. Just prior to the second goal, the concept of separatism is introduced, when one villager asks, in English, "What does Quebec want?" and another responds, "Quebec!" The irony and sarcasm is even more evident in production, as the stage directions and continued chant indicate:

> 2: What does Ottawa want?
> 4: (Accent anglais) Quebec![85]

The marked difference in the two pronunciations of the word Quebec represent the disparate visions of each side, while also playing out discordance on the stage.

The third goal is marked by a symbolic representation of the general visiting the Quebec Citadel. In this short scene, the referees bring out inflated crowns, decorated with the flags of different countries, and pass them to Quebec dignitaries. The dignitaries are uninterested in the crowns and continue to pass them off, until "La Marseillaise" begins to play. Then, an immense crown in the other tricolour – that of France – is brought out, at which point all the other crowns deflate. This scene symbolizes Québécois acceptance of de Gaulle as leader of the sole "mother country," France.[86]

Before Act 1 concludes, the fourth Quebec goal is scored, representing de Gaulle's immense public favour in Quebec. At the beginning of Scene 8, a group of men play hockey in the streets of Quebec City and discuss the events of the French president's visit.[87] Some of the men wish to go to see de Gaulle before he leaves for Montreal. By the end of the scene, all the players have become so obsessed with the prospect of seeing de Gaulle one last time that they leave the game to do so.[88] All of this leaves an American tourist onstage to ask, "Why are they so excited?"[89] – showing the cultural disconnect between anglophones and Québécois, while perhaps whispering at a closeness between anglophone Canadians and Americans.

The two Ottawa goals in *Le Chemin du Roy* are scored as a result of inaction by Quebec after de Gaulle's famous words uttered in Montreal: "Vive le Québec libre." The English make remarks like, "They're all talk" and they "throw stones and run away."[90] Shortly thereafter, de Gaulle's words are denounced in the House of Commons:

> 2: INIQUITY?
> 3: INSANITY?
> 5: INSPIDITY?
> 14: UNADVISABLE?
> 9: UNBEARABLE?
> 6: UNANSWERABLE?
> 4: UNACCEPTABLE!
> TOUS: UNACCEPTABLE![91]

This strong reaction marks the last point scored by Ottawa in the game,[92] but these words expressing outrage fall short, amounting to only two goals and, ultimately, a loss at the hands of Quebec in *Le Chemin du Roy*.

## THE SHIFTING SYMBOL OF *LES CANADIENS*, ACT 2

As Act 2 of *Les Canadiens* resumes, the date shifts to 15 November 1976, but instead of showing years, the scoreboard now indicates the time of day. Salutin's concluding act[93] is set on the day of the Quebec general election, which results in a Parti Québécois victory. In the play, as the final election results roll in, the Canadiens lose their metaphoric power as guardians of the people of Quebec. At the conclusion of the game on 15 November, the Canadiens hold up their sticks but they are no longer the weapons handed down from 1759.[94] Salutin posits that on that day the stick/torch was passed back to the people from the Canadiens. A woman tells one of the Canadiens players that the Québécois used to let surrogates like the Canadiens stand up for them, but after the election they will be able to do it for themselves.[95] Maurice Podbrey, then artistic director of Centaur Theatre, explained: "That night in a symbolic way les Canadiens ceased to be the emotional centre for the spirit of French Canadians."[96] As Miller astutely points out, the "francophones [of the play] are no longer content to live out fantasies of control over their own lives through Les Canadiens. Instead, the action has moved from the Forum to political action at the Paul Sauvé Arena" (where the PQ election celebration was held).[97] Melançon adds, "Instead of figurative success (hockey), Quebeckers have chosen literal success (politics)."[98] At the play's end, it is stated that hockey is "just a game [and the Canadiens are] just a hockey team."[99] Salutin's assertion that the symbolism of the Canadiens had changed in the relative time frame surrounding the election of the PQ is correct, as Jean Harvey confirms: "Between 1965 and 1990 the representative significance of the Canadiens would steadily diminish, partly as a result of changes in the structure of professional hockey, but even more because of political and social changes in Quebec."[100]

Yet in Canada hockey is more than a game, and in Quebec the Canadiens are not just a hockey team. Although diminished, the Canadiens' significance would not disappear altogether. And, as Emmanuel Lapierre shows in his chapter in this volume, language continues to be a hotly contested issue concerning the Canadiens in Quebec, where the expectation is that the team captain and the coach speak French.[101] In 2006 then Canadiens captain Saku Koivu "found himself in the crosshairs" of a battle in the media concerning his inability to speak French.[102] In the words of columnist and author Bruce Dowbiggin: "Never mind that Koivu had left significant pools of his blood on the ice in defence of the hockey honor of Montreal. Or that, gaunt and wan from chemotherapy, a bald Koivu had been feted by Canadiens' faithful with wave after wave of cheers on his return to the Bell Centre after starting treatment. Or that the Saku Koivu Foundation had raised enough money to buy a new PET/CT scanner for the Montreal General Hospital ... This is Quebec and the language kill shot is always in season in the political culture."[103]

In 2011 the Canadiens hired a unilingual anglophone, Randy Cunneyworth, as coach, prompting protests by fans outside the Bell Centre. As a result, General Manager Pierre Gauthier issued a public apology at a press conference, stating, "We're sorry if we offended anybody by hiring someone who is not bilingual."[104] According to Les Perreaux, writing in the *Globe and Mail*, the coach of the Montreal Canadiens is "quoted nearly as often as the Quebec Premier, and his decisions are scrutinized even more closely ... but when that man is the first in decades who can't speak a lick of French, the reaction is swift and merciless." The language issue exemplifies the fact that the Canadiens are not "simply a hockey team." They are, to quote a former editor of *La Presse*, Philippe Cantin, "an institution [with] responsibilities that go beyond being a hockey team."[105] With hockey possessing such rich significance for the people of Quebec, it is understandable why Salutin and Loranger and Levac have employed it as an effective symbol, metaphor, and rallying cry in their work. Within these plays, hockey is used creatively and adeptly to retell the rich history of Quebec resistance.

Today these works may be regarded as "museum pieces," unlikely to receive modern productions,[106] but to wipe the fog from the glass and look back onto their aged arena is a fascinating and worthwhile journey. Not unlike watching "Original Six" footage set in the Forum, these historic pieces of Canadian hockey drama are representative of styles and storylines from a bygone era. To continue the hockey comparison: watching these two plays is like watching tube-skated players with no helmets – it's just not done like that anymore. As is so often the case in Canadian theatre, to compare the styles of *Les Canadiens* and *Le Chemin du Roy* (written almost ten years apart) evinces the distinctiveness of Québécois drama and its anglophone cousin.[107] These are landmark works of drama, for French and English Canada, capturing the consuming cultural force that is hockey and giving it a socio-political message by putting it on the stage. By studying these bilingual hockey plays we come to appreciate the depth and complexity of the relationship we bear to our national winter sport and the commonalties that lie therein.

9

# RICHARD AND THE REST: QUEBEC IN HOCKEY FICTION

*Jason Blake*

Will Ferguson's *Beauty Tips from Moose Jaw: Travels in Search of Canada* takes the author into mysterious territory: Quebec. For Ferguson and for many other anglophones from *le reste du Canada*, that province may not be an exotic other, but it is nevertheless a little different. Ferguson uses hockey trivia to make some sense of one Quebec town. "What I know about Chicoutimi is this: it is the hometown of legendary goaltender Georges Vézina, who was renowned for keeping his cool under pressure. Vézina played for the Montreal Canadiens in their barnstorming glory days of the 1920s – which is to say, he *was* the team's defensive line. In one game, Vézina stopped seventy-eight out of seventy-nine shots, a record that still stands. They called him 'the Chicoutimi Cucumber.'"[1] This is superficial knowledge, to be sure, and yet such knowledge, acquired through old hockey cards and game programs and popular legends, helps map a large country. How many Canadians would know Saskatchewan's Floral, Manitoba's Flin Flon, Ontario's Parry Sound, Quebec's Thurso, or Nova Scotia's Cole Harbour were it not for Gordie Howe, the two Bobbys (Clarke and Orr), Guy Lafleur, or Sidney Crosby? Hockey helps Canadians navigate the country by letting us imaginatively connect disparate regions.

The national game is a connecting tissue also in literary works, and sometimes identifying a player's name is enough to provide a sense of place. "My Rousseau plays right wing," declares the zany narrator Demeter Proudfoot in Robert Kroetsch's 1969 *The Studhorse Man*. Narrating madly from a bathtub, Proudfoot dispenses with philosopher Jean-Jacques Rousseau in five short words. Not only does he prefer the Quebec-born hockey player Joseph Jean-Paul Robert "Bobby" Rousseau to the Genevan thinker, he takes possession of the hockey player by saying "*my* Rousseau." Allan Weiss's short story "Jean Beliveau Was Number Four," meanwhile, is even more explicit about cultural priorities in Canada. Preferring homegrown hockey heroes to the imported Great Men he learns about at school and from his bookish father, the child narrator says, "Beliveau, Worsley, Provost, Tremblay – these were names that meant something to me, not Caesar or Napoleon." The point is that foreign names of foreign leaders are meaningless to the New World child and that these luminaries of European history pale against the hometown excitement provided by the Montreal Canadiens. In Weiss's story, hockey culture and hockey names eclipse what the narrator would learn at school; moreover, hockey knowledge – that is, popular rather than "book knowledge" – helps make Canada's vast geography manageable.[2]

Taking into account both English-language and French-language hockey literature, this chapter examines where Quebec roosts in hockey fiction. Although hockey literature in English has been covered in studies by, among others, Michael Buma, Jamie Dopp, and Jason Blake, until very recently French-language hockey fiction remained tabula rasa in English-language scholarship. As Amy Ransom observes in her 2014 *Hockey, PQ: Canada's Game in Quebec's Popular Culture*, "in many English-language popular culture and literary texts, French-Canadians continue to appear just as marginalized and stereotyped as they did thirty-five years ago." The present chapter traces dominant patterns in bicultural nexuses in hockey fiction. In other words, it shows how francophone authors encode Canada in terms of Quebec and hockey, and how anglophone authors do the same in reverse. The chapter moves from considerations of hockey as an attractive but superficial map of Canada, from the fictionalized Maroons to the fictionalized Habs, and from franco-anglo solitudes to illusions of unity, before concluding with a brief musing on hockey's potential to inspire works of art. It argues that hockey is used by Canadian writers as a literary code that at times places Quebec in a broader Canadian consciousness.[3]

Hockey helps bind a vast and varied land because the New World child can identify more readily with hockey players. As with the just-cited Allan Weiss story and Kroetsch's "my Rousseau," hockey players are closer to us in imaginative time and space, and therefore more real, more tangible. The game also offers New Canadians a chance to integrate by playing hockey or at least joining the national conversation. This trope of integration is perhaps most baldly shown in Scott Young's Scrubs on Skates series, where Bill Spunska finds "acceptance faster than either of his parents" simply because he excels at hockey in his new country: "When he picked up the puck and started his big move, the people in a rink didn't care whether he came from Winnipeg or the moon."[4] Where someone was born, according to the mythology of acceptance and integration through sports, becomes irrelevant because games such as hockey unite.

Hockey fiction can also do a great deal to help unite a reading population. It can bridge the gap between popular or sporting culture and more traditionally artistic forms, including literature. Hockey stories and novels and poems can coax us into thinking about the Two Solitudes made famous by Hugh MacLennan's 1945 novel of the same title, they can invite us to acknowledge, for example, that Quebec might actually be a "distinct society," and they can invite us to explore the game imaginatively and critically. Hockey literature can be more intellectually fruitful than matching a nickname to a National Hockey League (NHL) player's birthplace, than learning some French (or English) words from the back of a bilingual O-Pee-Chee card.[5] However superficially or fleetingly, we non-Quebecers can identify with the Quebec "other."

However, in life and literature alike, some fans go too far in identifying with hockey and hockey heroes. A clear example is Clark Blaise's short story "I'm Dreaming of Rocket Richard." The story is unique in hockey literature because, though written in English, it is narrated from a francophone point of view, namely, through the eyes of a young Montreal boy. Though the boy wears "a Boston Bruins sweatshirt" whenever he goes to "to the Forum to watch the Canadiens play hockey," he adores Maurice Richard ("Despite the letters on the sweatshirt, I loved the Rocket. I loved the Canadiens fiercely"). Unlike the child narrator, the father is a caricature of a French Canadian, which indirectly accounts for the Bruins sweater – the boy dons the foreign sweater to distance himself from his father. Identifying intensely with Richard, though not yet in possession of any firm identity of his own, the (significantly) nameless narrator stops short of his father's idolatry: "My father's [Maurice Richard] tattoo was as long as my twelve-year-old hand, done in a waterfront parlour in Montreal the day he'd thought of enlisting. My mother had been horrified, more at the tattoo than the thought of his shipping out. The tattoo pictured a front-faced Rocket, staring at an imaginary goalie and slapping a rising shot through a cloud of ice chips." Where some might ink a lover's name into their flesh, the hyper-masculine and heterosexual father chooses the image of another male, perhaps as a protective amulet before heading off to the Second World War, perhaps as a sign of homosocial adulation (or perhaps because of drunken bad judgment). The narrator compares his father's tattoo to a "tribal marking" and worries that outsiders will think all francophone Québécois might have "one too," as though Richard were literally inked into Québécois flesh and not just into the cultural memory. As the narrator wryly comments during a visit to his cousins in the United States, "I would have preferred my father to walk shirtless down the middle of the street with a naked woman on his back."[6] Outside Canada, gaudy hockey tattoos suddenly look absurd. When not in hockeyville and not within accompanying tribal mentality, it is entirely unusual to ink portraits of men into your skin.

Hockey talk often claims that hockey is "natural" in the biological sense of being in our DNA. As Stephen Smith deadpans in *Puckstruck: Distracted, Delighted and Distressed by Canada's Hockey Obsession*, "hockey in the blood is a naturally occurring Canadian condition."[7] Even in jest, talk of genetics and bloodlines attempts to take hockey beyond history and culture to make it "natural," therefore beyond questioning. In this context, the Richard tattoo in "I'm Dreaming of Rocket Richard" is symbolically apt, because hockey is more like cattle branding or a "tribal marking" than a birthmark. Canadians are not born hockey stick in hand. The game is not biologically natural but cultural, since hockey is something we choose to play or watch.

And yet, though so many Canadian individuals have chosen hockey and hockey has become a collective national sporting choice, the game is not necessarily one of choice for all Canadians, everywhere. Since we cannot always avoid hockey-themed advertisements, or commentary, or vote-garnering politicians wearing the local team's colours, we often have hockey culture thrust upon us as the great Canadian narrative or a popular tale of the tribe. A real choice, in contrast, requires the availability of other options. In terms of unity, hockey is therefore often a forced unity, like a national anthem that is shared signifier but by no means an individual cultural choice.

Sometimes, as in Don Bell's non-fiction story "Hockey Night in Métabetchouan," hockey is the only cultural show in town. Though Bell praises the northern Quebec town's love of hockey, he immediately relativizes this praise: "There isn't a Museum of Fine Arts, there's no Chinatown, no bookstores."[8] In other words, in Métabetchouan, loving hockey is like loving the only other boy or girl in the village, or being forced into an arranged marriage. "Hockey Night in Métabetchouan" derives its charm from the local colour of the Saguenay-Lac-Saint-Jean region, in other words, in how it examines completely francophone surroundings made less strange by the hockey presence. Hockey is the vehicle through which the slightly exotic small-town Quebec environs are made familiar to the anglophone reading audience Bell is addressing. This common ground or hockey code, however, does not mean that hockey eradicates distinctions among viewers or players. On the contrary, hockey can highlight division.

Philosopher Tony Patoine zeroes in on this divisive aspect of the game. He points out that we often hear the facile equation "Hockey = identité canadienne," but asks, "Where does Québec fit in all this?"[9] In this volume, Fannie Valois-Nadeau comments similarly on a paradoxical facet of hockey in Canada: it was "at the very moment when its existence seemed challenged by the growing spectacularization and commodification of hockey in the 1990s" that hockey-as-nation was first examined by scholars. Still, as anyone familiar with hockey-happy Tim Hortons commercials can attest, commodification and national identity can go hand in hand – that is, one can sell doughnuts while simultaneously selling hockey and a simplified version of Canada.

But Canadians excel at layered identity, and although official multiculturalism has celebrated, sometimes fetishized,[10] multi-identities, the conservative hockey myth is essentialist in that it reduces all of Canada to sticks and pucks. In this equation, the abstract notion of "hockey" becomes flesh, and the national game becomes part of personal identity as well as national unity. That identification, however, is made possible precisely through the game's symbolic vagueness. Because hockey does not "mean" anything specific, there is room in the Canadian imagination for hockey to represent many concepts, to be a usefully nebulous metaphor for both life in Canada as a whole and life in Quebec.

## THE LITERARY HOCKEY CODE: *NOT* (YET) THE HABS

On the first page of *The Age of Longing* (1995), novelist Richard B. Wright craftily manipulates the reader by means of hockey trivia, leading those familiar with the hockey code down the wrong path. A former small-town athlete, one of the few anointed who has actually played in an NHL game, is spotted on the street. The children giddily whisper, "That's Buddy Wheeler. He played for Montreal and he won the Stanley Cup." The evocation of Montreal Stanley Cup glory is a ruse in this novel about broken hockey dreams, since Buddy Wheeler's team is *not* the Canadiens: "Of course, those children got it slightly wrong as most of us do when we hear stories. My father did play four games in the National Hockey League with Montreal. But it was the year *after* they won the Stanley Cup. And I am referring to a Montreal team that is now only a glimmering memory for a few old people. They were called the Maroons."[11] Like all legends, the Buddy Wheeler story has been bolstered by half-truths that are, in this case, strengthened by a community's desire to touch hockey greatness and dial into the national narrative. When tales are told and retold, they become anchored in a culture and eventually taken as gospel – that is, taken for granted and not critiqued. Playing four games "the year *after* [Montreal] won the Stanley Cup" is more than "slightly wrong." It is doubly wrong, since *not* winning the Cup means no ring, no glory. More importantly for this chapter, it is wrong because in popular memory and imagination the Maroons do not count as the *real* Montreal NHL team.

Edward F. Stack's vignette "A New Game" is another of the few literary works that refer to the Maroons, albeit solely as foils to the fabled Canadiens. "A New Game" takes place in the Montreal Forum, with the famed gallery ghosts lamenting its closing. "Howie Morenz, the greatest player of so many who had skated the ice of hockey's shrine," consoles the ghost of Saul, a wise man with a Jewish name, who had been a season-ticket holder over five decades. The story continues: "'Nothing is forever, Saul. You know that.' Saul slowly shook his misty visage as Howie [Morenz] went on, 'Remember how the Anglos hated the French when you were a kid? They sat on the opposite side of this building, cheering the Maroons against "les Canadiens"?' Nodding, Saul grinned, as did many of those gathered around, more and more of them as Howie spoke. 'When the Maroons folded, all Montreal became Habs fans, Anglos and French cheering "les Glorieux" together. We all said that could not be, but it happened.'"[12] As Stack's spectral spectators indicate, popular tradition sees the Maroons and other Montreal teams only as a side-act to the Canadiens, a muddled hockey prelude to "Les Glorieux" and its stable anglo-franco fan base. Ironically, in many written accounts, the myth of the "Flying Frenchmen" begins with the aforementioned Howard William Morenz, an anglo-Protestant from Mitchell, Ontario, who starred for the Canadiens (1923–34 and 1936–37). Stack's story, like most hockey fiction, parasitically weaves hockey traditions into its creative fabric. His Forum ghosts retell stories all hockey fans have heard, thereby supporting the communal story of hockey and making it a shared tale. It works according to a code, while also perpetuating that code through repetition.

Like Stack's story, Mordecai Richler's 1986 essay "Writers and Sports" contends that the Canadiens "didn't enter into legend until 1923–24, when Howie Morenz arrived." Richler's essay is in the same emphatic mode as Stack's ghost story. In fact, the two narratives work in tandem: in Stack, the Maroons fans and the Canadiens fans were "on opposite side[s]" of the Forum; in Richler, we read that Morenz's "fans, [who were] French-Canadian factory workers and railroaders, had once filled the Forum's cheap seats to the overflow." Is there a more convenient snapshot of Canadians working together, of unity, than francophones cheering heartily for an anglophone from Ontario? As Hugh MacLennan wrote in his novel *Two Solitudes*, French and English players exist in a promising line of Canada-defining hockey heroes: "Morenz, Joliat, Gagnon, Jackson, Smith – the whole lot of them are about the best artists this country ever turned out." MacLennan's list intermingles French- and English-sounding names to display biculturalism. And, as Richler and Stack show, hockey can be a balm to help quell linguistic hatreds – if only for the length of a game.[13]

### *The Most Frequent Hockey Reference*

It is a truth universally acknowledged that hockey in Quebec means the Canadiens, and *les Canadiens* means Maurice Richard. No comparable and sustained affinity between town and team, between province and player, exists in other hockey fiction, and perhaps only Babe Ruth's association with the Yankees comes close in North American sport. Remarkably for Canadian literature, Richard is a constant reference in English- *and* French-language writing; he is a rare Canada-wide reference point. However, whereas anglophone writers tend to respect Richard solely as a superb hockey player, French-speaking Québécois generally see him in broader social and political terms, as a "hero of the people."[14] Thus, the same player that is used in the service of a binding national story is also a dividing element.

Because Maurice Richard is so well known, hockey fiction does not spend much time introducing him. He is part of the sociolect. In "The Sportive Centre of Saint Vincent de Paul," for example, Hugh Hood refers to many NHLers by full name, last name, or nickname combined with last name (even "Gordie" is introduced as "Gordie Howe"). Last names are not needed for the Rocket: "In the Forum Tavern after the game, talking to Léon the waiter, we [i.e., the narrator and his friends] ask him to tell us who is the greatest player he ever saw, and he tells us the story of the time Maurice scored five." Instead of answering the question directly, Léon tells a story about the greatest player – as if the "who" should be self-evident – and notes that Richard the saviour "could score … on the Devil himself. If Maurice was dying and the goalie gave him the angle, he'd get up and score." The reference to the "Devil" and to the Lazarus-like rejuvenation of Richard has an intentionally religious air. Indeed, in a commentary on the story collection *Around the Mountain*, Hood states that this reference to Richard is among the "Christological allusions" that the "reader is supposed to notice."[15] Richard's skills are viewed as being supernatural and thus outside of history, like myth.

In the preface to his 1977 play *Les Canadiens*, Rick Salutin also speaks of Richard as something special: "I had thought Rocket would be one of the line of Canadien greats in the play … But it became clear that the Rocket was *sui generis*. He *was* the Canadiens, in some unique way." When Salutin was writing his play, Richard was long retired but not yet canonized. Some four decades after the play's premiere, and after the entrenchment of the Richard mythology, Salutin's claim appears naively simple because the Richard story has become fairly standardized over the years. That is why Emmanuel Lapierre is correct in arguing in his chapter that the dominant narrative in Quebec is of Richard as *l'idole d'un peuple*, as an embodiment of Québécois' aspirations for national affirmation. However, that particular embodiment of Richard does not mean that the Richard myth is stable. Like the commentators and play-by-play men who interpret the game for us, who tell us what we have just witnessed and interpret what it means, literature aids the mythologization process by handing stories down through generations or mediating the game to a larger audience.[16]

## *The Habs Are Special*

Jack Falla's 2008 novel *Saved* emphasizes the special relationship between Quebec and the Canadiens. "Playing hockey in Montreal was different from playing any sport anywhere else in North America," says the narrator, an NHL goalie.[17] This is a bold claim, given that the existence of any sport depends on unqualified adherence to standard rules, on continuity. Hockey literature and literary non-fiction constantly argue that the Canadiens are uniquely essential to Quebec's community lifeblood. Richler writes frequently of this lifeblood in his non-fiction hockey articles: "Once if the Canadiens won a Stanley Cup, something of a habit in the old days, the players who had turned the trick were either from Montreal or Thurso or Trois-Rivières or Chicoutimi, which is to say they were Quebeckers like the rest of us. They were *our* team." And, as he wrote in another article, most of the team's "star performers were Quebeckers born and bred." Richler conveniently ignores that already in the days of the "Original Six" many Habs stars were imports – exactly one-third of the famous "Punch Line" of Toe Blake, Elmer Lach, and Maurice Richard was "born and bred" in Quebec.[18] But to mention this too often or too loudly would muddy the waters. It would ruin the nostalgic mythology of the Canadiens as the homegrown "Flying Frenchmen."

About hockey nostalgia, Ken Dryden observes in *The Game* that "nothing is as good as it used to be," before adding a punchline: "and it never was." The "golden age of sports" is inevitably the pastoral age of one's childhood, of bygone eras when the players were purebred river-skaters, the salaries were laughably low, and at least the sporting world was honest and in order. Most sports fiction deals in such nostalgia, and Richler's novel *Barney's Version* occasionally uses this nostalgic background to produce refreshing humour as Barney Panofsky pines for Montreal's hockey past: "Those, those were the days … Fire-wagon hockey. Soft but accurate passes. Fast-as-lightning wrist shots. Defencemen who could hit … [Back then] *nos glorieux* were just about invincible [and] all they had to do was to leap over the boards in those red-and-white sweaters and the visiting team was a goner." François Gravel's adolescent novel *Le match des étoiles* also uses the trope of nostalgia, albeit without Richler's spicy quips about present-day "no-talent, chickenshit Canadiens … each one a multimillionaire." In Gravel's novel, Maurice Richard, Gordie Howe, and other hockey stars of the past face off against modern players who are portrayed as being dollar-hungry (the only way to convince the younger generation to play was to offer them a million dollars). *Le match des étoiles* includes a taxi driver who prefers to listen to tape recordings of old games, even though he already knows the outcome. His glib justification? "C'est plus intéressant" to hear play by play such as the following: "It's incredible, ladies and gentlemen, absolutely incredible, even with two players hanging onto his jersey, Maurice Richard continues ..." The understated critique that modern NHL hockey is less interesting is devastating because, despite faster players, harder slapshots, packaged glamour, and international flair, today's game is often thought to have lost its edge. Moreover, the fan's usual concern with results cedes to worrying about words, to an aesthetic consideration of commentators of yore establishing a code.[19]

## *Richard of the Habs, or the Habs of Richard?*

If the Montreal Canadiens are the "Lions in Winter," as writers Chrys Goyens and Allan Turowetz call them, Richard is the alpha male. Inventive versions of the man who constantly asserted he was "just a hockey player" monopolize francophone hockey fiction. Benoît Melançon's *Les yeux de Maurice Richard: Une histoire culturelle* studies how Richard differs from other hockey heroes of the past and how cultural products have aided his longevity. Almost three generations after Richard's final game in 1960, he remains a hockey icon. This is remarkable endurance – not least since many of today's "fans" never actually saw him play. Canada has mythologized the Rocket like no other hockey player, and few other Canadians. Richard has "a pan-Canadian following" and is a "veritable cult, in fact,"[20] states Melançon, and it is primarily thanks to Richard's exploits that the hallowed Canadiens sweater is known as "la Sainte-Flanelle." Aside from popular culture divas such as Céline Dion and Justin Bieber, and with the possible exception of prime ministers, no other Canadian crosses linguistic lines as easily as Maurice Richard does. "It is quite possible to live in Quebec today," writes Melançon, and have no inkling of the legendary strongman Louis Cyr (1863–1912). It is quite *probable* to live in such ignorance in the rest of Canada. Such ignorance is inconceivable when it comes to Richard, says Melançon: "Everybody knows him, or thinks they do." Although Melançon is writing about Quebec, the statement about how well known Richard is holds true for all of Canada. Richard is a touchstone available for all Canadians, a reference they can turn to in the way past generations turned to mythological or religious allusions.

Poets also tap into the hockey story. Al Purdy's 1976 "Homage to Ree-shard" is the finest English-language lyric depiction of the Rocket, with Purdy inventively and cleverly highlighting ambiguities within hockey culture, Canada and Quebec, even as he makes the game and the great Canadiens player immortal. Exceptionally in anglophone Canadian hockey fiction, "Homage to Ree-shard" admits to anglo-franco tensions, and these tensions are evident already in the title as Purdy spells Richard's name phonetically to reflect French syllabic stress. At the same time, the spelling hints at "re-sharding" or "re-fragmenting" of an icon, suggesting that Richard was somehow previously broken and that he requires a poet and reader to put him back together. For much of the poem, Purdy appears to be spinning an unsophisticated tale in which a single, representative Richard is a folk hero "bursting a straightjacket of six Anglos / riding his back a thousand miles / of ice to beat the Anglo goalie." In a neat reversal of how stereotypes usually surface, the anglophone poet reduces the English-speakers – his own people, so to speak – to types, to a bland "six Anglos." Moreover, the repetition of "Anglo" emphasizes the anglo-franco rift; the "thousand miles" leads Richard off the ice, well into anglophone Canada, and Purdy delivers a startling statement: "[Richard] waved his wand at Anglos Howe and Ezinicki / and made Quebec Canadian."[21] (Whether francophone Quebecers actually *wanted* to be "made … Canadian" is another matter.) Purdy's lines suggest a simplistic view of Canada as an essentially anglophone country, where Winnipeger Bill Ezinicki (representing a newer immigrant group, a family with eastern European roots) is somehow more Canadian than the *pure laine* Richard.

Yet, just when "Homage to Ree-shard" threatens to descend into an anglophilic vignette of national togetherness, one in which Quebec is assimilated into Canada, Purdy withdraws. "Rocket you'll never read this," he writes, with a touch of regret. Maurice Richard will never read it because the English-French language barrier remains formidable. Less famous than Purdy's "Hockey Players" – and its oft-quoted description of hockey being a "combination of ballet and murder" – "Homage to Ree-shard" is the more nuanced poem, and it uses hockey to examine part of Quebec. Purdy's words overcome the myopia that afflicts both sides of the anglophone-francophone hockey divide and depicts hockey as a binding sporting narrative, even if it is rife with violence, tension, repression, and linguistic disputes. Without sinking into political cant, Purdy uses Richard to teach us about Canada in political terms.

Not all of the textual or literary excitement around Richard occurred after he retired, and much ink was spilled while the celebrated hockey player was still active. In his 2011 *Maurice Richard*, Charles Foran imagines the Rocket during his playing days and uses the present progressive to place the reader in the past: there has been, Foran writes, "cultural activity lately swirling around [Richard's] image and career ... He is being discussed in books and magazines, in the lyrics of protest songs and on the stages of theatres. Motives are being attributed to his actions and words put into his mouth by people who had little to do with his actual professional life." The famously taciturn hockey player is more talked about than talking, and exists as a mediated and interpreted text of sorts more than as a social being.[22] Richard is fixed and dissected on the page, and strangers assume knowledge of the Rocket, ascribing "motives" to him, pinning him down, and verbally reinventing him. Similarly, Bernard Pozier's poem "Maurice Richard," which also attributes motives and desires to the man, has the Rocket longing for "The absolute joy of skating alone / Eyes in the heavens / Without rumour or goal / Free of all that hinders you."[23] The imaginative passages from Foran's biography and Pozier's poem are similar in that they show Richard as man-turned-text, the difference being that Pozier's literary Richard desires to break free of the constraints that come from being a mediated professional hockey player whose existence is cuffed and codified by others' perceptions.

Since his retirement, the Richard legend has been helped by time and popular media, by literature and money. Literally, in the case of the last, since the now-replaced Canadian $5 bill contained words from Roch Carrier's classic "The Hockey Sweater" and Sheila Fischman's translation: "Les hivers de mon enfance étaient des saisons longues, longues. Nous vivions en trois lieux: l'école, l'église et la patinoire; mais la vraie vie était sur la patinoire. [The winters of my childhood were long, long seasons. We lived in three places – the school, the church and the skating rink – but our real life was on the skating rink.]" The bill portrayed children playing shinny on a pond that could be anywhere in Canada, and the image neatly dispelled problems of geographical vastness. Moreover, because boys and girls are blithely playing together, hockey culture is temporarily devoid of sexism. True, there are also skaters and a lone tobogganer on the periphery, but if you folded the bill, the crease would bisect Maurice Richard's famous number 9 and Carrier's hockey words.[24] Money, which circulates among all Canadians in the way that mythology and a code about the Rocket does, is central to Canadian commerce. That hockey is in the forefront of the bill is a clear emblem of hockey's cultural centrality and of Richard's pivotal position in that narrative and system of allusions.

Carrier's "The Hockey Sweater," about a young Quebec boy who receives a Maple Leafs sweater as a result of a mail-order mix-up, is undoubtedly Canada's most famous short story. In other words, one can assume that almost every Canadian already knows the story. Originally titled "Une abominable feuille d'érable sur la glace" ("An abominable maple leaf on the ice"), Carrier's tale highlights linguistic tension and lack of knowledge about the "other." And yet it has managed to become a literary touchstone. As poet Bruce Meyer writes, "The Hockey Sweater" "has entered our national consciousness"[25] in the way that battles and signing of historical documents do. In a fine irony for a country dominated by English, a quintessentially French Canadian tale long rested in Canadian wallets. In addition, because the real Roch Carrier received a Maple Leafs sweater in a mail-order mix-up, the story sails very close to historical truth – our most famous *story* is only half-literary or half-fictional because there is a lurking truth-claim. The factual and the fictional coalesce, meaning that the boundaries between the real and the fictional blur.

Especially in hockey stories and novels, it is hard to chalk the divide between fiction and non-fiction, since most extensive literary accounts of Maurice Richard read like popular histories. In Jack Falla's novel *Saved*, the American narrator – like Falla himself – descends from one of the many Catholic French Canadians who left Canada between 1850 and 1940 in search of employment in the mills of New England. His grandmother adapts to life in the United States, but she preserves her love of the Canadiens and venerates the Rocket "as if he were the fleur-de-lis made flesh." Falla follows the overt allusion to Christ ("made flesh") with a page-long oral history, told in the voice of the narrator's grandmother: "Back then to be French-Canadian was to be consigned to an underclass of factory and mill workers forever under the thumb of English bosses. French-Canadians saw Richard, Montreal's biggest star, as a man who stood up to the English."[26] Saying that fact and fiction are antipodes does not work with the Richard story because, as Falla's novel shows, through repetition the Richard story has been uprooted from reality and replanted in mythical, quasi-religious territory.

Claude Dionne's 2012 novel *Sainte Flanelle, gagnez pour nous!* similarly mingles the historical and the religious, and the title alludes simultaneously to the Montreal Canadiens' uniform and the Ave Maria ("Sainte Marie, Mère de Dieu, / Priez pour nous"). In this novel, which spans three crucial decades in Quebec's history, Clément Belzile lives entirely for the Montreal Canadiens, for their history, even after he has grown up and become a schoolteacher. Born in 1947, Belzile recounts his life from his childhood in an orphanage to the time "Le Démon Blond" Guy Lafleur scored against a short-handed Boston team (a clear reference to the famed 1979 playoff game and the too-many-men-on-the-ice call, with Don Cherry behind the Bruins bench). The narrator is a Habs fan first and an educator second, meaning that his hockey addiction spills over into his professional life. His vocation or "spiritual calling" is to be a Habs fan; teaching just pays the bills.

Married to the team, Belzile skips school to attend a 1970s Stanley Cup parade, teaches in a Habs sweater to mark the twentieth-fifth anniversary of the Richard Riot, and generally finds himself in trouble for discussing hockey in the classroom. "It's not easy to combine sport with French class," notes the narrator. However, in spite of this novelistic claim, the overview of hockey literature written in French included within the same novel clearly shows that variations on the game are culturally and educationally significant – even if the staid school authorities are slow to realize it. Dionne begins his Cook's tour with Roch Carrier's story, but he also quotes extensively from poet and songwriter Félix Leclerc and novelist Pierre Gélinas, among others. Belzile entertains his students with lively tales of the Canadiens and saturates these tales with episodes of Quebec history, delighting and instructing in the venerable tradition of Horace's *Ars poetica*. Because hockey and hockey names are also pedagogically alluring, they encourage children to pick up books, suggesting that hockey culture is not just about escapism; it is also potentially edifying. More importantly, *Sainte Flanelle, gagnez pour nous!* shows how literary tales about hockey have become part of high culture; it is no longer radical to introduce sports fiction into the classroom. They have gained a cultural stamp of approval and therefore become part of the national narrative, and Maurice Richard, especially, has entered the Quebec and broader Canadian school canon.[27]

In *Sainte Flanelle*, unlike in Weiss's story "Jean Beliveau Was Number Four," hockey and formal education are not polar opposites. For the teacher, hockey literature in the classroom can attract students' attention and entice them into learning their province's history by being put to specific educational use. Like the Canadian hockey novels Michael Buma focuses on in *Refereeing Identity: The Cultural Work of Canadian Hockey Novels*, the texts Belzile chooses perform a cultural service. For example, in one passage Belzile explains to his class that Carrier's "The Hockey Sweater" is set during la Grande Noirceur, when the skating rink offered the sole distraction for the boys of Carrier's village – to which one bewildered pupil asks, "C'est quoi ça, la Grande Noirceur?" ("The Grande Noirceur? What's that?") Belzile replies with a rant about the formerly all-controlling Catholic Church, and concludes his outburst by pointing at the crucifix hanging from the classroom wall.[28] Whatever the teacher's views or biases, Dionne's novel shows a movement from ignorance to knowledge of a chapter in Quebec's history. This didacticism is mitigated by a profound irony: even as he rants against the church, Belzile has turned to idolizing hockey (which calls into question idolization because the object of reverence seems replaceable and therefore arbitrary) and especially Maurice Richard.

Maurice Richard was a lion on the ice, but mild on the pavement. These quiet ways made him easier to mythologize and glorify in literature precisely because he was not particularly outspoken or unambiguous in his political views, despite the undoubted pressure to articulate a sovereigntist position (and despite the columns he "wrote" criticizing NHL president Clarence Campbell).[29] Fans and writers could interpret him as they pleased. To quote again from Jack Falla's *Saved*, the narrator contemplates a picture of Richard as an art-lover might contemplate a Rembrandt or a Picasso: "Even in his seventies the Rocket's face was dominated by those piercing angry brown eyes. Angry at what? Opponents who routinely hacked and slashed him? Affronts to the French people? Both? I suppose fans could see whatever they were looking for."[30] Falla's series of questions shows how flexible textual interpretations of Richard have been. More directly than Falla's narrator does, Benoît Melançon examines how "the eyes of the Rocket have been a part of the popular imagination" and asks, "What does it mean?"[31] The proof that eyes cannot speak for themselves is this: writers in different periods read into those eyes entirely different qualities, seeing everything from muteness to pure determination. There is no such division with interpretations of Richard, since the Richard myth is malleable enough to let him be adopted by Quebec francophones (of whatever political stripe) and anglophones.

## WHAT'S MISSING FROM HOCKEY LITERATURE?

As Canadian literary critic Chelva Kanaganayakam noted in a 2009 lecture, "literary worlds … intersect with real worlds, and at some level they reflect or refract them."[32] Every play, poem, or novel exists in its own slow time, but it remains connected to the world and its social and political difficulties: "Literature might not have the solutions to our problems but it certainly alerts us to dimensions that we may have overlooked." Anglophone hockey literature does little "alerting" to Canada's real-world political problems, and for the most part this literature seems to exist in a social void. Playing into the myth that sports are a world apart, hockey literature generally foregoes political allegories of internecine struggle on the ice, or the political implications of the 1955 Richard Riot. If Richard's wish was to be "just a hockey player," English-language hockey fiction grants this wish, underscoring the idea of sport as a timeless realm beyond society and politics that is not governed by clock-time.

In a trio of narratives that touch upon the Riot or other Quebec hockey incidents – Pete McCormack's 1998 *Understanding Ken*, Mark Jarman's "Righteous Speedboat," and Michael McKinley's "Next Year" – there are significant silences, or topics that go unaddressed. McCormack's *Understanding Ken*, narrated by a young hockey player suffering under his parents' divorce and his over-bearing hockey father, delivers a facile account of the Richard Riot: "In 1955, Rocket Richard beat up a referee. When the Rocket got suspended for it, the people in Montreal were so mad they rioted like Arabs on TV … They named a riot after him! The Richard Riot. Like he did the best thing in the world. They didn't call it the Poor Sports Riot."[33] The boy's political naivety is evident in his blanket comparison of Montrealers to "Arabs on TV," which, in addition to sounding like handed-down parental prejudice, implies that Quebec is cryptically different from the rest of Canada and that "real" Canadians do not riot. The nameless narrator is a hockey-mad child who comfortably labels others and does not see past the famous name and historical event to consider political consequences. The passage thus transmits a half-truth by ignoring the political aspect of the historical event. The young narrator "sees" far less than the reader, which means that the novel rests on structural irony. We see more than the child does and, paradoxically, the political and social is made evident through its very absence.

Regardless of how blatant an absence might be, focusing on what is missing in individual works of literature is intellectually risky because it can mean ignoring what is actually *in* a story or novel. With that caveat in mind, we often are asked to look beyond what is written on the page, to reflect briefly on broader political and sociological implications in literature. In Mark Anthony Jarman's short story "Righteous Speedboat," a promising young player watches the 1991 NHL entry draft from a "loser bar." He watches Lindros being selected first overall by the Quebec Nordiques, and witnesses how the Toronto native "refuses their blue uniform, their lovely stone city."[34] Jarman's narrator is concerned primarily with money and his own hockey misfortune (the hockey establishment has blackballed him because he once punched a coach in the nose), and, though he mentions the young star's rejection of an entire "lovely stone city," he does not consider the symbolic repercussions of this. In Quebec, this rejection of a "lovely stone city" was read differently, namely as a rejection of an entire culture or "people." Lindros's decision not to play for the Nordiques was taken as anti-Quebec sentiment – and was trumped up in Quebec newspapers in the post-Meech Lake wash of resentment. Amy Ransom correctly notes that the Lindros affair was "a highly politicized (and profitable?) incident for Québec's media to jump on,"[35] making hockey and politics collide much as they did at the time of the Richard Riot.

Michael McKinley's "Next Year" is a third example of a hockey story with a naive narrator, a device that allows the writer to articulate opinions that would be deemed rude or coarse outside fiction. Thus, in McKinley's story, Dermot, "a prophylactically large thirteen year old" bully from Toronto, is vocal about his political views. Rather than ignoring politics, Dermot disgorges crude accounts about his Canada not including Quebec. McKinley uniquely satirizes anti-Quebec views, and Dermot's calumny is refreshing because he clearly states what his concept of Canada is and is not: "Montreal isn't really Canada because of all those Frenchies." Once again, Montreal is depicted as entirely different; the bicultural and bilingual city whose anglophone elite once ruled Canada is, laughably, excluded from the country. Through the bigoted voice of Dermot, McKinley reduces Canada to a cold place where anglophones can skate outside on natural ice. Though Canada has transcended such simplistic views of itself, still the hockey myth endures. More importantly, as Michael Buma notes about hockey writing in general, passages like McKinley's are rare in that they "def[y] the myth-making prescription of unity by depicting a national climate in which hockey expresses (rather than resolves) prevailing cultural and religious tensions." Rare as they are, such words are soil that can nourish future discussions about Canadian unity and Quebec's place within Canada. Dermot's fatuity demands engagement on the part of the reader precisely because the reader rejects the extreme viewpoint.[36]

## ILLUSIONS OF UNITY

Hockey fiction allows for more ambiguity than hockey scores and statistics do, and even page-turners such as Scott Young and George Robertson's novel *Face-Off* are at times skeptical about hockey-fuelled national unity. In *Face-Off*, up-and-coming NHL star Billy Duke lives at the centre of the Canadian hockey myth and thus has no interest in challenging the system that pays him to play. Yet, in spite of his interest in earning a living, Duke remains unconvinced about hockey's leading role in Canadian life: "I'd been brought up on the mystique of this one lousy, or great, or whatever, fact of Canadian life: Hockey Night in Canada. In the whole country right now it was the one common denominator between French and English, old and young, rich and poor, the hustler and the deacon's wife." Because this minor critique about unity through hockey is voiced by an NHL insider, it has added weight. Billy Duke is no anti-hockey firebrand, much less a commentator on Quebec or Canadian politics. As the passage above indicates, the slippery "mystique" of hockey is shapeless, by turns "lousy," "great," or "whatever." Shapeless as it is, *Hockey Night in Canada* is a slippery basis for national unity – even if, as Bruce Kidd writes, the weekly TV program did give "many people their strongest sense of pan-Canadian identity." Billy Duke may adopt an ironic stance toward his livelihood, but he does not unsettle the hockey myth or make us seriously question a key national symbol.[37]

As the title of this subsection hints, one grave danger of hockey as a national symbol is that it provides the *illusion* of unity while in fact promoting (or ignoring) cultural difference. And nowhere is this illusory aspect more evident than in the way that Quebec and the so-called Rest of Canada approach the game in cultural terms. In sports, the opposition or "other guy" is clearly marked and, especially when it comes to the Canadian national team, it is all too easy to embrace the idea that harmony on the ice translates to political and social harmony off the ice. For example, in his 1987 book *Country on Ice*, Doug Beardsley refers to a photo of anglophone Wayne Gretzky hugging francophone Mario Lemieux after the Montrealer scored a goal to defeat the Soviet Union in the 1987 Canada Cup. That photo, according to Beardsley, "did more for the English-French relations in this country than a rinkful of Canadian politicians." We can easily mock reading politics into a mere pass-and-shoot play, and point out that symbols are not of themselves a nation, and yet the symbolic pull should not be dismissed. As former commissioner of official languages Graham Fraser has commented, though Beardsley may seem hyperbolical or dewy-eyed in his description, "the sentiment may be true."[38]

A national symbol functions effectively only if it is flexible or vague enough to allow us to read into it what we desire. In contrast, Ian Orti's comic sketch "The Stanley Cup Conspiracy" is a fictional counterpoint to the theme of hockey as a national superglue. Unlike many literary hockey allusions, Orti concretely shows *how* hockey serves the political nation. In other words, because it is so specific, his story has a satirical bent. "The Stanley Cup Conspiracy" looks back to an event that many Toronto Maple Leafs fans might remember, when the Leafs and the Montreal Canadiens *almost* met in the finals. In fact, a specific hockey reference is required knowledge for the story to make much sense: "In the 1993 Stanley Cup semi-finals, when referee Kerry Fraser botched a call against Wayne Gretzky that cost Toronto a trip to the Stanley Cup Finals, fans in Toronto called it a league conspiracy to sell hockey to the south. They were only half right. It was indeed a conspiracy, but it was never about hockey." With the simplicity of motive that inspires any good conspiracy theory, Orti's fictional report intones: the overlooked penalty "was about federalism" because Fraser sent Gretzky and the Los Angeles Kings to the finals in order to sidestep national tragedy. Had Canada's Two Solitudes met in a Stanley Cup final, the 1995 referendum so narrowly won by the no-side would have had a different outcome. In Orti's version of the Stanley Cup tale, "the prospect of an entire country rallying behind a Quebec team against an American foe could allow federalists to show Quebec that there was an entire nation on their side." As noted, much hockey literature consists of retelling stories that fans already know. Such repetition is crucial for entrenching hockey history as myth, but reminding readers of, say, Paul Henderson's goal, risks becoming boringly nostalgic.

Orti takes the hockey narrative beyond nostalgia and imbues it with a clear meaning. His mock-serious tone, coupled with a political teleology, enlivens his adaptation of a real event. The Leafs' loss is given a purpose – redemption of a nation. Whereas David Adams Richards merely tells us in his non-fiction *Hockey Dreams* why "Hockey can save Canada" – "we see to the bottom of our heart there is no Gretzky without Lemieux" – Orti shows *how*. Of course, because Orti's tale is so obviously concocted to assuage the narrator's pain as a Leafs fan, and because the teleological explanation is delusion, the overriding tone is satirical. Hockey is, in the end, just a game, not a cure for whatever ails the country.[39] Orti's story comically highlights the illusory nature of using hockey as a simplistic emblem of Canada. "The Stanley Cup Conspiracy" is funny not least because so many similar tales are told entirely in earnest.

Sports are pithy markers of the individual or collective self, and in many ways hockey culture remains a repository of archaic patriarchal and sexist values. Like Belzile in Dionne's *Sainte Flanelle, gagnez pour nous!*, or the tattooed father in Blaise's "I'm Dreaming of Rocket Richard," we sometimes devote an astonishing amount of – perhaps too much – time, energy, and ink to the game. After all, a dollar spent on hockey means a dollar not spent on education, and bricks used for a hockey arena cannot be also be used for a concert hall. And yet, for all its superficiality, hockey is not an entirely unfortunate identity marker. Joining the hockey conversation by using a typically Canadian and/or Québécois code is easy, and hockey is therefore a more available conversational springboard among strangers than, say, pondering Margaret Atwood's survival theory or debating constitutional reform. The game is *relatively* inclusive – women and African Canadians have been playing for more than a century.[40] It is no longer surprising to see non-whites playing on *Hockey Night in Canada*. Most importantly, bickering about a hockey game is preferable to bickering about past historical borders or battles or making nation-state-style arguments about ethnicity-based nationalism, or speaking seriously about how neighbouring countries are genetically different.

Canada and hockey are changing, and many of the literary and the critical passages quoted in this chapter generally refer to a time when hockey meanings were more stable, simpler, more *codified*. During the "Original Six" era of the NHL, the Canadiens were the only Quebec team, and they always included a central core of francophone stars. Indeed, it was far easier then to reduce Canada to a land of Two Solitudes, the Toronto Maple Leafs versus the Montreal Canadiens. Kelly Hewson correctly notes that, before NHL expansion in 1967, the National Hockey League "effectively framed Canada with the Ontario and Quebec border. This is a geopolitical emblem of issues that continue to characterize Canada – those of centrism and western alienation."[41] Even when critiquing the game, much hockey fiction looks back to a romanticized, hockey-tinged childhood and reproduces a simplified view of the country as reflected in the dichotomy of Quebec and *le reste du Canada*.

Yet this simple dichotomy within Canada, and even within Quebec, has developed. The Canadiens sweater so crucial to Roch Carrier's story obviously still has monumental status in Quebec, but today, when most great francophone players are no longer playing in Quebec, much of this hockey identity discourse is dated, even when a francophone Quebecer wears the bleu, blanc, et rouge. Guillaume Corbeil's 2008 short story "L'île qu'on appelait L'Île" shows how the Montreal Canadiens' meanings have shifted; today, the Canadiens stand for something more global – perhaps for French Canada "in the world" – than parochial (witness the fact that the Montreal Bell Centre's Jumbotron flashes the players' country of origin during games, as if to underline Montreal's place in the world). Corbeil's self-conscious narrator ponders the appropriate hero for a story: "My first idea was to crown Saku Koivu as the greatest of modern Quebec heroes."[42] The Finnish import Saku Koivu as a hero of the people? There are doubts whether he even speaks French! Moving outward from literature to reality, it is clear that meanings and assumptions about the Canadiens are changing, as are assumptions about Quebec itself.

Shortly after the American conductor Kent Nagano took over the Montreal Symphony in 2006 – in hockey terms, during Koivu's lengthy tenure as team captain – there was a very public display of a changed meaning of the "Flying Frenchmen." One of Nagano's first concerts in Montreal included François Dompierre and Georges-Hébert Germain's *Les glorieux*. For the press photos, Nagano stood on the podium, dressed in a Canadiens sweater. The symphonic concert itself concluded with a multimedia display proudly emphasizing the diverse ethnic makeup of the modern Montreal Canadiens – the players said a few words in their native Russian, Czech, Finnish, and so on to emphasize the cosmopolitan flair of the Canadiens. With minimal tinkering, the corporate message of an inclusive Canada could adorn the walls of Halifax's Pier 21, now home to the Canadian Museum of Immigration. The message was that, as reflected in a modern hockey team, bilingual concerns had become a thing of the past for a modern multicultural or intercultural Quebec society, a topic generally missing in hockey literature.

Yet the real Canadiens' recent corporate focus on multicultural hockey is in some ways a return to the past, for the rise of high-level hockey in Montreal at the turn of the twentieth century was clearly tricultural. For most of the nineteenth century, Montreal sporting culture was very bourgeois and very English, and the English clubs would not admit or attract francophones and other "ethnics" (as Andrew Holman as well as Michel Vigneault observe in this volume, such exclusive policies would change). After the formation of the National in 1894, bourgeois francophones embraced "English" sports and English-style clubs. Despite lusty attempts in the 1860s to make lacrosse the Canadian national game, the rigid anglophone-dominated club structure precluded that sport from becoming a similar "link of loyalty to bind them to their home."[43] Such sporting exclusivity aided the rise of hockey as a pan-Canadian game and, as historian Gillian Poulter writes, even when lacrosse was losing "support because of dissention over amateurism and violence [sic!], ice hockey was growing in popularity among a wider range of groups – not just the middle classes ... but also teams made up of workers, French Canadians, and even 'other' groups."[44]

*New Yorker* columnist and Habs fan extraordinaire Adam Gopnik sees artistic potential in the Montreal hockey circles outlined by Vigneault in this volume, that is, in a hockey context that was sometimes tricultural:

> If anyone wanted to make a great Canadian movie – the great Canadian movie – it would be all about the hockey love triangle among the Montagnards [i.e. francophones], the Shamrocks [i.e. Irish Canadians], and the McGill Redmen [i.e. those anglophones able to attend university] in Montreal between 1900 and 1903. On the one hand all the prejudice and bigotry that kept these communities apart still existed, and at the same time there was an irresistible attraction, through the medium of this new sport of hockey, towards assimilation and joint effort ... Sport ... acts as a mirror for our divisions, but it also acts as a hammer that destroys them.[45]

Gopnik stresses the story's almost agentless potential ("if *anyone* wanted to make a great Canadian movie ..."), hinting that the powerful tale of the "hockey love triangle" can take flight on its own, regardless of the author. Armed with such material, any duffer with a pen could write a great hockey narrative.

Until now, Canadian culture has missed a fruitful opportunity to explore not division, not the "Two Solitudes," but how hockey can both link Canadians and help us transcend "prejudice and bigotry." In their herky-jerky way, literary and other artistic examinations of hockey can indicate our fault lines and "divisions" and allow us to move beyond them, without reducing hockey culture to the level of trading cards or to schlocky vignettes of national harmony. As the best of Canadian hockey literature shows, the potential of hockey codes does not lie in simplistic messages of an essentialist hockey-loving country, but in nuanced and critical examinations of the game in Quebec and *le reste du Canada*.

10

# *LA FORCE D'Y CROIRE*: THE LITERARY BATTLES OF GEORGES LARAQUE

—

*Paul Martin*

—

Cultural identities … are marked by time and place. There are models of identity culturally available to life narrators at any particular historical moment that influence what is included and what is excluded from an autobiographical narrative ... Life writers incorporate and reproduce models of identity in their narratives as ways to represent themselves to the reader ... The titles [of life narratives] announce a limit of identity that the narratives explore, exploit and explode.
Sidonie Smith and Julia Watson, *Reading Autobiography*[1]

The truth about stories is that's all that we are.
Thomas King, *The Truth about Stories*[2]

When, in January 2010, thirteen-year National Hockey League (NHL) veteran Georges Laraque was released by the Montreal Canadiens partway through his second, injury-riddled season with the team, he felt that he was "railroaded out of a game [he] loved, when [he] was still among the toughest in the league, by a coach [he] thought didn't understand the game."[3] The Canadiens chose to wait until June of that year to buy out Laraque's contract, thus preventing him not only from playing for another team but also from speaking out against how he felt he was treated by the team's management and coaching staff. Immediately after being released, Laraque tried to organize a press conference to tell his side of the story, but the Habs threatened to stop paying him and to take legal action.[4] Laraque's background as a black, bilingual Canadian born in Montreal made him a rare figure in the NHL. A player known for speaking his mind to the media, often against the wishes of the Habs' management, he was now unable to counter effectively General Manager Bob Gainey's explanation for the dismissal – namely, that "the team would be better without [him]" and that Laraque's "many distractions outside the ice" were a "nuisance to the team" and were keeping him from "doing the job [he'd] been hired for."[5] In the months leading up to his dismissal, Laraque had been criticized by the team's management and by some in the press as being a fighter whose strict adherence to a personal *code* prevented him from fighting as often as he might have; as Gainey told a journalist after Laraque's release, "I don't have a copy of Georges' code, I don't know what it is … I think the code is that you're here for your teammates. It's not your code, it's our code."[6] Being released from the Canadiens and having his integrity and commitment questioned in such a way was difficult for Laraque, especially since it occurred in the immediate wake of the massive earthquake in Haiti, the country from which his parents had emigrated. Though Laraque hoped to return to the NHL the following season, ongoing back troubles caused by two herniated discs forced him to announce his retirement in August 2010 at the age of thirty-three.

During the later years of his playing career, Laraque increasingly gained attention for his many apparent contradictions: a daunting and gifted enforcer who decisively won all but a half-dozen of his 130 fights in the NHL, Laraque also became known for being an outspoken vegan and a yoga-practising defender of animal rights. Whereas he gained notoriety in the NHL for how he seemed to contradict the long-standing stereotypes of the pro-hockey enforcer, his choices upon leaving the league cemented his reputation as a gentle giant. Less than a month after his release by the Canadiens, Laraque joined the Green Party of Canada, becoming its deputy leader just a few months later. He put much of his newly found free time into helping with relief efforts in Haiti, travelling there several times and, with the help of the NHL Players' Association, creating the "Hockey for Haiti" charity. That same spring, Laraque became a major investor in Crudessence, a raw vegan restaurant in Montreal. His entrepreneurial ventures continued in the next two years with an involvement in an artificial-ice business and the selling and promotion of the JuiceExtra juicer. The indefatigable Laraque also threw himself into social causes that showed him to be as much an activist as an athlete and entrepreneur; he slept on the street to draw attention to the plight of the homeless, provided the French narration for a documentary on animal rights and vegetarianism, shared a stage with the Dalai Lama, and, for a brief time in 2012, led the efforts to create a union for junior hockey players in the Canadian Hockey League. He also found new fame on the ice in *Battle of the Blades*, a popular television-reality show on the Canadian Broadcasting Corporation that brought together retired hockey players with figure-skating stars in a weekly pairs figure-skating competition. His success on that show led him to champion figure skating and to speak out about the toughness of the athletes involved. In the midst of all this, he also somehow managed to start a new career as a hockey analyst for the Quebec television network TVA.

Once he was free of the routine commitments of the hockey season and the restrictions placed on him by the Canadiens' vision of how a player should act in the public eye, the quantity of Laraque's other interests grew exponentially. By taking on so many seemingly divergent commitments, Laraque's already complex public persona became even more difficult to characterize. If the frenetic pace of his new life was a statement that he would not allow his identity to be subsumed by the dominant assumptions about what hockey players – and enforcers, in particular – are like, with the release of his autobiography in November 2011, Laraque finally seized the opportunity to tell his own story, to build a new narrative that would unite all of these disparate elements of his life. He was now free to take control over his own story and identity, just as he, having finished his hockey career, was now free from being labelled by others.

Published simultaneously in French and English as *Georges Laraque: La force d'y croire* and *Georges Laraque: The Story of the NHL's Unlikeliest Tough Guy*, Laraque's autobiography recounts, as one would expect, many details of his life that were previously unknown to his fans. Part chronicle of the major events of his life and career and part commentary on everything from violence in hockey and NHL politics to animal rights and the value of public service, the book suffers from trying to cover too much ground. The lack of an entirely cohesive narrative stems, at times, from the book's over-emphasis on the linear recounting of event after event – a not uncommon trait of many sports autobiographies – and a great many digressions. In the chapter entitled "Of Skating and Other Hobbies," for example, Laraque downplays the significance of his participation in *Battle of the Blades*. Rather than detailing how his foray into figure skating profoundly affected the Canadian public's perceptions of him and led to his further involvement and championing of the sport, he seems to lessen its importance by describing this part of his life alongside his comparatively trivial passion for Karaoke, an anecdote about how he fooled friends into thinking he could drink anyone under the table, and his dislike of country and rap music. The plethora of digressions in his narrative gives readers the sense that we are listening to Georges' voice, but they ultimately detract from his goal to show us that "how you start out does not determine where you end up."[7] Faced with the wide open net of the empty page and no one blocking his shot, Laraque ultimately fails to score – that is, he fails to create a narrative that draws cohesive and credible connections among all of the seeming contradictions in his life. The reader is left with a comprehensive view of Laraque's many achievements and opinions, but only a partial understanding of his character. Had he waited longer to write his autobiography, or had his editor and co-writer helped him to find a narrower focus, the story might have offered a clearer picture of how all these varying parts of his career connect. Yet these are easy criticisms to make, and they draw attention away from the agency Laraque seizes in telling his own story. The *act* of telling his own story, in other words, is as significant as its content. He battles to have his identity iterated in its full complexity and not reduced to any singular, easily identifiable trope – the NHL enforcer, the vegan animal activist, the Black athlete overcoming racism in sport.

Central to this project is the interplay between language and identity-making, an underlying theme that girds the autobiography from start to finish. Indeed, even the differing titles of the French and English versions demonstrate the challenges Laraque faces in trying to tell his own story when society and, likely, his publishers expect it to conform to their own expectations. The title *Georges Laraque: La force d'y croire* suggests a narrative that is inspirational and hints at how Georges relied on the power of his belief in himself to overcome the odds and achieve all that he has. *Georges Laraque: The Story of the NHL's Unlikeliest Tough Guy*, on the other hand, points directly to the contradiction between Laraque's skills and success as a fighter and his gentle, compassionate nature. The titles suggest very different narratives: one, the tale of a Québécois athlete's determination to make it to the NHL; the other, a more curious, anomalous, story of a gentle giant who became the NHL's most feared enforcer. These two distinct ways of spinning essentially the same story reveal as much about hockey's linguistic and socio-cultural contexts in Canada as they do about Laraque. As Smith and Watson note in *Reading Autobiography*, all "autobiographical acts take place at cultural sites where discourses intersect, conflict, and compete with one another … In these acts, the terms of the narrator-audience relationship are renegotiated as writers and practitioners develop new rhetorics of identity and strategies of self-presentation for being heard."[8] As we will see, the literary translating of an autobiography such as Laraque's – particularly when he and his co-writer are bilingual and themselves responsible for the translation – adds an additional layer of intersecting discourses to the autobiographical act.

## THE STORY (OF THE) GAME

Hockey is as rooted in narrative and interpretation as it is in action; it relies on words and language as much as it does on the body. As a game, it inspires us to tell stories, to analyze and comment on what we have seen as spectators or experienced as players. Yet its richness and complexity reveal to us with remarkable regularity the limits of any attempt to express the inexpressible. Perhaps because the game is such a fast and physically demanding one, where players shift continuously back and forth from attacking to defending at breakneck speed, words and language are poor tools to capture what happens on the ice. Both the power and the inadequacy of language, however, are ever present. The action on the ice is continuously filtered through narrative, whether it originates with the players trying to live up to what they told themselves they wanted to achieve, with the coaches trying to set and maintain an ever-shifting game plan or system, with the television and radio announcers interpreting the actions through play-by-play, with analysts replaying a key moment, or with fans disputing the referee's interpretation of a player's actions or intent. For every action that happens on the ice, there are many ways to describe it. As Richard Harrison notes in his essay "Between a Puck and a Showpiece," "while a baseball is small enough to hide in one hand, the structure of the play, focusing on the corridor between pitcher and catcher – and the batter's explosive intrusion – tells everyone where to focus their eyes to find the ball."[9] In hockey, by contrast, the continuous movement of players, the speed with which the puck can move between players and teams, challenges players and spectators to track the puck and forces the narrator to create a coherent narrative by discussing only a fraction of the events happening on the ice.

All forms of narrative rely heavily on context and perspective. Every viewer or participant in the game will have a different perspective and potential interpretation of the action. Add to this the context offered by the backstories of the different players on the ice, the situation of a single game within the larger context of a season, or the arc of a team's history, and one can see how a seemingly limitless combination of narratives renders impossible a singular, authoritative account of "what happened." And yet the impossibility of telling *the* story of the game is one of the things that makes watching sports so compelling. Its narratives are cultural work that demands analysis.

As Marie-Laure Ryan explains in her 1993 article "Narrative in Real Time: Chronicle, Mimesis, and Plot in the Baseball Broadcast," the retelling of the events of a game quickly fall into "the scripts, or scenarios, which define standard game-plots: the incredible Come-From-Behind Victory, the Fatal Error, the Heroic Feat, the Lucky Break Victory, the Unlikely Hero, the Inevitable Collapse, Overcoming Bad Luck, Persistence That Pays Off. These themes acquire existential significance through the metaphorical assimilation of victory to life and defeat to death. The broadcast is narrative to the extent that it configures the game by activating a script on the basis of some events, thereby marking these events as key plays in the game."[10] Which script gets "activated," of course, depends on the perspective and affiliations of the narrator. From the eyes of journalists and fans of the winning team, the story of the game might readily fall into a "Persistence That Pays Off" script; for the journalists writing for the hometown newspaper of the losing team and its fans, the dominant narrative might be "the Lucky Break Victory" or "the Inevitable Collapse."[11]

Players interviewed after a game often recount different (and sometimes conflicting) versions of the same event. While the clichés or standard scripts of the post-game hockey interview are quickly recognizable to anyone who has watched or listened to a few hockey broadcasts – "we just weren't able to get enough pucks on net" or "I thought we all gave 110 per cent tonight" or "we've just got to work better as a team" – one cannot assume in any way that these are the only interpretations the players make of the events on the ice or that players are inarticulate or ineffective storytellers. There are the discussions that go on between linemates of what happened in a particular shift on the ice, the interpretations a coach makes during or after the game, the stories that the players might continue to tell each other for years to come. Who gets to hear these stories and who is allowed to tell them is a matter of privilege. As in the oral stories and histories passed down among the First Nations, there are protocols or codes governing who can tell which story and which stories can be told outside of one's immediate community. Examples of such a code include not sharing a game plan with people outside the team, keeping what is said in the dressing room in the dressing room, and, in the case of a player who is benched or scratched, not speaking to the media about the specifics of his conversation with the coach. In the midst of the pressure to maintain these traditions, players often find themselves surrounded by myriad interpretations from the media and fans which may not correlate at all with what they know to be true. The silence of many players in the midst of so many conflicting narratives should not be mistaken for an inability or unwillingness to express themselves; rather, this silence comes out of a deep respect for language and its power, and a fear of misspeaking.

Some players, it seems, are content to continue to keep their stories to themselves after they retire. While it might be that the power of these codes remains in place after players leave hockey, it could also be that their reticence to tell their own story emerges from a deep understanding of the partiality of language and, ultimately, the ways in which any narrative necessarily reduces the complex nature of experience and "reality" into an overly simplistic and unsatisfying form. As the narrator, career minor-leaguer Bobby Bonaduce, reflects in Bill Gaston's novel *The Good Body*: "Language, simply, was not a route many [players] took. On the ice is where it really happened. The brilliance of some. All senses sparking, working at the widest periphery, aflame with danger and hope both, seeing the whole picture, the lightning-fast flux of friends and enemies, the blending of opportunity and threat. Words didn't stand a chance here. Words were candy wrappers, dead leaves."[12]

After years or even decades of listening to journalists and commentators turn action into words that have such little correlation to their experience of the game, it is understandable that many players would be reticent even to attempt to tell the story of "what *really* happened." This resentment on the part of players is summarized well in the words of Iz, the protagonist of Cara Hedley's hockey novel *Twenty Miles*: "Highlight reels are a lie. A hockey game writes its own Coles Notes, this much is true. It's like it's manufactured in an ephemeral package, ready to be butchered and filleted into three clean chunks, then chopped further, this massacre, then strung together in highlight reels – for those who missed it, for the illegitimate fans who believe that a hockey game is a list of the goals and fights, nothing else."[13]

Most former professional hockey players must simply have rejected the opportunity to tell their stories, given how words and language have failed them for so long. At the same time, other former players (a small minority) move quickly and easily into roles as television or radio analysts. It is as if, after years of being the ones hearing the stories told about what happened when they were on the ice, these players relish the opportunity, finally, to be the ones in control of the narrative. Fascinatingly, those who are most successful in this transition seem able to slide seamlessly into the language of the analyst; rather than fully bringing to the table their own experiences in the dressing room or on the ice, they display a facility at fitting the events into the dominant narrative structures. Whether or not, as Iz contends in *Twenty Miles*, the game on the ice is "the same story told over and over,"[14] stories told about hockey certainly seem to be part of a continuous and mostly unchanging set of narratives or scripts that players-turned-analysts rapidly adopt as their own. As Jason Blake argues in his chapter, hockey is a "binding" narrative, and yet it does offer potential as well as limitations.

In the face of so many outsiders telling stories that players know to be different from their own experiences, it is unsurprising that some athletes choose to write their autobiographies, typically after they have retired. In terms of the sheer number of sports memoirs, examples of a genre labelled the "jockography" by Bryan Curtis in the *New York Times*, there are surprisingly few written by hockey players. While baseball fans can read autobiographies by Jackie Robinson (*I Never Had It Made*, 1972), Mickey Mantle (*The Mick*, 1985), Babe Ruth (*The Babe Ruth Story*, 1948), Joe DiMaggio (*Lucky to Be a Yankee*, 1946), and Ty Cobb (*My Life in Baseball: The True Record*, 1961), only a handful of the greatest players in hockey history have chosen to tell their own stories in this way. These include Jean Béliveau (*Jean Béliveau: My Life in Hockey*, 1994), Wayne Gretzky (*Gretzky: An Autobiography*, 1990), Mario Lemieux (*Mario Lemieux: The Final Period*, 1997), Martin Brodeur (*Brodeur: Beyond the Crease*, 2007), and Ken Dryden, whose memoir of his time with the Montreal Canadiens, *The Game* (1983), remains perhaps the best book ever written about hockey. The hockey stars who never cared to put their story into their own words (as in probably all of the major sports) far outnumbers those who did. There are no autobiographies, for instance, of Maurice Richard, Jacques Plante, Guy Lafleur, Ray Bourque, Patrick Roy, or Mark Messier.

Many of the other former professional hockey players who have written autobiographies (or given their approval for ghost-written versions) seem to have done so out of a desire to share the unique aspects of their experience in and out of the sport. Aimed at younger readers, Willie O'Ree's *The Autobiography of Willie O'Ree: Hockey's Black Pioneer* (2000), for instance, is O'Ree's chance to tell his story of overcoming great odds in a way that might inspire young players. In *Why I Didn't Say Anything* (2006), Sheldon Kennedy recounts the story of his career and deals in detail with his efforts to overcome the devastation of having been sexually abused by Graham James, his coach in junior hockey. Kennedy's revelations about the sexual abuse in 1997 stunned the hockey world and the autobiography was Kennedy's opportunity to tell his story in full. In *Playing with Fire* (2009), Theo Fleury, who came forward much later as one of James's victims, describes his battle against drug and alcohol addiction and his efforts to overcome the psychological effects of sexual abuse. Although the recent memoir boom in English-language publishing has also hit the hockey world – recent examples include Johnny Bower's *The China Wall: The Timeless Legend of Johnny Bower* (2008), Stan Mikita's *Forever a Blackhawk* (2011), Bob Probert's *Tough Guy: My Life on the Edge* (2010), Derek Sanderson's *Crossing the Line* (2012), and Jeremy Roenick's

*J.R.: My Life As the Most Outspoken, Fearless, and Hard-Hitting Man in Hockey* (2012) – it remains true that autobiographies by former professional hockey players are fewer compared to other major sports.

The surge in autobiographies likely has more to do with changes in the literary marketplace than it does with hockey players' willingness to speak of themselves. When even the greatest players of all time – Wayne Gretzky was well known for doing this – routinely downplay their individual achievements to cast the spotlight on other teammates instead, it becomes clear that the dominant culture of hockey is one in which setting oneself before the team is seen as inappropriate and even crass. Bobby Orr, who famously shuns media attention and waited thirty-five years to tell his story in his own words, opens his 2013 autobiography *Orr: My Story* by recounting his discomfort on the day in 2010 when Boston unveiled the statue celebrating his 1970 Stanley Cup-winning goal, perhaps the most famous goal in Stanley Cup history: "The last thing I wanted to do was stand in front of a microphone and talk about myself or relive a moment of glory. I wasn't looking for praise, and I certainly wasn't there to take credit. If anything, I wanted to explain that the credit for that moment should be shared much more widely."[15] For many players, hockey's humble team-first mentality carries on into their lives after the game.

As his autobiography attests, Georges Laraque challenged this status quo both during and after his playing career. Continually slotted into a role as the team tough guy, Laraque nonetheless pushed the boundaries of the accepted ways for such players to act and, in particular, speak out in the NHL. Bold and seemingly fearless on and off the ice, Laraque battled (or at least purports to have battled) throughout his career to do things his way. This included speaking to the media and the public with an uncommon candour. Laraque's openness endeared him to fans and many journalists at the same time as it caused consternation among those in the NHL perturbed by his unwillingness to follow the code that demands that players either remain silent or utter little more than a series of interview clichés. Describing how the media would always seek him out for comments, Laraque admits that he chose not to limit what he would say: "I didn't have a secret recipe. I was simply saying everything that would come to my mind. And since clichés … never cross my mind, journalists knew they wouldn't get them from me … I wanted only one thing: that the fans paying my salary got the truth, not canned comments prepared by the media relations department. And even if I'd wanted to play the cliché game, I would have made a fool of myself – I'm just not fluent enough in that language to communicate in it."[16] Laraque's suggestion here that he is incapable of speaking the "language" of clichés is clearly disingenuous. His choice not to "play the cliché game" is, rather, one of a man seeking through language the agency he is not able to achieve in a game in which his role and his movements are predetermined, not only by the structure and rules of the game but also by those who control his ice time and, for the most part, the deployment of his fists.[17] Coaches could choose when and how Laraque was to play, but they and the team's management would have a much harder time forcing him to play a set part off the ice. When one starts to look at Laraque's autobiography as the story (and, in itself, an example) of his attempt to find "freedom" from stereotypes and constraining words like "goon" or "enforcer," *Georges Laraque: La force d'y croire / Georges Laraque: The Story of the NHL's Unlikeliest Tough Guy* becomes more complex than it first appears – in spite of the focus on the linearity of events. While the book fails to cohere fully around a central theme, a closer look at how language and identification played a profound role in Laraque's struggle for agency shows what makes his story compelling, even if it is occasionally discordant.

## FREE AGENCY

Through their autobiographies, many athletes (and their co-writers or ghost writers) suggest that their books will reveal to the reader the nature of their lives behind the scenes. Georges Laraque sets out to do this as well, but he also makes it clear that one of his primary objectives is to show his readers the discrepancy between the Laraque they have seen on the ice and what he is like in real life. After expressing his own personal dislike of baseball, he notes that he is nevertheless a huge admirer of Jackie Robinson and of how Robinson's autobiography reached a far wider audience than that of baseball fans: "Throughout my life I've always made a big distinction between the public person and the individual. You can respect the baseball player without respecting baseball … The book you're holding in your hands was written with the same intention in mind. On the one side is the Georges Laraque you saw in the NHL. And then there's the human being I am off the ice."[18]

Fascinating and telling in this passage is how Laraque references the materiality of the text – "[the] book you're holding in your hands" – and his aim for it to help supplant, or at least round out, the perceived persona of "the Georges Laraque" with a more three-dimensional understanding of his identity as a "human being."[19] The binary opposition he sets up between the persona and the person works its way through the book at nearly every level. He writes at numerous points about reputation and the ways in which others have projected certain assumptions on him that were not necessarily true. The results of some of these projections were extremely negative and hurtful, such as the terrible racism he faced, particularly as a young player, or the accusations by the press and by coaches late in his career with the Montreal Canadiens that he cared more about his activities off the ice than about hockey. Other elements of his reputation, created partly by him and partly by the media, worked in his favour.

In explaining his quick rise to becoming the most feared fighter in the NHL, Laraque discusses what it took to "make his name" in the league. Plagued by self-doubt when he was offered a roster spot with the Edmonton Oilers after his first training camp in 1995, Laraque lies to coach Ron Low and tells him he would prefer to return to junior to work on his skills. Struck by the fear of having to fight someone like Dave Brown, Laraque asks himself: "Was I really built to be an NHL tough guy? Did I really want to spend my life fighting these guys? … Guys [in junior] may have felt about me how I felt about Dave Brown. But in the NHL, the name on the back of my sweater didn't scare anyone. And having been on both sides, I knew better than ever that a reputation was more intimidating than a heavy fist. And a reputation is not an easy thing to get. Was I really ready to go through the battles it would take to make tough guys think about the name on my sweater?"[20] Though he had committed to play another year of junior, his public identity was changed by the act of signing his first professional contract. "On paper, I was a hockey millionaire … I wasn't the same Georges Laraque anymore."[21] It took a year back in junior and a couple of seasons playing mostly with the Oilers' farm team for Laraque's reputation as a fighter to become cemented. The chapter "Twenty-five

Seconds and the World Would Change" describes how Laraque's now famous fight against Buffalo Sabres' tough guy Rob Ray led to his ascension to a regular roster spot and his name being known around the league.

Interestingly, the battle between Laraque and Ray, "a first-class fighter, a bona fide NHL heavyweight with a league-wide reputation," begins with a war of words. Early in that game against the Sabres, Ray refuses to fight Laraque: "Since I was trying to build my *reputation* in the league, I gathered my courage and *asked* him if he wanted to fight. He *answered* with a no … That's how it works with tough guys. They respect each other enough that even if one of them *invites* another one to fight, the bout won't necessarily take place. The one who's invited simply has *to say* he doesn't feel like it … If he doesn't mess with the best players of the opposite team, he won't be worried for the rest of the game."[22] Not only is it fascinating to see here the dynamics of how crucial *language* is to determining the action of a fight or lack thereof, it is also important to note how the act of fighting in this instance is all about reputation rather than retaliation. When, late in the game, Ray breaks his word and attacks highly skilled Edmonton forward Bill Guerin, Laraque is "mad with rage."[23] After the game, consumed with anger and without thought of the legal implications of threatening to hurt another player, Laraque tells the media that Ray "was a coward, a man with no sense of honour. Moreover, I promised the entire universe that I was going to make him pay for what he had done and that I certainly wasn't going to ask for his permission next time to punch him in the head."[24] With rampant media attention leading up to the rematch between the teams a few days' later, Laraque found himself anxiously preparing to follow up on his words: "What had been said had been said. I had to live up to it. I tried to temper things a bit, but the journalists knew just what to ask in order to make my answers as provocative as possible. So I said yes, I was ready for him."[25] In the fight that inevitably ensued that night, Laraque proved that he had the powerful punches to back up his words: "He never got to hit me once … There wasn't a single hockey analyst who could have predicted what had happened. They were amazed to see that an inexperienced, twenty-two-year-old player had not only challenged one of the top fighters in the NHL, but had kept his promise to knock him down … In less than thirty seconds … I had built myself a solid reputation throughout the league. Nothing would be the same anymore, either for me or for the Oilers."[26]

If language was vital to the instigation of Laraque's infamous fight with Rob Ray, it was even more crucial to how the results of that fight would affect the rest of Laraque's career. Word of Laraque's promise and performance travelled quickly throughout the league. Without the events of that night being communicated to those who were not in attendance, the fight would have have had an impact only on that single game. Instead they reshaped Laraque's career, and his identity, at least in terms of how it was perceived by others; terms like "enforcer," "tough guy," "homme fort," "bagarreur," "fighter," and even "goon" were then forever associated with his name and, to his own chagrin, the limited role some coaches gave him.

If Laraque's fight against Ray, and the many other fights that followed, changed how others saw and labelled him, so too did another violent act, one that was not his own. As Laraque recounts in his book, the sickening act of violence that occurred on 21 February 2000, when Marty McSorley brutally struck Donald Brashear across the back of the head with his stick, began to change the public perception of those whose job it was ostensibly to protect other players and to alter, with violence, the flow of a game: "Public opinion, encouraged by the press, began mixing everything up. My acts on the ice, as well as those of other tough guys ... were now associated with McSorley's. For most observers from outside the hockey world we became the equivalent of bloodthirsty beasts, incapable of handling a puck, pursuing only one goal in life: hurt people! We kept hearing the same thing: the game didn't need that kind of player anymore."[27] This was one of many instances over the course of Laraque's career where others' interpretations of his actions on and off the ice shaped public perception of his role and identity. Frustrated by the attempts of others to define him, Laraque becomes more preoccupied with seizing control over his own narrative.

A decade later, in response to being released by the Canadiens in January 2010 and all that had been said about him by the team's management and both the French and English media, Laraque seized the opportunity to "give some facts about [his] side of the story" on the popular Québec television program *Tout le monde en parle*.[28] Broadcast on 31 January 2010, his comments on and approach to being released by his hometown team surprised many viewers. Speaking of hockey and its connection to his own identity, he argued: "Hockey is a sport, above all. I can't take it personally ... What I do on the ice, that doesn't define me as a person ... I help everyone, that's what is important to me. There are many other things in life than hockey." As he later notes about that interview, "the audience discovered then who I really was. I wasn't simply a *goon* who made a living punching people in the face because he loved it."[29]

Laraque writes at numerous points in the book that he hopes, by telling his own story, to replace the narrow conceptions of him as a "tough guy" with a more nuanced understanding of him as a complex and caring individual whose larger focus is "to influence for the better the course of the world."[30] He certainly achieves this on many levels, but the gentler image of what he is "really like" is complicated by the contradictions that lie throughout the book, particularly with respect to violence. Laraque does show, for instance, the negative sides to fighting in the NHL; he writes at length about the fear and anxiety he felt over the days and hours before he might have to fight, how some players took steroids in order to be stronger and more intimidating, the threat of being seriously injured in a fight, and the toll violence took on his contemporaries who played similar roles. It is important to recall that his book was published in the wake of the tragic and premature deaths of former NHL tough guys Derek Boogaard, Wade Belak, and Rick Rypien. Drawing a comparison between the Post-Traumatic Stress Disorder faced by soldiers – the "true heroes," he reminds the reader – returning home from war and the experiences of former NHL enforcers, Laraque argues that "it is urgent that we take some action to protect the NHL tough guys during and after their careers."[31] But, at the same time, Laraque in no way repudiates the role of fighting in hockey. Though he contends that fighters need to be better protected, he does not call for a reduction of violence in the game. Enforcers, in Laraque's eyes, are there to make sure that the "dirty stuff" is kept out of the game. The difference, he suggests, is that of intent. The league's most dangerous tough guys had a mutual respect for one another: "A great complicity keeps us united … And though I always *wanted* to win, I was never motivated by a desire to hurt anyone. That's not the same thing at all."[32] The possibility of someone getting seriously hurt in a fight, though, is real. Laraque's prowess and unmatched record of wins as a fighter means that he got the better of nearly everyone who tried to fight him. While he seems to have avoided the serious physical and mental trauma suffered by players such as Belak or Rypien, he contributed to the culture of violence that affected these players long after they left hockey. It is true that Laraque maintained and even helped foster an adherence among fighters to "the code" he outlines in the book. Yet, no matter how honourable or united the fighters are, Laraque's justification of fighting in the NHL seems out of step not only with the NHL today but also with his own commitment to helping the world through drawing attention, for example, to the suffering of animals and to other environmental concerns.

Perhaps the most unsettling contradiction in Laraque's book comes from his description of the physical abuse he received as a child from his father. Rather than the racism he suffered at the rink, Laraque points to his father's "tyrannical regime" as the "one thing that defined my childhood":[33] "My earliest memories of my father are of him instilling his fierce vision of discipline in his kids, and bending us to his will ... The slightest mistake any of his kids would make was sure to be severely punished. We had to suffer his chastisement every time he thought we'd gone off the right track he had planned for us. And by 'chastisement' I mean the physical kind, the kind most of us nowadays think is inappropriate. Unless, of course someone thinks that hitting a kid 50 times with the belt is a proper punishment ... When it came to raising his kids, there were no alternatives to belt smacking for my father."[34]

Laraque points to his father's own upbringing in Haiti as one of the sources of this behaviour – "[he] was simply repeating what he had gone through during his own childhood"[35] – and says that he was unwilling and unable "to adjust [his] social behavior to the customs and practices endorsed by the majority in Canada."[36] Because "[lack] of understanding is often the fastest route to racism," Laraque was troubled by how his father's violence appeared to his friends off the ice: "There was my father, conjuring negative stereotypes out of thin air with his barbarism. I was so ashamed of him that it was almost unbearable. I hated him more for the affronts he inflicted on us in front of others than for the actual punishments we were given."[37] One of the most striking parts of Laraque's story comes when, as a teenager, he is forced to decide for himself and his siblings which of his parents will retain full parental custody following their divorce. Despite the fact that the father "had almost never demonstrated any affection for [his children]" and "the only things [they] ever got from him were reprimands and belt-smacking sessions," Laraque asks the judge to give his father full custody. "I was deeply convinced," he writes, "that I had just made the right decision for our future."[38]

Laraque goes on to argue that his father's strict discipline and high standards helped his children to achieve excellence in athletics and in school. It is clear from Laraque's descriptions, though, that the father's demand for perfection had the opposite effect on his daughter's performance at track and field: "He wanted to motivate Daphney, but he ended up disenchanting her. He wanted her to dream, but he killed every possibility of doing so."[39] Laraque's decision for him and his siblings to remain with his father certainly did not make any of their childhoods more pleasant. In the end, unable to look back in any way but through the lens of a player who did achieve a professional career, he rationalizes this decision in an admittedly selfish way: "I hated my father's attitude and the way he was raising me. But if my goal was to reach the NHL one day, it could only be achieved under his severe supervision. Between the cuddling comfort my mother would have given me and the pathological harshness of my father, I had chosen."[40]

Laraque's own personality and behaviour today makes it abundantly clear that, aside from his strongly competitive nature, he has followed anything but his father's path of instilling fear and constant pressure in the lives of his own children. Speaking of his role as a father, Laraque pointedly notes that this particular cycle of family violence will end with him: "Never will my twin children ever have to suffer the belt-smacking torture. I'll never terrorize them that way. I strongly believe in different and better ways to raise my kids than getting the strap out every time something in their attitude doesn't comply with my standards."[41] The careful reader, however, cannot fail later on in the book to hear echoes of his father's example of punishment and retribution when Laraque talks about the need for teams to have enforcers to keep opposing players in line and to mete out punishment against those who transgress the boundaries of acceptable behaviour. He fails to see the parallels, or acknowledge them openly, but it is hard for the reader to ignore the similarity between the fear of violence that caused the young Georges Laraque to behave according to his father's standards and the way the presence on the bench of *the* Georges Laraque would cause other players to "show a lot of prudence."[42] As he came to be recognized in the NHL as "one of the toughest and most dangerous among my peers," Laraque contends, other players "began bodychecking my teammates, if not lightly, at least without putting all their energy and strength into it. Some would even miss them on purpose. Why? Because they knew a heavy hit would bring consequences they would prefer to avoid."[43] NHL "tough guys," he argues, "are not only useful but a necessity when it comes to keeping the game clean. We don't just punish dirty hits – we prevent them."[44] While it is vital to separate the "game" from "real life," the lines between the two are not as cut and dry as Laraque would have us believe. He, too, hints at this when he notes that becoming a father had a role in his decision to retire from the NHL: "It was tough doing something for a living I didn't want my kids to see. I'm not saying I had a problem with fighting in the game. But I didn't get into the game dreaming of being a fighter, and that is a complicated thing to explain to a kid."[45]

## THE POWER OF WORDS

Retirement and the writing of his own autobiography gave Laraque the freedom and opportunity to tell his story without having to worry about the constraints imposed by a team or the conventions of how a player should behave. His book is replete with observations he probably would not have dared to make while playing in the NHL. In some cases, such comments seem discordant when placed alongside Laraque's attempts to dispel stereotypes about everything from violence in hockey to the animal-rights movement. With respect to spirituality, for instance, he talks about how important it is "to always put ourselves in the shoes of the other before judging his or her actions in any way."[46] A page earlier, though, he talks about his rejection of the Catholic faith into which he was baptized: "Studying a bit more what [Catholicism] was really about … left me both sad and nauseated. Of all the religions in this world, I realized that it was one of the worst."[47] Despite professing his admiration for Jackie Robinson earlier in the book, he nonetheless dismisses the sport of baseball and takes a shot at what he perceives to be a lack of athleticism among some professional baseball players: "Half the players look like sumo wrestlers. They eat and chew gum or tobacco all game long and spend more time picking their noses than they do running ... When David Wells pitched his perfect game for the New York Yankees ... he was hungover from a boozing session the night before. That alone makes it a bit more difficult to take baseball too seriously. And what a paunch, for God's sake!"[48]

Interestingly, while the book received close attention from the media, neither of these provocative statements received any attention. The most controversial statements in the eyes of the press were those regarding the use of performance-enhancing drugs and human-growth hormone in the NHL ("quite a lot of [tough guys] did use [steroids], but other, more talented players did too"[49]) and Wayne Gretzky's performance as the coach of the Phoenix Coyotes ("[he] could hardly have been worse … It was frankly ridiculous.").[50] Despite his commitment to being as candid as possible, Laraque's harsh judgment of the coaching abilities of the greatest player in the history of the game risks undermining his readers' sympathy for him. That said, his publishers, and likely also Laraque and his co-author, Pierre Thibeault, recognized that controversy sells books. Laraque's statements about Gretzky and steroids use made headlines across Canada, as did his comments about the stress and anxiety he experienced as an NHL tough guy. The other aspect of the book that drew significant attention in the media was Laraque's discussion of the vicious racism he encountered as a young player. By comparing the version of this last part of Laraque's story in *Georges Laraque: La force d'y croire* to that in *Georges Laraque: The Story of the NHL's Unlikeliest Tough Guy*, we learn a great deal about not only the obstacles he overcame to make it to the NHL but also how public perceptions of him continue to challenge his ability to find true agency.

If Georges Laraque hoped to prove that he was much more than a feared fighter during his thirteen seasons in the NHL, writing about Léopold Sédar Senghor at the start of his autobiography certainly did not hurt. Laraque cites the famous Senegalese intellectual and the Négritude movement he founded in the 1930s with fellow poets and politicians Aimé Césaire and Léon Damas in order to make an important point about the power of language, intent, and the social contexts of words. Although the English and French versions of his book differ most in their first several pages, Laraque ultimately begins both with the story of how the racism he faced as a boy playing hockey made him determined to work hard enough to make it to the NHL.

*Georges Laraque: La force d'y croire* opens provocatively with the following passage:

> Negro. Five letters, one word.
>
> A word that echoed around me throughout my childhood and

throughout my adolescence. A word that voices shouted, screamed in my ear. Even when it was whispered, it never failed to astound me, to create a deafening din in the depths of my being. Always, the word was preceded by an epithet. "Dirty" recurred often. Sometimes it was accompanied by another type of qualification of the "hostie de nègre" type.[51]

Laraque says that later in life, through reading the work of Senghor and others from the Négritude movement, he came to understand "all the beauty and instrinsic grandeur of this word."[52] Here he articulates how a single word (*nègre*) can take on very different meanings depending on the intent of the speaker (expressing racist hatred versus empowering those of African origin to see "blackness" in a new way) and the context in which it is spoken (used by white bigots in the hockey rink versus employed by Black intellectuals to fight colonialist mentalities). This passage cleverly establishes the theme of Laraque reappropriating his identity and seizing agency by defining himself for others rather than accepting the determination of others. Readers will, ideally, come to see the single signifier ("*The* Georges Laraque") as referring to multiple signifieds (Georges the player, Georges the public figure, Georges the humanitarian, and so on), or, at least, a more complicated signified than they might have initially assumed.

The English version of this same passage (which, significantly, does not commence the book and is pushed farther into the opening chapter by an addition requested by the English publisher, Penguin Canada) brings us up against a challenging dilemma of translation. In English, the racist epithet used against Laraque, "nigger," does not have the same complexity as "nègre"; one cannot extricate the violent and hateful history from the English word, no matter the context. Describing how that word was used against him, often with a preceding word like "*fucking*" or "in a degrading short sentence,"[53] but how later in life he came to see "what truly constitutes the essence of the word *Negro*," the passage lacks the symmetry and power of the French.[54] Having ascribed the use of the English epithet against him as one of the reasons his "dreams had a slightly sharper focus" than those of his childhood teammates, he is unable in English to draw as clear a parallel between his drive to overcome these obstacles and the way he would later come to understand "negro" as a word of empowerment: "The cruel and racist words that buzzed around my mind during my youth were only meant to soil a beautiful word, a word full of history."[55] Translations, of course, always reveal the inexact and imperfect art of expressing ideas in words. What makes these passages more interesting than most in the book is that Laraque is trying to pay particular attention to the contingent meaning and use of a single word while communicating with both French-speaking and English-speaking audiences. This is particularly crucial because that single word is revealed to be one of the chief motivating factors behind Laraque's determination to succeed.

With respect to the issue of translation in Laraque's book(s), it is important to note that he and his co-author are credited with writing both the English and the French versions. One might presume that, because both men are native French speakers, they would have written the book first in French and had someone else translate into English. With no translator listed, one must assume Laraque and Thibeault wrote both the French and English versions of the text, an unusual situation to be certain. Unlike most translations, we cannot differentiate between the "original" text and the translation; neither of these books, then, appears to be a derivative or adaptation of the other. The books appear to be nearly identical in terms of their content and structure. Yet, upon closer examination, we can discern several significant differences between the books both in their titles and in the copy on their covers or dust jackets, as well as in their opening pages. These variances are much more than just stylistic changes. In fact, they create two fundamentally different reading experiences and, potentially, two very different perspectives of Georges Laraque. More important, they may reveal something about how French and English Canada – or at least two publishers from French and English Canada – are willing to conceive of hockey players as public figures. Paratextual elements, such as titles, covers, and dust jackets, as Gerard Genette and Philippe Lejeune have written,[56] provide us with instructions or, at the very least, strong suggestions as to *how* to read a text. These aspects of the paratext, that is to say the parts of the physical *book* outside of the *text*, are almost always determined by the publishers, who package the text the authors have given them in a way they think will be the most marketable. In the case of the English edition of the book, the publisher's editor also helped reshape the beginning of the text in a crucial way.

As discussed earlier, the subtitle of the French edition, *La force d'y croire*, signals that this will be a book about the overcoming of obstacles and the power of believing in one's dreams. The text on the back cover of the book clearly supports this idea:

> Throughout his career in the National Hockey League, Georges Laraque has demonstrated more than once that passion and determination can go a long way! For him, any dream is achievable when you have the strength to believe. Here, he gives us an autobiography in his own image, frank and direct. Racism, violence, religion, family, politics … No subject is taboo. This athlete tells us how he managed to make his way in a world where prejudice and discrimination was law. Turning now to the future, this former hockey player reveals all of his deepest convictions, his discovery of veganism, his many humanitarian projects, his positions on environmental matters … Beyond the imposing physique of the strong man, we discover a sensitive and committed intellectual, guided by steadfast values.[57]

It is worth noting that this text on the back cover says nothing about Laraque's career as a fighter. That part of his identity, of course, is well known, but aside from mentioning that Laraque shares his thoughts on violence and that he has the imposing physique of an NHL "homme fort," the cover describes him as a sensitive and engaged intellectual. The photos on the back cover, absent from the English cover, show Laraque celebrating after scoring a goal in Edmonton, participating in *Battle of the Blades*, representing the Green Party at a Gay Pride parade in Montreal, and being on stage with the Dalai Lama. Everything about the book cover and the rest of the paratext implies that this will not be a book focused on Laraque's role as an NHL enforcer.

The opening pages of the French edition support this as well. A brief introduction, titled "Un bon exemple," precedes the opening of the first chapter. This introduction establishes a parallel between the inspiration Laraque took from reading the story of Jackie Robinson and the role he hopes his own autobiography may play in the lives of his own readers: "As soon as I read the autobiography of Jackie Robinson, I dreamed of telling my story. I hope that my autobiography will be an inspiration for many of you, as much as Jackie's, which changed my life, was for me."[58] The book continues along this path of aligning Laraque's story with that of Robinson by opening the first chapter with the powerful and provocative passage about how extensively racism permeated his early life. By choosing to omit any mention of hockey in these opening lines and, indeed throughout the entire first section of this chapter (which goes on to discuss the Négritude movement and the battles of Malcolm X, Rosa Parks, and Martin Luther King, Jr), Laraque and his co-writer tell the reader unequivocally that this is not a routine hockey story but rather one of a man whose belief in following his dreams reaches far beyond sport.

If one of Georges Laraque's primary goals in writing his autobiography was to help readers think of him as being much more than an NHL enforcer, the title and opening pages of the English edition of the book are much less effective than those of *Georges Laraque: La force d'y croire*. Unhappy with the way the French version opened, Penguin Canada insisted on several key changes, all of which shift the focus toward Laraque's history as one of the most dominating fighters in recent NHL history.[59] The title *Georges Laraque: The Story of the NHL's Unlikeliest Tough Guy* removes any suggestion that the book is meant to inspire readers to follow their dreams. Furthermore, the use of the word "unlikeliest," perhaps to indicate that Laraque fails to live up to our stereotypes of NHL tough guys, may even seem to diminish his achievement of overcoming so many odds; it implies that his success is more an anomaly than an example of what one can accomplish with strong determination and hard work. The back cover of the book, unlike that of *La force d'y croire*, shows no photographic evidence of Laraque's many sides. Instead, it features a lengthy passage from chapter 9 in which Laraque talks openly of the fear and anxiety he and many other enforcers felt when preparing to fight. The passage ends with the following words: "It can be lonely, and it's always hard. I don't want to pretend to be a psychologist or to mention any names disrespectfully, but a number of tough guys who once dropped their gloves for a living have been in the headlines lately for the tragic way their lives came to an end. These guys had to call on their courage in ways other players don't, and I know that takes a huge toll."[60] Needless to say, this back-cover text paints a very different picture of the book than what one finds on the French edition.

Penguin counters the outer cover's focus on fighting with text on the dust jacket's inner flaps, something one does not find in the French edition. The inner-flap text begins with a question and answer in large, upper-case type: "THINK YOU KNOW NHL TOUGH GUY GEORGES LARAQUE? THINK AGAIN." The first three paragraphs of the text on the flap continue to focus on Laraque's prowess as a fighter: "*The Hockey News* named Laraque 'best fighter.' *Sports Illustrated* called him the league's '#1 enforcer.' Fans called him 'BGL' – for Big Georges Laraque. Ottawa Senators' pugilist Chris Neil called him 'probably the toughest in the league.'" By placing the emphasis on Laraque's pugilistic reputation before listing many of the ways in which that reputation does not match "who he really is," the flap text sets up the book as one that will discuss all of these sides of his career in detail. In that respect, the English description on the jacket flaps may well be more reflective of the book than the back cover of the French edition; there is a great deal in the book about Laraque's experiences in the NHL and the role that fighting played in his career. However, it also removes any expectation on the part of readers that they are about to read an inspirational text. These paratextual elements of the French and English editions, then, contextualize in strikingly different ways what the reader will encounter in the pages to follow.

The most striking difference between the English and French versions developed from the Penguin editor's insistence on a stronger focus at the start of the book on Laraque's NHL career.[61] As the English version opens, there is no introduction in which Laraque describes his aspiration for his own autobiography to be as inspirational to others as Jackie Robinson's was to him. Robinson is discussed, but not until five pages into the first chapter, which is entitled "A Good Example" (after the title of the book series for children that included the book on Robinson that Laraque read as a child). A matching passage is found in *La force d'y croire*, but when Robinson's name arises in the French edition, the readers already understand the significance of Robinson's "bon exemple" to Laraque; English-speaking readers, are left to draw a connection, if they can, between Robinson telling his story and Laraque wanting to do the same. In other words, in *Georges Laraque: The Story of the NHL's Unlikeliest Tough Guy*, Robinson is shown to be Laraque's hero only for what he achieved on the field and later as an advocate "for black people's causes,"[62] whereas in the French version we learn that Robinson was also an inspiration to Laraque for having written the story of his own life. Robinson, then, not only serves as a role model for Laraque's athleticism and activism, but also blazes a trail for him as a writer. Laraque sees in Robinson the power of claiming and telling one's own story about achieving one's dreams in the face of racism and seemingly impossible odds.

Most fascinating about the opening of the English book, however, is not the omission of the introduction but rather the addition of a new opening that pushes Laraque's powerful story of racism back a full page. Instead of confronting the reader head-on with the racist epithet used so frequently against him as a young player, Laraque sets up his story in an entirely different and more predictable manner. The book opens with Laraque describing a game in 1999 when, as an Oilers rookie, he lines up to fight Tony Twist: "a beast of a man. Two hundred and forty-five pounds of intimidation and aggression. His job is to scare grown men … in a moment I will drop my gloves and do battle with one of the toughest guys in the NHL? Why? That is a question that will take a whole book to answer."[63] Even though Laraque proceeds a few sentences later to explain that his dreams of reaching the NHL "had a slightly sharper focus … because someone called me a nigger,"[64] this opening passage dramatically alters the perspective one finds in the opening of *La force d'y croire*. Rather than starting immediately with the question of racism and understanding it as something much larger than hockey, *The Story of the NHL's Unlikeliest Tough Guy* begins with Laraque's role as a fighter and attributes his experiences of racism as one of the forces that helped motivate him to achieve all he did on the rink. By opening the book with a fight on the ice, Laraque and his co-writer make it more challenging for the English reader to get past the typical perception of him as a fighter with many other sides to him. In contrast, the French edition seems more effective from the outset in depicting Laraque as a complex individual for whom the NHL is but one side of his identity. The difference between these two perspectives becomes more subtle by the end of each book, since the editions are nearly identical after the opening chapter. It is interesting to speculate, however, about why these differences are there at all and what they imply about Laraque's quest to achieve true agency by telling his story.

Every publishing house has its own views on what a book needs in order to succeed on a commercial and/or aesthetic level. Most probably, Laraque, like many first-time authors, did not have the literary clout or desire required to refuse the changes suggested by his editor at Penguin. In order to have his book accepted by such a major international English-language publisher, he likely had little choice but to go along with its demands. In contrast, Laraque's publisher in Québec, Les Éditions de l'homme, is a vastly smaller and more independent press than the multinational conglomerate Penguin. Moreover, Laraque's celebrity status in Quebec, a province in which "the Habs are not only a hockey team … but also a religion,"[65] may have provided him the cultural capital to ensure that his book was as he wished it to be. The types of changes made to the English book on Penguin Canada's insistence, however, reveal much more than the extent of Laraque's influence in these two very different literary markets. The manner in which the English edition uses Laraque's status as a tough guy to frame the narrative suggests that Penguin felt that this angle would resonate more with English readers. Instead of challenging the popular assumptions about Laraque from the opening words, the English edition eases the reader into this process by starting with what, one presumes, is a more recognizable picture to the English reader: a young Laraque getting ready to fight one of the most intimidating fighters in the NHL. *La force d'y croire*, it would seem, has more faith in the reader to be engaged by an opening section that says virtually nothing about hockey but rather focuses on race, discrimination, and the overcoming of great odds. This may be because the latter narrative has all sorts of echoes of larger metanarratives in Quebec society. It applies not only to the history of francophone hockey stars like Maurice Richard overcoming prejudice and discrimination to achieve recognition and respect in the NHL, but also to the struggles (as Emmanuel Lapierre notes in this volume) faced by the Québécois people throughout much of their history. The idea of an athlete whose struggles against the odds is not only one of race and culture but also of language is anything but foreign to Quebec readers.

People "tell stories of their lives through the cultural scripts available to them," Smith and Watson remind us, "and they are governed by cultural strictures about self-presentation in public."[66] Both the French and English versions of the opening of Laraque's story, not to mention the paratextual elements of the title and cover text of each book, reflect "cultural scripts" of stories that correspond to each culture's expectations of what a hockey player's autobiography can be. Laraque's telling of his story never happens entirely on his own terms; no matter how provocative or seemingly unstructured the story is at times, he is still constrained by the restrictions imposed by the genre, his publishers, and his audiences. Yet this does not necessarily mean that, through his writing, Laraque fails to achieve a larger sense of agency, one that he rarely felt as a player. In considering any example of "life writing," Smith and Watson suggest that we ask "how do people change the narratives or write back to the cultural stories that have scripted them as particular kinds of subjects? How is this 'writing back,' this changing of the terms of one's representation, a strategy for gaining agency?"[67] If one revisits the stories he tells throughout *Georges Laraque: La force d'y croire* and *Georges Laraque: The Story of the NHL's Unlikeliest Tough Guy*, it becomes clear that Laraque sees his career and life as a journey that involves "writing back" against those "cultural scripts" that aimed to subordinate him through racism, to define what kind of role he would play on the ice, and to limit the kinds of activities he would undertake off the ice during and following his career. The writing of his autobiography, then, is only one of a lifelong series of attempts by Laraque to tell his own story on his own terms. That the project of writing the books succeeds on as many levels as it fails only makes each text all the more fascinating, particularly when they are looked at side by side.

# NOTES

## Introduction

1 Ignatieff, *Blood and Belonging*, 174.

2 Ibid., 176.

3 Marc Lavoie, *Désavantage numérique*, 14. "Est-il vrai que les hockeyeurs francophones sont trop petits, qu'ils ne sont pas suffisamment robustes, que leur jeu défensif est déficient, qu'ils deviennent invisibles quand l'enjeu est important?" Nonsense, says former NHLer Bob Sirois in his recent exposé on discrimination against francophones in elite-level junior and professional hockey. But this perceived physical deficiency continues to exist, he notes, as a conventional "truth" that allows anglophone owners, coaches, and fans to denigrate French Canadian players. See Sirois, *Discrimination in the NHL*. On the academic debate about discrimination against French Canadian elite players, see Lavoie, Grenier, and Coulombe, "Performance Differentials in the National Hockey League," 461–9; Longley, "Do English Canadian Hockey Teams Discriminate against French Canadian Players?" 217–20; and Krashinsky and Krashinsky, "Do English Canadian Hockey Teams Discriminate against French Canadian Players?" 212–16.

4 Gruneau and Whitson, *Hockey Night in Canada*.

5 Wong, "Proem," ix.

6 Harvey, "Whose Sweater Is This?" 29–52. See also Gitersos, "'Les frogs

sont menacés,'" 69–81; and, generally, Laurin-Lamothe and Moreau, *Le Canadien de Montréal.*

7 Léger, "Pour Sortir des Chemins de la résignation et de la servitude," 70–1. "Les ravages de la mentalité d'abdication"; "les exploits d'un joueur de hockey." Intellectuals held that Richard, the reluctant, working-class hero – a "busher" in mid-century parlance – with an unpolished demeanour, did not have the sort of exemplary character that was needed for a modernizing Quebec. "[Le Rocket] ne semble pas qu'il soit exactement ce qu'on peut appeler un 'prototype' de la civilisation, de la finesse et de la subtilité françaises" (The Rocket … does not exactly appear to be exactly what one can call a "prototype" of French civilization, delicacy and subtlety), one *Cité Libre* columnist offered in 1958. Cléobule, "Le Dangereux Tricolore," 44.

8 Godbout, "Pour se Déniaiser," 22. "Satisfaire sa fierté … avec des bingos pour les paroisses [et] héros du hockey."

9 Poisson, "La Langue: La soirée du Hockey," 721–4.

10 Harvey, "Sport and the Quebec Clergy, 1930–1960," 73–5.

11 Ibid., 81–2.

12 Quebecers' experiences of the iconic *Canadian* moment, the Summit Series, are explored in Simon Richard's *La série du siècle.*

13 Quoted in Harvey, "Sport and the Quebec Clergy," 85.

14 The FQHG changed its name to Hockey Québec in 1996. In the 1973 attempt at fusion, the united body became known as the Fédération de hockey sur glace du Québec (FHGQ). When it split, in 1974, the half of the organization constituted by old AHAQ members retained the name FHGQ – section majeure. Raymond Prince, "Prologue: Sur la route de la Fédération québécoise de hockey sur glace," 5; and Prince, "La naissance," 1. Both are typescript Histories of Hockey Québec provided to Andrew Holman by Sylvain B. Lalonde, directeur général, Hockey Québec, October 2011.

15 Bertrand openly, ardently campaigned for the Yes side in the referendum vote, organizing sixty prominent athletes and sportsmen into a Comité des athlètes pour le "Oui" as requested by Premier René Lévesque.

16 See François Béliveau, "Le ministre Lessard s'intéresse à une Équipe-Québec," *La Presse*, 25 September 1981, 8; "Équipe-Quebec est lancée!" *La Presse*, 19 August 1981, 12; "Le FQHG endosse Équipe-Québec," *La*

*Presse*, 2 October 1981, 18; "Guy Lafleur donne un coup de pouce," *La Presse*, 30 July 1981, 2; Réjean Tremblay, "Le projet d'Équipe-Québec: Bertrand s'est bien repris," *La Presse*, 20 August 1981, 9.

17 When NHL teams were accused of discrimination against francophone players in 1986, and when Canada's World Junior team selection was alleged to have slighted French Canadian talent in the 2000s, an independent Équipe Québec was proposed as the only satisfactory solution to the problem; Sirois, *Discrimination in the NHL*, 206, 208.

18 "Une nation, un club de hockey, dit Guy Bertrand," *Le Devoir*, 28 November 2006.

19 Graeme Hamilton, "Others Nations Pass on Challenge from Quebec-only Hockey Team," *National Post*, 9 March 2011.

20 In the summer of 2013, Parti Québécois Premier Pauline Marois declared her interest in seeing the Équipe-Québec project come to fruition, and appointed a two-person commission (Bob Sirois and André Matteau) to prepare a feasibility study. The *Rapport Sirois-Matteau* was financed by the Quebec government's Ministère de l'Éducation, du Loisir et du Sport and was submitted to a non-profit separatist advocacy body, the Conseil de la Souveraineté du Québec. See Ronald King, "Équipe Québec: l'idée fait son chemin," *La Presse*, 20 June 2013.

21 Patoine, "'*On est Canayen ou ben on l'est pas*,'" 19–20. The translation is by Scott Irving. The original: "Une Équipe Québec … entraînerait un fort sentiment identitaire collectif ; elle ferait partie d'une affirmation nationale concrete. Elle symboliserait par ses 20 joueurs un 'nous' québécois … qui, un soir donné, pourrait croiser le fer avec le 'nous' canadien, un duel qui susciterait au moins autant de passions que les affrontements de 1972 contre L'URSS."

22 See Melançon's *Les yeux de Maurice Richard*; Laurin-Lamothe and Moreau, eds., *Le Canadien de Montréal.*

23 Melançon, "Écrire Maurice Richard," 126. "Dépassent la personne de Richard et peuvent révéler quelque chose de la société Québécoise."

24 Bélanger, "The Last Game?" 299. Bélanger also argues that hockey culture in Quebec feeds a "specifically heterosexual, homophobic, and aggressive form of masculinity."

25 Baril, *Nos Glorieuses*; Detellier, *Mises au jeu*, 20, 47, 76, 240n86.

26 Ignatieff, *Blood and Belonging*, 176.

## Chapter One

The author's thanks go to the Center for the Advancement of Research and Scholarship at Bridgewater State University for support of the research for this chapter, to Dr Andrew Ross for his careful reading of an earlier draft, and to Gilbert Campeau, president of the DHL, who kindly allowed me access to the rich archive of documents housed in the DHL office, Aréna-Ronald-Caron, CEGEP Saint-Laurent, Montreal (hereafter A-R-C).

1 André Trudelle, "Impressions sur la Ligue Dépression," *22e Festival Sportif: Ligue de Hockey Depression*, 1955, 40: "Un plaisantin a dit un jour qu'il n'existait que deux importants compagnies au monde: le Pacifique Canadien et la religion Catholique. Il se trompait car il avait omis de mentionner la Ligue de hockey Dépression." All DHL festival/carnival programs, 1935–60, can be found in A-R-C.

2 Hood, "The Sportive Centre of Saint Vincent de Paul," 39.

3 Morrow and Wamsley, *Sport in Canada*, 140–3.

4 "Verdun Welcomes Skating Champion," *Montreal Gazette*, 11 March 1947, 13. The French-language coverage was equally glowing. See "Verdun recoît royalement Mlle Scott," *La Patrie*, 3 March 1947.

5 See, for example, Holman, ed., *Canada's Game*; Whitson and Gruneau, eds., *Artifical Ice*; Wong, ed., *Coast to Coast*; and Stevens and Holman, eds., "Rinkside."

6 See, for example, the Canadian Adult Recreational Hockey Association (CARHA), which started life in 1974 as the Canadian Oldtimers Hockey Association, http://www.carhahockey.ca/91/first-period (accessed 16 March 2013). In Quebec the term old-timers hockey is sometimes translated into the equally jocular term "has-been" hockey. In the case of the DHL, with an average player age of about thirty years, either term is a misnomer.

7 See, for example, Ignatieff, *Blood and Belonging*, 173–7; Gaston, *Midnight Hockey*.

8 See Gruneau and Whitson, *Hockey Night in Canada*; Lorenz and Osborne, "'Talk about Strenuous Hockey'"; Allain "'Real Fast and Tough'"; Barlow, "'Scientific Aggression.'"

9 One should not use the past tense here; the DHL has operated continuously since it was founded and still exists today, though it is arguably a very different creature. The original impetus for the league started with a group of friends from Saint-Adèle (including Conrad Archambault) who became the core of the DHL's Hobos.

10 "Ephemerides," *Ligue de Hockey Dépression presente son 19ième Festival Sportif*, 1952, 9, 47. Today's teams remain the Hobos, Grads, Sages, and Totem.

11 Having been built in 1929–30, the DHL moved into an arena that was almost brand new. Its opening was attended by Montreal Canadiens players. See "Historique CEGEP de St-Laurent," http://www.cegep-st-laurent.qc.ca/cegep/profil/historique/ (accessed 1 January 2016).

12 "Dépressionalités," *Bottin*, 1952–53, 2. This and all other DHL bottins, 1935–60, can be found in A-R-C.

13 "On joue pour s'amuser, tout en faisant la charité." On the history of the Saint-Vincent de Paul Society in Canada, see Gauvreau, "Forging a New Space for Lay Male Piety"; Fecteau and Vaillancourt, "The Saint Vincent de Paul Society and the Catholic Charitable System in Quebec."

14 This phrase was used repeatedly in the DHL discourse. See, for example, "Dépressionalités," *Bottin* 1951–52, 2. Whether *notre* refers to Canadians or *Canadiens* is hard to say; the double entendre made the term even more resonant.

15 Marshall, *Social Origins of the Welfare State*. The DHL's annual contributions were reportedly: 1935 ($300); 1938 ($350); 1939 ($250); 1943 ($700); 1944 ($1,000); 1945 ($1,250); 1947 ($4,500); 1949 ($1,600); 1950 ($1,500); 1951 ($2,500); 1953 ($2,000); 1954 ($2,500); 1955 ($2,500); 1956 ($2,500). See *Bottins*, 1935–56; 1945 festival program; and Louis Vien, Secrétaire SVP, to Monsieur le President, Ligue de Hockey Depression, 25 April 1939. These round figures betray the fact that DHL annual revenues amounted to more than the sums they donated to the SVP, but never by much. The DHL's *Rapport Financier* for 1945–46 shows that, after league expenses and the annual SVP donation, the league's balance was $521.57, which would have covered little more than start-up costs of the following season. *Rapport Financier de la Ligue de Hockey Depression*, Correspondence 1945–46, A-R-C. The relief of the poor in pre-1960s Montreal was a tangle of private, church-based, and municipal

institutions that were divided in orientation and responsibility by language. The onset of the Depression in the 1930s made poor relief an intense public problem but the reluctance of the state to encroach upon Catholic Church terrain (and to "own" the problem) helped to produce a patchwork of providers of indoor and outdoor relief. See Linteau, *L'histoire de Montréal depuis la Confédération*; Rumilly, *Histoire de Montréal*; Sancton, *Governing the Island of Montreal*.

16 See Kidd, "Brand-Name Hockey," in *The Struggle for Canadian Sport*.

17 Canadiens' General Manager Frank Selke and NHL presidents Frank Calder, Mervyn "Red" Dutton, and Clarence Campbell were honored guests at DHL functions. See, for example, *20ième Festival Sportif*, 1953, 2.

18 DHL players Pete Daigle and Edmond Lareau worked as goal judges in the Forum in 1952–53. "Dépressionalités," *Bottin*, 1952–53, 13.

19 DHL President Henry Richardson put in time at the Forum as a minor official in the rink's penalty box. "Les faits saillants de la saison 1958–59," *27e Festival*, 1959, 8.

20 NHL presidents were called upon to decide contested matters in the DHL: first, who could claim the league title in 1942, when two DHL teams finished the season with equal numbers of points; second, whether or not a goal was constituted when, in a freakish happening, a player's slapshot broke a puck in two, only one half of which made its way behind the goalkeeper and over the goal line. See "Red Pulls a Solomon in Split-Puck Debate," *Montreal Standard*, 26 February 1942. In 1947 the DHL officially adopted NHL rules as its own, ordering copies of the professional organization's rule booklet for distribution among its members. See Un Vieux de la Veille, "Événements Passés a L'histoire de la LHD" [sic], *Quatorzième Festival*, 1947, 47.

21 Jacques Beauchamp, "En Causant de la L.H.D. avec Les Canadiens," *21e Festival Sportif*, 1954, 10: "À tout événement, la ligue Dépression est fière d'avoir parmi ses admirateurs tous les membres du club de hockey Les Canadiens, l'orgueil des sportifs de la province de Québec." The article boasted that, besides Harvey and Béliveau, Canadiens Tommy Johnson, Bernard Geoffrion, Paul Masnick, and Baldy MacKay had all been in the Saint-Laurent Arena at one time or another to see the DHL action in the 1953–54 season. See also "Kenny Reardon du Canadiens …," "Dépressionalités," *Bottin*, 1949–50, 14. Maurice Richard and Bernard Geoffrion refereed games in the DHL on occasion. See

"Dépressionalités," *Bottin*, 1951–52, 13; "La Ligne du 'Punch,'" *20ième Festival Sportif*, 1953, 5.

22 Glen Harmon, Buddy O'Connor, Gerry Heffernan, Pit Morin, Nels Crutchfield, Paul Haynes, and Hector "Toe" Blake. See "Dépressionalités," *Bottin*, 1956–57, 18. Gerry McNeil, one-time goaltender for the Canadiens, coached for one year in the DHL after his retirement from the NHL. "McNeil devient coach dans la ligue Dépression," *La Patrie*, 30 September 1954, 21.

23 In addition to the *bottins*, the DHL printed a one-page typescript monthly bulletin that appears to have been for internal consumption only. See, for example, *L.H.D. Bulletin, Montreal, 4 janvier 1945*, Circulaires de la L.H.D, 1944–45, A-R-C.

24 "Dépressionalités," *Bottin*, 1946–47, 2; *Bottin*, 1949–50; "Publicistes," *Bottin*, 1951–52, 9; *Bottin*, 1953–54, 8–9; "L'Organisateur du Festival," *17ième Festival Sportif*, 1950, 6.

25 "Bienvenue à Nos Journalistes," *Bottin*, 1948–49, 12. See also "Nos Amis les Journalistes," *Bottin*, 1955–56, 9.

26 See "Depression Hockey League Organized Here," *Quebec Chronicle-Telegraph*, 13 October 1955, 11; "Dépressionalités," *Bottin*, 1947–48, 10; Roland Forget, Joliette, to La Directeur, La Ligue Depression, Montreal, 17 January 1945, LHD 1944 Correspondence, A-R-C; "Skating Has Started on Arena Hockey Rink," *L'Avenir* [Sept Îles], 21 October 1963, 7; "Commentaires Sportifs!" *La Gazette Valleyfield-Beauharnois*, 4 May 1961, 21.

27 For an analysis of this narrative, see Melançon, *Les Yeux de Maurice Richard*.

28 Harvey, "Whose Sweater Is This?"

29 Bélanger, "The Last Game?" 306.

30 See Connell, *Masculinities*; Goffman, *Presentation of Self in Everyday Life*. I am indebted to Cheryl MacDonald's recent PhD thesis "'You! You Can't say That!'" (Concordia University, Montreal, 2016) for her clear articulation of these concepts.

31 See Duhaime, "La construction du père Québécois"; Gossage, "Au nom du père," 59–60; and Gauvreau, *Catholic Origins of Quebec's Quiet Revolution*. The growing literature on the history of masculinity in French Canada includes Morton, "A Man's City"; Vacante, "Evolving Racial Identity and the Consolidation of Men's Authority in Early

Twentieth-Century Quebec"; Vacante, "Liberal Nationalism and the Challenge of Masculinity Studies in Quebec"; and Bienvenue and Hudon, "Pour devenir homme, tu transgresseras …"

32 Harvey, "Sport and the Quebec Clergy."

33 For example, Rev. Gérard Gendron, CSC, appears among the "Invités d'honneur" [sic] in the 1955, 1956, and 1960 DHL festival programs; he was joined by Rev. Père Lapalme in 1953. Curate Gédéon Sanche presented one of the league's trophies in 1951. "Potins," *18ième Festival Sportif*, 1951, 35: "Un facteur important des succès de notre organisation"; "a été la bienveillante coopération des Religieux de Ste-Croix, propriétaires de l'aréna St-Laurent." See also "Dépressionalités," *Bottin*, 1951–52, 2.

34 *8ième Carnaval Sportif*, 1941, 2: "À l'occasion de la fête de la 'St. Patrick,' la ligue offre ses meilleurs voeux à ses amis Irlandais."

35 "Nouvelles et Impressions," *Quatorzième Festival*, 1947, 11: "Il y a dans la Ligue 67 membres réguliers, soit 6 directeurs, 12 officiels, 44 joueurs et 6 instructeurs et gérants, de ce nombre, il y en a dix qui ont des noms a consonance anglaise, à savoir: Russell Newell, J.P. McConvey, Bill O'Brien, Jerry Sullivan, Rod. Merrill, Earl Smith, Louis Ferguson, Paul Haynes, Jerry Heffernan et Henry Richardson; tous sont des 'Citoyens Canadiens,' mais cinq sont canadiens-français, quatre canadiens-irlandais et un canadien-anglais."

36 The same sort of ambiguity is reflected in the DHL's attitude toward Canada's participation in the Second World War, "Canada's War." Montreal was home to both the country's largest open anti-war demonstrations and significant numbers of volunteers for the war effort, and the DHL reflected this mix. The results of one questionnaire circulated among the league's members in the fall of 1940, not long after the National Mobilization Resources Act was issued in June, authorizing universal registration for home defence, was telling. "Avez-vous fait votre entraînement militaire?" one question asked, anticipating, perhaps, an imminent exodus from team rosters. Of the forty-five responses gathered, thirty-three said "non"; two "non!"; five "oui"; and four left it blank. One player responded: "Je l'ignore." As the war progressed, and as former DHL players were killed and wounded in action, imprisoned as POWs, and celebrated as heroes, the league openly embraced them, sent them Christmas baskets, and lauded their sacrifices in the war effort in its *bottins* and as honoured guests at the annual festival. And once

peace resumed, all one-time DHLers-cum-war veterans were honoured with a special dinner at the downtown Windsor Hotel and guaranteed their old roster spots, if and when they should return. See "LHD 40–41," A-R-C; "Tableau d'Honneur: Anciens Membres de la L.H.D. dans les Forces Armées," *10ième Carnaval*, 1943, 14; ibid., *11ième Carnaval*, 1944, 16; "Dépressionalités," *Bottin*, 1943–44, 2; "Dépressionalités," *Bottin*, 1944–45, 2; "Membres de la Ligue de Hockey Depression en Service Actif," *12ième Festival*, 1945, 16; "Dépressionalités," *Bottin*, 1945–46, 2.

37 The racial "other" that DHL discourse did not embrace or claim is equally revealing. Here the evidence is rarer. French and Catholic, the DHL was also white. Its whiteness was obliquely asserted in the claim in "Dépressionalités" that speculated that, since one coach couldn't arrive at this year's festival in a limousine driven by a Black chauffeur, he had decided to come in a rickshaw driven by the only "Chinaman" in Nicolet County. "Saviez-vous que …" *Carnaval Sportif*, 1942, 10. Another gossip column called player Frank Daigneault, a veteran of several DHL teams, "le 'Juif Errant'" and congratulated the Hobos for accepting this "D.P." "Le Nez Fureteur," *22e Festival Sportif*, 1955, 34.

38 "Programme," *Quatorzième Festival*, 1947, 17.

39 *Bottin*, 1935; *Bottin*, 1943–44, 11; "Dépressionalités," *Bottin*, 1948–49, 15: "Cette Ligue … était entièrement composée de jeunes gens d'affaires et professionels de Montreal"; "Les avocats dament encore le pion dans la L.H.D., étant au nombre de douze, tandis qu'il y en a sept dans l'assurance, cinq comptables, quatre ingénieurs, deux médecins, un notaire, deux dentistes, et un optométriste."

40 One journalist, Bert Soulières of *Le Canada*, called them "l'élite de la ville de Montreal." "Opinion des Journalistes sur la L.H.D.," *Quatorzième Festival*, 1947, 9.

41 "Dépressionalités," *Bottin*, 1951–52, 14; "Dépressionalités," *Bottin*, 1945–46, 11; Beverley Mitchell, "Theatre Owner Played Tennis with the Stars," *Montreal Gazette*, 20 August 1989, D6.

42 "Hier … Aujourd'hui … Demain," *13ième Festival*, 1946, 6: "Plus d'une affaire importante y a pris ses germes"; "Quels précieux contacts!"

43 Behiels, *Prelude to Quebec's Quiet Revolution*, 15.

44 The words belong to Armand Richer of *La Presse*. Quoted in "Opinion des Journalistes sur la L.H.D.," *Quatorzième Festival*, 1947, 9.

45 "Dépressionalités," *Bottin*, 1942–43, 2: "En plus d'être une organisation de

sport et de charité, la Ligue Dépression a son rang dans l'échelle sociale … plus d'un mariage y a été enfanté."

46 For example, in December 1943, the executive ruled to expel Hobos' player Paul Beauchamps after complaints about his rough play from other teams and after a note from his own teammates requesting his removal. Ligue de Hockey Depression Inc. to Paul Beauchamps, 2 December 1943, 1943 file, A-R-C; Letter, "Les membres des HOBOS to Léopold Bernier," 2 December 1943, 1943 file, A-R-C. Most complaints in the 1930s and 1940s concerned rather minor matters, such as players playing without having paid dues in full or the condition of the ice at Saint-Laurent. On the former issue, see Rod Joly to Léo Bernier, 15 February 1946, Correspondence 1945–46; Jean Halde to M. le Secrétaire, 17 February 1947; and Jacques Archambault to Conseil Executif, 21 February 1947, all at A-R-C. On the latter matter, see Pierre H. Bélanger to Leo Bernier, 10 December 1943, A-R-C.

47 Rhéaume Brisebois, "La ligue Dépression, une sorte de Klu Klux Klan à rebours," unknown publication, 4 March 1952, clipping in DHL scrapbook, 1939–52, A-R-C: "Faire partie de la ligue Dépression est un honneur, une attribution dont même les plus humbles se glorifient, et avec raison. En se voyant inscrit au nombres de ses membres, on a l'impression qu'on vient de se joindre à un groupe tout à fait spécial, ne ressemblent en rien à la fierté que vous pouvez éprouver à vous sentir membre de tel ou tel club, organisation sociale, chevaliers de ci ou de ça. C'est une fraternité qui ressemble en quelque sorte à un Klu Klux Klan [sic] voué au bien."

48 See, for example, Pierre H. Bélanger to Rosaire Armand, 6 October 1944, LHD 1944 Correspondence, A-R-C.

49 DHL fees were $6.50 in 1936; $8.75 in 1940–41; $10 in 1943–46; $12.50 in 1946–47; $35 in 1952–53. La Direction to Cher Membre, 19 November 1936, untitled file, A-R-C; "Dépressionalités," *Bottins*, 1943–53.

50 On the founding of the QAHA, see Fred Kerner, "Quebec Amateur Hockey Body Reaches Quarter-Century Mark," *Montreal Gazette*, 19 January 1944, 14, cols, 5, 6. On its continued association with anglo-Quebec, see John Meisel and Vincent Lemieux, *Ethnic Relations in Canadian Voluntary Organizations*, Documents of the Royal Commission on Bilingualism and Biculturalism, 13 (Ottawa: Information Canada 1972). Qtd. in Harvey, "Sport and the Quebec Clergy," 85.

51 "Malgré que son organisation soit 'hors-la-loi,' en vertu de notre

constitution, Wilfrid sera le bienvenu parmi nous, cet hiver." See, for example, Registrar, QAHA, to H. Richardson, Vice-President, Ligue Depression, 1 December 1947, A-R-C; Dépressionalités," *Bottin*, 1950–51, 13. One QAHA attempt to court the DHL to join the provincial organization, in 1955, fell flat. See "Dépressionalités," *Bottin* 1955–56, 16.

52 See Leopold Bernier, President, to Rosaire Armand, 13 January 1948, A-R-C; "Secrétaire" to Rod Joly, 26 January 1948, A-R-C; St-L, "Secrétaire," to Gerald Sullivan, 30 December 1947, A-R-C.

53 "La ligue Dépression vraiment frustrée de la représentation aux Jeux Olympiques," *Le Petit Journal*, 19 Octobre 1947, 65, A-R-C. See also L. Bernier, President, to Al Pickard, President, Canadian Amateur Hockey Association, 9 October 1947, Correspondence 1947–48, A-R-C; A.W. Pickard, President, C.A.H.A., to L. Bernier, 12 October 1947, A-R-C; R. Norman Dawe, 1st Vice-President, C.A.H.A., to Leo Bernier, 24 October 1947, A-R-C. Pickard suggested to Bernier that, by October, the CAHA already had "certain plans" for a 1948 Olympic team and that the DHL bid might have received more serious consideration had it arrived earlier.

54 Roger Lacoste to Leopold Bernier, 18 June 1948. The questionnaire and responses can be found in "LHD Service Club," A-R-C: "Si vous cherchez à imiter les organisations déjà existantes, vous perdrez de votre prestige"; "un club … d'un genre différent."

55 Festival/carnival programs, 1935–60, A-R-C. One unattributed newspaper clipping promoting the 1949 festival promised a bizarre stick-swinging pantomime called "Richard vs. Ezinicki," an ice-dance rendering of a recent, real fight between the two NHLers. The ice dancers were dressed in Toronto Maple Leafs and Montreal Canadiens sweaters. See "Au Festival de la ligue Dépression ce soir," publication and date unknown, DHL scrapbook [c. 1940–54], A-R-C.

56 Mosse, *Image of Man*, 5. On the sporting body and masculine expression, see Park, "Muscles, Symmetry and Action," and Vertinsky, "Aging Bodies, Aging Sport Historians, and the Choreography of Sport History."

57 *Bottins*, 1942–56. With the 1956–57 issue, the DHL ceased publishing demographic statistics on players' ages, heights, weights, and marital status. On the meanings of historical anthropometry among hockey players, see Ross, Cranfield, and Inwood, "Defining the Sport-Industrial Body."

58 "Saviez-vous que," *8ième Carnaval Sportif*, 1941, n.p.; "Jean Halde," *La Patrie*, 7 March 1943, scrapbook, A-R-C: "le mastodonte Pitou St-Germain qui fait osciller la balance à 215 poids"; "Le 'Baquet' de la Ligue, Guy Lefaivre"; "l'embonpoint de Bernard Couvrette"; and Jean "Hippo" Halde, "le plus gros joueur de hockey."

59 "Prix," *8ième Carnaval Sportif*, 1941, 9: "Joueur le mieux Habillé."

60 "À La Session de la Chambre," *13ième Festival*, 1946, 35: "Notre 'Beau Brumel' [sic] est toujours la coqueluche de ces dames." Among the others who were labelled challengers for "le titre de Beau Brummel [sic]" were Roger Coquette, Earl Smith, and Gerry Dorais. See "Dépressionalités," *11ième Carnaval*, 1944, 13. George Bryan "Beau" Brummell was an early-nineteenth-century friend of the future King George IV, who gained notoriety in high society for foppishness in dress and appearance. See Kelly, *Beau Brummell.*

61 "La plupart de ce groupe n'avaient pas chausée patins depuis nombres d'années, hors de leurs tendres enfance au Collège." "Historique de la Ligue de Hockey Dépression" [typescript], 13 February 1939, LHD, 35–7, A-R-C.

62 *13ieme Festival*, 8. Caron's and Thibault's contracts are in "LHD Contrats 1946–47," A-R-C.

63 See, for example, "Toe Blake fait ses débuts dans la ligue Dépression," *La Presse*, 28 October 1952; "O'Connor et Blake, vedettes de la ligue Dépression," *Le Petit Journal*, November 1954. Clippings found in scrapbooks, A-R-C. See also "Pit Morin jouera pour les Sages de la ligue Dépression," *La Patrie*, 19 October 1955, 21; "Harmon jouera dans la ligue Depression," *La Patrie*, 24 October 1956, 24.

64 See "Chambre de Commerce Jr. Potins," *12ième Festival*, 1945, n.p.

65 *Festival Ligue de Hockey Dépression*, 1957–58, 16, 50.

66 "Dépressionalités," *Bottin*, 1952–53, 2: "Ce sont des variés passes de professionnels … je me demande comment je ferais jouer encore."

67 "Saviez-vous Que," *8ième Carnaval Sportif*, 1941, 7: "La Ligue Dépression semble favoriser le mariage."

68 The available average ages of DHL players were: 1942–43 (28.5); 1943–44 (29); 1944–45 (29); 1945–46 (29.5); 1946–47 (30); 1947–48 (31); 1948–49 (31); 1950–51 (31); 1951–52 (30); 1954–55 (31). Source: DHL *Bottins*, 1942–55.

69 "Le Ligue Dépression est de six ans plus vielle que la Ligue Nationale,"

the 1947–48 *Bottin* observed playfully. The average age of NHLers was twenty-six; the average age of DHLers, thirty-one. "Dépressionalités," *Bottin*, 1947–48, 10.

70 Emphasis added. "Dépressionalités," *Bottin*, 1948–49, 14: "L'on aura une occasion d'éprouver la valeur du mariage cette année"; "le champion gardien de but Pierre Bourgoin, un marié de juin dernier, évoluera pour la première fois comme membre de la catégorie *des gens sérieux*."

71 To celebrate the end of Rosaire Armand's bachelorhood, for example, a formal committee of DHLers was struck to plan a party and printed invitations entitled "R.I.P. Le 'Hobo' Rosaire Armand ne couchera plus sous les trains car il se marie …" were circulated: "R.I.P. 'Hobo' Rosaire Armand won't have to sleep under trains anymore, because he's getting married …" Ligue de Hockey Dépression Fonds, Bibliothèque et Archives nationales du Québec, Montreal.

72 The available marital status averages of DHL players were: 1942–43 (28 married [61 per cent]/18 bachelors [39 per cent]); 1943–44 (26 married [57 per cent]/20 bachelors [43 per cent]); 1944–45 (30 married [63 per cent]/18 bachelors [37 per cent]); 1945–46 (32 married [67 per cent]/16 bachelors [33 per cent]); 1946–47 (27 married [62 per cent]/17 bachelors [38 per cent]); 1947–48 (29 married [66 per cent]/15 bachelors [34 per cent]); 1948–49 (29 married [63 per cent]/17 bachelors [37 per cent]); 1949–50 (34 married [76 per cent]/11 bachelors [24 per cent]); 1950–51 (34 married [72 per cent]/13 bachelors [28 per cent]; 1951–52 (30 married [65 per cent]/16 bachelors [35 per cent]); 1953–54 (36 married [82 per cent]/8 bachelors [18 per cent]; 1954–55 (33 married [75 per cent]/11 bachelors [25 per cent]). Source: *Bottins*, 1942–55.

73 "Historique de la Ligue de Hockey Depression," [typescript] 13 February 1939, LHD, 35–7, A-R-C; *Bottin*, 1943–44: "très encouragés par leurs douces moitiés"; "victims de Cupidon."

74 André Racine, "Le Nez Fureteur," *22e Festival Sportif*, 1955; "Dépressionalités," *Bottin*, 1949–50, 14: "les célibataires 'tombent' les uns après les autres."

75 "Dépressionalités," *Bottin*, 1956–57: "Plus d'un mariage y a été engendré"; "des contacts d'affaires créées et des amitiés cimentées.

76 Duhaime, "'Les pères ont ici leur devoirs'"; Gossage, "Au nom du père?"

77 Available statistics for these years are as follows: 1942–43: 28 children;

1943–44: 34; 1944: 34; 1944–45: 38; 1945–46: 39; 1946: 38; 1946–47: 36; 1947–48: 40; 1948–49: 43; 1949–50: 54; 1950–51: 55; 1951–52: 40; 1953: 31; 1954–55: 47. Source: *Bottins*, 1942–55.

78 "Dépressionalités," *Bottin*, 1942–43, 10. See also "Dépressionalités," *Bottin*, 1947–48, 11; "Dépressionalités," *Bottin*, 1952–53, 15: "Bernard Couvrette and Eugene Brouillet sont les champions avec quatre enfants chacun."

79 "Potins," *17ième Festival*, 1950, 31: "Une autre preuve que la dénatalité affecte une nation."

80 See "Dépressionalités," *Bottin*, 1945–46, 11; *Bottin*, 1951–52, 15; *Bottin*, 1955–56, 33; *Bottin*, 1956–57, 19. But, like Barbara Ann Scott, it was as spectators – witnesses to the spectacle of manly self-making – that women were most needed by the DHL. This is expressed graphically in cartoonist Jacques Doyon's cover art in the 1942 festival program. On it, a DHL player in hockey gear and sweater emblazoned with all four team logos is surrounded by a newspaper photographer and journalist and, tellingly, five smiling female admirers. See *11ième Carnaval*, 1944.

81 "Dépressionalités," *Bottin*, 1954–55, 16.

82 "Un Quart de Siècle D'Activités," "Dépressionalités," *Bottin*, 1956–57, 1: "Tout comme un histoire d'un peuple, d'une nation, d'un pays, la L.H.D. à côté de ses heures célèbres, a connu des moments moins heureux, comme par exemple l'avènement du terrible conflit mondial de 1939 qui a décimé ses rangs; elle a connu aussi des intrigues et des guerres intestines qui ont même amené l'expulsion d'une équipe entière peu après sa fondation, et les pires troubles sous plusieurs domaines l'an dernier; mais tel pour un athlète olympique, ce dernier mille le plus ardu s'est terminé par un éclatant triomphe; la L.H.D. a survécu à ces embuches qui ont menacé son existence, pour s'en servir comme d'un tremplin et parvenir plus forte que jamais jusqu'à son JUBILE D'ARGENT."

83 "Dépressionalités," *Bottin*, 1956–57, 19.

84 *Bottin*, 1950–51, 2.

85 See *Bottin*, 1959–60; *Bottin*, 1957–58. The league instituted honorary members in 1944. See *11ième Carnaval*, 13.

86 See "Dépressionalités," *Bottin*, 1955–56, 16.

87 "Les faits saillants de la saison 1958–59," *27e Festival*, 1959, 24. As the old guard retreated from league control, some of the new executive

committee members (such as 1958 president Pierre Paquette) had themselves never played in the DHL. These people held even less basis for authority vis-à-vis the younger generation. See "Notre Festival 1959," *27e Festival*, 1959, 10.

88 "Nos enfants joueront dans la Ligue Dépression," "Dépressionalités," *Bottin*, 1951–52, 2. See also "Discours Prononcé par M. Léopold Bernier, lundi le 26 octobre 1948," typescript, LHD 50, A-R-C; "Dépressionalités," *Bottin*, 1948–49, 2.

89 See, for example, "Nombreux changements dans la ligue de hockey Dépression," *Montreal-Matin*, 23 October 1959; "Plusieurs nouvelles figures à la Ligue de hockey Dépression," *La Presse*, 24 October 1959; "Nombreux changements à la Ligue Depression," *La Presse*, 13 October 1960; scrapbook [1959–61], A-R-C.

90 See "Ice Festival," *Quebec Chronicle-Telegraph*, 5 February 1955, 6; "Équipe des As de la L.H.D.," *22e Festival Sportif*, 1955, 29.

91 This transition toward hyper-competitiveness in the DHL (and its lamentable consequences) was the same sort of slide experienced by Montreal's anglophone amateur clubs in earlier decades, and was warned against and decried publicly by some of its most respected spokesmen and commentators. These included Arthur Farrell in his 1899 book *Hockey: Canada's Royal Winter Game* (esp. 35, 42–3) and Montreal surgeon Sir Henry Gray in his 1933 address to the Montreal Amateur Athletic Association, "The Game of Hockey and Responsibility." See Farrell, *Hockey*, and Holman, "Curing Hockey's Ills."

92 The editor of "Dépressionalités" was amused (not alarmed) to discover that a rival old-timers league had refused admission to an ex-DHLer, Al Garbarino, "parce qu'il était trop rude." Dépressionalités, *Bottin*, 1953–54, 14.

93 Marc Thibault, "Le hockey est décidément trop rude," *Petit Journal*, 15 March 1953, 98.

94 "Dépressionalités," *Bottin*, 1954–55, 1, A-R-C.

95 Jacques Beauchamp, "Le Sport en Général," *Montréal-Matin*, 19 January 1956, 24: "On se demande maintenant si le fait de démantibuler son adversaire, de porter les bâtons trop élevés, de déclencher des combats sur la glace répond bien à la devise: 'L'ON JOUE POUR S'AMUSER.'" See also "'Le jeu est trop rude dans la L.H.D.': Marcel Tremblay," *La Presse*, n.d., 1956, clipping in LHD scrapbook, 1939–52, A-R-C.

96 André Trudelle, "L'instructeur Laviolette suspend pour une partie," January 1958 clipping in LHD scrapbook, 1939–52, A-R-C.

97 "Faits Saillants de la Saison 1955-56," *23e Festival*, 1956, 31.

98 "La charité et la sincérité, les deux belles traditions qui ont rendu la Ligue de Hockey Dépression célèbre ont disparu d'une façon notoire et alarmante … La majorité des nouveaux joueurs de la L.H.D. ne comprennent pas la raison d'être de la Ligue, 'On joue pour s'amuser, tout en faisant la charité.' Certain gérants ne se donnent même pas la peine d'expliquer à leurs joueurs quels sont les devoirs d'un membre. Avec une telle mentalité, on a affaibli dangereusement la structure de notre organisation au point de nuire grandement à sa subsistance." Léopold Bernier to Henry Richardson [copy], 5 April 1957, LHD 50, A-R-C. Richardson's response to Bernier is not known, but a sharply worded circular to prospective members instructing them on the league's aims and the expectations it had for each member followed soon thereafter. See Henry Richardson to Cher Ami de la L.H.D., n.d., Charles Mayer Fonds, Library and Archives of Canada, Ottawa.

99 "Pages Sportives," *La Presse*, 6 March 1959; scrapbook, "Ligue de Hockey Depression Inc., 1957–58," A-R-C.

## Chapter Two

This chapter was translated by Jason Blake.

1 Ross, *Joining the Clubs*, 9.

2 As hockey quickly spread across the country between 1895 and the First World War, it began to transcend class boundaries too, but only gradually, and it maintained much of its prescriptive "gentlemanly" imprimatur and its middle-class character. Hockey commentators, from (former Collège Sainte-Marie player) Arthur Farrell in his 1899 book *Hockey: Canada's Royal Game* to Sir Henry Gray in his 1933 address to the Montreal Amateur Athletic Club, worried continuously about hockey becoming plebeian in content and character. In French Canada, where hockey got a relatively late start and faced some opposition from Catholic clergy, hockey remained situated largely among the urban petit bourgeoisie, the francophone counterparts to the anglophone members of the Montreal Amateur Athletic Association, and those who attended the city's classical colleges and populated the first francophone sports associations, such

as the Association Athlétique d'Amateurs Canadiens-Français and the Association Athlétique d'Amateurs Nationale. See Metcalfe, *Canada Learns to Play*; Wong, *Lords of the Rinks*; Janson, *Emparons-nous du sport*; Holman, "Curing Hockey's Ills."

3 The only scholarly works to deal with early francophone hockey at any length are Guay, *L'histoire du hockey au Québec*, and Vigneault, "La naissance d'un sport organisé au Canada." In English, the following have touched briefly on the subject: Metcalfe, *Canada Learns to Play*; Gruneau and Whitson, *Hockey Night in Canada*; Wong, *Lords of the Rinks*.

4 The Amateur Hockey Association of Canada was formed in 1886–87 and was the first league. That league received the first Stanley Cup, won by the MAAA in 1893. When hockey was professionalized in 1906–07, the Stanley Cup trustees were not sure how to deal with the new hockey reality. For the 1884 Canadian Amateur Athletic Association's definition of "amateur," see Don Morrow et al., *A Concise History of Sport in Canada*, 181.

5 In 1885 the archbishop of Montreal, Mgr Édouard-Charles Fabre, banished tobogganing, among other physical activities, for its corrupting effects on French Canadian youth. Janson, *Emparons-nous du sport*, 36.

6 For an in-depth discussion, see Vigneault, "La naissance d'un sport organisé au Canada."

7 A prominent exception was Charles Lamothe, who by the end of the 1880s was captain of the Montreal Victorias.

8 "Collège classique," http://www.thecanadianencyclopedia.ca/en/article/college-classique (accessed 31 March 2016).

9 Pinto, "Ain't Misbehaving." For discussions of "manliness" and class considerations, see Barlow, "Scientific Aggression," 35–85, and Holman in this volume.

10 *Journal du Grand Conseil des Jeux*, Collège Ste-Marie, Archives SJCF, Saint-Jérôme.

11 Collège Sainte-Marie players, 1894: Jack Brennan, Arthur Farrell, John J. Harty, Walter Kiernan, D'Arcy McGee, Hugh Semple, Harry Trihey; 1895: Lorne Campbell, Dunstan Gray, William Hingston, D'Arcy McGee, John Meagher, William O'Brien, Harry Trihey; 1896: Arthur Farrell, Dunstan Gray, Georges Magnan, D'Arcy McGee, J. Mercier, William O'Brien, Ernest Pagnuelo, Harry Trihey. Mont Saint-

Louis players, 1895: Bauce, Louis Belcourt, Marcotte, Joseph Dostaler, Patrick McKenna, A. Monck, A. Panet, W. Peacock, Frank Tansey, F.X. Valade, R. Valade, Wilson. Saint-Laurent players, 1900: Henri Alleyn, Hervé Dagenais, Marion Horace Gohier, Rosaire Kent, Stephen Kent, J. Létourneau, F. Saint-Cyr. Sources: *La Presse* (1894–96, 1900), *La Patrie* (1894–96, 1900), *Montreal Daily Star* (1894–96, 1900), *Gazette* (1894–96, 1900).

12 The ethnic mix is implied by the names on the 1896 Orioles team roster, 1896: Louis Belcourt, Jack Brennan, Arthur Farrell, Dunstan Gray, Hudon, Walter Kiernan, Paul Lacoste, J. Mercier, E. O'Brien, Ernest Pagnuelo, Harry Trihey. Sources: *La Presse* (1896), *La Patrie* (1896), *Montreal Daily Star* (1896), *Gazette* (1896).

13 According to "Victoire du Collège Ste-Marie," *La Patrie*, 25 January 1899, 7, Louis Belcourt was a Sainte-Marie student.

14 The term "Old League" is used here because this league (Amateur Hockey Association of Canada, 1886–98; Canada Amateur Hockey League, 1899–1905; Eastern Canada Amateur Hockey Association, 1905–09) changed its name so many times between 1887 and 1910. The "Vieille ligue" is the term most often used by French-language newspapers of the time.

15 "Quelques joueurs du club de hockey Laval, de Montréal," *La Presse*, 10 February 1900, 3.

16 Guay, *L'histoire du hockey*, 129.

17 Université Laval at Montreal roster, 1900: Joseph Archambault, J.R. Bélanger, Hector Bisaillon, Raoul Bonin, Émilien Brais, Hector Dalbec, Henri Delorimier, Napoléon Dorval, Louis Hurtubise, P. Jobin, Paul Laflamme, Georges Magnan, Henri Ménard, Georges Molleur, Tassé. Sources: *La Presse* (1900), *La Patrie* (1900).

18 Gilles Janson and Normand Charbonneau, *Répertoire numérique simple du fonds de la Palestre Nationale*, Archives UQAM, March 1988.

19 The Montreal Amateur Athletic Association was formed in 1878 as a merger of three different clubs: Montreal Bicycle Club, Montreal Lacrosse Club, and Montreal Snowshoe Club. For the history of the club, see Morrow, *A Sporting Evolution: The Montreal Amateur Athletic Association, 1881–1981* (Montreal: MAAA 1981).

20 These tallies were drawn from newspaper game reports in *La Presse* (1895), *La Patrie* (1895), *Montreal Daily Star* (1895), and the *Gazette*

(1895). In 1896 there was a team called the Lilac from Mont Saint-Louis, with the same players as in 1895.

21 *Star*, 25 January 1895.

22 "Le National and Montreal South draw," *Star*, 14 January 1895.

23 "Le club National," *La Presse*, 3 April 1895, 4. "Tout indique que les Canadiens-français dans les choses du sport, comme dans toutes les autres sphères où se meut l'activité humaine, ne sont pas inférieurs aux autres races."

24 *Procès-Verbaux du National, 1895–1900*, Archives UQAM, 1P2–34.

25 "Le National, réorganisation de notre association athlétique," *La Patrie*, 1 March 1898, 7; "ce qui préoccupe maintenant les directeurs du National, c'est la formation des équipes de crosse."

26 "L'application du National, rejetée par la ligue intermédiaire de hockey qui préfère le Westmount à notre club," *La Patrie*, 11 December 1899, 2.

27 "Admission du National, du Montagnards et du PAAA," *La Presse*, 10 December 1900, 3.

28 "The Montagnards Club," *Gazette*, 27 November 1896.

29 "Le Montagnard, le nouveau patinoir," *La Presse*, 4 December 1897, 2. Note the masculine form of "patinoir," which was the contemporary usage.

30 The Montagnards 1898 rosters – Junior District League team: T. Bald, Charles Conrad, Eddy Cummings, Cusson, Denicourt, F. Dufresne, F. Nesbitt Jobin, Armand Lacroix, J. Mercier, A. Proulx, Rhéaume; City League team: Beaulieu, Hector Bisaillon, F. Charlebois, Joseph Coutlée, Eddy Cummings, Paul Laflamme, J. Moisan, Ed. Morin, Pelletier, Ed. Robert, Wall. Sources: *La Presse* (1898), *La Patrie* (1898), *Montreal Daily Star* (1898), *Gazette* (1898). It is has not proved possible to track down the players from the third team.

31 "At the Montagnards Rink," *Star*, 1 February 1899, 2. The more experienced Shamrock team won 7–4.

32 "La partie de samedi," *La Patrie*, 19 March 1900, 2. Except for Jobin and Bélanger, all the Montagnards players were from Université Laval. See J. Marier, "Le club de hockey Le Montagnards," *La Patrie*, 17 February 1900, 12.

33 And not just in hockey. As Donald Guay notes, referring to the National's lacrosse team: "To the various criticisms they receive about this subject, the directors of the club [the National] respond that it is

better to have a winning team that includes more English than a losing team consisting almost exclusively of French Canadians." ("Aux diverses critiques qu'ils reçoivent à ce sujet, les directeurs du club [le National] répondent qu'il vaut mieux avoir une équipe gagnante qui comprenne plusieurs Anglais, qu'une équipe perdante comprenant presque exclusivement des Canadiens français.") Guay, *Introduction à l'histoire des sports au Québec*, 92.

34 "The Game on the Ice," *Gazette*, 9 December 1899, 2.

35 "La partie de samedi," *La Presse*, 19 March 1900, 2.

36 "Admission du National, du Montagnards et de la PAAA," *La Presse*, 10 December 1900, 3.

37 "La première victoire, le Montagnards défait le National," *La Patrie*, 3 January 1901, 2. "L'équipe du Montagnard s'est montrée hier soir supérieure à celle du National, comme on s'y attendait bien un peu … ils se reconnaissaient un certain degré d'infériorité, mais cette infériorité, en réalité, n'existe que dans le manque d'ensemble des joueurs de l'attaque."

38 "Les Montagnards sont vainqueurs, mais les Montreal sont champions," *La Patrie*, 23 February 1901, 2.

39 *La Presse*, 21 December 1901.

40 Early Montreal anglophone hockey clubs seem to have been only a little more stable in their organization than the National and the Montagnards, likely because of the sound model that the MAAA provided them and because the vibrant culture of sport that thrived among English-speaking middle-class men in Victorian Montreal offered ample numbers of recruits. But this impression stands to be confirmed by more research. On Victorian sporting culture in Montreal, see, for example, Metcalfe, *Canada Learns to Play*; Poulter, *Becoming Native in a Foreign Land*; Morrow, "The Little Men of Iron."

41 Meanwhile, the Shamrocks and the PAAA wanted to have teams in the "Junior AHAC" in 1902. After having met with refusal, the two clubs asked the Montagnards to join them in forming a new junior league (See *La Presse*, 17 December 1901). The Montreal Junior Hockey League was comprised of six teams, namely, the Shamrocks, the PAAA, the Montagnards, Heather, the Crystal, and St Lawrence. The four players from the 1901 National team were on the Montagnards' junior squad, and four others were from Collège Sainte-Marie, which also explains the weakness of the National the previous year.

42 "La situation actuelle," *La Presse*, 15 January 1902, 3.

43 "Chez le Montagnard," *La Presse*, 18 December 1902, 3. "Il est absolument inutile d'appartenir à un corps où il ne saurait y avoir de l'avancement"; "Alors, à quoi bon faire partie d'une ligue qui n'occasionne que des dépenses? A quoi bon former des joueurs pour se les faire enlever par les clubs de la vieille ligue? … Le Montagnard aura cependant un club cette saison mais ce sera un club indépendant et il arrangera autant de parties que possible avec les clubs qu'il jugera à propos."

44 *La Presse*, 13 January 1902. "Hurtubise et Viau, les deux joueurs du Montagnard, faisaient merveille"; "Le premier sur la division d'attaque se faisait remarquer par ses courses hardies et son adresse étonnante ... enlever le caoutchouc à l'adversaire et s'élancer dans la direction opposée avec une vitesse étonnante ... Viau sur la défense … excella à débarrasser le terrain, à écarter le danger … et il les repoussa souvent d'un solide coup d'épaule."

45 "The Shamrocks' New Players," *Star*, 14 January 1902, 2.

46 "Du grabuge chez les hockeyistes," *La Patrie*, 1 December 1903, 2.

47 The following season, 1907, four of the six teams were semi-pro (though not MAAA and Victorias). This came at the same time of the "Athletic War" (1906–09). As to the question whether it was possible for amateurs to play with and against pro athletes and still remain "amateur," see Morrow, "A Case-Study in Amateur Conflict," 173–90.

48 Guay, *L'histoire du hockey au Québec*, 246.

49 Ibid.

50 The National team rosters, 1904 – Senior: Henri Ménard, Théophile Viau, Stephen Kent, Albert Prévost, J. Décary, Jack Laviolette, Wilfrid Viau, Joseph Dostaler, Didier Pitre; Intermediate: L. Mireault, Hector Collin, Didier Pitre, P. Kent, C. Clément, Albert Clément, Albert Millaire, Paul Laflamme, Wilfrid Viau, S. Bellerose, Joseph Dostaler, Brunet, A. Ducket, F. Desjardins. Sources: *La Presse* (1904), *La Patrie* (1904), *Montreal Daily Star* (1904), *Gazette* (1904).

51 "Le club de hockey National," *La Presse*, 2 April 1904, 11.

52 "Une réponse à M. Foran," *La Patrie*, 24 October 1904, 2.

53 "New Senior Club is Montagnards," *Gazette*, 26 October 1904, 2.

54 Montagnards, 1905: Henri Ménard, Théophile Viau, Rosaire Kent, Édouard Millaire, Albert Millaire, Hector Collin, L. Mireault, Pierre Champagne, Hector Desjardins, Albert Clément; National, 1905: Joseph

Cattarinich, Jack Ladéroute, Millette, Joseph Dostaler, Didier Pitre, W. Ladéroute, Préfontaine, Ernest Garon, Vendette, A. Duckett. Sources: *La Presse* (1905), *La Patrie* (1905), *Montreal Daily Star* (1905), *Gazette* (1905).

55 "Commentaires justes," *La Patrie*, 18 December 1905, 2.

56 There is almost no information to be found about the other National players.

57 *La Presse*, 20 January 1905.

58 "Les Nationals se retirent," *La Patrie*, 26 January 1905, 2. "Privés des services des bons joueurs sur qui ils fondaient leurs espérances et abandonnés de ceux qui devaient les encourager en autant qu'ils auraient mis sur pied une équipe digne d'encouragement, les directeurs du National ont résolu définitivement hier de se retirer de la ligue, de la C.A.H.L., tout en conservant le droit d'y appartenir de nouveau l'an prochain."

59 "La ligue est formée. Six clubs en feront partie," *La Patrie*, 12 December 1905, 2.

60 "Commentaires justes," *La Patrie*, 18 December 1905, 2.

61 Metcalfe, *Canada Learns to Play*, 123.

62 "Le Montagnard et sa position actuelle dans le monde du hockey," *La Presse*, 20 December 1905, 3. "Qu'avons-nous à y voir, et comment sommes-nous responsables de ce qui est arrivé dans la C.A.H.L., dont nous ne faisons pas partie? … Le National prêche la concorde, l'union en nous attaquant, nous conspuant, nous attaquant personnellement, en proclamant que le public est avec lui, et il n'a même pas de glace … M. Mercier [président du National] explique la défaite de son club par le fait d'un conflit d'ambitions entre certains clubs anglais et il prend une colonne pour l'expliquer … Il ne doit y avoir qu'un club canadien-français de hockey! Fort bien, nous sommes dans la Ligue [sic], nous avons nos joueurs, nous avons notre patinoire."

63 "Montagnards and Nationals Have Met," *Star*, 30 January 1906, 2.

64 "Montagnards Lost," *Gazette*, 30 January 1906, 2.

65 "Brillante victoire, le National anéantit le Montagnards hier soir," *La Patrie*, 30 January 1906, 2. "Nous avons un club canadien-français de première force et de taille à se mesurer avec ... les champions actuels."

66 Guay, *L'histoire du hockey au Québec*, 252.

67 "Le club Saguenay victorieux," *Le Progrès du Saguenay*, 1 March 1906. I

thank Guy Villeneuve for providing me with a copy of this article.

68 Guay, *L'histoire du hockey au Québec*, 252.

69 Team rosters, Montagnards and National, 30 January 1906 – Montagnards: R. Wright (goal), Doran (point), Stephen Kent (cover point), Ralph Mireault (forward), Rosaire Kent (forward), Pierre Champagne (forward), Charles Lunan (forward); National: Paul Lavigne (goal), Richard Duckett (point), Hector Dalbec (cover point), Albert Millaire (forward), Joseph Dostaler (forward), Édouard Millaire (forward), Wilfrid Viau (forward). Source: "Montagnard Lost," *Gazette*, 30 January 1906, 2.

70 Richard Duckett is considered to be francophone on the basis of a 1985 discussion with Zotique Lespérance, a former *Journal de Montréal* journalist who knew this player.

71 "Montagnards Resign from Federal League but Want to Keep the Franchise," *Star*, 9 February 1906, 2.

72 Guay, *L'histoire du hockey au Québec*, 253.

73 Diamond and Romain, *Hockey Hall of Fame*, 39.

74 Montagnards roster, 1907: Joseph Dostaler, Raymond Hébert, Gustave Lambert, W.E. Lannon, Joseph Leblanc, Jack Marshall, Henri Ménard, Édouard Millaire, Albert Prévost, F. Strike, Théophile Viau, Wilfrid Viau. Sources: *La Presse* (1907), *La Patrie* (1907), *Montreal Daily Star* (1907), *Gazette* (1907). Though their services would have been in high demand, there is no evidence that Marshall or the others were paid to play for the Montagnards.

75 "Montagnards Played Draw, Six All Score with Vics when Time Was Called," *Montreal Gazette*, 25 February 1907, 2.

76 "Une décision injuste," *La Patrie*, 7 February 1907, 2. The game was replayed on 20 February 1907.

77 "Le Montagnards se retire de la Ligue Fédérale," *La Presse*, 8 March 1907. "Après avoir été cruellement dupé maintes fois par les clubs de nationalités étrangères, le Montagnard, malgré le déficit qu'accusent ses livres, était décidé de continuer quand même la lutte parce qu'il entrevoyait le titre glorieux de champion de la Ligue Fédérale, mais ces jours derniers, ses adversaires jaloux qui n'avaient pu vaincre nos athlètes sur la glace résolurent d'anéantir leurs victoires dans les assemblées de ligue. Rien de plus facile et ils le comprirent bien, car le président de la

ligue se trouve en même temps représentant du club Cornwall ... C'est ainsi que le Montagnard se vit enlever successivement trois victoires par des protestations futiles et ridicules qui néanmoins trouvaient toujours des adeptes. Dernièrement, pour ne citer qu'un exemple, le Montagnard battait le Cornwall par un score de 7 à 3, ce dernier protesta sans rire qu'il y avait un joueur du Shamrock dans les rangs du Montagnard tandis que lui-même en eut deux pendant toute la saison et que les Victorias [Ottawa] veulent maintenant avoir l'équipe entière des Ottawa [Senators de la E.C.A.H.A.] à leur place ... Dans ces circonstances là, il était inutile pour le Montagnard de continuer à vaincre sur la glace pour être ensuite vaincu par les magnats de la ligue, mais il sera toujours glorieux de pouvoir proclamer bien haut qu'il n'a subi qu'une seule défaite cette année et encore faut-il ajouter qu'elle lui fut infligée par un referee [sic] intéressé et non par une équipe de joueurs."

78 "Le Montagnards. Il demandera à la Ligue Fédérale de lui accorder le titre de champion qu'il a gagné," *La Presse*, 7 December 1907, 15.

79 Only Eddie Robitaille (who appeared at the Quebec Bulldogs' training camp for the 1910 season but did not make the team) was a stranger to Montrealers. According to Durand's *La Coupe à Québec*, Robitaille played for the Pittsburgh Bankers of the International League; it is unclear whether he was from Quebec or Ottawa.

80 The National team line-up on 10 March 1909: Émile Coutu (goal), Université Laval; Jack Laviolette (point), Shamrocks; Didier Pitre (cover-point), Renfrew; Eddie Robitaille (forward), Pittsburgh; Édouard Lalonde (forward), Cornwall; Joseph Dostaler (forward), Université Laval; Alphonse Jetté (forward), Théâtre National Français. Source: "Le National fait bonne figure," *La Presse*, 11 March 1909, 3.

81 "Le National fait bonne figure," *La Presse*, 11 March 1909, 3. "Un millier de personnes environ a vu hier soir l'équipe canadienne-française qui jouait sous les couleurs du National, faire une vaillante lutte aux Wanderers, au patinoir [sic] Jubilée. Les ex-champions sont sortis victorieux de la rencontre par un score de 10 à 9, mais les joueurs canadiens ont démontré qu'ils étaient de taille à lutter avec les plus puissants clubs de la ligue professionnelle. Comme on peut se le figurer, le jeu de notre équipe manquait un peu d'ensemble, car ses membres avaient été recrutés à droite, et à gauche. Il n'y a aucun doute que si les mêmes joueurs pratiquaient quelque temps ensemble, ils formeraient

une formidable agrégation. Jetté a été toute une surprise. C'était là sa première partie senior, et il a accompli des prodiges. C'est une future étoile. La joute d'hier soir a démontré que la Ligue Professionnelle [sic] ferait une bonne acquisition en admettant l'an prochain le National dans ses rangs."

82 "French team fast," *Gazette*, 11 March 1909, 2.

83 Ibid.

84 *Constitution et règlements de l'Association Athlétique d'Amateurs Nationale de Montréal, 1910*, "Fonds Palestre Nationale," Archives UQAM.

85 "The Canadian Athletic Club held meeting," *Star*, 17 November 1908, 2.

86 "French Canadians Want to Be in with Senior Hockey," *Star*, 7 November 1908, 8.

87 O'Brien, *Les Canadiens*, 6.

88 "Five Leagues Here: Montréal Will Have a Big Bill of Senior Hockey This Week," *Gazette*, 27 November 1909, 2.

89 O'Brien, *Les Canadiens*, 7.

90 Mouton, *Les Canadiens de Montréal*, 21.

91 *Constitution et règlements de l'Association Athlétique d'Amateurs Nationale de Montréal*, 1.

92 Ibid., 1. "Néanmoins et nonobstant ce qui est ci-dessus, l'Association pourra employer un ou plusieurs joueurs professionnels qui ne devront pas être membres de l'Association, et ils pourront jouer pour l'Association ou contre les clubs ou associations qui pourront être les adversaires de l'Association, et ce sans préjudice à l'état d'amateur des membres de l'Association."

93 See "There Is Talk of Extending the National Hockey Association and Taking Another Club," *Star*, 15 December 1909, 2. The respective rosters were: Canadiens – Joseph Cattarinich, Jack Laviolette, Didier Pitre, Édouard Lalonde, Edmond Décarie, Arthur Bernier, Georges Poulin; National – Henri Ménard, L. Paré, Didier Pitre, Édouard Lalonde, Edmond Décarie, Émile Dubeau, Edgar Leduc.

94 "Une course peu banale," *La Patrie*, 13 December 1909, 2.

95 O'Brien, *Les Canadiens*, 9.

96 Ibid., 9. "Didier Pitre devra jouer avec le National," *La Patrie*, 4 January 1910, 2.

97 "The Pitre Decision and Lacrosse," *Star*, 26 February 1910, 14.

98 Janson and Charbonneau, *Répertoire numérique*, Archives UQA, 1988.

99 The CHA and NHA teams at the time of the merger were: CHA – All-Montreal, National, Shamrocks, Ottawa, Quebec); NHA – Canadiens, Wanderers, Cobalt, Haileybury, Renfrew. Sources: *La Presse* (1910), *Le Devoir* (1910), *Montreal Daily Star* (1910), *Gazette* (1910).

100 "Le National n'existe plus," *La Patrie*, 18 January 1910, 2. "1° que l'association se rende responsable de toutes les dettes contractées jusqu'ici par le Canadien; 2° que l'association joue toutes ses parties au Jubilee durant 3 ans; 3° que l'association paye la somme de $1,400 ou à peu près, dette contractée jusqu'ici par le Canadien; 4° que l'association paye aux joueurs du Canadien la somme de $6,200, ce qui représente le salaire des joueurs du Canadien pour la saison."

101 *Gazette officielle du Québec*, 1916, vol. 1, 880.

## Chapter Three

This chapter was translated by Jason Blake.

1 Holman, ed., *Canada's Game*, 4.

2 French Canadians and Québécois see the Montreal Canadiens as a symbolic justification of their existence, including the sense of a common struggle to defend the honour and pride of francophones. Québécois cultural nationalism was deployed after the 1940s in solidarity with French Canadian cultural nationalism. However, the two nationalist streams have differed in other respects, especially since 1967, when the Québécois nationalist movement distanced itself from the federalist French Canadian goal of defending the French language within Confederation. Québécois aspirations were aimed at statehood. See Martel, *Le deuil d'un pays imaginé*, 17–18, 139–65.

3 A. Smith, *Nationalism*; A. Smith, *National Identity*; Özkirimli, *Theories of Nationalism*.

4 Nielsen, "Un nationalisme culturel, ni ethnique ni civique," 143–59; Ipperciel, "La Suisse," 39–67; Seymour, *La nation en question*, 206; Billig, *Banal Nationalism*.

5 Lapierre, "À toi pour toujours?" 1–24.

6 Gagnon, Lecours, Nootens, eds., *Les nationalismes majoritaires contemporains*, 24–6.

7 Picoche and Marchello-Nizia, *Histoire de la langue française*, 31–5.

8 Anderson, *L'imaginaire national*, 87; Smith, *National Identity*, 81;

Dieckhoff, "Nationalisme politique contre nationalisme culturel?" 113–15.
9 Schleicher, "Education and Nationalism," 33.
10 Gellner, *Thought and Change*, 162–5.
11 Séguin, *Histoire de deux nationalismes au Canada.*
12 Martel and Pâquet, *Langue et politique au Canada et au Québec.*
13 Bégin, *Loyalisme et fanatisme.*
14 Martel and Pâquet, *Langue et politique au Canada et au* Québec, 13–14.
15 For comparative and international perspectives on sport and nationalism, see: Sugden and Bairner, "'Ma, There's a Helicopter on the Pitch!'"; Riordan, *Sport in Soviet Society*; Antohi, "De l'État-nation à l'État-parti roumain"; Mangan, "Imperial Education in British Tropical Africa"; Deville-Danthu, *Le Sport en noir et blanc*; MacClancy, "Nationalism at Play"; Duch, *Futbol, metàfora d'una guerra Freda*; Maclean, "Almost the Same but not Quite"; Morhouse, "Scotland against England"; Sen, "History without a Past."
16 Harvey, "Force physique, citoyenneté et réformisme modéré au Bas-Canada," 20.
17 Taché quoted in ibid., 81. "Faute d'exercice, et conséquemment de force et de rigueur, notre jeunesse devient craintive, irrésolue, moutonnière; et comment en serait-il autrement? Le courage et l'audace ne naissent-ils pas de la confiance qui, chez l'individu, n'est autre chose que la conviction intime de son habileté à vaincre tous les obstacles, à triompher de tous les dangers? Ainsi, sans exercice, point de force; sans force, point de confiance en soi; sans confiance en soi, point d'hommes vaillants, mais des êtres faibles lâches et pusillanimes …"
18 Janson, "Le sport comme enjeu national chez les Canadiens français, 1890–1920," 57–61.
19 Ibid.
20 In *L'Autorité*, 4 January 1914, 5, qtd. in ibid., 65. "Nous qui aimons les sports, les amusements sains et honnêtes, la gymnastique raisonnée qui fait des muscles d'acier, nous voulons des athlètes robustes, des Canadiens qui acquièrent [sic] par la pratique des sports l'esprit de discipline, l'audace et la ténacité indispensables pour triompher des obstacles de la vie. Nos champions du football, du hockey et de la crosse vont mettre en déroute les adversaires de la langue française."
21 Harvey, "Le clergé québécois et le sport," 73 Hudon; "Le Muscle et le Vouloir," 251.

22 Guay, *La conquête du sport*, 167; Harvey, "Le clergé québécois et le sport," 72.

23 Detellier, "Bonifier le capital humain," 478–81. "Ames d'or dans des corps de fer"; "affermir la puissance nationale."

24 Masson, *L'éducation physique, conditions et bienfaits corporels*, 1.

25 Masson, 24, in Detellier, "Bonifier le capital humain," 484–5; Baillargeon, "Entre la 'Revanche' et la 'Veillée' des berceaux," 120–1. "La lutte pour la vie devient de plus en plus âpre et difficile, et les hésitants, les faibles, les timides, sont rapidement relégués aux situations inférieures, cependant que les audacieux, les courageux, les hardis, s'imposent et s'assurent les bonnes positions, où ils se maintiennent par leur énergie, leur ténacité et leur esprit combatif … D'un côté, l'Anglo-Saxon est positif, hardi, tenace, froid, autoritaire, volontaire … mais âpre au gain; de l'autre côté, le Latin est poli, plus souple, un peu rêveur, réservé, idéaliste, ardent ..."

26 Black, "Évolution de l'image projetée par le Club de Hockey Canadien depuis ses origines jusqu'au mythe de la tradition glorieuse," 10.

27 There is great irony to this debate, since Power spoke fluent French and, as one contemporary critic wrote, was of "French-Canadian character" – unlike the unilingual Newsy Lalonde and Eugène Payan, who "spoke no French and were English in outlook and temperament." However, Lalonde and Payan had the advantage of *looking* francophone on a line-up sheet. On Rocket Power and linguistic outlook, see Jenish, *The Montreal Canadiens*, 48. On the difficulties of predicting a language on the basis of a name, see Vigneault's chapter in this collection.

28 *Le Devoir*, 13 February 1911, 4, qtd. in Black, "Évolution de l'image projetée par le Club de Hockey Canadien depuis ses origines jusqu'au mythe de la tradition glorieuse," 19. "Plusieurs journaux et surtout un nombre considérable de sportsmen ont protesté contre l'engagement de Rocket Power comme joueur du 'Canadien.' Ce n'est pas que Rocket ne soit pas un bon joueur de hockey. Au contraire, c'est un professionnel qui a sa valeur et si le public trouve étrange son engagement, c'est parce que le 'Canadien' est sensé représenter sur la glace les couleurs canadiennes-françaises uniquement. C'est du reste ce qui lui donne son cachet *et lui garde l'intérêt des nôtres.*" Emphasis in original.

29 *Le Devoir*, 14 February 1911, 5, 19. "une grave insulte," "une bourde," "un déshonneur."

30 Black, *Habitants et glorieux*, 60–9.
31 Goyens and Turowetz, *Lions in Winter*, 60.
32 "Comme si l'avenir de la nation était en jeu"; Black, "Évolution de l'image projetée par le Club de Hockey Canadien depuis ses origines jusqu'au mythe de la tradition glorieuse," 37, 83.
33 Richard and Fischler, *The Flying Frenchmen*, 21.
34 Valois-Nadeau, "Quand le cœur a ses raisons"; Patoine, "Sport et nationalisme"; Perrone, "The King Has Two Bodies"; Melançon, *Les yeux de Maurice Richard*; Sniec, "Les Canadiens de Montréal vus par les fans: une exploration en trois temps"; Laberge and Dumas, "L'affaire Richard/Campbell"; Bélanger, "Where Have the Ghosts Gone?"; Di Felice, "The Richard Riot"; Bélanger, "Le hockey au Québec"; Gunderson, "Memory, Modernity, and the City."
35 Poirier, "Hockey et identité au Québec," 183–5.
36 Gunderson, "Memory, Modernity, and the City," 16.
37 Lapierre, "Nationalisme culturel et performance dans l'histoire du Canadien de Montréal," 317–35.
38 Melançon, *Les yeux de Maurice Richard*, 185; Laberge and Dumas, "L'affaire Richard/Campbell," 31.
39 Les funérailles de Maurice Richard, http://archives.radio-canada.ca/emissions/443, 31 May 2000 (accessed 16 January 2011). "Ses exploits, ses buts spectaculaires ainsi que son désir de vaincre l'ont hissé au rang de héros de la nation canadienne française."
40 Relations internationales Québec, http://www.mrifce.gouv.qc.ca/en/protocole/funerailles (accessed 16 January 2011).
41 CBC, http://archives.cbc.ca/sports/hockey/clips/13334 (accessed 13 December 2010). "And, Maurice, I would say, in French, enjoy this peace, this eternal rest. We wish you that from the bottom of our hearts. *Merci*."
42 Ibid.
43 Admittedly, the CBC report is brief. And yet it is representative of a certain strain of reporting on Richard's death. As Jack Falla writes in "A Death in Montreal," on the day of Richard's funeral, "Canada's French and English were on the same sad page." *Open Ice*, 22. Roy MacGregor, meanwhile, subtly points out difference even within communal grieving: "We had lost a favourite uncle, a boyhood hero, a national treasure – the

word 'national' taking on a somewhat different context in the Saguenay than it had in the rest of the nation." *Canadians*, 102.

44 Beardsley, *Country on Ice*, 32.

45 Ramos and Gosine, "The Rocket," 16.

46 Ibid., 19.

47 Ibid.

48 Ibid., 9.

49 Melançon, *Les yeux de Maurice Richard*, 180.

50 André Laurendeau, "On a tué mon frère Richard," *Le Devoir*, March 21, 1955, 4. "They killed my brother Richard." "Le nationalisme canadien-français paraît s'être réfugié dans le hockey. La foule qui clamait sa colère jeudi soir dernier n'était pas animée seulement par le goût du sport ou le sentiment d'une injustice commise contre son idole. C'était un peuple frustré, qui protestait contre le sort … Or, voici surgir M. Campbell pour arrêter cet élan. On prive les Canadiens français de Maurice Richard. On brise l'élan de Maurice Richard qui allait établir plus clairement sa supériorité. Et cet 'on' parle anglais, cet 'on' décide en vitesse contre le héros, provoque, excite. Alors il va voir. On est soudain fatigué d'avoir toujours eu des maîtres, d'avoir longtemps plié l'échine. M. Campbell va voir. On n'a pas tous les jours le mauvais sort entre les mains; on ne peut pas tous les jours tordre le cou à la malchance." (The first two sentences of this translation are from Fred A. Reed's translation of Melançon's *Les Yeux de Maurice Richard*.)

51 Nick Auf der Maur, "Rocket Richard Riot Rocked Montreal 30 Years Ago This Week," *Gazette*, 15 March 1985, A2, republished in Auf der Maur, *A Montreal Life*, 218–19.

52 Sidney Katz, "The Strange Forces behind the Richard Hockey Riot," *Maclean's*, 17 September 1955.

53 Laberge and Dumas, "L'affaire Richard/Campbell," 36–43.

54 Di Felice, "The Richard Riot," i–ii.

55 Ibid., 29–33.

56 Ibid., 57–60.

57 Even a cursory look at the NHL's early rosters is revealing in this respect. In 1917–18, 8 of the 4 teams' 52 players (15 per cent) had French Canadian names (an admittedly rough but still useful hint at ethnicity). In 1927–28, 15 of the 10-team NHL's 158 players (9 per cent) had French Canadian

names. Finally, in 1937–38, 13 of the 8-team NHL's 173 players (7.5 per cent) had French Canadian names. If anything, the French Canadian presence declined during the NHL's early decades. See Hockey Database, "NHL Seasons," http://www.hockeydb.com/ihdb/stats/leagues/141.html (accessed 29 March 2016). There were exceptions, of course, such as Leo Dandurand, who skated as a referee in the NHA and was part owner of the Canadiens, 1921–30. See Barrette's *Léo Dandurand.*

58 Di Felice, "The Richard Riot," 81–7.

59 The equating of playing styles with ethnic characteristics was not unique to hockey. As Michael Oriard examines in his fine works on the cultural constructions of twentieth-century American football, sports writers were quite willing to imagine that race determined how the game was played. On the conflation of race and style of play in hockey, see Holman, "Telling Stories about Indigeneity and Canadian Sport."

60 Smythe was savvy, even ambivalent during the war. As Kelly McParland writes in *The Lives of Conn Smythe*, though many NHL players did military training, "very few took the next step and volunteered for service overseas" (189). Yet Smythe "*was* careful to ensure fans knew the Leafs were doing their duty, pumping out programs and promotional material with photos of Privates Broda and Davidson of the Toronto Scottish, Privates Nick and Don Metz of the Regina Rifles, and Private Wally Stanowski of the Winnipeg Rifles" (190).

61 J. Andrew Ross, in a thorough overview of professional hockey during the Second World War, points out that Bruins manager Art Ross believed Canadian teams, especially the Canadiens, were slack in aiding the war effort. In addition to publicly complaining about a cancelled Canadiens-Bruins "charity exhibition game," he "sarcastically referred to the Montreal Canadiens, whose players were mostly employed in Montreal war industries, as 'The Essential War Workers.'" Ross, "Arenas of Debate," 107–8.

62 Di Felice, 188, 190–2.

63 Elcombe, "Hockey New Year's Eve in Canada," 1287–1310; Patoine, "On est Canayen ou on l'est pas"; Noonan, "The Discourse of Hockey in Canada"; Zakus, "A Genesis of the Canadian Sport System in Pierre Trudeau's Political Philosophy and Agenda," 30–48; Gruneau and Whitson, *Hockey Night in Canada*; Harvey and Proulx, "Le sport et l'État

au Canada," 93–121; Macintosh, Bedecki, Franks, *Sport and Politics in Canada*, 210; Kidd, *The Political Economy of Sport*, 79.

64 For example, the Wickenheiser, Carbonneau, Chelios, Keane, Koivu, and Cunneyworth "affairs" and the matter of bypassing francophones in the draft. Martin Ouellet, "La classe politique dénonce la nomination d'un entraîneur unilingue," *La presse canadienne*, in *Le Devoir*, 20 December 2011, B6; Brian Myles, "Le Mike Lansing du hockey: Wake up, Capitaine Keane!" *La presse canadienne*, in *Le Devoir*, 14 September 1995, A1; *La Presse Canadienne*, "Français: Koivu avoue ne pas être parfait," in *Le Devoir*, 1 November 2007, A3. See also Réseau des Sports, http://www.rds.ca/zv2/: "Le Canadien et les Québécois," 23 June 2008; "Le Canadien ignore-t-il les Québécois?" 28 June 2010; "Damphousse souhaite plus de Québécois," 31 August 2010; "Patrick Roy: Le CH doit avoir plus de Québécois," 20 September 2010 (all accessed 4 May 2011).

65 The term is a translation of Michel Marois's "naturalistes" from *Les analyses de la dimension politique du sport*, 2, 5.

66 Namely, Henri de Baillet-Latour and Avery Brundage, in Milza, "Sport et relations internationales," 160.

67 Guttmann, "Sport, Politics and the Engaged Historian," 372. A recent example: sports commentator Claude Quenneville deemed the rampant politicization of sport among journalists and others to be a "danger": Radio-Canada, "Culture Physique,"15 September 2010, http://www.radio-canada.ca/emissions/culture_physique/2010-2011/archives.asp?date=2 (accessed 6 April 2011).

68 Cantelon and Gruneau, *Sport, Culture and the Modern State*, 19.

69 "Nous ne faisons pas de politique, nous jouons au hockey." Radio-Canada, Jean-François Chaumont, "Une partie intégrante de la mission," 16 September 2010, http://www.radio-canada.ca/sports/hockey/2010/09/16/005-habs-boivin-molson.shtml (accessed 2 October 2014).

70 Laurin-Lamothe, "La culture se joue-t-elle ici? Les implications de la corporation du Canadien de Montréal pour la société Québécoise."

71 Perrone, "The King Has Two Bodies," 95–9.

72 I thank a reviewer for pointing out the need to emphasize this point about paying for radio.

73 Perrone, "The King Has Two Bodies," 95–9.

74 Ibid., 95–9, 101–4.
75 Ibid., 95–6, 105–7.
76 Bélanger, "Where Have the Ghosts Gone?" 9, 30–1, and 141–2.
77 Ibid., 148–9, 152–3.
78 Ibid., 148–9.
79 Ibid., 157–65, 206.
80 Ibid., 205–8.
81 This and the next two quotations are from "Cent ans de Gloire / Hundred Years of Glory," in *Cent Ans des Canadiens de Montréal / Hundred Years of the Montreal Canadiens*. Emphasis added.
82 Martel et Pâquet, *Langue et politique au Canada et au Québec*, 130, 188.
83 Bourbonnais, *Champions*. For more on francophonizing, see Terry Vaois Gitersos in this volume.
84 Patrick Marsolais, "Ça suffit," *Cyberpresse*, 15 December 2009, http://www.cyberpresse.ca/debats/votre-opinion/200912/15/01-931301-ca-suffit.php (accessed 13 April 2012). See also n.57.
85 Radio-Canada, "La nomination d'un unilingue anglophone à la tête du Canadien suscite la controverse," 19 December 2011, http://ici.radio-canada.ca/nouvelles/societe/2011/12/19/001-cunneyworth-canadien-unilingue.shtml (accessed 16 October 2014); La Presse Canadienne, "La ministre St-Pierre dénonce la nomination d'un entraîneur-chef unilingue chez le Canadien," in *Le Devoir*, http://www.ledevoir.com/sports/hockey/338737/la-ministre-st-pierre-denonce-la-nomination-d-un-entraineur-chef-unilingue-chez-le-canadien (accessed 16 October 2014).
86 Le réseau des sports, http://www.rds.ca/zone-video/#cat=24&videoID=104688, January 2012 (accessed 13 April 2012).
87 Bélanger, "Where Have the Ghosts Gone?" 159.
88 The Montreal Canadiens corporate entity is owned by the Molsons, an anglo-Montreal family that is very important in Quebec. Does that entity wish to contribute to making Quebec a bilingual territory by means of its hockey team? Only the family can answer that question.
89 Lapierre, "Nationalisme culturel et performance dans l'histoire du Canadien de Montréal," 317–35.
90 Bélanger, "Where Have the Ghosts Gone?" 136.

Chapter Four

1 Laberge, "L'affaire Richard/Campbell," in Laruin-Lamothe and Moreau, eds., *Le Canadien de Montréal*, 13–30.
2 Patoine, "'*On est Canayen ou ben on l'est pas.*'"
3 Montreal Canadiens Children's Foundation *Report*, 19 (https://fondation.canadiens.com/wp-content/uploads/2014/07/rapport-annuel-10-11-eng.pdf) (accessed 4 January 2017).
4 Fondation des Canadiens, *Cuisiner avec les Canadiens*, 7.
5 On the contrary, some authors, like Fontan, Lévesque, and Charbonneau in "Les fondations privées québécoises," maintain that this tendency is relatively new compared to the anglophone side of Canadian society, where philanthropic behaviour is more inscribed in the tradition of most institutions.
6 Ibid.
7 King, "Doing Good by Running Well."
8 See, for example, Bélanger, "Le hockey au Quebec, bien plus qu'un jeu"; Melançon, *Les yeux de Maurice Richard*; Patoine, "'*On est Canayen ou ben on l'est pas.*'"
9 Montreal Canadiens Children's Foundation, *Report*, 2013–14.
10 Tracey, Phillips, and Haugh, "Beyond Philanthropy."
11 Sheth and Babiak, "Beyond the Game," 437.
12 Robinson, "Sport Philanthropy."
13 Montreal Canadiens Children's Foundation, *Report*, 2007–08, 9.
14 Talparu, qtd. in Sarah Boesveld, "Does a Donation Really Count if No One Sees You Giving?" *National Post*, 28 May 2012 (accessed 21 April 2017).
15 Sheth and Babiak, "Beyond the Game," 445.
16 http://canadiens.nhl.com/club/news.htm?id=490203.
17 http://canadiens.nhl.com/club/news.htm?id=612209. "Je me réjouis de la réalisation de ce projet exemplaire, qui nous est légué alors que nous amorçons les festivités de notre centenaire. Il illustre la volonté très forte des élus de LaSalle d'établir des partenariats gagnants en vue d'offrir aux citoyens et citoyennes des installations d'une grande qualité, accessibles et source de fierté pour tous, surtout" (http://canadiens.nhl.com/club/l_fr/news.htm?id=612206) (accessed 2 July 2013).
18 Michèle Ouimet, "Le Canadien en classe," *La Presse*, 10 February 2009, http://www.lapresse.ca/actualites/education/200902/09/01-825691-le-

canadien-en-classe.php (accessed 2 July 2013): "It is straight-out veiled publicity … Advertising to youth is forbidden. The Canadiens use an underhand approach to reach students. And the worst is that the Minister of Education encourages this practice by giving subsidies."

19 Ibid. "Le Canadien n'est pas une entreprise privée comme les autres, a-t-il souligné. Il fait partie de l'histoire. C'est une institution davantage qu'une entreprise."

20 Montreal Canadiens Children's Foundation, *Report*, 2010–11.

21 Montreal Canadiens Children's Foundation, *Report*, 2008–09, 15.

22 Robinson, "Sport Philanthropy,"15.

23 A case in point: on 16 September 2015, less than one year before being traded to the Nashville Predators, defenceman P.K. Subban announced the largest and most important donation ever made by a Canadian athlete. His pledge of $10 million to Montreal Children's Hospital monopolized all the charity-related media attention for several months, overshadowing the philanthropic actions of the other members of the Canadiens. Coordinated by Subban's own media team and marketing partners, this announcement was one of the first to be realized outside and without the collaboration of the Canadien's marketing and foundation divisions.

24 Montreal Canadiens Children's Foundation, *Report*, 2010–11, 3.

25 Ibid., 18.

26 Sheth and Babiak, "Beyond the Game," 442.

27 Berlant, *Compassion*, 1.

28 "Street Hockey de Rue," http://www.streethockeyderue.org (accessed 8 September 2012).

29 King, "Doing Good by Running Well," 297.

30 Berlant, *Compassion*; King, "Doing Good by Running Well."

31 Because of the links forged with French-language issues and the role that some intellectuals and fans attribute to the team during the emergence of the Quiet Revolution, the association between the Canadiens and the French-speaking Quebec nation seems to be obvious. See Black, *Habitants et glorieux*; Laberge, "L'affaire Richard/Campbell."

32 I present here just one perspective on this relationship. There are others as well.

33 Gruneau and Whitson, *Hockey Night in Canada*, 246.

34 See Valois-Nadeau, "Le Canadien de Montréal" ("The Montreal Canadiens as a Popular Object").
35 Williams, "Community," 76. Emphasis in original.
36 Anderson, *Imagined Communities*; Williams, "Community," 76.
37 Laberge, "L'affaire Richard/Campbell"; Melançon, *Les yeux de Maurice Richard.*
38 Berlant, *Compassion*, 3.
39 See Tracey, Phillips, and Haugh, "Beyond Philanthropy."

## Chapter Five

1 Jerry Trudel, "Le siège de Québec III," *Dimanche-Matin*, 4 April 1982, 32. "Le 13 septembre 1759, deuxième siège de Québec ou Wolfe et Montcalm laissent leur peau. Et un jour arrive que les Anglais deviennent maîtres pas chez eux et fondent 'The Gazette' et plus tard les Maroons. Les Maroons font une belle mort devant le Canadien et s'enfuient par la 401. Mais les fantômes des Plaines d'Abraham rôdent encore. Les Fleurdelysés s'emparent de Québec et insidieusement les Maroons renaissent sous le déguisement du Canadien. Astuce, ruse et boule de gomme! Et nous voici au siège de Québec III. Mais les troupes de Bergeron étaient décimées à la veille de la grande bataille. C'est qu'une semaine plus tôt, le général Berry avait ordonné à ses habits rouges de démoraliser l'ennemi avec incursions sournoises ... Quand même, le tonnerre gronde et les indigènes sont agités. L'intendant Filion à Québec tente de regrouper ses forces avec des soldats aguerris comme Wilfrid Paiement, Marc Tardif, Michel Goulet, Réal Cloutier, Alain Côté, Daniel Bouchard, une phalange de descendants des colons de la Nouvelle France auxquels, pour bonne mesure, on a ajouté trois mercenaires des vieux pays. Meanwhile back on St. Catherine St. West les Maroons passent leurs troupes en revue et pour la bataille de Québec et pour le repatriment de la Constitution. C'est avec fierté que défient au pas de l'oie devant le gouverneur Grundman les Robinson, Shutt, Napier, Wamsley, Acton, Wickenheiser, Langway, Englom, Brubaker, Nilan, Risebrough auxquels on a ajouté un Lafleur, un Tremblay, un Houle pour se conformer à l'article de la loi qui dit le français est acceptable 'where the number warrants.'"
2 Salutin, *Les Canadiens*, 27–45. See Frazer Andrews's chapter for a full consideration of this play.

3 This study examines the French-language media only, but an equally rich analysis could be undertaken by analyzing the hockey content in Montreal's *Gazette*, Quebec's only high-circulation English-language daily. By the same token, this study is limited to a socio-political analysis. An economic analysis, centred on the commercial context and marketing priorities of Molson and Carling O'Keefe, the Canadiens' and Nordiques' respective beer-brewing owners, would likewise be fascinating. During these years, Molson and O'Keefe were principal combatants in a Quebec "beer war" with their respective teams acting as commercial proxies. A sponsor of the Canadiens since the 1930s, Molson purchased the team outright in 1978. Now among NHL owners, Molson voted against the NHL's merger with the WHA (including O'Keefe's Nordiques) in 1979 and insisted on a television agreement that banned the Nordiques from receiving Hockey Night in Canada revenues for five years after the merger. "Molson, owner of the Canadiens, and Carling O'Keefe, owner of the Nordiques," *Gazette* writer Michael Farber wrote in December 1982 – in the thick of the on-ice rivalry – "are turning the playgrounds of this country into a battleground for a shrinking beer market." By 1982, Molson had claimed 38 per cent of the $500-million Quebec beer market, while O'Keefe claimed 32 per cent. But overall beer consumption in Quebec was declining in these years, from 130.76 litres per capita in 1980 to 119.23 in 1982. An intensification of beer commerce coloured and informed the broader social and political meaning of the Canadiens-Nordiques rivalry. But that particular aspect of this story awaits its historian. See Michael Farber, "Bitter Beer War Being Waged on Rinks, Fields," *Gazette*, 24 December 1982, B13–14; "Beer Companies Use Hockey in Their Fight for Customers," Regina *Leader-Post*, 28 December 1982, A17.

4 Neo-nationalism refers to the strain of Quebec nationalism centred on language, territoriality, and the urban experience that emerged in the 1960s and continues to predominate today. It is usually contrasted to "traditional" French Canadian nationalism, which was rooted in ethnicity, rural values, and religion. For an oft-cited look at the evolution of nationalism in Quebec, see Handler, *Nationalism and the Politics of Culture in Québec*.

5 Levine, *The Reconquest of Montreal*, 23–5.

6 Esman, "Ethnic Politics and Economic Power," 400.
7 For three very different perspectives on the Quiet Revolution, see Behiels, *Prelude to Quebec's Quiet Revolution*; Gauvreau, *The Catholic Origins of Quebec's Quiet Revolution, 1931–1970*; Gélinas, *La droite intellectuelle québécoise et la Révolution tranquille.*
8 Historian Sean Mills has described how the anti-imperialist writings of figures such as Andre Gunder Frank, Kari Levitt, Frantz Fanon, and Jean-Paul Sartre were distributed and eagerly consumed at union meetings. Mills, *The Empire Within*, 192.
9 Levitt, *Silent Surrender*, 147–8.
10 Vallières, *Choose!* 21.
11 Rouillard, *L'expérience syndicale au Québec*, 156. "Un levier de la lutte contre la domination capitaliste."
12 Ibid., 342–3.
13 Levine, *The Reconquest of Montreal*, 165.
14 Ibid., 167.
15 Ibid.
16 McRoberts, *Quebec: Social Change and Political Crisis*, 227–31.
17 Laurin, *Québec's Policy on the French Language Presented to the National Assembly and the People of Québec*, 52.
18 Ibid., 99.
19 Coleman, "From Bill 22 to Bill 101," 475–6.
20 Levine, *The Reconquest of Montreal*, 116–18.
21 Rouillard, *L'expérience syndicale au Québec*, 158. "Un frein à la subordination spécifique des travailleurs francophones en tant que travailleurs francophones."
22 Coleman, "From Bill 22 to Bill 101," 473. "La suprême affirmation du fait français en Amérique, la victoire de la nation québécoise sur l'occupant anglophone, l'annulation de la défaite des plaines d'Abraham, et le magna carta culturelle des Québécois."
23 Gagnon and Iacovino, *Federalism, Citizenship, and Quebec*, 98. Gagnon and Iacovino argue that "the jurisdictional battles of the Quiet Revolution and the linguistic conflicts of the 1970s culminated in a fully articulated discourse centred on citizenship in Québec."
24 These debates are ongoing. For example, the controversial adoption of a "code of conduct" by the small Quebec municipality of Hérouxville in 2007, criticized in some quarters as overtly racist, xenophobic, and

Islamophobic, kicked off another wave of debates about the nature of Quebec identity, and strongly suggested that the term Québécois continues for many to identify French speakers of French Canadian ethnic origin. See Nieguth and Lacassagne, "Contesting the Nation," 1–16.

25 Gitersos, "Les frogs sont menacés: Media Representations of the Nordiques and Canadiens, 1979–1981," 69–81.

26 See Claude Larochelle, "Jamais un Francophone au prix du talent," *Le Soleil*, 15 April 1980, B2. "À talent égal ... on choisira un francophone."

27 Claude Masson, "La thérapie des Nordiques," *Le Soleil*, 6 May 1982, A4. The fact that the Nordiques were owned by an English-Canadian brewery, Carling O'Keefe, was not mentioned.

28 Marc Lachapelle, "La victoire des Nordiques: un tonique pour le hockey junior majeur québécois," *Le Journal de Montréal*, 15 April 1982, 93.

29 Claude Cadorette, "Une boîte à surprise après les six premiers choix," *Le Journal de Québec*, 19 May 1982, 60.

30 Benoît Aubin, "La bataille des Nordiques," *L'actualité*, March 1980, 28.

31 Richard Milo, "L'arbitrage, un nouvel outil de négociations," *Le Devoir*, 27 January 1984, 11.

32 Ghyslain Luneau, "'Le p'tit Tigre' dans la jungle de Québec," *Le Journal de Montréal*, 24 May 1980, 70.

33 Michel Lemieux, "'Les ouvertures sont rares pour les Canadiens-français,'" *Dimanche-Matin*, 4 July 1982, 31; Maurice Dumas, "Nolet: un bon gars avec du caractère," *Le Soleil*, 17 July 1982, C2.

34 Canadian Press, "Les Anglophones ne se sentent pas chez eux à Québec," *La Presse*, 9 April 1980, D4.

35 Claude Larochelle, "Intégrer les Anglophones dans l'équipe," *Le Soleil*, 8 April 1980, B1.

36 Claude Larochelle, "Ferguson n'y échappe pas," *Le Soleil*, 15 April 1980, B2. "La dimension francophone *bien naturelle* de l'équipe."

37 Claude Larochelle, "Intégrer les Anglophones dans l'équipe," *Le Soleil*, 8 April 1980, B1. "L'intégration [des anglophones] prend un caractère particulier chez les Nordiques, une dimension qu'ont su éviter jusqu'ici les Canadiens de Montréal. À Montréal, les joueurs de language anglaise ont le West Island comme partage, et s'il y a des vedettes francophones comme Guy Lafleur faisant la razzia des trophées, il trouve également des athlètes du Québec pour assumer une bonne part du sale boulot ... A Québec, le travail obscur et éreintant est le lot de quelques anglophones

qui sont mal dans leur peau face aux vedettes aux plantureux revenus."

38 Claude Bédard, "Hart n'avait pas tort et n'avait pas raison," *Le Journal de Québec*, 12 April 1980, 66.

39 Claude Larochelle, "Jamais un Francophone au prix du talent," *Le Soleil*, 15 April 1980, B2. "Plusieurs athlètes du Québec et leurs familles ont vécu cette rude transition. Nombre d'entre eux ont été plongés dans un milieu d'une culture différente un peu partout en Amérique du Nord. Ils ont finalement tiré leur épingle de jeu sans que personne ne s'attendrisse sur leur sort. Comme je signalais à Gerry Hart récemment, l'athlète québécois qui débarque à Winnipeg ou Vancouver ne songe même pas à réclamer une proportion de francophones autour de lui et de demander des annonces en français à la patinoire!"

40 Canadian Press, "Thomas Alleges Nordiques Favouring French Players," *Gazette*, 26 September 1980, 35.

41 Canadian Press, "Encore un peu de fiel de Farrish," *La Presse*, 29 September 1980, C5.

42 Claude Larochelle, "Thomas ne faisait pas le poids," *Le Soleil*, 26 September 1980, A1. "Une vraie farce."

43 Claude Bédard, "Si les Francophones étaient aussi choyés," *Le Journal de Montréal*, 27 September 1980, 71. "Québec est une ville différente de toutes les autres en Amérique."

44 Jacques Dumais, "La bêtise de Thomas," *Le Soleil*, 27 September 1980, A6.

45 Réjean Tremblay, "Le Canadien a oublié le Québec," *La Presse*, 3 October 1980, B2.

46 Bernard Brisset, "Les 'frogs' sont menacés," *La Presse*, 4 October 1980, F2. Brisset charged that Quebec-based scouts were routinely ignored, and that Bert Templeton, the coach of the team's minor league affiliate in Nova Scotia and a key figure in the team's player-development scheme, was a confirmed francophobe. Brisset's assertion was seconded by *Le Soleil* scribe Claude Larochelle, and confirmed years later by Canadiens player Guy Carbonneau, who played for Templeton at this time. Claude Larochelle, "Ça gronde dans les parages du Forum," *Le Soleil*, 10 October 1980, C1; Jean Beaunoyer, "Carbonneau poursuit sa route sans jamais élever la voix," *La Presse*, 21 August 1982, C5.

47 Bernard Brisset, "Les 'frogs' sont menacés," *La Presse*, 4 October 1980, F2. "Évidemment, les Expos et les Alouettes n'ont pas à se préoccuper de la division linguistique dans leur rangs. Mais les amateurs se reconnaissent

dans leur équipe de hockey ce qui n'est pas le cas avec les deux autres formées de joueurs américains pour la plupart."

48 Marc Lachapelle, "'À talent égal, nous repêchons le Québécois,'" *Le Journal de Montréal*, 12 May 1982, 110. Canadiens General Manager Irving Grundman insisted that this had been the Canadiens' policy all along. This claim is untrue: in the 1980 draft, Canadiens' scouting director Ron Caron bluntly stated that the Canadiens did not consider the French fact in its personnel decisions." See Marc Lachapelle, "Séance d'entrée de la ligue nationale," *Le Journal de Montréal*, 11 June 1980, 125.

49 Réjean Tremblay, "Le Grand Serge amène avec lui un gros morceau de l'âme du Canadien," *La Presse*, 12 December 1981, H5. "D'ici deux ou trois ans, le Canadien sera moins qu'une équipe comme les autres."

50 See Tom Lapointe, "Larouche heureux d'être échangé," *Le Soleil*, 22 December 1981, B3.

51 Bernard Brisset, "Bloc-Notes," *La Presse*, 10 March 1982, sports section, 3. "Le ménage des frogs se poursuit chez le Canadien."

52 Ghyslain Luneau, "'Un simple concours de circonstances," *Le Journal de Montréal*, 10 March 1982, 111. "Il faut reconnaître que les Glorieux sont de moins en moins francophone"; "la liste s'allonge."

53 Réjean Tremblay, "La laine se fait rare," *La Presse*, 9 October 1981, sports section, 5.

54 The first reference I have found is in Claude Larochelle, "Les 'Maroons' s'interrogent comme jamais," *Le Soleil*, 23 December 1981, C1.

55 Réjean Tremblay, "Jean-D. ne perd pas de temps!" *La Presse*, 24 February 1982, sports section, 5.

56 Bernard Brisset, "Dan Daoust est cédé aux Voyageurs," *La Presse*, 8 October 1981, sports section, 9.

57 Ghyslain Luneau, "Dale Hoganson, blessé," *Le Journal de Québec*, 23 December 1981, 51.

58 Réjean Tremblay, for example, described Bowman as a tyrant who used language as a weapon against Québécois players. See Réjean Tremblay, "Docteur Bowman et Mister Hyde," *L'actualité*, March 1978, 37. At least one of Bowman's former players accused him of francophobia. See Claude Brière, "Un jour ou l'autre, il faudra régler le cas de Larouche," *Dimanche-Matin*, 21 October 1979, 54.

59 Canadian Press, "Le Canadien: une image à refaire," *Le Soleil*, 5 January 1982, C2.

60 Gilles Proulx, letter to the editor, *La Presse*, 12 January 1981, A7; Gilles Proulx, letter to the editor, *Le Devoir*, 13 January 1981, 12; Gilles Proulx, letter to the editor, *Le Journal de Montréal*, 15 January 1981, 10. "Actuellement, à l'heure de la francisation, l'équipe qui représente la deuxième ville française au monde compte 12 joueurs francophones contre 14 anglophones."

61 Gilles Proulx, letter to the editor, *La Presse*, 12 January 1981, A7; Gilles Proulx, letter to the editor, *Le Devoir*, 13 January 1981: 12; Gilles Proulx, letter to the editor, *Le Journal de Montréal*, 15 January 1981, 10. "Il ne s'agit pas d'éliminer les Anglais de Montréal ... mais simplement de respecter les proportions demographiques de la Metropole ... par example, nous pourrions avoir au sein du Tricolore au moins 14 joueurs francophones sur un total de 21, puisque Montréal est majoritairement française à 70%."

62 Réjean Tremblay, "Le dictateur des Canadiens," *L'actualité*, October 1979, 58.

63 Michael Farber, "Grundman a Winner despite Forum Heat," *Gazette*, 13 February 1982, F2. For another reference to the Forum as a synagogue, see Yvon Pedneault, "F.-X. fait des courses," *Le Journal de Montréal*, 27 July 1982, 68.

64 Université de Montréal theologian Olivier Bauer has recently published a book exploring, among other things, whether the Canadiens themselves constitute a religion. See Olivier Bauer's *Hockey as a Religion* and his "Le Canadien de Montréal est-il une religion," 20–80.

65 Réjean Tremblay, "Entre Roger Samson et Irving Grundman, un monde ...," *La Presse*, 20 June 1981, F2. "Un usurpateur de la haute finance."

66 Réjean Tremblay, "C'est ben nous autres!" *La Presse*, 10 November 1979, D2. "Des francophones, des anglophones, des Juifs qui contrôlent la patente."

67 Réjean Tremblay, "Entre Roger Samson et Irving Grundman, un monde ...," *La Presse*, 20 June 198, F2.

68 André Rufiange, "Mémo à Irving Grundman," *Le Journal de Montréal*, 13 April 1982, 11. It was reported that Grundman and his family were harassed in their seats and called "maudit Juifs" (damn Jews) by a few Nordiques fans. These depictions did not prevent other Grundman critics from using a different set of epithets: one letter to the editor in *La Presse* described the Canadiens' general manager as "Führer Grundman."

François Massue, letter to the editor, *La Presse*, 29 January 1980, A5.

69 Political scientist and historian Esther Delisle has published several controversial works discussing the relationship between pre-Quiet Revolution French Canadian nationalism, fascism, and anti-Semitism. See *The Traitor and the Jew* and *Myths, Memories, & Lies*. More recently, Mordecai Richler, who achieved literary fame through his vivid depictions of Jewish life in Montreal, criticized the neo-nationalist project for its perceived anti-Semitism in *Oh Canada! Oh Québec!*

70 Réjean Tremblay, "'Les gens s'arrêtent pour me serer la main. C'est bon,'" *La Presse*, 27 November 1982, D1. "Before leaving the Forum, I went to greet Irving's new boss, Mr. Corey, in person. We had been chatting for a while, in the centre of his office, when Mr. Grundman made his entrance. We had just finished an hour-long conversation. In French. [Grundman:] 'Excuse me, Ron, the lawer [sic] is waiting for us. We should go.' [Corey:] 'I'll be there in a few minutes.' Understood?"

71 Bernard Brisset, "Grundman choisit la stabilité," *La Presse*, 4 June 1981, sports section, 3. To his credit, Berry followed through with his promise.

72 For example, see Réjean Tremblay, "Molson et McCammon bougeront-ils enfin?" *La Presse*, 13 April 1981, sports section, 4.

73 Maurice Richard, "La réaction du Canadien m'a déçu," *Dimanche-Matin*, 7 June 1981, 45.

74 Claude Larochelle, "Retour du style Bowman au Forum," *Le Soleil*, 4 June 1981, C2. "Des citoyens de tradition anglo-saxonne, imprégnés de cet environnement où la language anglaise est l'instrument du travail."

75 "Gens du pays" was adopted by the Parti Québécois as an unofficial anthem. The song was prominently played at the official events that followed both the PQ's election victory in 1976 and the *non* side's referendum loss in 1980. See Lechaume, "Chanter le pays."

76 Jean Beaunoyer, "Bob Berry un 'loyaliste' tantôt sévére tantôt charmant," *La Presse*, 6 June 1981, F1.

77 Claude Larochelle, "Retour du style Bowman au Forum," *Le Soleil*, 4 June 1981, C2. "Plus que jamais, la langue de travail du club de hockey montréalais sera l'anglais."

78 François Béliveau, "Un coup de dé audacieux!" *La Presse*, 4 June 1981, sports section, 4. "Le Canadien, qui représente bien des traditions, a choisi de rester dans la lignée des Pollock, Toe Blake, Bowman, en embauchant Bob Berry à titre d'instructeur-chef, et poursuit comme le

gouvernement Trudeau le rêve d'un heureux mariage entre francophone et anglophone. Un rêve, puisque dans les faits, dans les petits mémos, la papeterie entre employés, les discussions entre joueurs et l'instructeur, l'anglais prédominera. L'image extérieure toutefois, celle que le bureau des relations publiques véhiculera, aura un cachet de bilinguisme."

79 Ibid.

80 Richard Chartier, "Ronald Corey déménage au Forum!" *La Presse*, 13 November 1982, D.

81 Claude Larochelle, "'Piraterie' entre Montréal et Québec," *Le Soleil*, 13 November 1982, F1. "Le francophone que le Canadien se devait d'aller chercher."

82 Marcel Gaudette, "Ronald Corey: son choix c'est Molson (air connu)," *Le Soleil*, 13 November 1982, F2.

83 Claude Brière, "Je suis un peu gêné," *Dimanche-Matin*, 21 November 1982, 52. "Comme s'il venait de sauver un monument historique de la démolition."

84 Réjean Tremblay, "Pourquoi s'amuse-t-on maintenant au Forum?" *La Presse*, 24 December 1982, C2. "L'image de Corey, celle d'un Québécois fonceur et moderne tranche nettement sur celle de M. Morgan McCammon ... Ronald Corey permet une forme d'identification entre l'amateur et son équipe. Dans l'imagination populaire, il est possible de se faire accroire que le Canadien appartient à ses citoyens."

85 The Montreal Forum was located just across Atwater Street from Westmount, a wealthy anglophone enclave associated with corporate Montreal.

86 This metaphor of eastward movement becomes even more salient in the context of the eastward move of Montreal's commercial core as a whole, spurred by the development of buildings such as Maison Radio-Canada and la Complexe Desjardins, from the anglophone west end closer to the francophone east end. See Demers, "Le nouveau centre-ville de Montréal," 209–35.

87 Predictably, perhaps, Berry was fired again in less than a year and replaced as head coach by Lemaire.

88 Réjean Tremblay, "'L'important, c'est d'être voulu,'" *La Presse*, 30 April 1983, D2.

89 Réjean Tremblay, "Corey a redonné le Canadien à son milieu," *La Presse*, 5 May 1983, sports section, 5.

90 Claude Larochelle, "'Purge' influencé par les Nordiques," *Le Soleil*, 14 April 1983, C1. "Une interminable éclipse … le français deviendra la langue du travail au Forum."

91 Claude Larochelle, "Savard s'installera en maître absolu," *Le Soleil*, 29 April 1983, C1. "A ébranlé les colonnes du temple, la longue tradition des Gorman, Selke, Pollock, Bowman, Grundman."

92 Réjean Tremblay, "'Savard est avec le Canadien pour les vingt prochaines années,'" *La Presse*, 29 April 1983, sports section, 5. "Ça faisait des décennies que le populo avait la désagréable impression que le Canadien appartenait 'aux autres,' qu'il était dirigé 'par les autres' et que lui, le monde ordinaire, n'était que toléré dans le Sanctuaire."

93 Réjean Tremblay, "Le Canadien à la reconquête du Québec derrière le général Corey," *La Presse*, 4 May 1983, sports section, 5. The article's subtitle read: "Les Nordiques repousées derrière leurs remparts" (The Nordiques are pushed back behind their defences).

## Chapter Six

1 Dave Stubbs, *Gazette*, 9 March 1996, 11.

2 Lisa Anne Gunderson, "Memory, Modernity, and the City," 57.

3 Red Fisher, *Gazette*, 11 March 1996, E3.

4 Ibid.

5 Vertinsky and Bale, *Sites of Sports*, 146.

6 William Northey played a role in establishing the Canadian Amateur Hockey Association (1914) and was president of the Montreal Athletic Association (1924) before founding the CAC, which built and managed the Forum. See Blevins, *The Sports Hall of Fame Encyclopedia*, 723.

7 See a short story of the Wanderers-Canadiens rivalry at http://notrehistoire.canadiens.com/opponent/Montreal-Wanderers (accessed 1 January 2017).

8 Goyens, *The Montreal Forum*, 12.

9 New ice-making technology was blamed on several occasions for these fires.

10 Gruneau and Whitson, *Hockey Night in Canada*, 94.

11 Ibid., 95.

12 For a history of the team, see Brown, *Montreal Maroons*.

13 *Gazette*, 28 December 1994, D2.

14 For most of the summer of 1968, the Forum had no roof and no walls. Goyens, *The Montreal Forum*, 101.

15 Ibid.

16 While many "odes" to hockey have suggested that the development of the sport occurred naturally in Canada, Richard Gruneau and David Whitson rightfully argue that hockey as a natural thing is only a myth. Although hockey may draw from the "northern mystique," Gruneau says, "the problem arises when Canadians' appreciation for hockey is mistaken for 'nature' rather than something that is socially and culturally produced." Gruneau and Whitson, *Hockey Night in Canada*, 26.

17 The association of hockey with religion has become quite a popular topic of historical inquiry. See Barreau and Bauer, *La religion du Canadien de Montréal*. This anthology examines hockey figures and events, and some pieces discuss the very serious possibility that hockey may be a religion. Of course, the links between the religious history of Quebec and the representativeness of the Canadiens for Quebec society and history are numerous and quite rich in symbolism and meanings.

18 Howie Morenz died in 1937 of complications resulting from an injury sustained during a hockey game. For a discussion of the official and unofficial causes of his death, as well as his commemoration, see Perrone, "The King Has Two Bodies."

19 Perhaps the Molson/Bell Centre gained some sentimental importance in the hearts of Montrealers when it served as a funeral home for Maurice "Rocket" Richard in 2000.

20 Guy Pinard, *La Presse*, 4 April 1991, A3. "On peut dire sans risquer de se tromper que la grande majorité des Québécois ont mis les pieds au Forum au moins une fois dans leur vie."

21 Ronald King, *La Presse*, 25 August 1989, A1. It was common knowledge that the demand for hockey tickets was far greater than what the Forum could offer. Fred Steer, vice-president of administration and finance for the Canadiens, explained to one disgruntled fan that "the red seats are sold in advance of each season to season ticket holders and getting one through the regular channel, such as the Forum box office and Ticketron, is impossible." Ray Doucet, *Gazette*, 1 May 1989, F10. Doucet reported further that "unless you're a visiting head of state or somebody equally distinguished, don't bother calling the Forum for tickets." Ray Doucet, *Gazette*, 16 May 1989, A3.

22 Ronald Corey, cited by Jack Todd, *Gazette*, 25 August 1989, A3.

23 Ronald Corey, cited by Ronald King, *La Presse*, 25 August, 1989, A1. "Le prochain édifice devra poursuivre la tradition d'excellence du Canadien."

24 Ronald King, *La Presse*, 1 February 1990, Sports 6, "Rivalité Est-Ouest, Francophone-Anglophone."

25 The group was called PRO-EST (Société de promotion et de concertation socio-économique de l'Est de Montréal) and was supported by the federal minister of labour, Jean Corbeil, a few politicians (both Liberals and members of the Parti Québécois) from the east end, and, unsurprisingly, the Régie des installations olympiques. Conrad Bernier, *La Presse*, 31 January 1990, A4. It should be noted that *La Presse* spent quite a lot of time and ink debating the new location of the Forum, and, strangely enough, not nearly as much on what the old Forum meant. *La Presse* commissioned a valuation of several potential sites in 1989 and concluded that the Olympic park was "l'emplacement idéal." *La Presse*, 7 September 1989, A1.

26 Jack Todd, *Gazette*, 31 January 1990, A3.

27 *Gazette*, 28 December, 1994, D2.

28 Pat Burns, qtd. by David Johnston, *Gazette*, 11 December 1990, F1.

29 Robert Magne, project architect, qtd. by François Béliveau, *La Presse*, 10 November 1993, S9. "Le défi était de créer un ensemble cohérent et urbain à partir des composantes du site qui comprennent, outre le nouveau Forum (l'élément générateur), la gare Windsor, le terminus des trains de banlieue, l'édifice de la Tour du Terminus et la place publique nommée les Cours Windsor."

30 Many opposed any modification/restoration of Windsor Station and decried the construction of a brand new building beside the historic station. Most vocal of these opponents was Michael Fish, president of the Friends of Windsor Station. See Jean-Pierre Bonhomme, *La Presse*, 3 January 1992, A5.

31 Yvon Laberge, *La Presse*, 11 March 1995, A12. "Bien casqués et chaudement vêtus, ils ne se traînent pas les pieds, eux. En fait, ils sont tout le contraire de la poignée de jeunes millionnaires biens casqués et drapés de flanelle – toute sainte soit-elle – qui éliront domicile là en mars 1996." "La Sainte-Flanelle" is another nickname for the team, one that does not translate well!

32 Ibid. The announcement for the construction of the Deloitte Tower (not Windsor Tower) was published on 13 July 2012. See http://www.cadillacfairview.com/Notesdata/HR/CF_LP4W_LND_WebStation.nsf/page/Construction+of+Downtown+Montreal+Office+Tower+to+Commence+asCadillac+Fairview+and+Deloitte+Sign+Lease+Agreement (accessed 14 September 2012). The announcement for the Tour des Canadiens was made on 16 July 2012. See http://www.cadillacfairview.com/Notesdata/HR/CF_LP4W_LND_WebStation.nsf/page/Emblematic+residential+building+to+be+built+in+montreal (accessed 14 September 2012).

33 *La Presse*, 16 November 1994, A7. See also *Gazette*, 24 November 1994, 3.

34 *Gazette*, 23 May 1995, B2.

35 High and Lewis, *Corporate Wasteland*, 25.

36 Restaurant and business owners of the area estimated revenue losses between 10 and 40 per cent. This forced some owners to hike up their prices to cover for the decreasing sales, while others made desperate pleas to the city for lowering taxes. Katherine Wilton, *Gazette*, 9 March 1996, A1.

37 François Seigneur, marketing consultant for the Canadiens, cited by Michael Farber, *Gazette*, 4 April 1991, F1.

38 Another consequence of this move, which certainly did not draw as much sympathy, was the fact that the city of Westmount would have to compensate for about 1.5 million dollars' worth of parking tickets issued to Forum patrons. Nick Auf der Maur, *Gazette*, 1 September 1995, B3.

39 *Gazette*, 7 September 1989, C2.

40 Both the *Gazette* and *La Presse* provided extensive coverage of the events surrounding the closing of the Forum and the opening of the Molson Centre. *La Presse* asked its readers to send in their memories of the Forum. Both newspapers also featured several pieces by Quebec and Canadian personalities, from hockey and beyond, recounting their memories of the Forum.

41 Michael Farber, *Gazette*, 4 April 1991, F1.

42 To be fair, however, some comments about the choice of name were actually positive, mostly because the Molson name also had great historical significance for the city. Hickey argued that "it is a tribute to a prominent family which has contributed to the sporting, economic and cultural fabric of Montreal over a 200-year period." Pat Hickey, *Gazette*, 14 December 1995, C9.

43 Perrone, "Le processus d'héroïsation du Rocket," 67–8.
44 Jean Dion in *Le Devoir*, 12 March 1996, A1. "L'argent a parlé et les fantômes se sont tus."
45 Jack Todd, *Gazette*, 11 March 1996, E3.
46 Maurice Richard, qtd. by François Béliveau, *La Presse*, 9 March 1996, G2, "Je n'aime pas ça passer pour un fantôme."
47 Bell, "The Ghost of Place," 831.
48 Stewart, "Nostalgia – a Polemic," 227.
49 Bélanger, "Where Have the Ghosts Gone?" See esp. chapter 4 on capital accumulation.
50 Jackson, "A Sense of Place, a Sense of Time," 24.
51 Jay Bryan, *Gazette*, 29 June 1989, D1.
52 Réjean Tremblay, *La Presse*, 25 August, 1989, Sports 4.
53 Walter Buchignani, *Gazette*, 8 July 1989, A1.
54 Derek Drummond, *Gazette*, 8 February 1992, K2.
55 Yves Létourneau, *La Presse*, 27 August 1989, Sports 11.
56 High and Lewis, *Corporate Wasteland*, 93.
57 Nora, "Between Memory and History," 12.
58 High and Lewis, *Corporate Wasteland*, 95.
59 Red Fisher, *Gazette*, 11 March 1996, E3.
60 *Gazette*, 1 March 1996, B2.
61 Pat Hickey, *Gazette*, 25 August 1989, A1; and David Johnston, *Gazette*, 4 February 1996, A5.
62 *Gazette*, 1 October 1995, B2.
63 Jack Todd, *Gazette*, 13 February 1996, D1.
64 Borer, "Important Places and Their Public Faces," 221.
65 Michael Fish, *Gazette*, 28 May 1995, B2.
66 Gare Joyce, *Globe and Mail*, 15 March 1996, D4.
67 David Johnston, *Gazette*, 19 February 1991, A1.
68 Walter Buchignani, *Gazette*, 8 July 1989, A1.
69 Players in the 1940s and 1950s often had to find a second job to supplement their hockey income. Richard kept his job as a welder for the first few years of his hockey career.
70 Michael Farber, *Gazette*, 4 April 1991, F1.
71 Francine Grimaldi, *La Presse*, 6 March 1996, E1.
72 Jack Todd, *Gazette*, 13 February 1996, D1.

73 Lysiane Gagnon, *La Presse*, 12 March 1996, B3.
74 David Johnston, *Gazette*, 23 April 1993, A4.
75 Lysiane Gagnon, *La Presse*, 12 March 1996, B3. "Trop caverneux, trop sonore, trop luisant et trop métallique."
76 Stewart, "Nostalgia – a Polemic," 227.
77 Graham Watt, letter to the editor, *Gazette*, 1 March 1996, B2.
78 Michel Laliberté, *La Presse*, 13 March 1996, A1. "Pour meubler mon bar."
79 Louis Lefebvre and Joseph Rasmussen, letters to the editor, *Gazette*, 26 September 1995, B2.
80 Ibid.
81 Don MacPherson, *Gazette*, 5 March 1996, B3.
82 Qtd. in Patrice Groulx, *Pièges de la mémoire*, 65.
83 Admittedly, the Canadiens won the Stanley Cup in 1993, a win that took everyone by surprise given the team's lacklustre performances since the last Stanley Cup win of 1986. And one must qualify the term "lacklustre" here, because it is relative to the history of the team rather than to actual results. Indeed, the team reached at least the Conference Division semifinals every year between those two cup wins. But fans in Montreal are notorious for criticizing the team for bringing home anything less than the Cup.
84 Derek Drummond, *Gazette*, 8 February 1992, K2.
85 *La Presse*, 6 March 1996, S8. "Pour moi, le Forum c'est mon père et moi, enfant."
86 David Howes, interviewed by Mark Abley, *Gazette*, 22 January 1994, B1.
87 Nathalie Petrowsky, *La Presse*, 13 March 1996, A5. "Appartient aussi à nous, les filles."
88 Yves Létourneau, *La Presse*, 27 August 1989, 11. "Quand jeunes, fanatiques que nous étions, nous avions la chance d'approcher les guichets du Forum et de nous offrir un billet, même debout, nous n'avions qu'une idée en tête: franchir au plus vite les tourniquets et jeter un coup d'oeil sur ce qui se passait en dedans, sur la patinoire."
89 *La Presse*, 7 February 1996, S1. "Rusé placier."
90 Lysiane Gagnon, *La Presse*, 12 March 1996, B3. "Ce que nous cherchons, ce sont les regards, les sifflements et autres témoignages d'appréciation dont pourraient nous gratifier la fine fleur des collèges classiques masculins."
91 *La Presse*, 2 February 1996, S3. "En main propre."

92 *La Presse*, 8 February 1996, s5.

93 *La Presse*, 2 February 1996, s3. "Les alentours du Forum sont déserts. On s'adresse à un préposé aux tourniquets. 'Pas de problème,' qu'il nous fait."

94 Mathias Brunet, *La Presse*, 10 February 1996, G4.

95 Gunderson, "Memory, Modernity and the City," 104.

96 Ibid., 107. The last time the Toronto Maple Leafs had hoisted the Stanley Cup was in 1967.

97 Every issue revives an aspect of Montreal history: the French and English divide over the choice of a unilingual anglophone coach in March 2012 (see http://www.lapresse.ca/le-droit/sports/canadien/201112/19/01-4479297-imperatif-francais-et-la-ministre-st-pierre-sinsurgent.php) or the class divide when the construction of the Canadiens Tower began in July 2012 (see http://www.montrealgazette.com/news/Mike+Boone+Condos+displace+Habs+legends/6947034/story.html) (both accessed 7 August 2012).

98 Bell acquired the Molson Centre in 2002 and changed its name in September of that year. See http://www.bce.ca/news-and-media/releases/show/molson-centre-to-become-the-bell-centre-in-september (accessed 14 September 2012).

99 Sophie Gironnay, *Le Devoir*, 30 March 1996, D12. "Ni beau ni laid, ni renversant, ni catastrophique … plutôt sympa, un peu bedonnant, mais hospitalier. Un vrai bon Québécois moyen, quoi!"

100 *Gazette*, 11 August 1996, A2.

101 Réjean Tremblay, *La Presse*, 25 August 1989, 4. "L'âme n'est pas dans la brique, elle est dans l'esprit de l'équipe."

## Chapter Seven

1 Héroux and Pagé, *Lance et compte*, 62.

2 Detellier, *Mises au jeu*.

3 Irigaray, *Parler n'est jamais neutre* and *Sexes et genres à travers les langues*, to cite only two of many examples.

4 Baillargeon, *Brève histoire des femmes au Québec*; Vacante, "Liberal Nationalism."

5 Héroux and Pagé, *Lance et compte*, 25.

6 Ibid., 48; see also Bélanger, "The Last Game?" and Harvey, "Whose Sweater Is This?"

7 Héroux and Pagé, *Lance et compte*, 36. “Cette histoire québécoise de pure laine.”

8 This concept acknowledges the basic meaning of the term (a specific national audience recognizes itself in the images portrayed on screen) as well as Gilles Deleuze's complexification of the concept as applied to film studies. Felicity J. Colman offers a very lucid description of the latter: “Recognition occurs through complex processes, and is not just a matter of viewing an image on a screen. Rather, that image must contain the processes of thought within it to be affective, actionary, perceivable.” Colman, “Cinema,” 151.

9 Skinner, “Television in Canada: Continuity or Change?” 7–8.

10 Héroux and Pagé, *Lance et compte*, 21–2.

11 Savoie, *Thatcher, Reagan, Mulroney*.

12 P. Fortin, “L'économie du Québec,” 40–1.

13 Héroux and Pagé, *Lance et compte*, 30.

14 Bonneville, “Jean-Claude Lord: Interview,” 16.

15 Like the Canadiens, who won the last two of their twenty-four Stanley Cups in 1986 and 1993, the Nordiques entered a slump in the 1980s, failing even to make the playoffs from 1987 to 1992, the period of *Lance et compte*'s original broadcasts.

16 Claude Héroux and Martine Pagé claim that the series consistently broke viewing records (*Lance et compte*, 7): for season two, the series averaged 2,481,000 viewers (ibid., 151); episode 12 of season three garnered 3,227,000 viewers (ibid., 185). Series reruns aired during the 1995 NHL lockout attracted as many or more viewers as would have an actual game (ibid., 229). Hugo Dumas, reporting for La Presse.ca, notes that *Le Grand Duel*'s season finale in late November 2009 garnered a 50 per cent audience share in Quebec, with 1,788,000 viewers (Dumas, “Fin des émissions”).

17 Space limitations restrict my discussion to the series' dialogue. The original music composed for the first series by Guy Trépanier, however, features English-language pop-rock songs which also foreground the discourse of winners and losers.

18 Héroux and Pagé, *Lance et compte*, 76, 134.

19 Ibid., 65.

20 Ibid., 83.

21 Ibid., 104.

22 Ibid., 154. "Nous réalisons ce que le CRTC dit souhaiter: diffuser une production pancanadienne adoptée par les téléspectateurs d'un océan à l'autre." Héroux specifically blames Tom Curzon, then public-relations director of the CBC, for sabotaging the show's success outside Quebec; the producer finds particularly misguided the state network's plan to broadcast the second season of *He Shoots! He Scores!* after the Saturday evening *Hockey Night in Canada* NHL match, a decision that led to varying (and sometimes quite late) broadcast times. Héroux also implies that even Canadians can become glutted on too much hockey: "Who can watch three hours of live hockey then stay tuned for an hour-long fiction series also set in the hockey world?" ("Qui peut arriver à regarder trois heures de hockey en direct puis rester à l'antenne pour une heure d'une fiction qui se déroule elle-même dans le monde du hockey?") Ibid., 153.

23 Ibid., 62.

24 Ibid., 67.

25 Ibid.

26 Ibid., 105.

27 Ibid., 106.

28 Acknowledging the influence of McGill sociolinguists Mela Sarkar and Lise Winer, I substitute "Vernacular Quebec French" for what they term "NonStandard Quebec French" in order to avoid any implied value judgment. Sarkar and Winer, "Multilingual Codeswitching in Quebec Rap," 179–80.

29 Lubin, "The Politics of Language in Quebec," 174–80.

30 Bouchard, "The Sociolinguistic History of French in Quebec," 161–3.

31 Therrien, "Evolution du langage dans le cinéma québécois."

32 Sarkar and Winer, "Multilingual Codeswitching in Quebec Rap."

33 Sanaker, *La Rencontre des langues dans le cinéma francophone*, 57.

34 *LCII*: 26. "On joue pour notre pays, pis ce pays-là s'appelle le Canada!"

35 Yvan Lamonde provides an overview of this concept and the surrounding debates; whereas some strains of Québécois nationalism turn toward France as a pole of identification to distinguish franco-Québécois culture from the continent's dominant anglo-American culture, others have turned to the notion of the "American" – broadly defined as relating to the Americas (rather than the limited definition appropriated by the United States to refer to its inhabitants and culture)

– to differentiate North American French-speaking cultures and peoples from the "French from France." Lamonde, "Quebec's Americanicity."

36 Bouchard, "The Sociolinguistic History of French in Quebec," 157.

37 Ibid.

38 Carrière, "Américanité et cinéma québécois," 23.

39 Melançon, "La Langue du hockey à travers les âges."

40 Héroux and Pagé, *Lance et compte*, 73. "L'entraîneur du National au langage coloré."

41 Coates, *Men Talk*, 46.

42 Bonneville, "Jean-Claude Lord: Interview," 18–19.

43 Payant, "La Force des formes," 86.

44 *LCI*: 2.

45 See Macdougall, "Facing Off," for a thorough discussion of language in the popular film *Bon Cop, Bad Cop*. And for an analysis of that film's use of hockey, see Ransom, *Hockey, PQ*, 9–17.

46 Bouchard, "The Sociolinguistic History of French in Quebec," 164–5.

47 Jenish, *The Montreal Canadiens: 100 Years of Glory*, 50.

48 Sirois, *Discrimination in the NHL*, 87–8.

49 Ransom, "*Plus ça change* …," in *Hockey, PQ*, 84–117.

50 The original *Lance et compte* series represents a pioneering work; other prime-time serials of the period, like *Duplessis* (1978), *Les Tisserands du pouvoir* (1988), or *Les Filles de Caleb* (1990), tended to exploit historical settings. Indeed, *Lance et compte* opened up the field for subsequent television dramas set in professional milieus and in the present day, such as *Scoop* (1992) and *Omertà* (1996–99). See Émond, "La Représentation du genre masculin et du genre féminin dans le téléroman Québécois," 52.

51 Lamoureux, *L'Amère Patrie*, 137. "Une recomposition imprévue des rôles sociaux de sexe."

52 Baillargeon, "Quebec Women of the Twentieth Century," 241–44; Lamoureux, "The Paradoxes of Quebec Feminism."

53 Vacante, "Liberal Nationalism and the Challenge of Masculinity Studies in Quebec," 101.

54 Parent, "Féminisation et masculinisation des titres de professions au Québec."

55 Vacante, "Liberal Nationalism," 100.

56 Cf. Connell, *Gender and Power*; Sabo, *Sex, Violence and Power in Sports*.

57 Marshall, "Gender, Narrative and National Identity," 55.

58 Sova, *Women in Hollywood*, 21.

59 Elsewhere, I discuss the racial stereotyping involved in Beauchesne's sometimes Sambo-like characterization; see Ransom, *Hockey, PQ*, 93.

60 *LCI*: 1. "C'est fini les parties de fesses avec vos blondes; il faut les oublier."

61 *LCI*: 1. "Je pense que j'suis même pas capab."

62 *LCI*: 6. "Lâche les petites filles! T'as plus les jambs ... Marc, le hockey, c'est une belle game, arrête de la maganer!"

63 Lamoureux, *L'Amère Patrie*, 137. "Un mouvement de virilisation des hommes."

64 Vacante, "Liberal Nationalism," 97.

65 Ibid.

66 Bélanger, "The Last Game?" 299.

67 Connell, "An Iron Man," 83.

68 Ibid., 94.

69 Waugh, *The Romance of Transgression in Canada*, 192.

70 Barrette, "La Télévision est hockey!" 40. "Le grand portrait de famille qui s'élabore autour du sport national."

71 Baillargeon, *Brève Histoire des femmes au Québec*, 181–213.

72 Green, "Léa Pool's *La Femme de l'hôtel* and Women's Film in Québec," 49.

73 See ibid.; M.E. Fortin, "The *En Tant que femmes* Series."

74 Marshall, "Gender, Narrative and National Identity," 52.

75 Bonneville, "Jean-Claude Lord: Interview," 16. "Le rôle d'une femme de quarante ans, beaucoup plus dynamique."

76 Héroux and Pagé, *Lance et compte*, 151.

77 Ibid., 150. "Des femmes de tête, des professionnelles, indépendantes."

78 As Iris Marion Young explains in terms of the cultural and individual significance of the breast (Young, "Breasted Experience"), Suzie's battle is not just with cancer but, having undergone a partial mastectomy, also with Western societies' fetishization of the breast – not just by men but by women as well. Thus, at first unable to see the changes made to her body by the life-saving surgery as anything other than a mutilation of her very self, Suzie must learn to accept her changed appearance and refuse the notion that a decrease in her cup size also diminishes her femininity. This storyline not only allows Marc Gagnon to redeem himself, but it also breaks media taboos, not about showing breasts themselves (full nipple shots occur from season one on), but about

showing only *fetishized* images of breasts. In an astonishing scene that perhaps reflects the French-inflected, more open relationship with the body prevalent in contemporary Quebec, as opposed to the more puritanical American and anglo-Canada one, a post-operative Suzie offers her naked but scarred and wounded breast to Marc to kiss, a scene shot with an actual cancer survivor as Orsini's body double (Dumas, "La fin des émissions").

79 See Ransom, "Real Men Play Hockey: Sport, Masculinity, and National Identity in the *Les Boys* Films," in *Hockey, PQ*, 118–57.

80 Using the statistical methodologies of sociology, Émond calculated the percentage of sequences that Jacques Mercier appeared in professional situations to be 90 per cent of the time; in contrast, Béliveau appeared in such situations only 77 per cent of the time, and there was a much greater amount of narrative time spent on her personal relationships. Similarly, in terms of the various settings in which characters appear in the show, whereas Mercier appeared in "sites of power" as much as 13.5 per cent of the time, Béliveau appeared only 2.2 per cent of the time. Furthermore, Béliveau appeared in "sites of exchange" – suggesting relationality – three times as often as Mercier did. Émond, "La Représentation du genre masculin et du genre féminin dans le téléroman québécois," 61, 64.

81 *LCI: 2*. "Le travail, ça passe avant les affaires du coeur, Ginette."

82 Fuller, "Vamp, the Homebody, and the Upstart," 183.

83 Vacante, "Liberal Nationalism," 103.

84 Ibid.

85 The other flawed character in the post-2000 iterations of *Lance et compte* is Mathias Ladouceur, upon whom Valérie preys after Danny's death; the series blames his failures on a coach's sexual abuse when he was a teenager, and thus also invokes the homophobic elements of Quebec nationalism. See Vacante, "Liberal Nationalism," 102.

86 See Strachan, "37 Years Ago, a Female Journalist Won the Right to Do Her Job."

87 See Disch and Kane, "When a Looker Is Really a Bitch."

88 *LCII: 11*. "Si tu étais une vraie femme ..."

89 Héroux and Pagé, *Lance et compte*, 210.

90 Anouk Bélanger also addresses this issue in a hockey-related context in "The Last Game?"

91 Edensor, *National Identity, Popular Culture and Everyday Life*, 20, 23.

## Chapter Eight

1 Ayot, et al. *Arena: The Art of Hockey*, 2008. Exhibition, Art Gallery of Nova Scotia. For a succinct overview of hockey as literary metaphor, see Kennedy's "Hockey as Metaphor in Selected Canadian Literature."

2 Pryer, "The Aesthetics and Erotics of Hockey," 73.

3 Gowdey, *Riding the Roar of the Crowd*, x.

4 Stompin' Tom Connors's "The Hockey Song," the Tragically Hip's "Fifty Mission Cap," Tom Cochrane's "Big League," and Pierre Letourneau's "Maurice Richard," to name a few.

5 Kennedy, ed., *Going Top Shelf*, 10.

6 See Blake, *Canadian Hockey Literature*. For an exhaustive database of hockey writing, see David McNeil's *Hockey in Print*, http://david-mcneil.ca/hockey/HIP/HIP_current.html (accessed 15 September 2016).

7 This chapter does not cover Simard's *La soirée du fockey* or Germain's *Un pays dont la devise est je m'oublie*. For a description of Germain, see Melançon, *The Rocket*, 143–6.

8 In the introduction to *Les Canadiens*, Salutin refers to himself as a "lifelong Maple Leafs fan" (11), and Benoît Melançon identifies Salutin as "looking at Quebec from the outside" (146). Although I consider myself to have considerably better taste in teams than Salutin does, being in what can best be described as a long-term relationship with the Montreal Canadiens, because I am predominantly anglophone I also approach hockey and theatre in Quebec from an outsider's vantage point.

9 Kidd and Macfarlane, *The Death of Hockey*, 4.

10 Dryden and MacGregor, *Home Game*, 19.

11 Adams, "The Game of Whose Lives?" 71.

12 Robidoux, "Imagining a Canadian Identity through Sport," 218–19.

13 Miller, "Two Versions of Rick Salutin's *Les Canadiens*," n.p.

14 Dryden and MacGregor, *Home Game*, 19.

15 Miller, "Two Versions," n.p.

16 Nardocchio, *Theatre and Politics*, 64.

17 Salutin, *Les Canadiens*, 22.

18 Ibid.

19 According to Miller's "Two Versions," both Theatre Passe Muraille and Neptune productions were extensively edited to "reflect an apolitical view of the play" (n.p.).
20 Miller, "They Shoot! They Score," 148.
21 Nardocchio, *Theatre and Politics in Modern Quebec*, 64.
22 Salutin, *Les Canadiens*, 27.
23 Nardocchio, *Theatre and Politics*, 64.
24 Qtd. in Salutin, *Les Canadiens*, 7.
25 Ibid., 21.
26 Qtd. in ibid., 12.
27 Ibid., 12. The cover art, by Bill Featherstone, clearly alludes to Benjamin West's 1770 *The Death of General Wolfe*. Even more striking is the Canadiens player in the foreground, since he is aiming his hockey stick as if it were a rifle – a symbol from the script.
28 Ibid., 13.
29 Qtd. in ibid., 13.
30 Harvey, "Whose Sweater Is This?" 34.
31 Miller, "Two Versions," n.p.
32 Linteau, *The History of Montreal*, 165.
33 Loranger and Levac, *Le Chemin du Roy*, 21.
34 Ibid., 22.
35 Ibid., 23.
36 Salutin, *Les Canadiens*, 27.
37 Gina Mallet, "*Les Canadiens* a Rousing Opening," *Toronto Star*, 21 October 1977.
38 Max Wyman, "Arts Club Shoots, It Scores," *Vancouver Sun*, 21 April 1978.
39 Miller, "Two Versions," n.p.
40 Renate Usmiani argues "that historical drama in Quebec up to this point serves mainly the function of demythification." "The Playwright as Historiographer," 127.
41 Loranger and Levac, *Le Chemin du Roy*, 22.
42 Max Wyman, "Arts Club Shoots, It Scores," *Vancouver Sun*, 21 April 1978.
43 Salutin, *Les Canadiens*, 27.
44 Ibid., 28.
45 Dickinson and Young, *A Short History of Quebec*, 49.
46 Salutin, *Les Canadiens*, 12.
47 Ibid., 39.

48 Dickinson and Young, *A Short History*, 109.
49 Miller, "Two Versions," n.p.
50 Salutin, *Les Canadiens*, 42.
51 McKinley, *Hockey: A People's History*, 7.
52 Dickinson and Young, *A Short History*, 251.
53 Salutin, *Les Canadiens*, 45.
54 Ibid.
55 Ibid., *Les Canadiens*, 48–9.
56 Dowbiggin, *The Meaning of Puck*, 41. For more on the financial aspects, see Ross, *Joining the Clubs*, 38.
57 Ibid.
58 Salutin, *Les Canadiens*, 52.
59 Jenish, *The Montreal Canadiens*, 43.
60 Salutin, *Les Canadiens*, 55.
61 Jenish, *The Montreal Canadiens*, 46.
62 Salutin, *Les Canadiens*, 91. On the shift from a francophone to a mixed fan-base, as shown in literature, see Jason Blake's chapter in this volume.
63 Salutin, *Les Canadiens*, 94.
64 Dickinson and Young, *History of Quebec*, 296.
65 Salutin, *Les Canadiens*, 102.
66 Ibid., 106.
67 Ibid., 109.
68 Jenish, *The Montreal Canadiens*, 146.
69 Salutin, *Les Canadiens*, 110.
70 Melançon, *The Rocket*, 148.
71 Salutin, *Les Canadiens*, 111.
72 Ibid. In his introduction (14) Salutin attributes this quote to Tim Burke of the *Gazette*. The same interpretation has been put forward by a few (sports-leaning) sources: Jean Harvey, who cites Alain-G. Gagnon and M.B. Montcalm, calls the Richard Riot the "spark that fuelled later and more explicitly political protests … that would lead to the Quiet Revolution" ("Whose Sweater Is This?" 39). In his 29 November 1999 *Sports Illustrated* article, "Loud Start to the Quiet Revolution," Michael Farber refers to the riot as a "harbinger" of the election of Lesage and the Quiet Revolution (124). The title of Farber's article is borrowed from another *Gazette* writer, Red Fisher, whom he quotes as saying, "If that was the start of the Quiet Revolution, it wasn't very quiet."

73 Melançon, *The Rocket*, 149.
74 Salutin, *Les Canadiens*, 111.
75 Nardocchio, *Theatre and Politics*, 64.
76 Ibid., 64.
77 Qtd. in ibid., 132.
78 Qtd. in ibid., 135. The difficulty on the part of anglophone reviewers to acknowledge *Le Chemin du Roy* as theatre suggests the advanced quality of Quebec drama (and its audience) in the late 1960s. At that time, English Canadian drama was just on the verge of establishing itself, an early example being George Ryga's *The Ecstasy of Rita Joe,* which premiered in 1967 and was one of the first English Canadian plays to address a Canadian social problem: the plight of our First Nations. For more on the establishment of a Canadian voice in theatre, see Don Rubin's winter 1974 *Canadian Theatre Review* article "Creeping toward a Culture: The Theatre in English Canada Since 1945," where he asserts that, in 1967, "French language Canada seems to have achieved its cultural identity some years earlier." Qtd. in Rubin, ed., *Canadian Theatre History*, 323.
79 Loranger and Levac, *Le Chemin du Roy*, 60.
80 Thomson, *Vive le Québec Libre*, 197.
81 Ibid., 51.
82 Loranger and Levac, *Le Chemin du Roy*, 70.
83 Ibid., 71.
84 Godin, *Daniel Johnson*, 216.
85 Loranger and Levac, *Le Chemin du Roy*, 70.
86 Ibid., 76–7.
87 Ibid., 83.
88 Here, the political struggle overshadows the game. Salutin reaches a similar conclusion in *Les Canadiens*, since in Act 2 players and fans alike stop paying undivided attention to a hockey game at the Forum – they are, instead, following live updates of the 1976 provincial election.
89 Loranger and Levac, *Le Chemin du Roy*, 84.
90 Ibid., 119.
91 Ibid., 121.
92 Ibid.
93 Act 2 centres on fictional Canadiens player Dave Kirk as he prepares for the game that night: attending a French class, taking a nap and

experiencing a nightmare, and discussing the election in the dressing room with teammates.

94 Salutin, *Les Canadiens*, 170.

95 Ibid., 173.

96 Podbrey, *Half Man, Half Beast*, 71.

97 Miller, "Two Versions," n.p.

98 Melançon, *The Rocket*, 149.

99 Salutin, *Les Canadiens*, 177.

100 Harvey, "Whose Sweater Is This?" 39.

101 Salutin and Dryden address the dichotomous situation of non-francophones playing for the Canadiens in Act 2 when a group of English speaking players attend French class. The substitute French teacher, Mme Miron, has all but given up on trying to teach the players ("Oublier! Forget it! C'est pas la peine! It's not worth the trouble!" [128]) when she realizes that her "pauvres étudiants" are in fact "nos Canadiens" (126). Miron then acknowledges the "special situation" and tries a "different approach" whereby she placates the team with a childish song instead of teaching them more conversational French: "Mes joueurs ont tous des beaux patins … / Des beaux patins … / Et pis skate, skate, skate … / Patine plus vite …" (131). Salutin's stage directions question the perceived double standard – "singing and learning Bilingualism can indeed be fun, but does it really solve anything?" – and only Kirk seems concerned with Miron's shift in attitude: "She doesn't like us when we're English, but she likes us fine when we're the Canadiens" (132).

102 The details of which can be found in Dowbiggin, *Meaning of Puck*, 26–30.

103 Ibid., *Meaning of Puck*, 28.

104 Qtd. in Bill Beacon, "Habs GM Apologizes for Unilingual Coach," *Globe and Mail*, 3 January 2012. On the Cunneyworth affair, among others, see the chapters by Amy Ransom and Julie Perrone in this volume.

105 Qtd. in Les Perreaux, "In Montreal, No French behind the Bench," *Globe and Mail*, 19 December 2011.

106 In a mid-1980s interview with Albert-Reiner Glaap, Salutin himself noted, "There's always the danger, the risk when writing something like [*Les Canadiens*] that it'll date." He did, however, add, "I think it was wonderful to be as contemporary as I was and I would trade in the timeliness for the timelessness you get when you go in another direction." Glaap, "Interview with Rick Salutin, author of *Les Canadiens*," 15.

107 Quebec drama, with an authentic Québécois voice, was being produced in the late 1940s (a seminal example being Gratien Gélinas's *Tit-Coq*, 1948); English Canadian drama wouldn't follow suit until almost two decades later. Groundbreaking French-language companies, like Théâtre du Rideau Vert (1949) and Théâtre du Nouveau Monde (1951), were, again, established before their English relatives, such as Toronto Workshop Productions (1959) and Theatre Passe Muraille (1968).

## Chapter Nine

1 Ferguson, *Beauty Tips from Moose Jaw*, 188.

2 Kroetsch, *The Studhorse Man*, 122; Weiss, "Jean Beliveau Was Number Four," 8.

3 Buma, *Refereeing Identity*; Dopp and Harrison, eds., *Now Is the Winter*; Blake, *Canadian Hockey Literature*; Ransom, *Hockey, PQ*, 6.

4 Scott Young, *A Boy at the Leafs' Camp*, 10. The other two books in the famous series are *Scrubs on Skates* and *Boy on Defence* (as well as *That Old Gang of Mine*, a pulp novel with saucy language, saucier scenes, and grown-up boys).

5 Recent non-fiction such as Bruce Dowbiggin's *The Meaning of Puck*, Khan's *Of Hockey and Hijab*, and Kennedy's *My Country Is Hockey* uses hockey as an inroad to examining Canada; each observes Quebec through a hockey lens.

6 Blaise, "I'm Dreaming of Rocket Richard," 30, 35.

7 Smith, *Puckstruck*, 20.

8 Don Bell, "Hockey Night in Métabetchouan," 35. On the "naturalness" of the game, see Gruneau and Whitson, *Hockey Night in Canada*.

9 Patoine, "*On est Canayen ou ben on l'est pas*," 10. Patoine's playful false dichotomy does not seem to admit layered identity. The English is taken from Scott Irving's 2015 translation, *Hockey and Philosophy*, 4.

10 For the most spirited view on this topic, see Bissoondath's *Selling Illusions*.

11 Wright, *The Age of Longing*, 1.

12 Stack, "A New Game," http://ceauthors.com/eAnthology.pdf (accessed 8 December 2016). The story takes place just before the Canadiens relocated to the Molson Centre. On whether Morenz's popularity and stardom was aided by his early demise (and also on ghosts), see Perrone,

"The King Has Two Bodies," 95–110. See also Emmanuel Lapierre's chapter in this volume.

13 The dates do not support Stack's narrative: the Maroons' final season in the National Hockey League was 1938; Morenz died in 1937. See Stack, "A New Game"; Richler, "Writers and Sports," 249; MacLennan, *Two Solitudes*, 319. On *Two Solitudes* and "unity-by-hockey," see Buma, *Refereeing Identity*, 120–1.

14 Given that most Quebec hockey writing focuses on the glory years of the Montreal Canadiens, Richard's prominence is understandable; even so, Jean Béliveau is a distant second in terms of literary cameos in French-language hockey literature, and Guy Lafleur appears only here and there.

15 Hood, "The Sportive Centre of Saint Vincent de Paul," 124, 21.

16 Salutin, *Les Canadiens*, 10. For a book-length examination of what goes into making a mythology, see Melançon's *Les yeux de Maurice Richard*.

17 Falla, *Saved*, 214. Michael Buma points out that the "device" of an American narrator "allows Falla to engage in an unusual level of exposition about the game's history and cultural importance to Canada." *Refereeing Identity*, 118. Such precision slows down the narrative flow, since lengthy explanations about popular legends are tedious.

18 Richler, "Cheap Skates," 143; Richler, "The Fall of the Montreal Canadiens," 254; Richler, "Writers and Sports," 97–9.

19 Dryden, *The Game*, 73. Richler, *Barney's Version*, 121; Gravel, *Le Match des étoiles*, 12. "C'est incroyable, mesdames et messieurs, absolument incroyable, même avec deux joueurs accrochés à son chandail, Maurice Richard continue à patiner …"

20 The quotations used here are from *The Rocket: A Cultural History of Maurice Richard*, Fred A. Reed's translation of Melançon's *Les yeux de Maurice Richard*, 6. On theology and the Habs, see Barreau and Bauer's 2009 volume *La religion du Canadien de Montréal* (*Hockey as a Religion*, 2011). Bauer argues that the hockey team's iconic status gained from Quebec's post-Quiet Revolution exodus from Catholicism. See also Melançon, *The Rocket*, 191.

21 Purdy, "Homage to Ree-shard." To be clear, Purdy's phonetic playfulness is miles away from the doggerel tradition of William Henry Drummond, or Wilson MacDonald of "Monsieur Joliat" infamy: "Morenz 'e go lak' one beeg storm; / Syl Mantha's strong and fat. / Dere all ver' good, but none ees quite / So good as Joliat." Available at *Representative Poetry*

*Online* (sic!). http://rpo.library.utoronto.ca/poems/monsieur-joliat (accessed 8 December 2016).

22 I thank an anonymous reviewer for pointing this out.

23 Foran, *Maurice Richard*, 13. The translation is Pozier's own. The French: "De patiner simplement à jamais / Seul / Les yeux dans les cieux / Sans rumeurs et sans but / Libre de toute entrave." Bernard Pozier kindly provided me with a copy of his poem.

24 Of course, Richard's rival, anglophone Gordie Howe, also wore number 9. Howe fans could therefore pretend that the girl's sweater on the bill evokes "Mr. Hockey."

25 Meyer, *The Time of the Last Goal*, 49. Because this story has been analysed very often, I give it short shrift here. See Blake, *Canadian Hockey Literature*, 21–2.

26 Falla, *Saved*, 90.

27 Dionne, *Sainte Flanelle, gagnez pour nous!* 115. "Pas façile de marier le sport avec un cours de français." Melançon, in "Écrire Maurice Richard," writes of Richard's "entrée dans le canon scolaire canadien et Québécois" (27).

28 Ibid., 123, 187. Melançon, *The Rocket*, 208.

29 On popular media's role in creating meaning and myth, especially as meanings change over time, see Melançon, "Écrire Maurice Richard." Wayne Johnston's short story "The Montreal Canadiens" is in the voice of a sportswriter who was writing for the *Montreal Gazette* while Richard was "'writing' a column, too. It was called *Le Tour du* Chapeau" (34).

30 Falla, *Saved*, 214.

31 Melançon *The Rocket*, 27.

32 Kanaganayakam, "Snarling the Gardiner," n.p.

33 McCormack, *Understanding Ken*, 209. The infamous Vancouver riot after the 2011 Stanley Cup finals adds irony to the narrator's naive statement. John Ralston Saul muses, meanwhile, while speaking of a nineteenth-century riot, that in Canada "our stable, middle class democracy ... hates to be reminded of riots." Saul, *Louis-Hippolyte LaFontaine and Robert Baldwin*, 21.

34 On the literary role of the Nordiques, including a very thorough analysis of the Lindros affair in literature, see Ransom's chapter "'The Nordiques Have Disappeared!' Hockey, Science Fiction, and Nationalist Fantasies in Quebec" in her *Hockey, PQ*.

35 Jarman, "Righteous Speedboat," 234. In "Hockey et politique, même combat!" Jean-Claude Simard points out that, post-Quiet Revolution, Québécois had to be *either* federalist or separatist, and that hockey was folded into this dilemma (39). As Terry Gitersos elucidates in his chapter in this volume, the Nordiques, with their fleur-de-lys logo, were viewed as *the* separatist team; for many they had replaced the Montreal Canadiens as the signifier of the modern aspirations of Québécois, and to this day one is for either the departed Nordiques or the Canadiens.

36 McKinley, "Next Year," 53, 60; Buma, *Refereeing Identity*, 114–15. Buma is not commenting on "Next Year" but on Wayne Johnston's comic novel *The Divine Ryans*. Johnston writes, "When Montreal was playing Toronto at the Forum, it was not a hockey game, but a holy war, a crusade carried on nationwide TV, Rome's Canadiens versus Canterbury's Maple Leafs, 'the heathen Leafs against the Holy Habs.'" Johnston, *The Divine Ryans*, 77.

37 Young and Robertson, *Face-Off*, 76; Kidd, *The Struggle for Canadian Sport*, 259.

38 Beardsley, *Country on Ice*, 42; Fraser, interview with author, 3 July 2012. Fraser added the telling qualifier: "I can't think of a rinkful of Canadian politicians actually contributing much to English-French relations."

39 Orti, "The Stanley Cup Conspiracy," 43; Richards, *Hockey Dreams*, 234–5.

40 Mary Louise Adams bluntly and accurately states, "[Hockey] is part of the obfuscating construction of the so-called 'ordinary Canadian,'" before adding, "[I]f hockey is life in Canada, then Canada remains decidedly masculine and white." Adams, "The Game of Whose Lives?" 14. Anouk Bélanger, meanwhile, focuses on Quiet-Revolution-era Quebec and concludes that hockey aided "the construction of a specifically heterosexual, homophobic and aggressive form of masculinity." Bélanger, "The Last Game?" 284.

41 Hewson, "You Said You Didn't Give a Fuck about Hockey," 192.

42 See Harvey, "Whose Sweater Is This?" 29–52. "Ma première idée consistait à sacrer ici Saku Koivu le plus grand héros québécois moderne." Corbeil, "L'île qu'on appelait L'Île," 63. On Koivu's French and the political repercussions, see Patoine, "*On est Canayen ou ben on l'est pas*," 21. See also Frazer Andrews' chapter in this volume for a theatrical take.

43 The "link of loyalty" quotation is from Englishman George Beers, who

worked hard in the mid-nineteenth century to establish lacrosse as the "national game of Canada." For a brief overview of lacrosse vs. hockey in a literary context, see Buma, *Refereeing Identity*, 6–9; for a thorough historical account, see Morrow and Wamsley's chapter on lacrosse in *Sport in Canada: A History*.

44 Poulter, *Becoming Native in a Foreign Land*, 18. The "other groups" include the "the Eurekas and the Young Jubilees who played for the Coloured Championship of Halifax and Dartmouth in 1895" (ibid.).

45 Gopnik, *Winter*, 159.

## Chapter Ten

1 Smith and Watson, *Reading Autobiography*.

2 King, *The Truth about Stories*.

3 Laraque, *Georges Laraque: The Story of the NHL's Unlikeliest Tough Guy*, 241.

4 Ibid., 235.

5 Ibid.

6 "Canadiens Part Ways with Heavyweight Georges Laraque," *Toronto Star*, 21 January 2010.

7 Laraque, *The Story of the NHL's Unlikeliest Tough Guy*, 339.

8 Smith and Watson, *Reading Autobiography*, 164.

9 Harrison, "Between a Puck and a Showpiece," 156.

10 Ryan, "Narrative in Real Time," 145.

11 Ibid.

12 Gaston, *The Good Body*, 42.

13 Hedley, *Twenty Miles*, 146.

14 Ibid., 140.

15 Orr, *Orr: My Story*, 2–3.

16 Laraque, *The Story of the NHL's Unlikeliest Tough Guy*, 300.

17 Ibid., 300.

18 Ibid., 8.

19 Ibid.

20 Ibid., 77.

21 Ibid., 79.

22 Ibid., 102. Emphasis added.

23 Ibid., 103.

24 Ibid.
25 Ibid., 102–3.
26 Ibid., 107.
27 Ibid., 125.
28 Ibid., 242.
29 "Le hockey c'est un sport, avant tout. Je ne peux pas le prendre d'un coté personnel … Ce que je fais sur la patinoire, ça ne me définit pas comme personne … J'aide [tout] le monde, c'est ça qui pour moi est tant important. Il y a beaucoup d'autres choses dans la vie que l'hockey." Ibid., 243.
30 Ibid., 331.
31 Ibid., 135.
32 Ibid., 134.
33 Ibid., 11.
34 Ibid., 12.
35 Ibid.
36 Ibid., 14.
37 Ibid., 15.
38 Ibid., 25.
39 Ibid., 26.
40 Ibid., 31.
41 Ibid., 13.
42 Ibid., 129.
43 Ibid., 128.
44 Ibid., 129.
45 Ibid., 241.
46 Ibid., 248.
47 Ibid., 246–7.
48 Ibid., 9.
49 Ibid., 132.
50 Ibid., 192.
51 Ibid., 11. "'Nègre.' Cinq lettres, un mot. Un mot qui résonna autour du moi durant toute mon enfance et toute mon adolescence. Un mot que des voix crièrent, hurlèrent à mes oreilles. Même lorsqu'il était chuchoté, il ne manquait jamais de m'abasourdir, de créer un vacarme assourdissant au plus profond de mon être. Toujours, ce mot était précédé d'une épithète. 'Sale' revenait souvent. Parfois, il était accompagné d'un autre type de qualification, du genre 'hostie de nègre.'"

52 Ibid. "Toute la beauté et la grandeur intrinsèque de ce mot."
53 Laraque, *The Story of the NHL's Unlikeliest Tough Guy*, 2.
54 Ibid., 2.
55 Ibid., 3.
56 See Genette, *Paratexts*, 11–13.
57 "Tout au long de sa carrière au sein de la Ligue nationale de hockey, Georges Laraque a démontré plus d'une fois que la passion et la détermination peuvent mener loin! Pour lui, tout rêve est réalisable lorsqu'on a la force d'y croire. Il livre ici une autobiographie à son image: franche et directe. Le racisme, la violence, la religion, la famille, la politique ... Aucun sujet n'y est tabou. L'athlète raconte comment il est parvenu à se frayer un chemin dans un monde où les préjugés et la discrimination faisaient loi. Se tournant maintenant vers l'avenir, l'ancien hockeyeur dévoile tout de ses convictions profondes, de sa découverte du végétalisme, de ses nombreux projets humanitaires, de ses prises de position écologiques … Au-delà du physique imposant de l'homme fort, découvrez un intellectuel sensible et engagé, guidé par des valeurs inébranlables."
58 Laraque, *La force d'y croire*, 9. "Dès que j'ai lu l'autobiographie de Jackie Robinson, enfant, j'ai rêvé de raconter mon histoire … J'espère que mon autobiographie sera une source d'inspiration pour un grand nombre d'entre vous, autant que le fut pour moi celle de Jackie, qui a changé ma vie."
59 Laraque, Georges, interview with author, 27 January 2012.
60 Laraque, *The Story of the NHL's Unlikeliest Tough Guy*, 127.
61 Laraque, Georges, interview with author, 27 January 2012.
62 Laraque, *The Story of the NHL's Unlikeliest Tough Guy*, 6.
63 Ibid., 1.
64 Ibid., 1–2.
65 Bauer, *Hockey as a Religion*, 48.
66 Smith and Watson, *Reading Autobiography*, 235.
67 Ibid.

# BIBLIOGRAPHY


Adams, Mary Louise. "The Game of Whose Lives? Gender, Race, and Entitlement in Canada's 'National Game.'" In David Whitson and Richard Gruneau, eds., *Artificial Ice: Hockey, Culture and Commerce*. 71–84. Peterborough, ON: Broadview Press 2006.

Allain, Kristi. "'Real Fast and Tough': The Construction of Canadian Hockey Masculinity." *Sociology of Sport Journal* 25, 4 (2008): 462–71.

Anderson, Benedict. *L'imaginaire national: Réflexions sur l'origine et l'essor du nationalisme*. Paris: La Découverte 2002 (1983).

– *Imagined Communities: Reflections on the Origins and Spread of Nationalism*. London: Verso 1983.

Antohi, Sorin. "De l'État-nation à l'État-parti roumain: Le sport instrument de conscience nationale." *Quasimodo* 3–4 (1997): 101–8.

Auf der Maur, Nick. *A Montreal Life*. Montreal: Véhicule Press 1998.

Ayot, Pierre et al. ARENA: *The Art of Hockey*. Exhibition. Halifax, Art Gallery of Nova Scotia. 2008.

Baillargeon, Denyse. *Brève histoire des femmes au Québec*. Montreal: Boréal 2012.

– "Entre la 'Revanche' et la 'Veillée'des berceaux: Les médecins québécois francophones, la mortalité infantile et la question nationale, 1910–1940." *Canadian Bulletin of Medical History/Bulletin canadien d'histoire de la médicine* 19 (2002): 113–37.

– "Quebec Women of the Twentieth Century: Milestones in an Unfinished

Journey." In Stephan Gervais, Christopher Kirkey, and Jarrett Rudy, eds., *Quebec Questions*. 231–48. Don Mills, ON: Oxford University Press 2011.
Baillargeon, Normand. *La vraie dureté mental: Hockey et philosophie*. Québec: Les presses de l'université Laval 2009.
Baillargeon, Normand, and Christian Boissinot, eds. *Hockey and Philosophy*. Trans. Scott Irving. Ottawa: University of Ottawa Press 2015.
Baril, Lynda, *Nos glorieuses: Plus de cent ans de hockey féminin au Québec*. Montreal: Les Éditions La Presse 2013.
Barlow, John Matthew. "'Scientific Aggression': Irishness, Manliness, Class, and Commercialization in the Shamrock Hockey Club of Montreal, 1894–1901." In John Chi-Kit Wong, ed., *Coast to Coast: Hockey in Canada to the Second World War*. 35–85. Toronto: University of Toronto Press 2009.
Barreau, Jean-Marc, and Olivier Bauer, eds. *La religion du Canadien de Montréal*. Montreal: Éditions Fides 2009.
Barrette, Pierre. "La Télévision est hockey!" *24 images* 152 (2011): 40–1.
Barrette, Rosaire. *Léo Dandurand, Sportsman*. Ottawa, Ontario: Le Droit 1952.
Bauer, Olivier. "Le Canadien de Montréal est-il une religion." In Jean-Marc Barreau and Olivier Bauer, eds., *La religion du Canadien de Montréal*. 29–80. Montreal: Éditions Fides 2009.
– *Hockey as a Religion: The Montreal Canadiens*. Champaign, IL: Common Ground Publishing 2011.
Bean, Kellie. *Post-Backlash Feminism: Women in the Media since Reagan-Bush*. Jefferson, NC: McFarland 2007.
Beardsley, Doug. *Country on Ice*. Victoria, BC: Polestar Press 1987.
Bégin, Pierre-Luc. *Loyalisme et fanatisme: Petite histoire du mouvement orangiste canadien*. Québec: Éditions du Québécois 2008.
Behiels, Michael. *Prelude to Quebec's Quiet Revolution: Liberalism versus Neo-Nationalism, 1945–60*. Montreal and Kingston, ON: McGill-Queen's University Press 1985.
Bélanger, Anouk. "Le hockey au Quebec, bien plus qu'un jeu: analyse sociologique de la place centrale du hockey dans le projet identitaire des Québécois." *Loisir et Société* 19, no. 2 (1996): 539–57.
– "The Last Game? Hockey and the Experience of Masculinity in Quebec." In Philip White and Kevin Young, eds., *Sport and Gender in Canada*. 292–309. Toronto: Oxford University Press 1999.

– “Where Have the Ghosts Gone? Sports Venues and the Political Economy of Memory in Montreal.” PhD thesis, Simon Fraser University, 1999.

Bélanger, Anouk, and Fannie Valois-Nadeau. “Entre l’étang gelé et le Centre Bell.” In Normand Baillargeon and Christian Boissinot, eds., *La vraie dureté du mental: Hockey et philosophie*. 73–94. Quebec City: Les Presses de l’Université Laval 2009.

Bell, Don. “Hockey Night in Métabetchouan.” In Dale Jacobs, ed., *Ice: New Writing on Hockey*. 33–47. Edmonton: Spotted Cow Press 1999.

Bell, Michael Mayerfeld. “The Ghost of Place.” *Theory and Society* 26, no. 6 (1997):813–36.

Bergero, Léandre. *The History of Quebec: A Patriote’s Handbook*. Toronto: NC Press 1975.

Berlant, Lauren. *Compassion: The Culture and Politics of an Emotion*. New York and London: Routledge 2009 (2004).

Bienvenue, Louise, and Christine Hudon. “Pour devenir homme, tu transgresseras…: Quelques enjeux de la socialisation masculine dans les collèges classiques québécois (1880–1939).” *Canadian Historical Review* 86, no. 3 (2005): 485–511.

Billig, Michael. *Banal Nationalism*. Thousand Oaks, CA: Sage Publications 1995.

Bissoondath, Neil. *Selling Illusions*. Revised Edition. Toronto: Penguin Canada 2002.

Black, François. “Évolution de l’image projetée par le Club de Hockey Canadien depuis ses origines jusqu’au mythe de la tradition glorieuse.” MA thesis, Université de Montréal, 1992.

– *Habitants et glorieux: Les Canadiens de 1909 à 1960*. Laval: Éditions Mille-Îles 1997.

Blaise, Clark. “I’m Dreaming of Rocket Richard.” In Doug Beardsley, ed., *Our Game: An All-Star Collection of Hockey Fiction*. 30–7. Victoria, BC: Polestar 1997.

Blake, Jason. *Canadian Hockey Literature*. Toronto: University of Toronto Press 2010.

Blevins, David. *The Sports Hall of Fame Encyclopedia*, vol. 1. Lanham, MD: Scarecrow Press 2012.

Bonneville, Léo. “Jean-Claude Lord: Interview.” *Séquences* 128 (1987): 12–20.

Borer, Michael Ian. “Important Places and Their Public Faces:

Understanding Fenway Park as a Public Symbol." *Journal of Popular Culture* 39, no. 2 (2006): 205–24.

Bouchard, Chantal. "The Sociolinguistic History of French in Quebec." In Stephan Gervais, Christopher Kirkey, and Jarrett Rudy, eds., *Quebec Questions*. 153–67. Don Mills, ON: Oxford University Press 2011.

Bourbonnais, Jean. *Champions: Le rouge et le bleu*. Film. Production La Presse Télé 2007.

Brown, William. *The Montreal Maroons: The Forgotten Stanley Cup Champions*. Montreal: Véhicule Press 1999.

Buma, Michael. *Refereeing Identity: The Cultural Work of Canadian Hockey Novels*. Montreal and Kingston: McGill-Queen's University Press 2012.

Cantelon, Hart, and Richard S. Gruneau. *Sport, Culture, and the Modern State*. Toronto: University of Toronto Press 1982.

Carrier, Roch. *Le Chandail de Hockey*. Toronto: Livres Toundra 1979.

– "The Hockey Sweater." Trans. Sheila Fischman. In Doug Beardsley, ed., *Our Game: An All-Star Collection of Hockey Fiction*. 15–17. Victoria, BC: Polestar 1997.

– *Our Life with the Rocket: The Maurice Richard Story*. Trans. Sheila Fischman. Toronto: Penguin 2001.

Carrière, Louis. "Américanité et cinéma québécois." *Ciné-Bulles* 14, no. 3 (1995): 20–3.

*Cent Ans des Canadiens de Montréal/Hundred Years of the Montreal Canadiens*. DVD. Dir. Christopher Paine. Warner Home Video 2009.

Cha, Jonathan. "La ville est hockey: De la hockeyisation de la ville à la representation architecturale: Une quête urbaine." *Journal de la société pour l'étude de l'architecture au Canada* 34, no. 1 (2009): 3–18.

Cléobule. "Les Dangereux Tricolore." *Cité Libre* (1958): 44.

Coates, Jennifer. *Men Talk: Stories in the Making of Masculinity*. Malden, MA, Oxford, and Melbourne: Blackwell Publishing 2003.

Coleman, William D. "From Bill 22 to Bill 101: The Politics of Language under the Parti Québécois." *Canadian Journal of Political Science* 14, no. 3 (1981): 475–6.

Colman, Felicity J. "Cinema: Movement – Image – Recognition – Time." In Charles J. Stivale, ed., *Key Concepts*. 141–56. Montreal and Kingston: McGill-Queen's University Press 2005.

Connell, R.W. *Gender and Power: Society, the Person and Sexual Politics*. Stanford, CA: Stanford University Press 1987.

– "An Iron Man: The Body and Some Contradictions of Hegemonic Masculinity." In Michael A. Messner and Donald F. Sabo, eds., *Sport, Men, and the Gender Order*. 83–96. Champaign, IL: Human Kinetics 1990.
– *Masculinities*, 2nd ed. Berkeley: University of California Press 2005.
Connor, Walker. "Beyond Reason: The Nature of the Ethnonational Bond." *Ethnic and Racial Studies*, 16, no. 3 (1993): 373–89.
Corbeil, Guillaume. "L'île qu'on appelait L'Île." In Guillaume Corbeil, ed., *L'art de la Fugue*. 63–73. Quebec City: L'Instant Même 2008.
Delisle, Esther. *Myths, Memories, and Lies: Québec's Intelligentsia and the Fascist Temptation, 1939–1960*. Trans. Madeleine Hébert. Westmount, QC: Robert Davies Multimedia 1998.
– *The Traitor and the Jew: Anti-Semitism and Extremist Right-Wing Nationalism in Québec from 1929 to 1939*. Trans. Madeleine Hébert, Claire Rothman, and Käthe Roth. Montreal: R. Davies Publishing 1993.
Demers, Clément. "Le nouveau centre-ville de Montréal." *Cahiers de géographie du Québec* 27, no. 71 (1983): 209–35.
Detellier, Élise. "Bonifier le capital humain: le genre dans le discours médical et religieux sur les sports au Québec, 1920–1950." *Revue d'histoire de l'Amérique française* 62, nos. 3–4 (2009): 478–81.
– *Mises au jeu: Les Sports féminins à Montréal, 1919–1961*. Montréal: Les éditions du remue-ménage 2015.
Deville-Danthu, Bernadette. *Le Sport en noir et blanc: du sport colonial africain dans les anciens territoires français d'Afrique occidentale (1920-1965)*. Paris and Montreal: L'Harmattan 1997.
Diamond, Dan, and Joseph Romain, *Hockey Hall of Fame*. Toronto: Doubleday Canada 1980.
Dickinson, John, and Brian Young. *A Short History of Quebec*. Montreal and Kingston: McGill-Queen's University Press 2008.
Dieckhoff, Alain. "Nationalisme politique contre nationalisme culturel?" In Alain Dieckhoff and Christophe Jaffrelot, eds., *Repenser le nationalisme: Théories et pratique*. 105–29. Paris: Presses de Sciences Po[.] 2006.
Di Felice, David. "The Richard Riot: A Socio-Historical Examination of Sport, Culture, and the Construction of Symbolic Identities." MA thesis, Queen's University, 1999.
Dionne, Claude. *Sainte Flanelle, gagnez pour nous!* Montreal: VLB Éditeur 2012.

Disch, Lisa, and Mary Jo Kane. "When a Looker Is Really a Bitch." In Susan Birrell and Mary G. McDonald, eds., *Reading Sport: Critical Essays on Power and Representation.* 108–43. Boston, MA: Northeastern University Press 2000.

Dodds, Jeramy. "Canadæ." *Geist* 84 (spring 2012): 52. Also available at http://www.geist.com/fact/poetry/canadae/ (accessed 8 December 2016)

Dopp, Jamie, and Richard Harrison. *Now Is the Winter: Thinking about Hockey.* Hamilton, ON: Wolsak and Wynn 2009.

Dowbiggin, Bruce. *The Meaning of Puck: How Hockey Explains Modern Canada.* Toronto: Key Porter Books 2008.

Dryden, Ken. *The Game.* 3rd ed. Toronto: McClelland and Stewart 1999.

Dryden, Ken and Roy MacGregor. *Home Game: Hockey and Life in Canada.* Rev. ed. Toronto: McClelland & Stewart 1994.

Duch, Jordi Salvador. "Futbol, metàfora d'una guerra Freda: Un estudi antropològic del barça." PhD thesis, Rovira and Virgili University, Tarragona, Spain, 2004.

Duhaime, Vincent. "La construction du père québécois: Le discours du mouvement familial et l'expérience des pères, 1945–1965." MA thesis, Université de Montréal, 2000.

– "'Les pères ont ici leur devoirs': Le discours de movement familial québécois et la construction de la paternité dans l'après guerre, 1945–1960." *Revue d'histoire de l'Amérique française* 57, no. 4 (2004): 535–66.

Dumas, Hugo. "La fin des émissions. " *La Presse.ca.* 25 November 2009. http://www.lapresse.ca/debats/chroniques/hugo-dumas/200911/25/01-924897-fin-des-emissions.php (accessed 17 July 2012).

Durand, Marc. *La Coupe à Québec, les Bulldogs et la naissance du hockey.* Quebec City: Éditions Sylvain Harvey et Commission de la capitale nationale du Québec 2012.

Edensor, Tim. *National Identity, Popular Culture and Everyday Life.* Oxford: Berg 2002.

Elcombe, Tim. "Hockey New Year's Eve in Canada: Nation-Making at the Montreal Forum." *International Journal of the History of Sport* 27, no. 8 (2010): 1287–1310.

Elliott, Richard, and Joseph Maguire. "'Net Gains': Informal Recruiting, Canadian Players and British Professional Ice Hockey." In Joseph Macguire and Mark Falcous, eds., *Sport and Migration: Borders, Boundaries, and Crossings.* 102–11. New York: Routledge 2011.

Émond, Sophie. "La représentation du genre masculin et du genre féminin dans le téléroman québécois: Le cas de *Lance et compte*." MA thesis, Université Laval, 2009.
Esman, Milton J. "Ethnic Politics and Economic Power." *Comparative Politics*, 19, no. 4 (1987): 400.
Falla, Jack. "A Death in Montreal." In *Open Ice: Reflections and Confessions of a Hockey Lifer*. 1–28. Mississauga, ON: John Wiley and Sons 2008.
– *Saved*. New York: Thomas Dunne Books 2008.
Farrell, Arthur. *Hockey: Canada's Royal Winter Game*. Montreal: C.R. Corneil 1899.
Fecteau, J. M., and É. Vaillancourt. "The Saint Vincent de Paul Society and the Catholic Charitable System in Quebec (1846–1921)." In Michael Gauvreau and O. Hubert, eds., *The Churches and Social Order in Nineteenth- and Twentieth-Century Canada*. 195–224. Montreal and Kingston: McGill-Queen's University Press 2006.
Ferguson, Will. *Beauty Tips from Moose Jaw*. Toronto: Vintage Canada 2005.
Flanders, Laura, ed. *The W Effect: Bush's War on Women*. New York: Feminist Press 2004.
Fontan, Jean-Marc, Benoît Lévesque, and Mathieu Charbonneau. "Les fondations privées québécoises: Un champ de recherche émergent." *Lien social et Politiques* 65 (2011): 43–64.
Foran, Charles. *Maurice Richard*. Toronto: Penguin 2011.
Fortin, Marie-Ève. "The *En Tant que femmes* Series, the Film *Souris, tu m'inquiètes*, and the Imaging of Women's Consciousness in 1970s Quebec." In Thomas Waugh, Michael Brendan Baker, and Ezra Winton, eds., *Challenge for Change: Activist Documentary at the National Film Board of Canada*. 117–35. Montreal and Kingston: McGill-Queen's University Press 2010.
Fortin, Pierre. "L'économie du Québec." In Guy Lachapelle and Robert Comeau, eds., *Robert Bourassa: Un bâtisseur tranquille*. 40–63. Quebec City: Les Presses de l'Université Laval 2003.
Fraser, Graham. *Sorry I Don't Speak French: Confronting the Canadian Crisis That Won't Go Away*. Toronto: Douglas Gibson Books 2006.
Fuller, Linda K. "Vamp, the Homebody, and the Upstart: Women and the Language of Baseball Films." In Linda K. Fuller, ed., *Sport, Rhetoric, and Gender: Historical Perspectives and Media Representations*. 185–97. New York: Palgrave Macmillan 2006.

Gagnon, Alain-G., André Lecours, and Geneviève Nootens, eds. *Les nationalismes majoritaires contemporains: identité, mémoire, pouvoir.* Montreal: Éditions Québec Amérique 2007.
Gagnon, Alain-G., and Raffaele Iacovino. *Federalism, Citizenship, and Quebec: Debating Multiculturalism*. Toronto: University of Toronto Press 2007.
Gaston, Bill. *The Good Body*. Dunvegan, ON: Cormorant Books 2000.
– *Midnight Hockey*. Doubleday Canada 2006.
Gauvreau, Michael. *The Catholic Origins of Quebec's Quiet Revolution, 1931–1970*. Montreal and Kingston: McGill-Queen's University Press 2005.
– "Forging a New Space for Lay Male Piety: St. Vincent de Paul Societies in Urban Quebec and Ontario, 1846–1890." *Histoire sociale / Social History* 42, no. 83 (2009): 35–67.
Gélinas, Xavier. *La droite intellectuelle québécoise et la Révolution tranquille*. Quebec City: Les Presses de l'Université Laval 2007.
Gellner, Ernest. *Nations and Nationalism*. Ithaca, NY: Cornell University Press 1983
– *Thought and Change*. London: Western Printing Services 1964.
Genette, Gérard. *Paratexts: Thresholds of Interpretation*. Trans. Jane E. Lewin. Cambridge, UK: Cambridge University Press 1997.
Germain, Jean-Claude. *Un pays dont la devise est je m'oublie*. Montreal: VLB 1976.
Gervais, Stéphan, Christopher Kirkey, and Jarrett Rudy, eds. *Quebec Questions: Quebec Studies for the Twenty-First Century*. Don Mills, ON: Oxford University Press 2011.
Gitersos, Terry Vaios. "Les frogs sont menacés: Media Representations of the Nordiques and Canadiens, 1979–1981." *Sport History Review* 40, no. 1 (2009): 69–81.
Glaap, Albert-Rainer. "Interview with Rick Salutin, author of Les Canadiens." *Der fremdsprachliche Unterricht: Wissenschaftliche Grundlegung, methodische Gestaltung*, 101 (1990): 15.
Godbout, Jacques. "Pour se Déniaiser." *Cité Libre* 12, no. 41 (1961): 22–3.
Godin, Pierre. *Daniel Johnson 1964–1968: La difficile recherche de l'égalité*. Montreal: Éditions de l'homme 1980.
Goffman, Erving. *The Presentation of Self in Everyday Life*. Garden City, NJ: Anchor 1959.

Gopnik, Adam. *Winter: Five Windows on the Season*. Toronto: Anansi 2011.
Gossage, Peter. "Au nom du père? : Rethinking the History of Fatherhood in Quebec." *American Review of Canadian Studies* 44, no. 1 (2014): 49–67.
Gowdey, David. "Foreword." In David Gowdey, ed., *Riding on the Roar of the Crowd: A Hockey Anthology*. ix–xi. Toronto: Macmillan 1989.
Goyens, Chrys, and Allan Turowetz. *Lions in Winter*. Scarborough, ON: Prentice-Hall Canada 1986.
Goyens, Chrystian. *The Montreal Forum: Forever Proud*. Montreal: Les Éditions Effix 1996.
Gravel, François. *Le Match des étoiles*. Montreal: Les Éditions Québec Amérique 1996.
Green, Mary Jean. "Léa Pool's *La Femme de l'hôtel* and Women's Film in Québec." *Québec Studies* 9 (1989–90): 49–62.
Greenfeld, Liah. *Nationalism: Five Roads to Modernity*. Cambridge, MA: Harvard University Press 1992.
Grondin, Jean. "La métaphysique du hockey." In Normand Baillargeon and Christian Boissinot, eds., *La vraie dureté du mental: Hockey et philosophie*. 116–28. Quebec City: Les Presses de l'Université Laval 2009.
Groulx, Patrice. *Pièges de la mémoire: Dollard des Ormeaux, les Amérindiens et nous*. Montreal: Éditions Vents d'Ouest 1998.
Gruneau, Richard, and David Whitson. *Hockey Night in Canada: Sport, Identities and Cultural Politics*. Toronto: Garamond Press 1993.
Guay, Donald. *La conquête du sport: Le sport et la société québécoise au XIXe siècle*. Montreal: Lanctôt 1997.
– *L'histoire du hockey au Québec: Origine et développement d'un phénomène culturel*. Chicoutimi, QC: Les Éditions JCL 1990.
– *Introduction à l'histoire des sports au Québec*. Montreal: VLB Éditeur 1987.
Gunderson, Lisa Anne. "Memory, Modernity, and the City: An Interpretive Analysis of Montreal and Toronto's Respective Moves from Their Historic Professional Hockey Arenas." MA thesis, University of Waterloo, 2004.
Guttmann, Allen. "Sport, Politics and the Engaged Historian." *Journal of Contemporary History* 38, no. 3 (2003): 363–75.
Gzowski, Peter. *The Game of Our Lives*. Toronto: McClelland and Stewart 1981.
Handler, Richard. *Nationalism and the Politics of Culture in Québec*. Madison: University of Wisconsin Press 1988.
Harrison, Richard. "Between a Puck and a Showpiece: Spectator Sport and

the Differing Responses to Hockey (and Its Absence) in Canada and the United States – A Canadian Poet Looks at the Fate of the Game." In Andrew C. Holman, ed., *Canada's Game: Hockey and Identity*. 151–60. Montreal and Kingston: McGill-Queen's University Press 2009.

– "Elegy for the Rocket." In *Hero of the Play: 10th Anniversary Edition*. 95. Toronto: Wolsak and Wynn 2004.

Harvey, Jean. "Le clergé québécois et le sport, 1930–1960." In Jean Harvey and Hart Cantelon, eds., *Sport et pouvoir: les enjeux sociaux au Canada*. 69–88. Ottawa: Les Presses de l'Université d'Ottawa 1988.

– "Force physique, citoyenneté et réformisme modéré au Bas-Canada." *Bulletin d'histoire politique* 11, no. 2 (2003): 77–85.

– "Sport and the Quebec Clergy, 1930–60." In Jean Harvey and Hart Cantelon, eds., *Not Just a Game: Essays in Canadian Sport Sociology*. 69–87. Ottawa: University of Ottawa Press 1988.

– "Whose Sweater Is This? The Changing Meanings of Hockey in Quebec." In David Whitson and Richard Gruneau, eds., *Artificial Ice: Hockey, Culture and Commerce*. 29–52. Peterborough, ON: Broadview Press 2006.

Harvey, Jean, and Roger Proulx. "Le sport et l'État au Canada." In Jean Harvey and Hart Cantelon, eds., *Sport et pouvoir: les enjeux sociaux au Canada*. 93–121. Ottawa: Les Presses de l'Université d'Ottawa 1988.

Hedley, Cara. *Twenty Miles*. Toronto: Coach House Press 2007.

Héroux, Claude, and Martine Pagé. *Lance et compte: Les dessous d'une grande réussite*. Montreal: Flammarion Québec 2006.

Hewson, Kelly. "'You Said You Didn't Give a Fuck about Hockey': Popular Culture, the Fastest Game on Earth and the Imagined Canadian Nation." In Jamie Dopp and Richard Harrison, eds., *Now Is the Winter: Thinking about Hockey*. 187–203. Hamilton, ON: Wolsak and Wynn 2009.

High, Steven, and David W. Lewis. *Corporate Wasteland: The Landscape and Memory of Deindustrialization*. Ithaca, NY: Cornell University Press 2007.

Hobsbawm, Eric. *Nations and Nationalism since 1780: Programme, Myth, Reality*. Cambridge: Cambridge University Press 1990.

Holman, Andrew C., ed. *Canada's Game. Hockey and Identity*. Montreal and Kingston: McGill-Queen's University Press 2009.

– "Curing Hockey's Ills: Sir Henry Gray's Address to the Montreal Amateur Athletic Association, March 1933." In *Findings/Trouvailles*, January 2016. http://www.champlainsociety.ca/

curing-hockeys-ills-sir-henry-grays-address-to-the-montreal-amateur-athletic-association-march-1933/ (accessed 8 December 2016).
– "Telling Stories about Indigeneity and Canadian Sport: The Spectacular Cree and Ojibway Indian Hockey Barnstorming Tour of North America, 1928." *Sport History Review*, 43, no. 2 (2012): 178–205.
Hood, Hugh. "The Sportive Centre of Saint Vincent de Paul." In Doug Beardsley, ed., *Our Game: An All-Star Collection of Hockey Fiction*. 117–29. Victoria, BC: Polestar 1997.
Hudon, Christine. "Le Muscle et le Vouloir: Les sports dans les collèges classiques masculins au Québec, 1870–1940." *Historical Studies in Education/ Revue d'histoire de l'éducation*, 17 no. 2 (2005): 243–63.
Ignatieff, Michael. *Blood and Belonging: Journeys into the New Nationalism*. Toronto: Penguin Canada 1993.
Ipperciel, Donald. "La Suisse: Un cas d'exception pour le nationalisme? / Switzerland: An Exceptional Case of Nationalism?" *Swiss Political Science Review* 13, no. 1 (2007): 39–67.
Irigaray, Luce. *Parler n'est jamais neutre*. Paris: Minuit 1985.
– *Sexes et genres à travers les langues*. Paris: Grasset 1990.
Jackson, J.B. "A Sense of Place, a Sense of Time." *Design Quarterly* 164 (spring 1995): 24–7.
James, C.L.R. *Beyond a Boundary*. London: Serpent's Tail 2000.
Janson, Gilles. *Emparons-nous du sport: Les Canadiens français et le sport au XIXe siècle*. Montreal: Guérin 1995.
– "Le sport comme enjeu national chez les Canadiens français, 1890–1920." In Michel Sarra-Bournet, ed., *Les nationalismes au Québec du XIXe au XXe siècle*. 57–61. Saint-Nicolas, QC: Les Presses de l'Université Laval 2001.
Jarman, Mark Anthony. "Righteous Speedboat." In Doug Beardsley, ed., *Our Game: An All-Star Collection of Hockey Fiction*. 233–43. Victoria, BC: Polestar 1997.
Jenish, D'Arcy. *The Montreal Canadiens: 100 Years of Glory*. Toronto: Anchor Canada 2009.
Johnston, Wayne. *The Divine Ryans*. Toronto: Vintage 1990.
– "The Montreal Canadiens." In Paul Quarrington, ed., *Original Six: True Stories from Hockey's Classic Era*. 34–61. Toronto: Reed Books Canada 1996.
Kanaganayakam, Chelva. "Snarling the Gardiner: Managing and Celebrating

Multiculturalism in Canada." Keynote lecture delivered at "Managing Diversity and Social Cohesion: The Canadian Experience, 5th International CEACS Conference, Sofia, Bulgaria, October 2009. 16–18.

Kelly, Ian. *Beau Brummell: The Ultimate Man of Style*. New York: Free Press 2013.

Kennedy, Brian. *My Country Is Hockey: How Hockey Explains Canadian Culture, History, Politics, Heroes, French-English Rivalry and Who We Are as Canadians*. Edmonton: Argenta Press 2011.

Kennedy, Michael, P.J. "Hockey as Metaphor in Selected Canadian Literature." *Textual Studies in Canada* 12 (1998): 81–94.

– "I Am Hockey." In Michael Kennedy, ed., *Going Top Shelf: An Anthology of Canadian Hockey Poetry*. 19–22. Surrey, BC: Heritage House 2005.

– *Words on Ice: A Collection of Hockey Prose*. Toronto: Key Porter 2003.

Khan, Sheema. *Of Hockey and Hijab: Reflections of a Canadian Muslim Woman*. Toronto: Tsar Publications 2009.

Kidd, Bruce. *The Political Economy of Sport*. Ottawa: CAHPER [1979].

– *The Struggle for Canadian Sport*. Toronto: University of Toronto Press 1995.

Kidd, Bruce, and John Macfarlane. *The Death of Hockey*. Toronto: New Press 1972.

King, Samantha. "Doing Good by Running Well: Breast Cancer, the Race for the Cure, and New Technologies of Ethical Citizenship." In Jack Z. Bratich, Jeremy Packer, and Cameron McCarthy, eds., *Foucault, Cultural Studies and Governmentality*. 295–316, Albany: State University of New York Press 2003.

– "Pink Ribbon Inc.: Breast Cancer Activism and the Politics of Philanthropy." *International Journal of Qualitative Studies in Education* 17, no. 4 (2004): 473–92.

King, Thomas. *The Truth about Stories: A Native Narrative*. Toronto: House of Anansi Press 2003.

Krashinsky, Michael, and Harry A. Krashinsky. "Do English Canadian Hockey Teams Discriminate against French Canadian Players?" *Canadian Public Policy* 23, 2 (1997): 212–16.

Kroetsch. Robert. *The Studhorse Man*. Markham, ON: PaperJacks 1977.

Laberge, Suzanne. "L'affaire Richard/Campbell: le hockey comme vecteur de l'affirmation francophone québécoise." In Audrey Laruin-Lamothe and Nicolas Moreau, eds., *Le Canadien de Montréal: Une légende repensée*. 13–30. Montreal: Les Presses de l'Université de Montréal 2011.

– "The Richard/Campbell Affair: Hockey as the Catalyst for Quebec Francophone Affirmation." In Nicolas Moreau and Audrey Laurin-Lamothe, eds., *The Montreal Canadiens: Rethinking a Legend*. 9–24. Trans. Howard Scott. Toronto: University of Toronto Press 2015.

Laberge, Suzanne, and Alexandre Dumas. "L'affaire Richard/Campbell: Un catalyseur de l'affirmation des Canadiens français." *Bulletin d'histoire politique* 11, no. 2 (2003): 30–44.

Lamonde, Yvan. "Quebec's Americanicity." In Stéphan Gervais, Christopher Kirkey, and Jarrett Rudy, eds., *Quebec Questions: Quebec Studies for the Twenty-First Century*. 80–91. Don Mills, ON: Oxford University Press 2011.

Lamoureux, Diane. *L'Amère Patrie: Féminisme et nationalisme dans le Québec contemporain*. Montreal: Remue-ménage 2001.

– "The Paradoxes of Quebec Feminism." In Stephan Gervais, Christopher Kirkey, and Jarrett Rudy, eds., *Quebec Questions*. 307–23. Don Mills, ON: Oxford University Press 2011.

Lapierre, Emmanuel. "Nationalisme culturel et performance dans l'histoire du Canadien de Montréal." *Globes* 15, nos. 1–2 (2012): 317–35.

– "À toi pour toujours? Le Canadien de Montréal comme enjeu national d'une guerre culturelle." MA thesis, Université de Montréal, 2012.

Laraque, Georges, and Pierre Thibeault. *Georges Laraque: La force d'y croire*. Montreal: Les Éditions de l'Homme 2011.

– *Georges Laraque: The Story of the NHL's Unlikeliest Tough Guy*. Toronto: Viking Canada 2011.

Lasorsa, Steve. *La Rivalité Canadien-Nordiques*. Quebec City: Les Presses de l'Université Laval 2011.

Laurin, Camille. *Québec's Policy on the French Language Presented to the National Assembly and the People of Québec*. Quebec City: Éditeur officiel du Québec 1977.

Laurin-Lamothe, Audrey. "La culture se joue-t-elle ici? Les implications de la corporation du Canadien de Montréal dans la société québécoise." In Audrey Laurin-Lamothe and Nicolas Moreau, eds., *Le Canadien de Montréal: Une légende repensée*. 93–106. Montreal: Les Presses de l'Université de Montréal 2011.

Lavoie, Marc. *Désavantage numérique: Les francophones dans la LNH*. Hull, QC: Vents d'ouest 1998.

Lavoie, Marc, Gilles Grenier, and Serge Coulombe. "Performance Differentials in the National Hockey League: Discrimination versus Style-of-Play Thesis." *Canadian Public Policy* 18, no. 4 (1992): 461–9.

Lechaume, Aline. "Chanter le pays: sur les chemins de la chanson québécoise." *Géographie et Cultures* 21 (1997): 45–58.

Lefevre, Henri. *The Production of Space*. Cambridge, MA: Blackwell 1991.

Léger, Jean-Marc. "Pour Sortir des Chemins de la résignation et de la servitude." *L'Action nationale* (10 September 1956): 66–73.

Levine, Marc V. *The Reconquest of Montreal: Language Policy and Social Change in a Bilingual City*. Philadelphia: Temple University Press 1990.

Levitt, Kari. *Silent Surrender: The Multinational Corporation in Canada*. Toronto: Macmillan of Canada 1970.

Linteau, Paul-André. *L'histoire de Montréal depuis la Confédération*. Montreal: Boréal 1992.

– *The History of Montreal: The Story of a Great North American City*. Trans. Peter McCambridge. Montreal: Baraka Books 2013.

Longley, Neil. "Do English Canadian Hockey Teams Discriminate against French Canadian Players?: A Reply." *Canadian Public Policy* 23, no. 2 (1997): 217–20.

Loranger, Françoise, and Claude Levac. *Le Chemin du Roy*. Ottawa: Lemeac 1969.

Lorenz, Stacy, and Geraint B. Osborne. "'Talk about Strenuous Hockey': Violence, Manhood, and the 1907 Ottawa Silver Seven-Montreal Wanderer Rivalry." *Journal of Canadian Studies*, 40, no. 1 (2006): 125–56.

Lubin, Martin. "The Politics of Language in Québec." In Stephan Gervais, Christopher Kirkey, and Jarrett Rudy, eds. *Quebec Questions*. 168–83. Don Mills, ON: Oxford University Press 2011.

MacClancy, Jeremy. "Nationalism at Play: The Basques of Vizcaya and Athletic Club de Bilbao." In Jeremy MacClancy, ed., *Sport, Identity and Ethnicity*. 183–92. Oxford: Berg 1996.

MacDonald, Cheryl. "'You! You Can't Say That!': Understandings of Gender and Sexuality and Attitudues towards Homosexuality among Male Major Midget AAA Ice Hockey Players in Canada." PhD thesis, Concordia University, Montreal, 2016.

MacDonald, Wilson Pugsley. "Monsieur Joliat" [1940]. *Representative Poetry Online*. http://rpo.library.utoronto.ca/poems/monsieur-joliat (accessed 8 December 2016).

Macdougall, Heather. "Facing Off: French and English in Bon Cop, Bad Cop." *Reconstruction: Studies in Contemporary Culture* 11, no. 1 (2011). http://reconstruction.eserver.org/111/Macdougall.shtml (accessed 12 September 2014).

MacGregor, Roy. *Canadians: A Portrait of a Country and Its People*. Toronto: Penguin Canada 2007.

Macintosh, Donald, Tom Bedecki, and C.E.S. Franks. *Sport and Politics in Canada*. Montreal and Kingston: McGill-Queen's University Press 1987.

Maclean, Malcolm. "Almost the Same but Not Quite … Almost the Same but Not White: Maori and Aotearoa / New Zealand's 1981 Springbok Tour." Kunapipi, *Journal of Post-Colonial Writing*, 23, no. 1 (2001): 69–82.

MacLennan, Hugh. *Two Solitudes*. Toronto: Macmillan 1945.

Maguire, Joseph. "Blade Runners: Canadian Migrants and European Ice Hockey." In Joseph Macguire and Mark Falcous, eds., *Sport and Migration: Borders, Boundaries, and Crossings*. 141–56. New York: Routledge 2011.

Mangan, J.A. "Imperial Education in British Tropical Africa." In William J. Baker and J.A. Mangan, eds., *Sport in Africa. Essays in Social History*. 141–46. New York and London: Africana Publishers Company 1987.

Marois, Michel. *Les analyses de la dimension politique du sport: Un examen critique*. Département de science politique de l'Université de Montréal 1988.

Marshall, Bill. "Gender, Narrative and National Identity in *Les Filles de Caleb*." *Canadian Journal of Film Studies / Revue canadienne d'études cinématographiques*, 2, nos. 2–3 (1993): 51–65.

Marshall, Dominique. *The Social Origins of the Welfare State: Quebec Families, Compulsory Education, and Family Allowances, 1940–1955*. Waterloo, ON: Wilfrid Laurier University Press 2006.

Martel, Marcel. *Le deuil d'un pays imaginé: Rêves, luttes et déroutes du Canada français*. Ottawa: Les Presses de l'Université d'Otawa 1997.

Martel, Marcel, and Martin Pâquet. *Langue et politique au Canada et au Québec: Une synthèse historique*. Montreal: Boréal 2010.

Masson, Raoul. *L'éducation physique, conditions et bienfaits corporels*. Lauzon: Société québécoise d'histoire du loisir 1981.

McCormack, Pete. *Understanding Ken*. Vancouver: Douglas and McIntyre 1998.

McKinley, Michael. *Hockey: A People's History*. Toronto: McClelland and Stewart 2006.

– "Next Year." In Doug Beardsley, ed., *Our Game: An All-Star Collection of Hockey Fiction*. 52–60. Victoria, BC: Polestar 1997.

– *Putting a Roof on Winter: Hockey's Rise from Sport to Spectacle*. Vancouver: Greystone 2000.

McParland, Kelly. *The Lives of Conn Smythe: From the Battlefield to Maple Leaf Gardens*. Toronto: McClelland and Stewart 2011.

McRoberts, Kenneth. *Quebec: Social Change and Political Crisis*. 3rd ed. Toronto: McClelland and Stewart 1993.

Melançon, Benoît. "Écrire Maurice Richard: Culture savante, culture populaire, culture sportive." *Globe: Revue internationale d'études québécoises* 9, no. 2 (2006): 1–27.

– "La Langue du hockey à travers les âges." *L'Oreille tendue*. http://oreilletendue.com/2011/04/04/la-langue-du-hockey-a-travers-les-ages-comme (accessed 15 July 2012).

– *Langue de puck: abécédaire du hockey*. Montreal: Del Busso Éditeur 2014.

– "Maurice Richard Expliqué aux Enfants." In Benoît Melançon, Geneviève Lafrance, and Yan Hamel, eds., *Des mots et des muscles! Représentations des pratiques sportives*. 13–30. Québec: Éditions Nota bene 2005.

– *The Rocket: A Cultural History of Maurice Richard*. Trans. Fred A. Reed. Toronto: Greystone Books 2009.

– *Les yeux de Maurice Richard: Une histoire culturelle*. Montreal: Fides 2006.

Melançon, Benoît, Geneviève Lafrance, and Yan Hamel, eds. *Des mots et des muscles! Représentations des pratiques sportives*. Québec: Éditions Nota bene 2005.

Metcalfe, Alan. *Canada Learns to Play*. Toronto: McClelland and Stewart 1987.

Meyer, Bruce. *The Time of the Last Goal: Why Hockey Is Our Game*. Windsor, ON: Black Moss Press 2014.

Miller, Mary Jane. "They Shoot! They Score?" *Canadian Drama / L'Art dramatique canadien* 4, 2 (Fall 1978): 140–49.

– "Two Versions of Rick Salutin's *Les Canadiens*." *Theatre Research in Canada* 1, no. 1 (1980): n.p.

Mills, Sean. *The Empire Within: Postcolonial Thought and Political Activism in Sixties Montreal*. Montreal and Kingston: McGill-Queen's University Press 2010.

Milza, Pierre. "Sport et relations internationales." *Relations internationales* 38 (1984): 155–74.

Moreau, Nicolas, and Audrey Laurin-Lamothe, eds. *The Montreal*

*Canadiens: Rethinking a Legend*. Trans. Howard Scott. Toronto: University of Toronto Press 2015.

Morhouse, H.F. "Scotland against England: Football and Popular Culture." *International Journal of the History of Sport*, 4, 2 (1987): 189–202.

Morrow, Don. "A Case-Study in Amateur Conflict: The Athletic War in Canada 1906–09," *British Journal of Sports History* 3, no. 2 (1986): 173–90.

– "The Little Men of Iron: The 1903 Montreal Hockey Club." *Canadian Journal of History of Sport* 12, no. 1 (1981): 51–65.

– *A Sporting Evolution: The Montreal Amateur Athletic Association, 1881–1981*. Montreal: Montreal Amateur Athletic Association 1981.

Morrow, Don, et al. *A Concise History of Sport in Canada*. Toronto: Oxford University Press 1990.

Morrow, Don, and Kevin B. Wamsley. *Sport in Canada: A History*. 2nd edition. Don Mills, ON: Oxford University Press 2005.

Morton, Suzanne. "A Man's City: Montreal, Gambling and Male Space in the 1940s." In T. Myers et al., eds., *Power, Place and Identity*. 170–82. Montreal: Montreal History Group 1998.

Mosse, George L. *The Image of Man: The Creation of Modern Masculinity*. New York: Oxford University Press 1996.

Mouton, Claude. *Les Canadiens de Montréal*. Montreal: Éditions La Presse 1986.

Nardocchio, Elaine F. *Theatre and Politics in Modern Quebec*. Edmonton: University of Alberta Press 1986.

Nieguth, Tim, and Aurélie Lacassagne. "Contesting the Nation: Reasonable Accommodation in Rural Québec." *Canadian Political Science Review* 3, no. 1 (2009): 1–16.

Nielsen, Kai. "Cultural Nationalism: Neither Ethnic Nor Civic." *Philosophical Forum* 28, nos. 1–2 (1997): 42–52.

– "Un nationalisme culturel, ni ethnique ni civique." In Michel Sarra-Bournet, ed., *Le pays de tous les Québécois: Diversité culturelle et souveraineté*. 143–59. Montreal: VLB Éditeur 1998.

Noonan, Kerry. "The Discourse of Hockey in Canada: Mythologization, Institutionalization, and Cultural Dissemination." MA thesis, Carleton University, 2002.

Nora, Pierre. "Between Memory and History: Les Lieux de Mémoire." *Representations*, 26 (spring 1989): 7–24.

O'Brien, Andy. *Les Canadiens*, Montreal: McGraw-Hill 1972.

Orr, Bobby. *Orr: My Story*. New York: G.P. Putnam's Sons 2013.
Orti, Ian. "The Stanley Cup Conspiracy." *Matrix* 89 (spring 2011): 43.
Özkirimli, Umut. *Theories of Nationalism. A Critical Introduction*. New York: Palgrave Macmillan 2010 (2000).
Parent, Monique. "Féminisation et Masculinisation des Titres de Professions au Québec." *La Linguistique: Revue de la Société Internationale de Linguistique Fonctionnelle / Journal of the International Society of Functional Linguistics* 30, no. 1 (1994): 123–35.
Park, Roberta J. "Muscles, Symmetry and Action: 'Do You Measure up?' Defining Masculinity in Britain and America from the 1860s to the early 1900s." *International Journal of the History of Sport* 24, 12 (2007): 1604–36.
Patoine, Tony. "'*On est Canayen ou ben on l'est pas*': Hockey, Nationalism, and Identity in Québec and Canada." In Normand Baillargeon and Christian Boissinot, eds., *Hockey and Philosophy*. 3–23. Trans. Scott Irving. Ottawa: University of Ottawa Press 2015.
– "'On est Canayen ou ben on l'est pas': Hockey, nationalisme et identités au Québec et au Canada." In Normand Baillargeon and Christian Boissinot, eds., *La vraie dureté du mental: Hockey et philosophie*. 9–25. Quebec City: Les Presses de l'Université Laval 2009.
– "Sport et nationalisme: une perspective québécoise et canadienne." MA thesis, Université de Montreal 2008.
Payant, René. "La force des formes: Vidéo et télévision." *Études françaises* 22, no. 3 (1986): 83–99.
Perrone, Julie. "The King Has Two Bodies: Howie Morenz and the Fabrication of Memory." *Sport History Review* 41 (2010): 95–110.
– "Le processus d'héroïsation du Rocket." MA thesis, Université du Québec à Montréal 2008.
Picoche, Jacqueline, and Christiane Marchello-Nizia. *Histoire de la langue française*. Paris: Nathan 1989.
Pinto, Barbara S. "Ain't Misbehaving: The Montreal Shamrock Lacrosse Club Fans, 1868 to 1884." MA thesis, University of Western Ontario, 1990.
Podbrey, Maurice. *Half Man, Half Beast: Making a Life in Canadian Theatre*. Montreal: Véhicule 1997.
Poirier, Christian. "Hockey et identité au Québec: L'évolution contrastée d'un sport national." In Jean-Pierre Augustin and Claude Sorbets, eds., *La culture du sport au Québec*. 183–209. Talence: Éditions de la Maison des sciences de l'Homme d'Aquitaine 1996.

Poisson, Jacques. "La Langue: La soirée du Hockey." *L'Action nationale* (11 April 1962): 721–4.

Poliquin, Daniel. "Pour qui prends-tu?" In Marc Robitaille, ed., *Une enfance-blue-blanc-rouge*. 115–18. Montreal: Les Éditions les 400 coups 2000.

Poulter, Gillian. *Becoming Native in a Foreign Land: Sport, Visual Culture and National Identity, Montreal 1840–1885*. Vancouver: UBC Press 2009.

Pryer, Allison. "The Aesthetics and Erotics of Hockey." *Canadian Women Studies* 21, no. 3 (2002): 73–6.

Purdy, Al. "Hockey Players." In Michael Kennedy, ed., *Going Top Shelf: An Anthology of Canadian Hockey Poetry*. 25–6. Surrey, BC: Heritage House 2005.

– "Homage to Ree-shard." In *Bursting into Song: An Al Purdy Omnibus*. Windsor, ON: Black Moss Press 1982.

Ramos, Howard, and Kevin Gosine. "The Rocket: Newspaper Coverage of the Death of a Cultural Icon, a Canadiens Hockey Player." *Journal of Canadian Studies / Revue d'études canadiennes* 36, no. 4 (2002): 9–31.

Ransom, Amy J. *Hockey, PQ: Canada's Game in Quebec's Popular Culture*. Toronto: University of Toronto Press 2014.

Reines, Philip. "The Emergence of Quebec Cinema: A Historical Overview." In Joseph I. Donohoe, Jr, ed., *Essays on Quebec Cinema*. 15–33. East Lansing: Michigan State University Press 1991.

Richard, Maurice, and Stan Fischler. *The Flying Frenchmen: Hockey's Greatest Dynasty*. Upper Saddle River, NJ: Prentice Hall/Hawthorn 1971.

Richard, Simon. *La série du siècle: Septembre 1972*. Montreal: Les Éditions Hurtubise 2002.

Richards, David Adams. *Hockey Dreams: Memories of a Man Who Couldn't Play*. Toronto: Anchor 2001.

Richler, Mordecai. *Barney's Version*. Toronto: Knopf 1997.

– "Cheap Skates." In *Dispatches from the Sporting Life*. 141–7. Toronto: Knopf 2002.

– "The Fall of the Montreal Canadiens." In *Dispatches from the Sporting Life*. 241–74. Toronto: Knopf 2002.

– *Oh Canada! Oh Québec! Requiem for a Divided Country*. Toronto: Penguin Books 1992.

– "Writers and Sports." In *Dispatches from the Sporting Life*. 93-104. Toronto: Knopf 2002.

Riordan, James. *Sport in Soviet Society: Development of Sport and Physical Education in Russia and the USSR*. Cambridge: Cambridge University Press 1977.

Robidoux, Michael. "Imagining a Canadian Identity through Sport: A Historical Interpretation of Lacrosse and Hockey." *Journal of American Folklore* 115, no. 456 (2002): 209–36.

Robinson, Rebecca. "Sport Philanthropy: An Analysis of Charitable Foundations of Major League Teams." MA thesis, University of San Francisco, 2005.

Ross, J. Andrew. "Arenas of Debate: The Continuation of Professional Hockey in the Second World War." In John Chi-Kit Wong, ed., *Coast to Coast: Hockey in Canada to the Second World War*. 86–131. Toronto: University of Toronto Press 2009.

– *Joining the Clubs: The Business of the National Hockey League to 1945*. Syracuse, NY: Syracuse University Press 2015.

Ross, J. Andrew, John Cranfield, and Kris Inwood. "Defining the Sport-Industrial Body: The Historical Stature of Major League Hockey Players, 1909–2010." Essay manuscript.

Rouillard, Jacques. *L'expérience syndicale au Québec: ses rapports à l'État, à la nation et à l'opinion publique*. Montreal: VLB Éditeur 2009.

Rubin, Don, ed., *Canadian Theatre History: Selected Readings*. Toronto: Copp Clark 1996.

Rumilly, Robert. *Histoire de Montréal*. Montreal: Fides 1974.

Rutherford, Paul. *When Television Was Young: Prime Time Canada, 1952–1967*. Toronto: University of Toronto Press 1990.

Ryan, Claude. *Les classes moyennes au Canada français*. Montreal: Éditions de l'Action Nationale 1951.

Ryan, Marie-Laure. "Narrative in Real Time: Chronicle, Mimesis and Plot in the Baseball Broadcast." *Narrative* 1, no. 2 (1993): 138–55.

Sabo, Don. *Sex, Violence and Power in Sports: Rethinking Masculinity*. Freedom, CA: The Crossing Press 1994.

Salutin, Rick. *Les Canadiens*. Vancouver: Talonbooks 1977.

Sanaker, John Kristian. *La Rencontre des langues dans le cinéma francophone: Québec, Afrique subsaharienne, France, Maghreb*. Quebec and

Paris: Presses de l'Université Laval / L'Harmattan 2010.
Sancton, Andrew. *Governing the Island of Montreal*. Berkeley: University of California Press 1985.
Sarkar, Mela, and Lise Winer. "Multilingual Codeswitching in Québec Rap: Poetry, Pragmatics and Performativity." *International Journal of Multilingualism*, 3 no. 3 (2006): 173–92.
Saul, John Ralston. *Louis-Hippolyte LaFontaine and Robert Baldwin*. Toronto: Penguin Canada 2010.
Savoie, Donald J. *Thatcher, Reagan, Mulroney: In Search of a New Bureaucracy*. Pittsburgh: University of Pittsburgh Press 1994.
Schleicher, Klaus. "Education and Nationalism." In H. Herb Guntram and David H. Kaplan, eds., *Nations and Nationalism: A Global Historical Overview, Vol. 1, 1770–1880*. 29–42. Santa Barbara, CA: Abc-Clio 2008.
Séguin, Maurice. *Histoire de deux nationalismes au Canada*. Montreal: Guérin 1997.
Sen, Satadru. "History without a Past: Memory and Forgetting in Indian Cricket." In Stephen Wagg, ed., *Cricket and National Identity in the Postcolonial Age*. 94–109. London and New York: Routledge Taylor and Francis Group 2005.
Seymour, Michel. *L'institution du langage*. Montreal: Les Presses de l'Université de Montréal 2005.
– *La nation en question*. Montreal: Éditions de l'Hexagone 1999.
Sheth, Hela, and Kathy M. Babiak. "Beyond the Game: Perceptions and Practices of Corporate Social Responsibility in the Professional Sport Industry." *Journal of Business Ethics* 91 (2010): 433–50.
Simard, André. *La soirée du fockey. Le temps d'une pêche. Le vieil homme et la mort*. Montreal: Leméac 1974.
Simard, Jean-Claude. "Hockey and Politics, Same Battle!" In Christian Boissinot and Normand Baillargeon, eds., *Hockey and Philosophy*. 25–42. Trans. Scott Irving. Ottawa: University of Ottawa Press 2015.
– "Hockey et politique, même combat!" In Normand Baillargeon and Christian Boissinot, eds., *La vraie dureté du mental: Hockey et philosophie*. 27–42. Quebec City: Les Presses de l'Université Laval 2009.
Sirois, Bob. *Discrimination in the NHL: Quebec Hockey Players Sidelined*. Montreal: Baraka 2010.
Skinner, David. "Television in Canada: Continuity or Change?" In David

Ward, ed., *Television and Public Policy: Change and Continuity in an Era of Global Liberalization*. 3–26. New York: Lawrence Erlbaum / Taylor and Francis 2008.
Smith, Anthony D. *National Identity*. Reno: University of Nevada Press 1991.
– *Nationalism. Theory, Ideology, History*. Cambridge: Polity Press 2010 (2001).
Smith, Sidonie, and Julia Watson. *Reading Autobiography: A Guide for Interpreting Life Narratives*. 2nd ed. Minneapolis: University of Minnesota Press 2010.
Smith, Stephen. *Puckstruck: Distracted, Delighted and Distressed by Canada's Hockey Obsession*. Vancouver: Greystone Books 2014.
Sniec, Monika. "Les Canadiens de Montréal vus par les fans: Une exploration en trois temps." MA thesis, Université de Montréal, 2004.
Society for International Hockey Research. *Pucklore*, Kingston, ON: Quarry Press 2010.
Sova, Dawn B. *Women in Hollywood: From Vamp to Studio Head*. New York: Fromm International 1998.
Stack, Edward F. "A New Game." In M.D. Benoit, ed., *Looking in ... Portraits of the Canadian Soul*. http://ceauthors.com/eAnthology.pdf (accessed 8 December 2016).
Stevens, Julie, and Andrew Holman, eds., "Rinkside: New Scholarly Studies on Ice Hockey and Society," *Sport in Society* 16, no. 3 (2013): 1–3.
Stewart, Kathleen. "Nostalgia – A Polemic." *Cultural Anthropology* 3, no. 3 (1988): 227–41.
Strachan, Maxwell. "37 Years Ago, a Female Journalist Won the Right to Do Her Job." *Huffington Post*, 25 September 2015, http://www.huffingtonpost.com/entry/melissa-ludtke-locker-rooms-sports-journalism_us_56057c26e4b0dd8503074f2e (accessed 8 December 2016).
Sugden, John, and Alan Bairner, "'Ma, There's a Helicopter on the Pitch! Sport, Leisure and the State in Northern Ireland." *Sociology of Sport Journal* 9 (1992): 154–66.
Taché, Sir Étienne-Paschal. *Du développement de la force physique chez l'homme*. Ed. Donald Guay. Lauzon: Société québécoise d'histoire du loisir 1981.
Talparu, Margrit. "Philanthropy Chic: The Emergence of Conspicuous Giving." Paper presented at the Canadian Communication Association Annual Conference, Waterloo, ON, 30 May 2012.
Therrien, Denyse. "Evolution du langage dans le cinéma québécois des

années 60 à 80." In William C. Wees and Michael Dorland, eds., *Words and Moving Images*. 191–202. Montreal: Mediatexte 1984.
Thomson, Dale C., *Vive le Québec Libre*. Toronto: Deneau 1988.
Tracey, Paul, Nelson Phillips, and Helen Haugh. "Beyond Philanthropy: Community Enterprise as a Basis for Corporate Citizenship." *Journal of Business Ethics* 58 (2005): 327–44.
Tremblay, Victor-Laurent. "Masculinité et hockey dans le roman québécois." *French Review* 78 (2005): 1104–16.
Usmiani, Renate. "The Playwright as Historiographer: New Views of the Past in Contemporary Québécois Drama." *L'art dramatique canadienne / Canadian Drama* 8, no. 2 (1982): 117–28.
Vacante, Jeffery. "Evolving Racial Identity and the Consolidation of Men's Authority in Early Twentieth-Century Quebec." *Canadian Historical Review* 88, no. 3 (2007): 414–38.
– "Liberal Nationalism and the Challenge of Masculinity Studies in Quebec." *Left History* 11, no. 2 (2006): 96–117.
Vallières, Pierre, *Choose!* Trans. Penelope Williams. Toronto: New Press 1972.
Valois-Nadeau, Fannie. "Le Canadien de Montréal: un objet populaire, des représentations et des traditions." In Audrey Laurin-Lamothe and Nicolas Moreau, eds., *Le Canadien de Montréal: Une légende repensée*. 75–91. Montreal: Les Presses de l'Université de Montréal 2011.
– "The Montreal Canadiens as Popular Object: Representations of Tradition." In Nicolas Moreau and Audrey Laurin-Lamothe, eds., *The Montreal Canadiens: Rethinking a Legend*. 64–79. Trans. Howard Scott. Toronto: University of Toronto Press 2015.
– "Quand le cœur a ses raisons: Analyse de la construction mythique du club de hockey Le Canadien de Montréal." MA thesis, Université du Québec à Montréal, 2009.
Vance, Jonathan. *A History of Canadian Culture*. Toronto: Oxford University Press Canada 2009.
Vertinsky, Patricia. "Aging Bodies, Aging Sport Historians, and the Choreography of Sport History." *Sport History Review* 29 (1998): 18–29.
Vertinsky, Patricia, and John Bale, eds. *Sites of Sports: Space, Place, Experience*. New York: Routledge 2004.
Vigneault, Michel. "La naissance d'un sport organisé au Canada: Le hockey à Montréal, 1875–1917." PhD thesis, Université Laval, 2001.
Waugh, Thomas. *The Romance of Transgression in Canada: Queering*

*Sexualities, Nations, Cinemas*. Montreal and Kingston: McGill-Queen's University Press 2006.

Weiss, Allan. "Jean Beliveau Was Number Four." *Loomings* 1, no. 1 (1979): 2–12.

Whitson, David, and Jon Horne. "Underestimated Costs and Overestimated Benefits? Comparing the Outcomes of Sports Mega-Events in Canada and Japan." In John Horne and Wolfram Manzenreiter, eds., *Sports Mega-Events: Social Scientific Analyses of a Global Phenomenon*. 73–89. Malden, MA: Blackwell Publishing 2006.

Whitson, David, and Richard Gruneau. "Introduction." In David Whitson and Richard Gruneau, eds., *Artificial Ice: Hockey, Culture and Commerce*. 1–25. Peterborough, ON: Broadview Press 2006.

Williams, Raymond. "Community." In *Keywords: A Vocabulary of Culture and Society*. New York: Oxford University Press 1976.

Wong, John Chi-Kit. *Lords of the Rinks*. Toronto: University of Toronto Press 2005.

– "Proem." In John Chi-Kit Wong, ed., *Coast to Coast: Hockey in Canada to the Second World War*. xii–xiv. Toronto: University of Toronto Press 2009.

Wong, John Chi-Kit, ed. *Coast to Coast: Hockey in Canada to the Second World War*. Toronto: University of Toronto Press 2009.

Woods, Hanford. "The Drubbing of Nesterenko." In Doug Beardsley, ed., *Our Game: An All-Star Collection of Hockey Fiction*. 244–59. Victoria, BC: Polestar 1997.

Wright, Richard B. *The Age of Longing*. Toronto: HarperCollins 1995.

Young, Iris Marion. "Breasted Experience: The Look and the Feeling." In Rose Weitz, ed., *The Politics of Women's Bodies: Sexuality, Appearance, and Behavior*. 179–91. New York: Oxford University Press 2010.

Young, Scott. *A Boy at the Leafs' Camp*. Toronto: McClelland & Stewart 1989. First published 1953.

– *Boy on Defence*. Toronto: McClelland & Stewart 1989. First published 1953.

– *Scrubs on Skates*. Toronto: McClelland & Stewart 1985. First published 1952.

– *That Old Gang of Mine*. Don Mills, ON: Fitzhenry & Whiteside 1982.

Young, Scott, and George Robertson. *Face-Off*. Toronto: Macmillan 1971.

Zakus, Dwight H. "A Genesis of the Canadian Sport System in Pierre Trudeau's Political Philosophy and Agenda." *Sport History Review* 27 (1996): 30–48.

# CONTRIBUTORS

FRAZER ANDREWS works at Athabasca University. A theatre man, his most recent production is *Cowboy: A Cowboy Story*, which featured at the 2016 Edmonton Fringe Festival.

JASON BLAKE is a professor in the English Department at the University of Ljubljana. He is the author of *Canadian Hockey Literature*.

TERRY VAIOS GITERSOS is an independent researcher based in Toronto, Ontario. He is interested in the intersection of sport and national identity, in Quebec and elsewhere.

ANDREW C. HOLMAN is a professor of history and director of the Canadian Studies Program at Bridgewater State University in Massachusetts.

EMMANUEL LAPIERRE is a doctoral candidate in the History Department at l'Université Laval à Québec. His current research focuses on political demonstrations in Montreal (1955–69).

PAUL MARTIN is the faculty development coordinator at MacEwan University in Edmonton, Alberta. He also teaches in MacEwan's Department of English. The primary focus of his research is the literatures of Canada. His book *Sanctioned Ignorance: The Politics of Knowledge Production and the Teaching of the Literatures of Canada* (2013) won the 2013 Gabrielle Roy Prize for the best book-length work of Canadian literary criticism published in English.

JULIE PERRONE is an independent researcher and communications professional working in Montreal. Her research interests are national identity, sport history, masculinity, and public memory.

AMY J. RANSOM is a professor of French at Central Michigan University. She is the author of *Hockey, PQ: Canada's Game in Quebec's Popular Culture* and is currently working on a book on memory, territory, and identity in twenty-first-century Quebec film.

FANNIE VALOIS-NADEAU is a post-doctoral fellow in communication studies at Concordia University, Montreal. Her research interests are cultural studies, sport-media studies, and memory studies. Her current work interrogates the links between cultural practices and the politico-economic issues within sport industries to understand new forms of engagement circulating in the professional sport milieu and more broadly in popular culture.

MICHEL VIGNEAULT is a lecturer at the Université du Québec à Montréal (UQAM) and McGill University (in the physical education and kinesiology departments). His current research is hockey history, with the principal focus on French-English relationships in Montreal hockey.

# INDEX